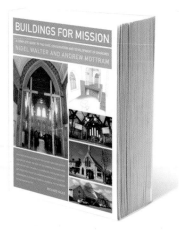

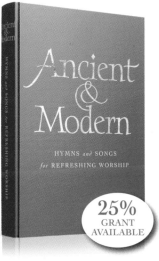

The Sign

The nationwide church magazine supplement

Enhance your parish magazine with quality articles, book reviews, reflections, puzzles and each month's Lectionary.

Order print copies

A 16-page supplement ready to send –
just add local content!
Less than 11p per copy.

Email: ruth.hunter@hymnsam.co.uk
Call: 01603 785911

The Sign Online

Pick and choose articles from
our easy-to-use website.
Your first year's subscription
is just £10!

Visit: www.the-sign.co.uk

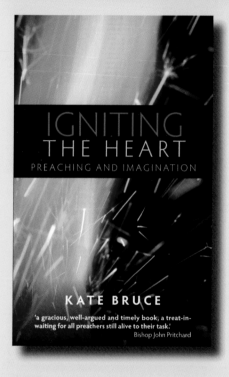

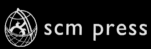

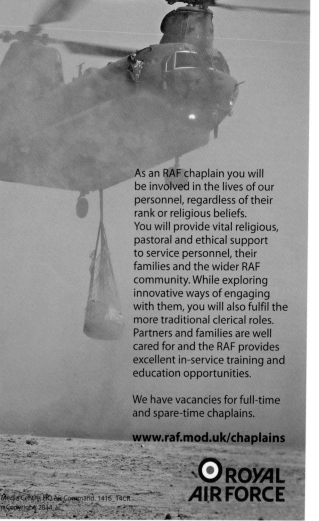

Could You Be Their Chaplain?

As an RAF chaplain you will be involved in the lives of our personnel, regardless of their rank or religious beliefs. You will provide vital religious, pastoral and ethical support to service personnel, their families and the wider RAF community. While exploring innovative ways of engaging with them, you will also fulfil the more traditional clerical roles. Partners and families are well cared for and the RAF provides excellent in-service training and education opportunities.

We have vacancies for full-time and spare-time chaplains.

www.raf.mod.uk/chaplains

ROYAL AIR FORCE

The Canterbury Preacher's Companion 2017

Sermons for Sundays, Holy Days,
Festivals and Special Occasions
Year A

Michael Counsell

CANTERBURY
PRESS
Norwich

First published in 2016 by the Canterbury Press Norwich
Editorial office
108-114 Golden Lane
London, EC1Y OTG

Canterbury Press is an imprint of Hymns Ancient &
Modern Ltd (a registered charity)
13a Hellesdon Park Road
Norwich, NR6 5DR, UK

www.canterburypress.co.uk

British Library Cataloguing in Publication data

A catalogue record for this book is available
from the British Library

Scripture quotations are mainly drawn from the New Revised
Standard Version Bible © 1989 by the Division of Christian
Education of the National Council of Churches of
Christ in the USA
Readings are from *Common Worship: Services and Prayers
for the Church of England*, which is copyright © The
Archbishops' Council 2000: extracts and edited extracts are
used by permission.
Readings for days not covered by that book are from
Exciting Holiness, second edition 2003, edited by Brother
Tristram, copyright © European Province of the Society of
Saint Francis, 1997, 1999, 2003, published by Canterbury
Press, Norwich; see www.excitingholiness.org

ISBN 978 1 84825 851 8

Typeset by Manila Typesetting
Printed and bound in Great Britain by
Ashford Colour Press Ltd, Gosport, Hampshire

Contents

Preface   xvii

How to Read Music   xix

SUNDAYS

Unless otherwise stated, the readings and the verse numbers of the psalms are taken from *Common Worship: Services and Prayers for the Church of England* (Church House Publishing, 2000), with revisions, and are for Year A.

2016

Nov. 27   First Sunday of Advent, Year A,
          The Year of Matthew
          Principal Service: Matt. 24.44
             Matthew's vision   2
          Second Service: Matt. 24.23
             Is the world coming to an end today?   4

Dec. 4   Second Sunday of Advent
          Principal Service: Matt. 3.1–2
             Remorse → forgiveness → progress   7
          Second Service: 1 Kings 18.21
             Elijah and Mendelssohn   9

Dec. 11   Third Sunday of Advent
          Principal Service: Isa. 35.6
             Streams in the desert   12
          Second Service: Acts 13.26
             Preaching to Jews   14

Dec. 18   Fourth Sunday of Advent
           Principal Service: Matt. 1.18
             The troubled town   16
           Second Service: Rev. 22.20–21
             Come, Lord Jesus!   19

Dec. 25   Christmas Day
           Set I: Luke 2.11 On screen   23
           Set II: Titus 3.4–5 The Gloom family's
             Christmas circular   25
           Set III: Heb. 1.1–2 Have faith   28
           Second Service: Phil. 2.6–7 or
             Luke 2.11 Virgin birth   30

2017
Jan. 1   Second Sunday of Christmas
           (The Naming and Circumcision of Jesus)
           Principal Service: Isa. 63.9
             New beginnings   33
           Second Service: Phil. 2.5–7
             God's idea of humanity   35

Jan. 8   Baptism of Christ (First Sunday of Epiphany)
           Principal Service: Ps. 29.3
             Voices from heaven   37
           Second Service: Ps. 46.10
             Be still and know   40

Jan. 15   Second Sunday of Epiphany
           Principal Service: Isa. 49.6
             A light to the nations   42
           Second Service: Gal. 1.15–16
             Christianity in Russia   44

Jan. 22   Third Sunday of Epiphany (Week of Prayer
           for Christian Unity)
           Principal Service: 1 Cor. 1.10, 13
             Unity through baptism   47
           Second Service: Ps. 33.1, 3
             Singing to God a new song   49

Jan. 29   **Fourth Sunday of Epiphany** (or Candlemas)
Principal Service: John 2.6–9
  Gallons of guilt and gallons of grace   51
Second Service: Ps. 34.17
  The Lord hears them?   54

Feb. 5   **Fourth Sunday before Lent** (Proper 1)
Principal Service: Matt. 5.17
  Law of Moses or law of love?   56
Second Service: Eph. 4.22–24
  The old life and the new life   58

Feb. 12   **Third Sunday before Lent** (Proper 2)
Principal Service: Matt. 5.27–28 Adultery   61
Second Service: Amos 3.5, 7
  Reasons to believe   63

Feb. 19   **Second Sunday before Lent**
Principal Service: Gen. 1.31 Giving to God   65
Second Service: Rev. 4.2
  The Blessed Damozel   68

Feb. 26   **Sunday next before Lent**
Principal Service: Matt. 17.1–3
  The Law and the prophets   71
Second Service: Ps. 84.9
  One day in your courts   73

Mar. 1   **Ash Wednesday**
Joel 2.13 Miserable sinners   76

Mar. 5   **First Sunday of Lent**
Principal Service: Matt. 4.1 Personality   79
Second Service: Ps. 50.14
  A sacrifice of thanksgiving   81

Mar. 12   **Second Sunday of Lent**
Principal Service: John 3.3, 16–17
  Born-again Christians   83
Second Service: Num. 21.5–7
  Grumbling   86

Mar. 19	**Third Sunday of Lent**	
	Principal Service: Rom. 5.10	
	Reconciliation	88
	Second Service: Josh. 1.1, 7	
	Be bold, be strong	90
Mar. 26	**Fourth Sunday of Lent**	
	(or Mothering Sunday)	
	Principal Service: Eph. 5.8	
	Milton's 'Ode on his blindness'	93
	Mothering Sunday: Tobit 4.1–5	
	Motherliness	96
Apr. 2	**Fifth Sunday of Lent**	
	Principal Service: John 11.25–26	
	Wake up and smell the coffee	98
	Second Service: Matt. 20.26–28	
	Everybody's slave	100
Apr. 9	**Palm Sunday**	
	Principal Service: Matt. 27.11–12	
	Illegal legalities	103
	Second Service: Isa. 5.1–3	
	Vineyard religion	106
Apr. 10–12	**First Three Days in Holy Week**	
	Isa. 49.6 The Court of All Nations	108
Apr. 13	**Maundy Thursday**	
	1 Cor. 11.23–24 Where's the body?	111
Apr. 14	**Good Friday**	
	Ps. 22.1–2 Suffering	113
Apr. 15–16	**Easter Vigil**	
	Exod. 15.1–2 The Exultet	116
Apr. 16	**Easter Day**	
	Principal Service: Ps. 118.15–17	
	Is anyone there?	119
	Second Service: S. of Sol. 8.6	
	Love and death	121

Apr. 23   **Second Sunday of Easter**
           Principal Service: John 20.21–23
               Resurrection in John's Gospel   124
           Second Service: Ps. 30.3
               Resurrection in daily life   126

Apr. 30   **Third Sunday of Easter**
           Principal Service: Luke 24.15–16
               Sunset to sunrise   128
           Second Service: Haggai 2.9
               Herod's Temple   131

May 7   **Fourth Sunday of Easter**
           Principal Service: 1 Peter 2.25
               A popular shepherd   133
           Second Service: Eph. 2.13–14
               A contract with everyone   135

May 14   **Fifth Sunday of Easter**
           Principal Service: 1 Pet. 2.4–5 Living stones 138
           Second Service: Rev. 21.1–2
               Old Jerusalem and new   140

May 21   **Sixth Sunday of Easter** (Rogation Sunday)
           Principal Service: 1 Pet. 3.19 Spirits in prison 143
           Second Service: Zech. 8.4 Old age   145

May 25   **Ascension Day**
           Eph. 1.20–21 or Acts 1.9 Thrones   149

May 28   **Seventh Sunday of Easter**
           (Sunday after Ascension Day)
           Principal Service: John 17.5 Celebrity   151
           Second Service: Mark 16.15
               or Ps. 47.7 All the earth   153

June 4   **Day of Pentecost** (Whit Sunday)
           Principal Service: 1 Cor. 12.4
               Gifts of the Spirit   156
           Second Service: Acts 2.17–18
               Visions and dreams   158

June 11   **Trinity Sunday**
Principal Service: 2 Cor. 13.11, 13
   Fellowship   160
Second Service: John 16.5, 7
   Incomprehensible   163

June 18   **First Sunday after Trinity** (Proper 6)
Principal Service: Matt. 9.35–36
There could be trouble ahead   167
Second Service: Luke 11.24–26
   The return of the demon   169

June 25   **Second Sunday after Trinity** (Proper 7)
Principal Service: Matt. 10.29, 31
   Do not be afraid   171
Second Service: Luke 14.18 Too busy   174

July 2   **Third Sunday after Trinity** (Proper 8)
Principal Service: Matt. 10.40–42
   A cup of cold water   176
Second Service: Luke 17.33–36 Punishment   178

July 9   **Fourth Sunday after Trinity** (Proper 9)
Principal Service: Matt. 11.28
   Restless without God   181
Second Service: Luke 18.41–42 Blindness   183

July 16   **Fifth Sunday after Trinity** (Proper 10)
Principal Service: Matt. 13.20–21 Shallow   185
Second Service: Luke 20.1–2 Authority   188

July 23   **Sixth Sunday after Trinity** (Proper 11)
Principal Service: Rom. 8.18
   God knows best   190
Second Service: Ps. 67.5 Other faiths   193

July 30   **Seventh Sunday after Trinity** (Proper 12)
Principal Service: Matt. 13.31–32
   Destined to grow   195
Second Service: 1 Kings 6.11–12
   Solomon's Temple   198

Aug. 6   The Transfiguration of Our Lord
          Eighth Sunday after Trinity (Proper 13)
          The Transfiguration: Luke 9.28
              God's will, not mine   200
          Second Service: Acts 13.5
              What we owe to the Jews   203

Aug. 13   **Ninth Sunday after Trinity** (Proper 14)
          Principal Service: Matt. 14.24–25
              Impossible miracles   205
          Second Service: 1 Kings 12.16–17
              Two kingdoms   207

Aug. 20   **Tenth Sunday after Trinity** (Proper 15)
          Principal Service: Matt. 15.14
              Humour and holiness   210
          Second Service: Acts 16.14
              A letter to Paul from Philippi   212

Aug. 27   **Eleventh Sunday after Trinity** (Proper 16)
          Principal Service: Rom. 12.4–5
              The Church is the Body of Christ   214
          Second Service: Acts 17.22–23 Islam   217

Sept. 3   **Twelfth Sunday after Trinity** (Proper 17)
          Principal Service: Rom. 12.12 Pain and hope   219
          Second Service: 2 Kings 7.9 Sharing good news   222

Sept. 10 **Thirteenth Sunday after Trinity** (Proper 18)
          Principal Service: Rom. 13.10 Do or die   224
          Second Service: Acts 19.19 Magic   226

Sept. 17 **Fourteenth Sunday after Trinity** (Proper 19)
          Principal Service: Matt. 18.21–22 Forgiveness   229
          Second Service: Acts 20.33–35
              Giving and receiving   231

Sept. 24 **Fifteenth Sunday after Trinity** (Proper 20)
          Principal Service: Matt. 20.1 Work   234
          Second Service: Acts 26.12–15
              God speaks to us   236

Oct. 1   Sixteenth Sunday after Trinity (Proper 21)
            (Alternatively the Dedication Festival)
            Principal Service: Phil. 2.7–8 Humble   239
            Second Service: 1 John 2.22 Heresies   241

Oct. 8   Seventeenth Sunday after Trinity (Proper 22)
            Principal Service: Phil. 3.12–14
            Perseverance of athletes   244
            Second Service: 1 John 2.9–11 Harmful sin   246

Oct. 15   Eighteenth Sunday after Trinity (Proper 23)
            Principal Service: Phil. 4.6 Man Friday   249
            Second Service: 1 John 3.2 See you in heaven   251

Oct. 22   Nineteenth Sunday after Trinity (Proper 24)
            Principal Service: Matt. 22.17–21
            Church and State   254
            Second Service: Prov. 4.1, 5
            Fathers' wisdom   256

Oct. 29   Last Sunday after Trinity (Proper 25)
            (Alternatively Bible Sunday
            or the Dedication Festival)
            Principal Service: Matt. 22.37–40
            Which comes first?   258
            Second Service: Eccles. 11.7–9 Youth and age   261

Nov. 5   All Saints' Sunday
            Principal Service: Rev. 7.9–10
            Saints beyond number   263

Nov. 5   Fourth Sunday before Advent
            Principal Service: Micah 3.9–10 Guy Fawkes   265
            Second Service: Dan. 7.11
            Decline and fall   268

Nov. 12   Third Sunday before Advent
            (Remembrance Sunday)
            Principal Service: 1 Thess. 4.18
            Changing one's mind about Advent   270
            Remembrance Sunday: Matt. 5.43–45
            God with us   272

Nov. 19	**Second Sunday before Advent**	
	Principal Service: Zeph. 1.12	
	Punished by God	275
	Second Service: Rev. 1.5	
	Heirs and successors	277
Nov. 26	**Christ the King**	
	Principal Service: Matt. 25.31–32	
	Overseas aid	280
	Second Service: Matt. 28.18	
	Philosophers may sing	282

SERMONS FOR SAINTS' DAYS
AND SPECIAL OCCASIONS

Readings are from *Common Worship*, or from *Exciting Holiness* by Brother Tristam SSF, second edition, Canterbury Press, 2003.

2016		
Dec. 26	**St Stephen, Deacon, First Martyr**	
	Acts 7.53 Opposition	286
Dec. 27	**St John, Apostle and Evangelist**	
	John 21.20, 24 The Beloved Disciple	288
Dec. 28	**Holy Innocents**	
	1 Cor. 1.27 Child death	290
2017		
Jan. 1	**Naming and Circumcision of Christ**	
	Luke 2.21 Joking about somebody's name	293
Jan. 6	**Epiphany**	
	Matt. 2.2 The star is love	295
Jan. 18–25	**Week of Prayer for Christian Unity**	
	Eph. 4.1–3 Post-denominational	297
Jan. 25	**Conversion of St Paul**	
	Jer. 1.5 From Jerusalem to Athens	299

Feb. 2   Presentation of Christ in the Temple (Candlemas)
Luke 2.22 Purification   302

Mar. 1   St David, Bishop of Menevia, Patron of Wales
Matt. 16.24–26 St David's prayer   305

Mar. 17   St Patrick, Bishop, Missionary, Patron of Ireland
2 Cor. 4.1 Ireland before Patrick   307

Mar. 20   St Joseph of Nazareth (transferred)
Matt. 1.24–25 Adoption   309

Mar. 25   Annunciation of Our Lord
to the Blessed Virgin Mary
Luke 1.34 Divine rape?   312

Apr. 24   St George, Martyr, Patron of England (transferred)
2 Tim. 2.3 Everybody needs a hero   314

Apr. 25   St Mark the Evangelist
Mark 13.12–13 John Mark's mother's house   316

May 1   SS Philip and James, Apostles
John 14.8 May Day   319

May 15   St Matthias the Apostle (transferred)
1 Cor. 4.5 Three judgements   321

May 31   Visit of the Blessed Virgin Mary to Elizabeth
Luke 1.39–40 Modern verse   323

June 12   St Barnabas the Apostle (transferred)
Acts 11.20–24 Epistle of Barnabas   327

June 15   Day of Thanksgiving for the Institution
of Holy Communion (Corpus Christi)
1 Cor. 11.25 Thicker than water   329

June 24   The Birth of St John the Baptist
Luke 1.80 Desert saints   332

June 29   SS Peter and Paul, Apostles
           Zech. 4.12–14 Conflict in the Church   334

July 3   St Thomas the Apostle
           Hab. 2.4 Gospel of Thomas   336

July 22   St Mary Magdalene
           John 20.17–18 Authority   339

July 25   St James the Apostle
           Acts 12.1–2 St James' bones?   341

Aug. 6   The Transfiguration of Our Lord
           (see page 200)   344

Aug. 15   The Blessed Virgin Mary
           Luke 1.52–53 Human rights   344

Aug. 24   St Bartholomew the Apostle
           Luke 22.26 Unknown saints   346

Sept. 14   Holy Cross Day
           John 3.14–15 Salvator Mundi   349

Sept. 21   St Matthew, Apostle and Evangelist
           Prov. 3.13–14 Love or gold?   351

Sept. 29   St Michael and All Angels
           John 1.51 Guardian angels   354

Oct. 18   St Luke the Evangelist
           2 Tim. 4.11 Luke's letter to Paul   356

Oct. 28   SS Simon and Jude, Apostles
           Eph. 2.19–20 A shipwrecked apostle   358

Nov. 1   All Saints' Day
           Heb. 12.22–23 Where prayer has been valid   361

Nov. 2   Commemoration of the Faithful Departed
           (All Souls' Day)
           Lam. 3.31–33 Bereavement trauma   363

Nov. 8   **Saints and Martyrs of** (our own nation)
          Isa. 61.9 or Ecclus. (Ben Sira) 44.1
              A Christian nation?   365

Nov. 30   **St Andrew the Apostle**
          Matt. 4.20 Instant obedience   367

          Harvest Festival
          Ps. 65.3 Just enough   370

          Sermon for a Wedding
          Rom. 12.1, 10 All give, no take   372

          Sermon for a Baptism or Christening
          Prince George   374

          Sermon for a Funeral or Memorial Service
          Ps. 23 The Lord is my shepherd   376

          **Address for an Atheist's Funeral
          or Memorial Service**
          Socrates   379

Scripture Index to Sermon Texts   381
Author Index   385
Subject Index   387

Preface

My love for Jesus grew alongside my love for music, and the two have continued to reinforce each other. For many in our congregations, the musical part of the service is one of the most attractive aspects, which draws them to come regularly. Some non-churchgoers are drawn to attend church in the first place by the beauty of the music, in carols, anthems or the ordinary hymns in some small church. The music does not have to be perfectly performed, though we should always honour God by doing our best. In the words attributed to St Augustine, 'Those who sing the praises pray twice.' So we should always try to sing sincerely.

But there are others who claim to be 'tone-deaf', like the woman in the humorous poem who said, 'I'm going where heavenly anthems are ringing – but me having no voice I shan't join in the singing.' But many experts claim that is not true. Anyone, they say, can learn to sing in tune if they breathe correctly, produce the sound in the top of their mouths and not in their throats, and learn to listen to their own voice and bring it closer to the note they hear from the piano or their teacher. This has been proved by the formation of community choirs recently, first on television, and then in many areas in town and country across the nation. People who thought they could never sing, find that, with a little encouragement, they can produce a sound which is pleasing to themselves and no longer produces agony in their neighbours.

One of the beauties of the community choirs is that you do not have to read music in order to join. This must always remain so, as their task is to draw those with no or little musical education to discover the enjoyment to be found in singing together. But after they have found this joy, some, though not all, will want to explore more deeply. How about singing in two parts, with half the singers singing the tune and the others singing different notes which 'harmonize', to make a pleasant sound against them? How about singing a melody which develops in interesting ways which it is hard to memorize? What happens when the tune makes a big leap up or down but you find it hard to remember how far? How do you know at which point in the piano introduction you should begin to sing? And if you have learnt to sing, you might like to listen to the interplay of different instruments in a group, band or orchestra, or even learn an instrument yourself.

As I have suggested, there is a strong connection between music and religion. It is no accident that artists and poets have represented heaven as being full of angels singing. In music we experience a joy which is beyond logic, and a form of communication which does not depend on words. So it is to be encouraged if a minister or members of the congregation, if they do not already know, want to learn how to read music. It will deepen their intellectual and spiritual pleasure in worship. So as the latest in my series of 'How to . . .' articles, I have written one this year on 'How to read music'. You are welcome to study it on your own, or make 'not-for-sale' photocopies for others who have expressed an interest. Encourage shy people to take it up, to give them confidence. Wouldn't it be wonderful if the church organist or some other musical church member could run a series of lessons for anyone whom you can enthuse to come, or even for the whole congregation?

In addition, in the introductions to the different seasons, I have expressed thoughts which might attract you to various types of music, not only hymns, which are associated with that theme. 'Alleluia! Sing to Jesus!'

Michael Counsell

How to Read Music

PART 1

Singing is fun

Singing is fun! When we are small, we listen to somebody singing a song or humming a tune, and we try to copy what they do. With luck, we find somebody who says, 'Well done! But you haven't got it quite right. Listen carefully to these few notes. Now sing them back to me. No, the first note needs to be higher, and the second note a little lower.' We try this a few times until the correct tune sticks in our memories. If you didn't do this when you were young, try to find somebody who will play that game with you now. This is known as 'learning by ear'.

But singing from a piece of paper is even more fun, because it widens your opportunities for learning new tunes, on your own or in a group. You don't have to learn this, but it will enormously increase your pleasure in discovering new songs.

Notes on a keyboard

The easiest way to learn the notes is to get access to a piano or an electronic keyboard. Look at the white keys and the black keys. The black keys come in groups of two and three. The white key to the left of a group of two black keys is always called 'C'. (It would seem more logical if we started at A, but this system of writing music was invented centuries ago, when melodies were different from what we are used to.) Count the white notes from one C to the C above it: CDEFGABC. Including the first C and the last C that is eight notes; we call it an 'octave'. Study the picture below for a long time, memorizing where each note comes in relation to the groups of black notes. Then pick out a note on the keyboard at random, and try to name it without looking at the diagram. Sing them too at the same time. It is worth taking a long time until this is fixed in your mind.

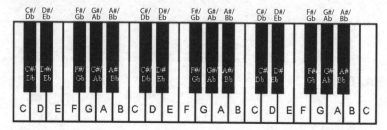

Notes on paper

Each of these notes on the keyboard (and in your voice) is represented on paper by a dot in a particular place on five lines and the gaps between them. The five lines are called a 'stave', and the lines from bottom to top are EGBDF, which you can remember as the initials of the phrase 'Every Good Boy Deserves Fun'. The spaces correspond to the notes FACE (spelling the word . . . well, that is obvious). Notes which are too high or low to fit on to the stave are added with the help of little 'leger lines' running through, above or below the notes. Spend some time learning to recognize each line and space, playing them on a keyboard if possible, and singing them from bottom to top; this is known as 'the scale of C', though most singers will find the lowest or highest notes beyond their reach.

Now sing 'Three blind mice', ignoring everything else other than noticing how the notes go up and down, sometimes far apart, sometimes only just a little bit, depending on how far apart they are on the stave:

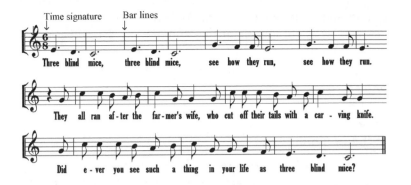

The long and the short of it

Now look at the different symbols used in musical notation. First, *the note lengths*: a white note looking like an egg lying on its side (there aren't any in 'Three Blind Mice') is called by our American cousins a 'whole note' (I shall use the American names to begin with, as they are easy to understand, but in the next illustration, the old European names, which you hear often in this country, are below the American names). A whole note lasts as long as 2 half notes, which are white notes with a stem (a vertical line attached to them); and the same as 4 quarter notes (black notes with a stem); or as 8 eighth notes (a black note with a single tail (or flag) flying off the end of it); or 16 sixteenth notes with two tails (not in 'Three Blind Mice') and so on. Often two or more quarter notes have their tails joined by a beam, especially if you sing two notes to the same syllable. A dot after a note means it is half as long again; so the half-note at the beginning would normally equal four eighth notes, but a dotted half-note equals six eighth notes. If you are not singing, the length of your silence will be marked with a 'rest', see the symbols on this illustration:

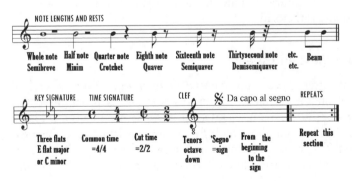

You should make sure you are thoroughly familiar with the above paragraphs before looking at the more advanced teaching in the rest of this article.

PART 2

In the beginning

The first symbol you see in the 'Three Blind Mice' music, looking a bit like an '&' sign, is actually an ornate calligraphy letter G, because it starts on the second line up, which is G. The name of the sign is the 'treble clef'. After that is the time-signature, which looks like a fraction, six-eighths; it tells you there are six of the notes with a single tail (the 'eighth notes') in every bar. The bar is the box between two vertical lines, and there is a stress (a note sung a little louder) at the beginning of every bar, to mark the rhythm. In this case there is also a more gentle stress on the fourth beat of the bar: ONE two three four five six; EVer you see such a. An accent sign > means emphasize it by singing it a bit louder; a tenuto sign like a hyphen (–) shows it should be stressed and held for its full length or slightly longer; and marcato like a ^ or alternatively like a V means stamp on it as though you were marching. Staccato, marked by a dot over the note, means detached.

Major and minor

The notes from C up to C and down again are described as the C major scale. C is called the tonic note of this scale. But if you play E flat instead of E, A flat instead of A, and B flat instead of B going up but B natural coming down, that is called the minor scale; it is usually rather sad.

Loudness and speed

The letters *pp* are pronounced *pianissimo* and mean very soft; *p* is pronounced *piano* and means soft; *mp* is pronounced *mezzo-piano* and means moderately soft; *mf* is pronounced *mezzo-forte* and means middling loud; *f* is pronounced *forte* and means loud; and *ff* is pronounced fortissimo, meaning very loud. Two diverging lines mean 'getting louder', or it may be written as *crescendo* or *cresc.*; two converging lines mean 'getting softer', or it may be written as *diminuendo* or *dim*. *Poco* means 'a little'; *accelerando* or *accel.* means 'getting faster'; *ritardando* or *rit*. means 'getting slower'; *Presto* means 'very fast'; *Allegro* means 'fairly fast'; *Andante* means 'fairly slow'; and *Largo* means 'very slow'.

Other symbols

A curved line (called a 'tie'), joining two notes to the same syllable, means that they are to be sung continuously one after the other without a break. A curved line over a long series of notes (a 'slur') means sing it as a single phrase, with no breaths, smoothly or *legato*. Breaths are usually only taken where there is a comma or a full stop in the words. Singers often pencil in an upright line or a tick to show when to breathe. A semicircle with a dot in the centre (*fermata*) means pause, or hold this note or rest until the conductor tells you when to stop.

Sharps and flats

A pair of notes with a black note between them on the keyboard (e.g. C and D) are described as being a whole tone apart, but two notes like B and C, or E and F, with no black note between them, are a much smaller interval apart, called a semitone; listen to it and see. A hash sign # before a note (called a sharp) means sing the semitone above it; so C sharp is the black note to the right of C. A lower-case b (called a flat) before a note means sing it a semitone lower; so C sharp is the same note as D flat. Once a composer has marked a note as C sharp, all the other Cs in that bar are changed to C sharp without needing to be marked. If composers want to cancel that before the end of the bar, they add a 'natural' sign, meaning 'go back to playing the white note on the keyboard' (see the next illustration, and the paragraph below on key signatures).

Key signature

So far we have been talking as though everything was in the key of C major, starting and ending on C, with no sharps or flats. If you play or sing an octave beginning on G, you have to replace all the Fs by F sharps; this is done by putting a 'key signature', consisting of one F sharp # symbol, at the beginning of the first line of music after the treble clef sign; this applies to every bar of the piece except in bars which have an F natural in them, or there is a new key signature marked part way through the piece. This process goes up a major fifth (seven semitones) at a time: C major is no sharps; G major is one sharp, D major is two, A major is three, E major is four, B major is five, F sharp major is six and C sharp major has seven sharps. Going down: C major has no flats; F major is one flat; B flat major is two flats, E flat major is three, A flat major is four, D flat major is five, G flat major is six, and C flat major is seven flats.

There is a similar arrangement for minor keys, but starting on the note three semitones below the start note of the major key with the same key signature. So A minor is no sharps; E minor is one sharp, B minor is two, F sharp minor is three, C sharp minor is four, G sharp minor is five, D sharp minor is six and A sharp minor has seven. Going down: A minor has no flats; D minor is one flat; G minor is two flats, C minor is three, F minor is four, B flat minor is five, E flat minor is six, and A flat minor is seven flats.

Voices

The highest women's voice is called soprano; lower women's voices are contraltos, sometimes called just altos. High men's voices are called tenors, and the lowest of all are basses. Some men train themselves to ignore what happened in their teens when their voices broke, and sing *falsetto*, when they are called altos and sing the same notes as the contraltos. Normally when only one voice is singing from a line of music, the stems of the notes point upwards from C up to B; either way on B; and point downwards for notes above B; see 'Three Blind Mice'. But if two voices are singing from the same line, such as sopranos and altos, the stems are up for the sopranos and down for the altos. If tenors have a line to themselves they often use the treble clef with a tiny figure 8 at the bottom of it, to indicate that they actually sing an octave lower than the notes which are written. But if tenors and basses are singing from the same line, it is marked by the bass clef, which is a calligrapher's F, believe it or not, with the two dots representing the cross strokes of the letter, and the sign beginning on the second line down. For the bass clef, the lines are, from the bottom, GBDFA or Good Boys Deserve Fun Always, and the spaces are ACEG or All Cows Eat Grass. If both are singing from the same line, the stems of the tenor notes point upwards and the stems of the bass notes point down. The line of each voice is often distinguished by the letters SATB, for soprano, alto, tenor and bass.

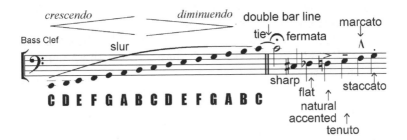

Intervals

You can practise the different rising and falling intervals by singing to yourself the first two notes of the following songs:

Semitone or minor second: UP (C–D flat) Jaws; It's been a hard day's night

Semitone or minor second: DOWN (C–B flat) Joy to the world; Shall we dance?

Tone or major second: UP (C–D) Happy birthday; Silent night

Tone or major second: DOWN (E–D) Mary had a little lamb; The first Nowell

Minor third: UP (C–E flat) Oh where, oh where has my little dog gone?; Kum Ba Yah

Minor third: DOWN (G–E) Hey Jude; Jesus loves me, this I know

Major third: UP (C–E) Oh when the saints; While shepherds watched

Major third: DOWN (E–C) Swing low, sweet chariot; Good night, ladies

Perfect fourth: UP (G–C) Amazing grace; Here comes the bride

Perfect fourth: DOWN (C–G) Born free; Oh come all ye faithful (notes 2–3)

Augmented fourth: UP (C–F sharp) Maria (West Side Story)

Augmented fourth: DOWN (C–F sharp) Police siren

Perfect fifth: UP (C–G) Twinkle, twinkle, little star

Perfect fifth: DOWN (G–C) For all the saints (notes 1 and 4)

Minor sixth: UP (C–A flat) Go down, Moses

Major sixth: UP (C–A) My Bonnie lies over the ocean; Dashing through the snow

Minor or diminished seventh: UP (C–B flat) There's a place for us (*West Side Story*)

Minor or diminished seventh: DOWN (C–D) Donkey's hee-haw

Major seventh: UP (C–B) Bali Hai (South Pacific)

Octave: UP: (C–C) Somewhere over the rainbow (*The Wizard of Oz*)

Octave: DOWN: (C–C) There's no business like show business (notes 2–3)

Practice

Now you know all this, borrow as much printed music as you can, and preferably a recording of the song also, and learn to recognize the names of the notes, the feeling of the intervals and the swing of the rhythm, and you will be well on the way towards 'sight-reading', which means knowing from the printed music what you are going to sing even before it is played or sung over to you.

If you search on Google for 'How to read music' you will find several sites which cover this subject in different ways, and you may like to compare them.

YEAR A, the Year of Matthew

*(Year A begins on Advent Sunday
in 2016, 2019, 2022 etc.)*

ADVENT

We strike one of the hardest problems in church music at the very beginning of the church year. At Christmas we celebrate the coming of Jesus into the world at Bethlehem. For many centuries the celebrations began on Christmas eve and included the 'Twelve days of Christmas', finishing on the eve of the Epiphany (5 January). Preceding that celebration, there were four Sundays of solemn preparation for the coming of Christ, in various different ways, called Advent. To be honest, if we are humble, any of us who was told they would shake hands with Jesus tomorrow would be terrified – we know we are not good enough, and we want to say sorry for the bad things we have done, before he comes. So Advent is a penitential season, an opportunity to confess our sins and receive God's forgiveness. So we do not sing the 'Glory to God in the highest' during Advent; the church hangings are purple, and some church music refers to the Last Judgement: 'Lo, he comes with clouds descending'; 'Soon and very soon'; 'Sleepers, wake', with J. S. Bach's cantata on those words. And here comes the second problem: many Christians now do not believe there will be a Last Judgement, though they may not say so for fear of offending simple souls. At some point we need to point out that Jesus comes to us every day of our lives, with forgiveness, grace and blessing, and at our death to welcome us to heaven. So we should concentrate on more hopeful hymns, looking to the coming of Jesus to forgive and save: 'Christ is surely coming' (Land of hope & glory); 'Come and see the shining hope' (Marching through Georgia); 'Come thou long expected Jesus'; 'Hark, a herald voice is sounding'; 'Hark, the glad sound! the Saviour comes'. The themes of the readings on the four Sundays of Advent include: Prophecy ('Long ago, prophets knew'), John the Baptist ('On Jordan's bank the Baptist's cry'), Joseph and the Angel ('Joseph dearest, Joseph mine, Joseph was an old man' (The Cherry Tree Carol)), and the Annunciation ('The angel Gabriel from heaven came'). But there is a third problem: people want to sing Christmas carols during Advent, and who are we to stop them? The shops fill with Christmas goods in August and remove them at Christmas for the New Year sales; schools that have carol services fit them in before the end of term. The most we can hope for is to keep carols for the carol services, and take a not-too-solemn approach to the Sundays. And Handel's *Messiah* is suitable for any season.

First Sunday of Advent   27 November 2016
Principal Service   **Matthew's Vision**
Isa. 2.1–5 Nations will seek the Temple; Ps. 122 Let us go up to the Temple; Rom. 13.11–14 Lay aside the works of darkness; Matt. 24.36–44 The coming of the Son of Man

> *'[Jesus said,] "Therefore you . . . must be ready, for the Son of Man is coming at an unexpected hour."' Matthew 24.44*

Matthew

St Matthew's Gospel was written for Jews who had become Christians, or were thinking about it. We can tell that because of the number of quotations from the Old Testament, and some typically Hebrew turns of phrase, indicating that the writer's first language was Hebrew; but it was written in Greek, so they were probably living at some distance away from Jerusalem. St Mark's was the first Gospel to be written, and Matthew and Luke copied huge chunks of it word for word; yet each added sections of their own which Mark had omitted. The Gospels include words of Jesus about what is going to happen in the future; Mark collects them into a single chapter, Mark 13; Luke copies this in chapter 21, with additions; Matthew does the same in Matthew 24 and 25, part of which we have read today. When he writes critically of 'the Jews', we should remember that he himself was Jewish, as was Jesus, who constantly criticized the priests, the Pharisees and the Sadducees, who were extreme nationalists and hated the Christians. The priests had refused to accept Jesus as the Messiah when he rode into Jerusalem on a donkey; so Jesus replies that although they were hoping Jerusalem would have a glorious future, the opposite would be the case, and not one stone would be left upon another. The obvious questions on everybody's lips, then, were: what will happen, and when will it occur?

Jerusalem destroyed

There are two alternative answers to this: some verses support one and some support the other explanation. Probably Jesus spoke about both things, and his disciples wove them together. The two explanations are:

1   The Destruction of Jerusalem, in AD 70; and
2   The coming of the kingdom of God.

Jesus quite clearly warned his fellow Jews that if they continued to resist the Roman Empire, the Empire would destroy the Jewish nation. Jesus opposed narrow nationalism, and recommended that different races should cooperate for the benefit of everybody. What Jesus had predicted came to pass in AD 70, when the Jews rose up in revolt, and so the Romans destroyed the Temple and burnt Jerusalem to the ground, forbidding any Jew from entering the city ever again. This vindicated Jesus as a prophet, and warned the Jews against excessive attachment to their national symbols. It warns all of us against trying to impose our will on others by the use of force.

The kingdom of God

The second thing which Jesus predicted was the coming of the kingdom of God. But those words were understood in several different ways. To begin with, many Jews thought the Lord would send a Messiah, a great king and general, who would destroy their enemies in battle and set up a Jewish empire in place of the Roman one.

3

But Jesus had already rejected a military role, which was the exact opposite of the kingdom of love that he talked about. So when he told us to pray, 'thy will be done, thy kingdom come, on earth as it is in heaven,' did he mean he would suddenly reappear on earth and divide its inhabitants into good and bad, the bad to be destroyed and the good to reign with him on earth for a thousand years? If so, why hasn't it happened yet; and if it isn't going to happen in our lifetime, what does it matter to us? Or did he mean that we should strive towards a human society in which justice rules and unselfish love abounds? We are still a long way from that ideal world, and it may not happen in our lifetime; but if we are wholeheartedly working in that direction, then we are doing what God wants us to. So we shall be unafraid to die, whenever that happens, because we know that the ideal society already exists in heaven, and that Jesus will welcome us at whatever point in our lives we happen to die. So the words of Jesus are not just relevant to what happened 2,000 years ago, nor to what will happen in the far distant future – they are an urgent warning to us about what we do this very day. The word 'Advent' means 'coming'; are you working towards the coming of the kingdom of God?

All-age worship

Make a poster, with coloured crowns: Jesus comes: to earth at Christmas; to our hearts when we pray; to our souls when he takes us to heaven; to this planet when we build an ideal world.

Suggested hymns

And did those feet in ancient time?; Lo, he comes with clouds descending; Sleepers wake, a voice is calling; The Lord will come and not be slow.

First Sunday of Advent   27 November 2016
Second Service   Is the World Coming to an End Today?
Ps. 9 The Lord judges the world; Isa. 52.1–12 How beautiful upon the mountains; Matt. 24.15–28 False messiahs

> '[Jesus said,] "If anyone says to you, 'Look! Here is the Messiah!' or 'There he is!' – do not believe it."' Matthew 24.23

Peanuts

Charles Schulz, in one of his 'Peanuts' cartoons, has a character say, 'Don't worry about the world coming to an end today – in Australia it's already tomorrow'! That is cute, and a necessary warning to people who live in a perpetual state of anxiety. But the logic is faulty, because 1am in Australia is the same moment as 1pm here, and any world-shattering event which occurred at what we call 1 p.m., could be observed by those on the opposite side of the globe as happening in the middle of the night, on whichever side of the international dateline they happen to be. (I think.) But his serious message is worth heeding: don't live in a state of perpetual panic, because it will prevent you doing all the good things you could be attempting.

For us

But there are several reasons why the world as we know it could end *for us* on this day or on some other day, but within our lifetime. Here are just a few; most of them are avoidable:

- We could be killed in a road accident; what is popularly called 'walking under a bus'. Careless, to say the least.
- We could have a heart attack. Usually you already know that you have the symptoms that make that likely, but some patients refuse to accept the warnings, or, as we say, 'live in denial'.
- We could be in a building which collapses; there have been too many examples of this recently, and usually they were because those in authority neglected to carry out regular inspections.
- We could be the victims of an earthquake, a strong gale, a hurricane or a tsunami. We may think there is nothing we can do about this, but past history has shown us where the earthquake zones lie, and where the low land is which is frequently subject to flooding. We don't have to build our houses there, or force poor people to do so. If we do, we must ensure that they are built of strong materials which can resist such forces.
- We could be the victims of climate change. This may be a natural fluctuation, or it may be caused by human pollution of the atmosphere. In either case, if we could lessen the effects by reducing our carbon emissions, we are committing a wicked sin against our children and grandchildren by failing to do so.

- We could starve, or die of thirst, because we have destroyed the environment by cutting down the rainforest, covering green fields in concrete, or neglecting our wildlife. Or if we neglect the unequal distribution of human resources, the people in the developing world whom we are starving to death will demand to enter our country and share our wealth.
- We could go down with a disease, which could be prevented if we devoted more funds to research.
- You could . . . well, you get the point!

Be ready

Why should I read such a list in a sermon? My purpose is not to make you gloomy, but to make you prepared. Some causes of death cannot be avoided; but for others, we are just burying our heads in the sand if we refuse to take simple precautions. Have the electric cables in your house checked periodically – that sort of thing.

Advent

If you are a Christian, you ought not to be afraid of death, because the Bible tells us it is the gateway to eternal life, to a world where all is peace and joy, where we shall meet again in love those who have gone there before us. Advent is a good time to think of how Jesus may come to us at any moment; but we should not be afraid. If you look at the life-expectancy figures in our grandparents' days, you would realize that many of us are lucky to have reached the age we are, when very few lived that long in the past. So surely we should enjoy life to the full for as long as we can, thanking God for all the good things which happen to us, and looking forward in hope to the day when God thinks we are ready to enter into eternal life. Listen to Jesus; don't listen to the gloom merchants, or to those who raise false hopes of eternal health in this world. Jesus said, 'If anyone says to you, "Look! Here is the Messiah!" or "There he is!" – do not believe it.' But Jesus is the true Messiah, and we can trust him to tell us the truth about life after death.

Suggested hymns

Come, thou long expected Jesus; Hark, the glad sound, the Saviour comes; How lovely on the mountains are the feet of him; Joy to the world.

Second Sunday of Advent 4 December

Principal Service **Remorse → Forgiveness → Progress**
Isa. 11.1–10 A shoot from the stump of Jesse; Ps. 72.1–7,
18–19 Give the King your righteousness; Rom. 15.4–13
Hope from the Bible; Matt. 3.1–12 John the Baptist preaches
repentance

> 'John the Baptist appeared in the wilderness of Judea, proclaiming,
> "Repent, for the kingdom of heaven has come near."' Matthew
> 3.1–2

Perfectionism

What a lot of time we waste trying to defend our own reputation!
If the least hint of criticism is levelled against us, we metaphorically leap to the portholes of our ship, cutlass in our mouth, trying
to beat away the slightest allegation against the perfection that
we see in our own character. Our self-respect seems to depend
on believing that there is not the tiniest flaw in our personality.
Does somebody say we forgot something? Nonsense, we have a
perfect memory. Is it alleged that we have been inconsiderate? Of
course not; we look after number one, as anybody does who has
any sense; but if at any time that leaves us, we are delighted to do
somebody else a favour, provided that they are eternally grateful
to us. It is all 'me', 'me', 'me'; and we devote our lives to fooling
the rest of the world that there is not a single fault in us. Of course
I exaggerate, but surely you can see a trace of that defensiveness in
your own life?

Handicap

Other people may get cross with us for never admitting that we
have any faults. More likely they will chuckle behind their hands at
how ridiculous we are. But the real problem with those who cannot admit their deficiencies is that it becomes a handicap, which
prevents them moving forward. You cannot improve your own
character if you do not see that it needs improving. You get stuck
in immaturity, if you are not prepared to work honestly towards a
more mature opinion of yourself. So the first step towards behaving as an adult is to admit that you have occasionally done wrong,
possibly unintentionally, but more likely because you have been so

7

busy presenting yourself to the world as an angel to notice what effect your words and actions are having on the people around you. Now I know what you're thinking: 'I'm not at all like that, but I know somebody who is.' Uh-uh, you've fallen into the trap again, judging other people but refusing to judge yourself.

John the Baptist

The message of John the Baptist, which we heard in today's Gospel reading, is summed up in one word: 'Repent!' His fellow Jews thought that, because they were descended from Abraham, they were sinless; it was only those filthy foreigners who, if they wanted to be admitted to God's Chosen People, needed to have their sins washed away in what was called Gentile baptism. 'No', said John sternly; all have sinned, so all must repent, and be baptized. You only need to be baptized once; but after that you must be constantly self-critical, and always repentant.

Forgiveness

Admitting your faults is a stepping-stone towards repentance. Normally, but not always, the next step is to confess to other people that you have wounded them, and ask them to forgive you. Then you must say sorry to God. There is no need for constant remorse; once your sins have been confessed, God forgives them, and it is self-centred of the sinner to bring them up again.

Progress

But as John well knew, remorse leading to forgiveness is the only way towards progress in life. Broken relationships litter our path, because neither side will say 'I'm sorry', and neither party will reply, 'I forgive you.' And these remembered resentments drag like a ball and chain on our feet, stopping us from progressing towards maturity and true happiness. In Advent, we think of the coming of Christ, and his cousin John said that when Jesus was born, the kingdom of heaven had drawn near. But it is by our kind deeds that the kingdom of justice and love will come on earth, so John told us to produce loving behaviour, arising out of our repentance, like fruit growing from a healthy tree, 'fruits which prove our repentance'.

So remember: the only way forward is to acknowledge your faults, say sorry, and ask for forgiveness, from those you have hurt, and from God. That path leads to release from the past, with great joy and freedom. So the apparently gloomy message of John, which we proclaim in Advent, is in fact the path to happiness.

All-age worship

Each is invited to write, on a paper, things they have done wrong in the past week, fold it and put it in a jar, unread by anyone else. Tell God you are sorry, and put the contents of the jar through a shredder to show that God has wiped them from his memory.

Suggested hymns

Hark, the glad sound! the Saviour comes; O come, O come, Emmanuel; On Jordan's bank the Baptist's cry; The kingdom of God is justice and joy.

Second Sunday of Advent 4 December
Second Service Elijah and Mendelssohn
Ps. 11 The righteous Lord loves righteousness [28 The Lord has heard my prayer]; 1 Kings 18.17–39 Elijah and the prophets of Baal; John 1.19–28 The testimony of John the Baptist

> *'Elijah . . . came near to all the people, and said, "How long will you go limping with two different opinions? If the LORD is God, follow him; but if Baal, then follow him." The people did not answer him a word.' 1 Kings 18.21*

Decision time

In Advent we prepare for the coming of Jesus at Christmas, so there are references in the readings to St John the Baptist, whose task it was to 'prepare the way of the Lord'. At this service the first reading is the story of the prophet Elijah, presumably because he, like John after him, challenged the people of Israel to make a fresh start, fully committed in total loyalty to the Lord their God; Elijah said, 'How long will you go limping with two different opinions? If the LORD is God, follow him; but if Baal, then follow him.' Other prophets are mentioned before Elijah, but he is the first whose deeds and character are fully described. And what a character! Tremendous courage and authority, yet a very human self-doubt and vulnerability.

Life

In case you have forgotten, Ahab, King of Israel, stopped following the Lord God, with his demands for ethical behaviour, preferring the many baalim, the fertility gods of the neighbouring nations, who brought a promise of fulfilling his sexual and physical desires. Many people today desert the worship of the one true God for similar reasons. So Elijah confronted Ahab and threatened him with a long drought unless he changed his ways. Then Elijah fled to the Brook Cherith, where the ravens fed him, and on to the widow of Zarephath, where they lived on the endless supply of oil in the widow's 'cruse' – not a sea journey, but an old name for a jug! The widow's son died; so Elijah brought him to life again with a sort of artificial respiration. Elijah sends for King Ahab to meet him, and Ahab calls him 'You troubler of Israel'. 'No, you are the one who troubles Israel,' replies Elijah. 'Call all the prophets of Baal to meet me on Mount Carmel for a fire-lighting competition.' The prophets perform a limping dance around the altar of Baal, but their offering does not catch fire. Elijah mocks them, saying, 'Perhaps your all-too-human god has gone to relieve himself.' He prays to the Lord: fire comes down from heaven and burns up the sacrifice, the altar and the ground around it. In one of the most unpleasant scenes in the Bible, Elijah then kills all the prophets of Baal. Next he tells his servant to look out for a rain cloud. When they see one, 'no bigger than a man's hand', Elijah runs all the way to Jezreel, the then-capital of Israel, overtaking Ahab just as the clouds burst, drenching the parched land. Ahab's wife, Jezebel, threatens to kill Elijah, so again he flees for his life. Growing old, he chooses Elisha to be his servant; then he ascends in a chariot to heaven; the cloak of Elijah fell on Elisha.

Mendelssohn

As if that wasn't a wonderful enough tale on its own, it was then set to some of the world's most beautiful music, composed by

Mendelssohn. Felix Mendelssohn-Bartholdy was born in 1809, the grandson of the famous Jewish philosopher Moses Mendelssohn. He was brought up a Christian, but his devotion to study owed much to the family's Jewish roots. His conducting of Bach's *St Matthew Passion* brought Bach's music back to public attention when it had been forgotten for more than a century. Ten times Mendelssohn visited Britain, including a trip to the Hebrides where he wrote what is popularly known as *Fingal's Cave*. He was a great favourite of Queen Victoria, who may have been among those who tried to persuade him to write oratorios in the style of Handel's popular *Messiah*. His first, *St Paul*, was performed in Germany, but Mendelssohn's *Elijah* was first performed in Birmingham Town Hall.

Oratorio

Inspired by the story in the Bible, Mendelssohn's *Elijah* contains some of the finest melodies he wrote; and the music brings out the deep meaning of the words. Among the memorable sections are:

- 'Lord! bow thine ear to our prayer!'
- 'If with all your hearts ye truly seek Me'
- the quartet 'Cast thy burden upon the Lord'
- many wonderful choruses, including 'Baal, we cry to thee'
- 'He, watching over Israel, slumbers not nor sleeps'
- 'Be not afraid, saith God the Lord'
- 'Thanks be to God'
- 'Lift thine eyes'
- 'He that shall endure to the end'
- and many others.

What an inspiration to follow Elijah's courage in confronting wickedness without fear; bearing bold witness to God; and clinging tenaciously to our hope, when our faith weakens in times of affliction!

Suggested hymns

Long ago, prophets knew; People, look east; The people that in darkness sat; Ye servants of the Lord.

Third Sunday of Advent 11 December
Principal Service **Streams in the Desert**

Isa. 35.1–10 Healing in the desert; Ps. 146.4–10 Healing and salvation, *or Canticle*: Luke 1.46–55 Magnificat, God's justice; James 5.7–10 Wait in patience; Matt. 11.2–11 Jesus' teaching about John the Baptist

> *'Waters shall break forth in the wilderness, and streams in the desert.' Isaiah 35.6*

Isaiah chapter 35

Our first reading today was probably not written by the prophet Isaiah, I am trying to make this as simple as possible, so please take my word for it that Isaiah chapter 35 was written when the Jews were in exile in Babylon. If you accept that, then suddenly a set of puzzling words make brilliant sense when read in context. The Jews thought the Lord God had abandoned them, and they had lost hope. This, they thought, was the end of God's Chosen People. No, wrote the anonymous prophet, the Lord still has a plan for you. He will come and destroy Babylon, and in the midst of the trackless desert, a highway will be built from Babylon to the ruins of Jerusalem, which will be rebuilt:

> Say to those who are of a fearful heart, "Be strong, do not fear! Here is your God. He will come with vengeance, with terrible recompense. He will come and save you." Then the eyes of the blind shall be opened, and the ears of the deaf unstopped; then the lame shall leap like a deer, and the tongue of the speechless sing for joy. For waters shall break forth in the wilderness, and streams in the desert; the burning sand shall become a pool, and the thirsty ground springs of water; the haunt of jackals shall become a swamp, the grass shall become reeds and rushes. A highway shall be there, and it shall be called the Holy Way; the unclean shall not travel on it, but it shall be for God's people . . . the redeemed shall walk there. And the ransomed of the LORD shall return, and come to Zion with singing; everlasting joy shall be upon their heads; they shall obtain joy and gladness, and sorrow and sighing shall flee away.

Well, in 538 Cyrus King of Babylon signed a decree allowing the exiles to return; they marched across the desert, and somehow found enough to drink. The Lord didn't destroy Babylon, and there were no actual streams in the desert, but otherwise the prophecy was spot on, and this poem brought a message of hope, without which they might never have taken the first steps on the homeward journey.

New Testament

That was what this chapter meant to those who first read it; but Jesus and the writers of the New Testament took it much deeper. Jesus opened the eyes of several blind people. Revelation describes the destruction of Babylon. John the Baptist appeared in the desert, saying he was called to prepare the way of the Lord; he used water to bring believers to new life. Redeemed is another translation of the word 'ransomed'. But above all, Jesus quoted many of these phrases, and other passages from Isaiah, to describe the kingdom of God which he had come to bring:

> The Spirit of the Lord is upon me, because he has anointed me to bring good news to the poor. He has sent me to proclaim release to the captives and recovery of sight to the blind, to let the oppressed go free, to proclaim the year of the Lord's favour . . . Today this scripture has been fulfilled in your hearing.

Jesus taught his disciples to build such an ideal society on earth.

Today

Today, too, the Bible calls us to work towards social justice. We seem to be in exile in a sinful world; but take courage, one day God will come to save us. That is the theme of this Advent season, and we think of God coming to us as our Saviour when Jesus was born in Bethlehem. But the ideal society didn't come straight away, and still it has not yet arrived. But we are making progress, and we must go on working towards universal justice. We may not achieve it in this world, but God's kingdom does exist in the afterlife, in heaven. So in Advent we also look forward, each of us, to the day when Jesus will welcome us to his heavenly kingdom. Then our long exile on earth will be over, and our spiritual blindness will be cured. Then:

> the ransomed of the LORD shall return, and come to Zion with singing; everlasting joy shall be upon their heads; they shall obtain joy and gladness, and sorrow and sighing shall flee away.

All-age worship

Write down what we would have to do to make our country as fair and just as it is in heaven.

Suggested hymns

Christ is surely coming (Land of hope and glory); I cannot tell why he whom angels worship; Soon and very soon; Thou didst leave thy throne.

Third Sunday of Advent   11 December
Second Service   Preaching to Jews

Ps. 12 Social injustice [14 The fool has said]; Isa. 5.8–30 Social injustice; Acts 13.13–41 Paul preaches to Jews; *Gospel at Holy Communion*: John 5.31–40 Jesus' teaching about John the Baptist

> '[Paul began his sermon], "My brothers, you descendants of Abraham's family, and others who fear God, to us the message of this salvation has been sent."' Acts 13.26

Antioch

In the book called the Acts of the Apostles, St Luke describes the journeys of his friend St Paul all across the Roman Empire. The places he visited were all different. In today's reading, Paul and Barnabas arrive at Pisidian Antioch. There were several cities in the Empire named after the successful Emperor Antiochus, so they were distinguished by a second name, usually the district where they were situated. Pisidia was on the very edge of the Empire, keeping watch against the warlike tribes beyond the nearby border. The Romans there were mostly soldiers, or civil servants. There was no reason why many Jews should go there, except, of course, that they never missed an opportunity to do business; so they met in a small synagogue, the foundations of which have been discovered among the ruins. It was here that Paul was invited to preach.

God-fearers

Among the congregation there were also a number of what the Jews called 'god-fearers'. These were non-Jews who were attracted by Jewish culture and morality, worshipped the one God, and followed the Law, except that they were not willing to be circumcised; they were kept on the edges of the worshipping community. So Paul began his sermon: 'My brothers, you descendants of Abraham's family, and others who fear God, to us the message of this salvation has been sent.'

Adapting

But as any preacher will tell you, you can't preach the same sermon to different types of congregation. Here, St Paul, who was himself Jewish, gives us an example of how he preached to Jews, which wasn't at all like what he said to those who were quite unfamiliar with the Jewish Scriptures; for an example of that, see his sermon at Athens. You might think that this sermon doesn't concern you if you are not Jewish, but you are wrong. Everything that Jesus did was thought out in Jewish terms, and everything Paul and the other apostles taught was originally in a dialect of the Hebrew language, so you cannot understand any of it unless you make an effort to understand how Jews in those days reasoned.

Planned

The first point is that God does not act on impulse; he has a carefully worked-out plan, which he has been applying steadily down the centuries. St Paul began at the Exodus from Egypt. God chose the descendants of Abraham not for any virtue of their own, but because they had nothing, and were completely dependent on his mercy. The escape from Egypt showed them clearly that their God is a god who saves. No matter what a mess we get ourselves into, if we repent and pray to him, God will rescue us. God gave them kings, and from David's descendants promised a Messiah. Jesus came, fulfilling all the predictions of the prophets. But he would save us, not from tyrants, but from slavery to those bad habits which we call sin, and the guilt which follows. Baptism was a symbol of forgiveness, offered by the Jews to non-Jews who converted; but John the Baptist taught that even faithful Jews needed to repent and be forgiven. Yet those who believe they are chosen and virtuous are at greatest danger, and the people whom Jesus had come to save turned on him and had him condemned to death. But God raised Jesus from the dead and offered immortality to all who believe in him. This was a bit much for the people in the synagogue to swallow at one gulp. They begged Paul to continue the following week. But the next week crowds of non-Jews – Romans and Greeks – gathered to hear Paul's message of free forgiveness to all. The Jews in the synagogue were angry at losing their privileged status. As they had turned on Jesus, now they turned on his apostle, and drove him from the area. Meanwhile, however, many non-Jews were converted, and Paul saw that is the direction in which his future mission lay.

Lesson

What does this mean for us non-Jews? It means that God has a plan, from the very beginning, for us as a group and you as an individual, but we need to respond in faith and obedience for God to bring it to fulfilment. And never dare to think for one moment that you hold a privileged position, because of your religion, your race or your social group; or you may fall as the Jews did, and need to be born again if God is to rescue you.

Suggested hymns:

God is working his purpose out; Jesus shall reign, where'er the sun; The God of Abraham praise; We sing the glorious conquest.

Fourth Sunday of Advent   18 December
Principal Service   **The Troubled Town**
Isa. 7.10–16 The sign of Immanuel; Ps. 80.1–8, 18–20 Restore your people; Rom. 1.1–7 Sent to preach the gospel of salvation; Matt. 1.18–25 The birth of Jesus, Joseph's dream

'Now the birth of Jesus the Messiah took place in this way . . .'
Matthew 1.18

Pilgrims

Jesus was born on Christmas Day, but for a week or more beforehand, his heavily pregnant mother Mary was jolting along the rough roads on the back of a donkey. So the coming of God into the world was already marked by suffering and official oppression. His birth in Bethlehem and resurrection in Jerusalem made them the two holiest cities for Christians around the world, and pilgrims started visiting them from at least AD 333, when the Pilgrim of Bordeaux visited Jerusalem and found it had been completely destroyed by the Roman army in AD 70. By the time Egeria went there in 381 there were swarms of pilgrims everywhere. St Jerome translated the Bible into Latin in the cave next to that where Jesus was born in Bethlehem. Christians have always wanted to see the places mentioned in the Bible, so that they can better imagine the background to the stories.

Commerce

But pilgrims need looking after: they want food and somewhere to sleep, and souvenirs to remind them where they have been. Obligingly, the local people supplied their needs, and the economy of Bethlehem was transformed from shepherding to tourism. Some people are disappointed in the Holy Land, because they think it no longer looks like the pictures in the Sunday school books. Sorry, dears; it never did. Of course, now there are armed Israeli soldiers on every corner, and you can't move for people trying to sell you things. But in the time of Jesus, there were armed Roman soldiers on every corner, and you couldn't get into the Temple, for the crowds of money-changers and dove-sellers. You misunderstand the Gospels if you ignore those facts.

Christians

But things have changed drastically in recent years. Not long ago 90 per cent of the population of Bethlehem were Arab Christians, mostly Roman Catholics converted by the Franciscan friars who have been there since the fifteenth century. Many of them were craftsmen, skilled at carving olive wood and inlaying it with mother-of-pearl. They made rosary beads and crosses, but also some large beautifully carved models of the Church of the Holy Sepulchre. But since the Israeli occupation, Bethlehem's residents cannot get a permit to cross the high wall which snakes its way around royal David's city, across the fields where they used to keep their flocks and grow crops. Jerusalem is only six miles away; yet they are lucky if they get a permit to go there once a year. They cannot export their products, and the pilgrims come for an hour or so through the border gate with an Israeli tour company. In this situation, many of the Christian population, unable to make a living, have emigrated, and Bethlehem's population is now three-quarters Muslim. On the whole they get on well together, facing a common threat, but some have wondered whether in a few years there will be any Christians at all in the land where Christianity was born. Bethlehem now has a life of suffering, like that of the Saviour who was born there.

Phillips Brooks

In 1865, when the American Episcopal priest Phillips Brooks, later to become a bishop, visited Bethlehem, he rode on horseback along the top of the ridge in the moonlight – possibly the route along which Mary rode her donkey – and was so struck by the calm atmosphere surrounding the birthplace of Jesus, that he wrote the carol 'O little town of Bethlehem':

> O little town of Bethlehem,
> how still we see thee lie!
> Above thy deep and dreamless sleep
> the silent stars go by . . .
> How silently, how silently,
> the wondrous gift is given . . .

Anyone who knows what Bethlehem is like now almost chokes over those words. A recent pilgrim revised the first verse to read:

> The troubled town of Bethlehem,
> so long a scene of strife,
> hears God's 'No More!' to weary war
> which dogs its daily life,
> and Muslim, Christian, Jew all call
> on God to bring release,
> for here was born on Christmas morn
> the fragile Prince of Peace.

© 2007 Michael Counsell

You may not want to sing those words in church. But when you read the pretty stories of the nativity, remember that Bethlehem was a place of pain for Mary, Jesus, and still is for some. For some in this congregation, still grieving over the death of someone they love, Christmas is no longer a happy time. But if we pray, God will give us an inner peace and strength which will carry us through the difficult times.

All-age worship

Tie a pillow on your tummy, and ride piggy-back on someone larger than yourself. Imagine what it was like for Mary on the donkey. Learn 'Little donkey . . .'.

Suggested hymns

Little donkey; 'The Kingdom is upon you!'; Thou whose almighty word; Wake, O wake! With tidings thrilling.

Fourth Sunday of Advent   18 December
Second Service   **Come, Lord Jesus!**
Ps. 113 God blesses the barren [126 Sow in tears, reap with joy]; 1 Sam. 1.1–20 Hannah conceives Samuel; Rev. 22.6–21 Come, Lord Jesus!; *Gospel at Holy Communion*: Luke 1.39–45 Mary visits Elizabeth

> *'The one who testifies to these things says, "Surely I am coming soon." Amen. Come, Lord Jesus!' Revelation 22.20–21*

Bishop Robinson

John Robinson was a divinity lecturer in Cambridge; then, in the 1960s, Bishop of Woolwich. His most controversial book was *Honest to God*, but it was not his best. His monograph called *The Body* was useful in disentangling the difference between the flesh and the body in the New Testament. But at Advent, which means 'coming', we should take a closer look at a short book he wrote called *Jesus and his Coming*. There are several ways in which Jesus comes to us, he wrote. Jesus came to us at Christmas, and in his life, death and resurrection, and in the coming of the Holy Spirit. He comes to each one of us when we die. He comes to us in the crises of our lives, and of human history. And some day, in some way, when human life ends on this planet, that will be his final involvement with our earthly existence. Some of his sayings refer to one of these, and some apply to another, and we misunderstand the Bible if we fail to disentangle them.

Revelation

The coming of Christ is the main theme of the book of Revelation. It is the last book of the Bible, and the last words of this book are '"Surely I am coming soon." Amen. Come, Lord Jesus! The grace of the Lord Jesus be with all the saints. Amen.' But what did St John the Theologian, who wrote Revelation, actually believe about the coming of Christ? Which coming was he referring to?

Code

The first thing to remember is that it was written in code. John was a political prisoner, condemned to slavery in the quarries on the island of Patmos. Somehow he managed to smuggle out a document, containing letters to seven Christian congregations he was connected with, in the Province of Asia, in what we now call Turkey. He knew them well, named several individuals in the congregations, and gave them warnings appropriate to their situation at that time. They were beginning to experience persecution from the Roman Empire, and basically John wanted to tell them not to worry, because no empire lasts for ever. But he would be executed for treason if he wrote that in clear; for it was the Roman Empire who had sent him to Patmos. So he used an old trick, writing about visions in symbolic poetry, using references to the Old Testament which would mean nothing to a Roman soldier who intercepted it. This was called apocalyptic writing, from a word meaning 'no longer hidden', or in other words, 'revealed'.

Apocalyptic

An early example was when someone tacked a manuscript, which we know as Isaiah 40 and onwards, on to the end of a copy of the writing of the prophet Isaiah several centuries earlier. This was sent to the Jewish exiles in Babylon, encouraging them that the Babylonian Empire will not last for ever, and one day God will lead them back across the wilderness to Jerusalem. So 'prepare in the wilderness the way of the Lord'. When St John, in the Revelation, writes about the destruction of Babylon, which was then long past, he is referring to the decline and fall of the Roman Empire, which at that time was still in the future.

Come

There are symbolic descriptions of the worship of God in heaven, which would encourage the persecuted churches to believe that there *is* life after death, and all those who believe in Jesus will enjoy 'the heavenly Jerusalem' where all will be happiness and love. Many Christians believe that the New Jerusalem, coming down to earth from heaven, is a reference to future historical events. But that is impossible; anything as heavy as a city could not possibly be kept above the clouds; and if Jesus and John meant that it was to happen 'soon', then they were both grievously mistaken, because after 2,000 years it has still not happened. More likely, they both referred to an ideal society of self-sacrificing love. *Whenever* we die, we should like to be found busily building such a society, whether or not it comes to fruition in this life. So when we say with St John, 'Come, Lord Jesus', we mean several things:

> come to me when I have a problem;
> come to destroy the unjust civilizations which oppress us;
> come and help us to build a society in which everyone, includ-
> ing me, obeys God as our king; and
> come to me in mercy when I die.

Suggested hymns

Hark, what a sound, and too divine for hearing; Hills of the North, rejoice; The advent of our King; Thy Kingdom come, O God.

CHRISTMAS, EPIPHANY AND CANDLEMAS

Probably the most popular piece of Church music for TV viewers at Christmas is the Service of Nine Lessons and Carols from King's College Chapel in Cambridge. Many churches try to copy this format, though the readings will probably be from a modern translation of the Bible, and unless you are blessed with a choir, some of the choral settings of the carols which King's has made famous will be beyond the ability of the congregation. But this does not matter; it is the total experience that counts. Most people make a willing suspension of disbelief during the readings, realizing that it doesn't really matter whether the stories are historically true or not; in fact, that is rather a distraction from the real point of the story, which is that 'God loved the world so much that he gave . . .', gave Jesus to show us that God's character is unblemished love. Enjoy as many of the choir carols as you can, but for the congregation you would do better to choose from popular collections like the Bethlehem Carol Sheets (www. embracechristmas.org or phone 01227 811646).

'The Epiphany' means 'The Revealing', and the festival falls on 6 January. This is the Greek Orthodox Christmas, but in the West we concentrate on the visit of the wise men to Bethlehem. If you are going to observe this feast on the Sunday nearest to 6 January, you would be wise not to sing carols about the magi at Christmas, and save them for Epiphany-tide. Examples are: 'As with gladness men of old'; 'From the eastern mountains'; 'O worship the Lord in the beauty of holiness'; and 'We three kings of orient are'. But each Sunday between 6 January and 2 February is in the Epiphany season. The Persian Magi were the first foreigners to worship Christ, when we think about the worldwide mission of the Church, with hymns like 'God forgave my sin' ('Freely, freely'); 'God is working his purpose out'; 'God's Spirit is in my heart' ('Go tell everyone'); 'Hail to the Lord's anointed'; 'Hills of the north, rejoice'; 'In Christ there is no east or west'; and 'Jesus shall reign, where'er the sun'.

Then on 2 February or the nearest Sunday we celebrate the Presentation of Christ in the Temple. As the old man sang 'Lord, now lettest thou thy servant . . .', ending, 'To be a light to lighten the Gentiles,' this is a festival of light called Candlemas. We sing hymns like 'Christ is the world's true light'; 'Faithful vigil ended'; 'In a world where people walk in darkness'; 'Jesus bids us shine'; 'Lead, kindly light'; 'Light of the minds that know him'; 'Lord, the light of your love is shining' ('Shine, Jesus, shine'); 'O gladsome light, O grace'; 'Of the Father's love begotten'; 'Sometimes a light surprises'; 'The Spirit lives to set us free' ('Walk in the light'); 'This little light of mine'; 'We are marching in the light of God'.

Christmas Day Sunday 25 December
Any of the following sets of readings may be used on the evening of Christmas Eve and on Christmas Day: Set III should be used at some service during the celebration. Set I **On Screen**
Isa. 9.2–7 A child is born; Ps. 96 Tell of his salvation; Titus 2.11–14 Salvation has come; Luke 2.1–14 [15–20] The birth and the shepherds

> *'[The angels said to the shepherds,] "To you is born this day in the city of David a Saviour, who is the Messiah, the Lord."'*
> *Luke 2.11*

Competition

'The Nativity Factor' describes itself as a short film competition, sponsored by a commercial television production company called ITN Productions, together with Jerusalem Productions, one of the Sainsbury family charities. They ask entrants to tell the story of the birth of Jesus on film in their own unique way. Normally, videos are between 30 seconds and 3 minutes long, and are judged on 3 criteria: creativity, style and story. There are 4 categories for which prizes are given: adult (over 19), 14–19, and 13 and under, and an all-age group for very short films lasting no more than 6 seconds! This started several years ago, and my information may be out of date; if that is your scene, you can look it up on www.nativityfactor.com.

Styles

Looking at past entries, I see that retellings of the nativity story on screen have been submitted in rap style; featuring characters in jeans and hoods as the angels argue over who is going to tell Joseph that his fiancée has not been unfaithful; as animations with puppets or with pencil drawings or Lego™ bricks; filmed by the Israeli wall in modern Bethlehem; as 'A Space Godyssey'; with dinosaurs, and so on.

Reactions

I am sure these ideas have had a mixed reception. Some of you will say it is irreverent to make our Saviour and his Blessed Mother the subject of humour. Some will add that the Gospels contain an accurate historical account of what happened, and it is wrong to tamper with that, otherwise people may begin to doubt whether it ever happened at all. I can sympathize with that, and admire the piety from which those opinions undoubtedly spring. But I also admire the imagination and creativity of those who have found new ways of telling an old story. Ask yourself, what was the point of telling the story in the first place? Surely it was not to give an exact historical narrative – St Luke gets the bit about the census completely wrong, but who cares? – it was to make people ask, what does the idea of God becoming a human being, because he loves us, mean to me today? Matthew and Luke are the only two Gospels to describe the birth of Jesus: Mark begins his Gospel at the Baptism of Jesus, and John refers to it in the mystical words, 'The Word became flesh'. St Paul and the other New Testament writers do not mention it at all. But all are agreed that God became human somewhere in Palestine, and that has huge repercussions for each one of us. Any way we can make people sit up and think afresh about that is good.

Nativity plays

Nativity plays performed by small children are a delight, and cause thousands of people every Christmas to hear again the traditional story. But it is very easy when children are involved to get tied up in the minor details, and lose track of the central message. I am delighted that people with strong faith or no faith at all come to see the traditional performance, but most of them think of it as an ancient fairy tale, with no basis in fact and no relevance to our own lives whatever. But if just a few people think really deeply about the message that God our Creator loves us so much that he actually stripped himself of his glory and somehow became human, it will make a colossal difference in the way that many people live their lives in the twenty-first century. Anything is good which helps us contemplate the mystery that God made us because he wanted creatures to love who would love him in return. God came to earth to break down all the barriers which separate us from him, and to fill our hearts with love for one another. Then we shall be ready to pass into another world where all is love. For that is the message of Christmas; not disputes over whether the wise men were kings, and how many of them there were. I am not asking you to enter the 'Nativity Factor' competition. But I do beg of you to set aside a few minutes in the next few days to ponder how *you* would retell the story of God becoming human, in ways that would attract the men and women in the street who seldom think of God except at Christmas time.

All-age worship

Together, try to retell the story of the birth of Jesus in a modern way which concentrates on the message of love.

Suggested hymns

Christians, awake! salute the happy morn; I danced in the morning; O little town of Bethlehem; Unto us a boy is born!

Christmas Day   Sunday 25 December
Set II   The Gloom Family's Christmas Circular

Isa. 62.6–12 Prepare a way; Ps. 97 God comes to rescue his people; Titus 3.4–7 Salvation by grace; Luke 2.[1–7] 8–20 Shepherds go to Bethlehem

> *'When the goodness and loving-kindness of God our Saviour appeared, he saved us, not because of any works of righteousness that we had done, but according to his mercy, through the water of rebirth and renewal by the Holy Spirit.' Titus 3.4–5*

Circular letters

Many people at Christmas time save themselves having to write to each of their friends by compiling a circular letter, in which they list all the boring things they have been doing in the past year, and posting it or emailing it to everyone on their address list. I want you to imagine that what I am reading to you now is the Christmas circular from a family with the apt surname of G. L. Double O. M. – the GLOOM family. From George and Gladys Gloom, Grandpa Gloom, Gregory and Glenys:

Dear friends, former friends and sworn enemies,

We're too late to wish you a happy Christmas. We know how much you enjoy reading a full and detailed account each year of what each member of the GLOOM family has been doing. But we weren't able to produce our circular letter in time for Christmas this year. We seldom have a very happy Christmas in the GLOOM family, but due to a peculiar series of circumstances this year has been unusually difficult.

It all began on Christmas Eve when Grandpa GLOOM refused to let anyone help him fetch the Christmas tree down from the loft. Carrying the tree on his shoulder he accidentally pushed the ladder to one side, so that he had one leg on the attic floor and across the hatch. Grandpa didn't break anything when he eventually let go of the tree and fell on to the landing. He *claimed* he'd strained a muscle, and sat in his usual chair for the rest of the day, growling at anybody who came near him. Gregory's mum kept calling him to help her in the kitchen preparing the Christmas dinner. He refused, saying that's her job, that's what mums are for. He said he had an urgent appointment to play football down at the park. As he dribbled his ball out of the front door, he knocked over the table and smashed some expensive glass ornaments.

So that left his sister Glenys GLOOM to sweep the glass up and calm her father down. She complained that a girl never gets any time to enjoy herself at Christmas, what with telephoning all her friends, squeezing her pimples and trying to get her make-up straight.

Gladys, the mother of the GLOOM tribe, grumbled that she was stuck in the kitchen, because the others wanted to enjoy themselves. 'Enjoy themselves! At Christmas!' she said.

'When there's so much work to be done!' Her husband, George GLOOM, thought the main purpose of Christmas was to show off that your house was better decorated than your neighbours'. So he went to the shops to buy more decorations, when he passed the church. Outside there was a poster. *'Stronger family, better world,'* it said. *'Fix the world. Start in church this Christmas.'* So on Christmas Day he dragged the whole GLOOM family, kicking and screaming, to the service. He reckoned that should fix them.

We enjoyed the carols, and everybody seemed very friendly. The vicar said what was wrong with the world is that people are too selfish. He said Christmas was the answer. We were thinking: 'Not the GLOOM family's Christmas, that's the worst time of the year for us.' Then we realized he meant the Baby in the manger. He said if anything could fix the world it was a God who was completely unselfish. Who gave up everything and was born in a stable. And there was Mary, his mum. All she cared about was doing what God wants. And Joseph never grumbled. Well, not like the GLOOMs do. So the vicar said, if every family could become unselfish, like the Holy Family, then the world would be fixed already.

So the GLOOM family decided we'd give it a try. If the baby Jesus could fix our family of selfish layabouts in one day, fixing the world would only take him about, say, 2,000 years. We've decided to change our surnames by deed poll. No longer the GLOOM family, but the GLADs. Mum says she'll like being called Gladys Glad.

So that ends our family circular letter this year. We hope you all, friends and enemies alike, will join us in building strong, unselfish families, as the first step towards fixing the world. A Glad and Happy Christmas, everyone!

All-age worship

Write a letter to your friends, telling them what made you happy this Christmas.

Suggested hymns

Away in a manger, no crib for a bed; Come and join the celebration; God rest you merry, gentlemen; Joy to the world, the Lord is come!

Christmas Day 25 December
Set III Have Faith

Isa. 52.7–10 The messenger of peace; Ps. 98 God's victory; Heb. 1.1–4 [5–12] God speaks through a Son; John 1.1–14 The Word became flesh

'Long ago God spoke to our ancestors in many and various ways by the prophets, but in these last days he has spoken to us by a Son.' Hebrews 1.1–2

Paradox

My dictionary defines a paradox as something which appears to be absurd, but is actually true. Really gripping thrillers grab your attention by means of paradox. And the story of Christmas, often called 'The greatest story ever told', is full of it. We are told in the Letter to the Hebrews that this is the story of the birth on earth of the second most powerful being in the universe, the Son of God. Yet the events in the 'little town of Bethlehem' seem quite disproportionate to such a world-shattering event. The woman chosen to give birth to this phenomenon is neither regal, wise nor wealthy, but a naive, unmarried teenager. The first people to hear the news are not A-list celebrities or powerful media reporters, but a huddle of low-paid agricultural workers on the night shift! Would you have expected God to bungle this public-relations exercise to such an extent?

The message

No! But then, each of these paradoxes reinforces the message that God was trying to get across. By sending his Son to be born on earth, God is proclaiming the good news of his love to every single member of the human race, the wealthy and the underprivileged, the clever and the stupid alike. So it needs to be expressed in words of one syllable. Yet at the heart of this message is a startling idea which is totally unexpected. God chose to enter this world, not in power and great glory, but as a suffering servant – a human being whose flesh will feel the agony of human pain while bringing deep joy and contentment to those for whom he will have to die.

Illogical

That is what makes Christmas such a paradox: it is cramming two completely opposite ideas into one human frame: worldly and divine, God and man, sharing one brain and one body. That is not an idea which materialistic people of today find easy to accept. The United Kingdom, which used to be called a Christian country, grows more and more secular. And although the secularists claim to bring greater tolerance for all types of people, that seems to exclude accepting anyone who adheres to the Christian faith. Faith brings many blessings, and a deeper understanding of who we are and why we are here; but our understanding of the universe suffers a painful tumble when we pull the carpet of faith from underneath our own feet. The atheists say that faith is illogical; but faith is the foundation-stone of our civilization. Human freedom is best defended by the leaders of a nation which holds on to certain core values which everybody believes are worth protecting.

Roots

Throughout history, it has been values drawn from the Old Testament and the New Testament which were the basis of British culture. It is the teaching of the Bible which has led our rulers, whether they realized it or not, to insist on public honesty, care for the needy, and liberty of conscience. If we lose touch with these roots, and forget the faith from which they are drawn, we do not increase human liberty – we erode the foundations on which liberty rests.

Effects

The effects of national withdrawal from faith have been a growth in shallow materialism, a cheapening of our respect for love and beauty, and a devotion to money and celebrity. We call bad behaviour 'evil', but are unable to define what is wrong about it, still less why we should abstain. But it was into a world of shallow materialism and vicious power struggles that Jesus was born. It was to a world like ours that he brought the message of faith. The paradox that the all-powerful God is interested in the doings of ordinary people, and shares in their suffering, still needs to be proclaimed loudly today. The only way to change our selfish behaviour is to bring people to believe in a God of love. And that is the message of Christmas. It survived through centuries of hatred, but is now in danger of being lost because of sheer indifference and neglect. Cling to the paradoxical message of Christmas, and shout it from the rooftops: God is a God of love; and he became human at Christmas time to show that he loves every single one of us with a love deeper than we can ever imagine. Happy Christmas!

All-age worship

Make a big red cardboard heart and write on it 'God's love for me'. Then put it in the manger in the Christmas crib in place of the Christ-child.

Suggested carols

Love came down at Christmas; O come, all ye faithful; The God whom earth and sea and sky; The great God of heaven is come down to earth.

Christmas Day   25 December
Second Service   Virgin Birth

Morning Ps. 110 This day of your birth, 117 Steadfast love; Evening Ps. 8 Out of the mouths of babes; Isa. 65.17–25 A new creation; Phil. 2.5–11 Jesus emptied himself *or* Luke 2.1–20 Shepherds go to Bethlehem (*if it has not been used at the Principal Service of the day*)

> 'Christ Jesus . . . though he was in the form of God . . . emptied himself . . . being born in human likeness.' Philippians 2.6–7; or

> 'To you is born this day in the city of David a Saviour, who is the Messiah, the Lord.' Luke 2.11

Is it true?

In the Nicene Creed we declare that Jesus 'came down from heaven, was incarnate from the Holy Spirit and the Virgin Mary, and was made man'. At the heart of the Christmas good news is the fact that Jesus was completely human, and yet that 'God was in Christ, reconciling the world to himself.' The stories of his birth, in the Gospels of Matthew and Luke, are told so as to emphasize this point. They both state that Mary was a virgin, who had never had sex with a man; but that is not the main point of the story. Several books have recently been published suggesting that these two Gospels, perhaps basing their versions on a story which was then going around the Christian community, added the detail of the virgin birth to show that this was a fulfilment of Old Testament prophecies. This is not intended to be an attack on the Christian gospel, or to weaken the simple faith of ordinary believers. If I report what some modern scholars are writing, you do not have to agree; but I hope it will make you think more deeply about what the Bible actually teaches.

Silence

The first worrying thing for traditionalists is that the events of the birth of Jesus are not mentioned anywhere else in the New Testament other than these two Gospels. St Mark starts with the baptism of Christ; John says that 'the word was made flesh' and reports that the mother of Jesus was standing by the cross; St Paul emphasized that Jesus, who was in the form of God, was born in human likeness, and that he was 'born of a woman'. All of them mention that Jesus had brothers and sisters. If they had heard of the virgin birth, why did they not mention it?

Prophecy

The main reason why Matthew and Luke report it is because of a single prophecy in the Old Testament. Isaiah 7.14 in the King James Bible reads:

Therefore the Lord himself shall give you a sign; Behold, a virgin shall conceive, and bear a son, and shall call his name Immanuel.

But in those days, the word we translate as 'virgin' also meant a young woman or a girl. So the NRSV Bible correctly translates that verse: 'Look, the young woman is with child and shall bear a son, and shall name him Immanuel.' Isaiah was probably referring to King Ahaz's new wife, and promising the Jews that their oppression by Assyria would not last longer than nine months, after which they would be rescued, and would be able to say, 'God is on our side – God is with us!' It was not that Isaiah was predicting the birth of Jesus, but that Matthew and Luke recognized that his words were reflected in the incarnation, when truly the God of heaven came to live with us on earth.

Heroes

Another thought in their minds must have been that in the ancient world, many heroes were thought to have had miraculous births, and even the Emperor Augustus was said to have been fathered by the god Apollo in the form of a serpent. The evangelists wanted to show that Jesus was in no way inferior to the Roman emperors. Scientific laws were unknown, so miracles were regarded not as unscientific but more as God overruling the random acts of nature to ensure that the right wonder happened at the right time in the right place. One of the problems with the virgin birth story for today is that although parthenogenesis happens in nature, the offspring, as is the case with worker ants, are always female. This is because the genome in normal births consists of X-chromosomes derived from the mother and Y-chromosomes from the father. Where did Jesus get the Y-chromosomes, essential in a male baby, from?

Poetic

The concept of historical accuracy was hardly understood in those days. Many books about events in the past were deliberately written in the genre of poetic symbolism. So it is perfectly possible to be a Christian, believing that Christ was God incarnate, while uncertain about the historical accuracy of the nativity story. The message of Christmas is that God loves us, and God's Son came to earth to save us. Believe in that, and disputes about historicity no longer matter.

Suggested hymns

From heaven you came; Hark! the herald angels sing; It came upon the midnight clear; Long ago, prophets knew.

Second Sunday of Christmas   1 January 2017

(The Naming of Jesus (see page 293) can be observed on 1 January; or on 2 January, in which case 1 January is called Christmas 2 but the readings are those for Christmas 1.)

Principal Service   **New Beginnings**

Isa. 63.7–9 God's presence brings salvation; Ps. 148 Let all creation praise the Lord; Heb. 2.10–18 The suffering of Jesus brings salvation; Matt. 2.13–23 Flight into Egypt

> *'It was no messenger or angel but his presence that saved them; in his love and in his pity he redeemed them; he lifted them up and carried them all the days of old.' Isaiah 63.9*

Nazareth

St Matthew seems not to have known that Joseph and Mary, as St Luke tells us, had lived in Nazareth before they went to Bethlehem. Matthew sees everything as a fulfilment of prophecy, and Jesus, the new King of the Jews, had to be born in the same village where King David was. But when King Herod heard this, he was determined to kill all the children of Bethlehem, so the Holy Family had to flee to Egypt. That reminded Matthew of the words in Hosea, in which God says, speaking about the Exodus, 'When Israel was a child, I loved him, and out of Egypt I called my son.' So Joseph, Mary and Jesus were refugees, and had to make a new beginning in a foreign country. Then, when King Herod died, they wanted to return to Bethlehem, but, hearing that Archelaus was ruling over that area, who was even more cruel than his father, they turned north and settled in Nazareth in Galilee. Even if St Luke is correct in saying that they had lived there before, this was also a new beginning, because then they had been unmarried and childless, now they had to face the disapproval of their neighbours, because Mary had not been married when her child was born. This year, Christmas Day is a Sunday, so the following Sunday falls on New Year's Day, so 'New beginnings' is a fitting theme for our thoughts.

Incarnation

When Jesus was born, God was making a new beginning also. He had spoken through the prophets, persuading the Jewish people that there is only one God, who wants his people to obey his laws. But they had not succeeded in spreading this message to the rest of the world, as God had planned; nor had they fully understood that what God commands us to do is to show unselfish love to all our neighbours. If they would not listen to his message through prophetic middle-men, then he would come to dwell among them and tell them himself. That was a very startling new beginning. Isaiah had also written about the Exodus, words that find their fulfilment in the incarnation of Jesus, 'It was no messenger or angel but his presence that saved them; in his love and in his pity he redeemed them; he lifted them up and carried them all the days of old.' And in the New Testament, the Letter to the Hebrews tells us that God's Son 'had to become like his brothers and sisters in every respect, so that he might be a merciful and faithful high priest in the service of God, to make a sacrifice of atonement for the sins of the people.' No longer would we look to the daily sacrifice of animals to bring us forgiveness and salvation; now, the once and for all sacrifice by Jesus of his own life on the cross would do that.

Naming

January 1st is also the date when we commemorate the circumcision and naming of Jesus. When it falls on a Sunday, however, we can transfer that celebration to the following day. Just as when we christen babies in church today, this ceremony represented for the Jews a new beginning as a member of God's family: in their case as children of Abraham, in ours, as members of God's family the Church. At both ceremonies, the baby is officially given their name. It may have been chosen for him or her by their parents beforehand, but now the whole local community recognizes the child as a new individual.

God's help

There may be other new beginnings later in our lives, when we commit ourselves more deeply to Christ in faith and love. But in each case we are not alone; the Son of God, who made a new beginning when he was born as a human being, stands beside us as our brother

34

to hold our hand, and gives us strength to cope with all the challenges we face in the new year, our new life, or our deeper commitment to God. Never be afraid to make a fresh start. Your life up till now may have been OK, but there is always room for improvement, and with the help of the incarnate Christ we can always do better. That is what God's new beginning at Christmas was all about.

All-age worship

Make New Year cards, wishing our friends God's loving help in the year to come.

Suggested hymns

God is working his purpose out; I heard the voice of Jesus say; To the name that brings/of our salvation; The Virgin Mary had a baby boy.

Second Sunday of Christmas   1 January 2017
(See note above on page 33.)
Second Service   **God's Idea of Humanity**
Ps. 132 The Son of David; Isa. 49.7–13 These shall come from far away; Phil. 2.1–11 Born in human likeness; *Gospel at Holy Communion*: Luke 2.41–52 Jesus aged 12

> *'Let the same mind be in you that was in Christ Jesus, who, though he was in the form of God, did not regard equality with God as something to be exploited, but emptied himself, taking the form of a slave, being born in human likeness.' Philippians 2.5–7*

Likeness

St Paul wrote that Jesus was 'born in human likeness'. It is an odd word to use. We commonly say about a photograph, 'Look, it's a very good likeness!' By which we mean that the image closely resembles the actual features of the sitter. Or perhaps we mean, 'It corresponds with the mental image I already had in my brain of this person, and shows up the character I imagine them to have.' St Paul also says that, in heaven, before Christ came to earth, he was in the 'form of God', but when he descended to earth, he took 'the form of a slave', which many people thought to be the lowest form of human life. 'Likeness' could be translated 'resemblance' or 'image'; 'form' translates the Greek word which we now use in science fiction, when a being 'morphs' from one shape to another. But I doubt whether St Paul was troubled about the exact meaning of the words he used; what he was trying to do was conjure up in his readers' imaginations a sense of awe at the amazing thing which happened that first Christmas day.

Incarnation

What St Paul is saying is that, before he came to earth, Jesus was exactly the same as God his Father; they were identical, there was no distinguishable difference between them. It was rather as though God was a community, Father, Son and Holy Spirit, joined together so closely in love that they thought the same and decided together and acted together as one. But then God took the decision to come down to earth so that he could talk to us in terms we could understand, and show us his love in a visible form. So Jesus gave up, temporarily, his sameness with the God in heaven, and became completely human. What people thought when they saw Jesus was, 'That's a very good likeness to a slave, with all the slave's humility, no false pride, and readiness to jump to it whenever his owner gives him a command and do exactly what he is told.' What an amazing leap that was, morphing in one night from being an all-powerful God to being a human baby, and a few years later the spitting image of a human slave!

Lord

A little further on, Paul says that the reason for Christmas was so that 'every tongue should confess that Jesus Christ is Lord'. Now 'Lord' is the translation in our Bibles for the Jewish name of God, which they would not pronounce for fear of breaking the commandment against taking 'God's name in vain'. So Paul wants, because he knows that God wants, that everybody in the whole world should accept that Jesus is the spitting image of God. Well, that is not completely true, because God is invisible; but their characters are the same. God our Father has the same loving heart as Jesus, the same burning desire to make the world a better place for humans to live in, and the same readiness to forgive us our sins and help us to become completely unselfish, like Jesus was . . . and is. 'Jesus is Lord' means 'Jesus is the same as God', and is the basic Christian creed. Saying it and meaning it makes you a Christian, and of course leads you into complete obedience to God your boss, in response to God's complete love for you. But soon, people began to try to define exactly what 'Jesus is Lord' means, and started quarrelling about it, calling those who chose a different form of words 'heretics'. So the simple gospel was lost in a morass of philosophy and theology which nobody could understand.

Image

I came across a quotation the other day, though I can't trace where it comes from. It goes like this: 'Christmas is what man means by God, and what God means by man.' To make it less sexist, I think we should change it to:

> The human Jesus, who came to earth on the first Christmas Day, gives us the correct idea of what God is like, and shows us what God thinks human beings should be like.

I think that will do for the Christian creed, and would save us a lot of argument.

Suggested hymns

Jesus is Lord – Creation's voice proclaims it; Lord, for the years; Thou didst leave thy throne; Thy hand, O God, has guided.

Baptism of Christ (*First Sunday of Epiphany*)
8 January
(If 8 January is a Sunday, The Epiphany may be transferred to the Sunday. If so, The Baptism of Christ is transferred to Monday 9 January.)
Principal Service **Voices from Heaven**
Isa. 42.1–9 God gives his Spirit to his servant; Ps. 29 The voice of the Lord is over the waters; Acts 10.34–43 Anointing by the Holy Spirit; Matt. 3.13–17 The baptism and anointing of Jesus

> *'The voice of the Lord is upon the waters; the God of glory thunders; the Lord is upon the mighty waters.' Psalm 29.3 (Common Worship)*

Listening

A Christian set off to the airport one day when, unknown to every-body, a terrorist act was planned. Suddenly she heard a clear voice from heaven telling her not to go. So she stayed at home, and heard on the news that a bomb had been smuggled into the airport. If it had gone off it would have killed many people; fortunately it didn't. This left her with two puzzles. If God knew in advance the bomb was being planted, why didn't he know that the attempt would fail? And why didn't God warn all the other people who were going to the airport that day? To the first, she reasoned that by giving us free will, God has prevented himself from knowing what choices we shall make, and has to allow for everything. To the second question, she answered that perhaps God did speak to everyone, but they weren't listening.

Voices from heaven

Voices from heaven seem very rare these days. But perhaps they are quite common, only we drown them out by all the noise with which we surround ourselves. I wonder what God has been trying to say to me today, and to you, but neither of us was paying any attention? There was a voice from heaven when Jesus was baptized, yet the crowd thought it was the sound of thunder. But Jesus heard his Father's voice, saying, 'This is my Son, the Beloved, with whom I am well pleased.'

Meaning

The whole Christian gospel is summed up in those words. They are based on quotations from the Old Testament. We say every week in the Creed that we believe that Jesus is the Son of God, and our Muslim friends are shocked, because the Qur'an tells them that God has no sons. But we have no idea what that means, because God is above mere human words. The Muslims are right: our God is not like the randy pagan gods who went round begetting semi-divine babies on every maid they met. Nor was Jesus a god pretend-ing to be human. But God is a community of three persons bound together by love, with one mind and one will. And just as 'sons of destruction' in Hebrew means 'destructive people', so 'Son of God' means a divine human being. In Psalm 2, God addresses the king of the Jews with the words, 'You are my son, this day I have begotten you.' Now that they no longer had a king, the Jews interpreted those words as a promise of the coming Messiah. In Isaiah 42, God says, 'Here is my servant, whom I uphold, my chosen, in whom my soul delights; I have put my spirit upon him; he will bring forth justice to the nations.' So the words, 'With whom I am well pleased', identify Jesus with the suffering servant who saves his people by his willingness to die for them. Jesus is both the Messiah, and the suffering servant; in other words, the Servant King.

Listen to him

St Mark and St Luke, in their Gospels, add three more words to Matthew's report of what the voice from heaven said at the baptism of Christ: 'listen to him'. We do not often hear a voice from heaven, or if we do, we are usually too busy to pay attention. But Jesus speaks to us in the prodding of our conscience; the inner conviction that we know what he wants us to do; in our daily Bible reading; and in silent prayer. Sometimes God speaks to us through the words of our family and friends, encouraging and warning us. They may not realize that God is using them as his spokespeople. Yet in all these ways, the voice of God from heaven is saying the same thing to us: 'Jesus is my Son, my Beloved, with whom I am well pleased; listen to him.'

All-age worship

Record on a laptop etc. the words you think a mother might use to tell her baby she loves it, or a husband might say to his wife; a teacher telling the class to quieten down and pay attention; your friends telling you to look after yourself. Then download it to a CD, and write on it, 'God's words to me'.

Suggested hymns

From heaven you came (The Servant King); Guide me, O thou great Redeemer; I heard the voice of Jesus say; When Jesus came to Jordan.

Baptism of Christ (*First Sunday of Epiphany*)
8 January
Second Service   **Be Still and Know**

Ps. 46 There is a river, 47 King over the earth; Joshua 3.1–8,
14–17 Crossing the Jordan; Heb. 1.1–12 Superior to angels;
Gospel at Holy Communion: Luke 3.15–22 Baptism with the Spirit

> *'Be still and know that I am God.'* Psalm 46.10 (Common
> Worship)

Be still

I often wonder how the psalms are chosen for this service. This
Sunday is dedicated to the baptism of Christ in the River Jordan,
so the Old Testament passage about Joshua crossing that river is
obviously relevant. Psalm 46 contains a verse about a river. Then
there is a verse telling the enemy nations to stop shouting at God
and start to listen, and that reminds us that the voice of God was
heard at Christ's baptism. 'Be still and know that I am God,' says
the Psalmist. And that reminds me of an article I read in the *Satanic
Times*. What am I doing reading the *Satanic Times*, you ask? Well,
if you are engaged in a war, the more intelligence you can gather
about your enemy, the easier it is to foil his strategy of attack.

Satan's meeting

Satan arranged an international conference of demons, said the
article. He addressed them like this: 'We can't stop people praying.
We can't stop them reading their holy books. So far, we haven't
been able to prevent them developing a personal relationship with
their God. Once that relationship has been formed, we no longer
have any power over them. So I want you to let them keep the
outward show of religion, but make sure they are so busy that they
never have time to develop this closeness with God. What you must
do is distract them,' Satan shouted. 'Make them so busy that they
never have a moment to be alone with their God, or keep their relationship with him vital and strong.'

'How can we do that?' yelled the demons.

'Occupy their time with things that don't really matter,' replied
Satan. 'Think up projects to busy their brains with. Tempt them

to spend money they haven't got, then take out loans they will never be able to repay. Push them into such an extravagant lifestyle that they cannot survive unless the wives go out to work, and the husbands have their noses to the grindstone for 12 hours every day in a 6- to 7-day working week,' continued Satan. 'That will never leave them enough time to spend with their children. Then their families will begin to fall apart, and coming home will give them no respite from the pressures of their working lives. Fill their brains with greedy desires, so that they have no time to listen to God's still, small voice. Tell them it will help them to relax if they play recorded music, at home or when they are travelling, or play computer games in every spare minute. Teach them that it is normal to watch television for hour after hour. Fill the shops and restaurants with meaningless music, until they have no time to think about their God, let alone talk with him. Persuade them that it is politically incorrect to mention God in public. Develop an advertising industry which fills every square inch and every moment with adverts, and interrupt their television programmes every few minutes for a 'commercial break'. Push dozens of pieces of junk mail through their letterboxes every day. Fill the magazines and newspapers with pictures of skinny models till they think nobody can be beautiful unless they are constantly dieting. Never let them walk in the countryside in case they notice how beautiful God's creation is. If they do go to church, involve them in snide gossip and criticizing others, so that they never learn to love their neighbours. Keep them so busy supporting various charities that they have no time to ask for God's help, even in the good things they do. Before long, they will try to do everything in their own strength, sacrificing their own health and the well-being of their family for a set of abstract ideas,' Satan continued. 'Then they will do our work for us, leaving us nothing to do but sit by and grin at what fools they all are!' He laughed with glee.

The demons set about the tasks he had set them diligently, until everyone in the world was rushing around in ever-decreasing circles. Nobody had any time any more to 'Be still and know that I am God'. Nobody had any time left over to tell other people that God loves each one of us, and can change our lives for the better if only we will relax and let him do so. Do you think that Satan's plan has been successful? Decide for yourself! Oh, and as you will have guessed, the *Satanic Times* is a joke!

Suggested hymns

As the deer pants for the water; Amazing grace! How sweet the sound; Be still and know that I am God; Thou didst leave thy throne.

Second Sunday of Epiphany   15 January
Principal Service   **A Light to the Nations**
Isa. 49.1–7 The servant a light to the nations; Ps. 40.1–12 I spoke of your salvation; 1 Cor. 1.1–9 Called to be saints; John 1.29–42 Andrew brings Peter

> *'I will give you as a light to the nations, that my salvation may reach to the end of the earth.' Isaiah 49.6*

Exile

The Holy Land was settled by 12 tribes. The Bible claims that all 12 were united under King David and his son King Solomon, but there is no archaeological proof that this was so. Under their successors, the two southern tribes were known as Judah, and the ten in the north were called Israel. In 722 BC the Assyrian army from what is now northern Iraq conquered the ten tribes of Israel, and took many of them into exile. There they intermarried with the locals, and ceased to exist as a nation; they are referred to as the Ten Lost Tribes. Many Assyrian people settled in their place, and intermarried with the remaining Israelites. The result was a thoroughly mixed population, with its capital in Samaria. The good Samaritan was a descendant of this mixed-race population, and the whole area became known as 'Galilee of the Gentiles', meaning foreigners. Forty years later, the two southern tribes were conquered by an army from Babylon, in southern Iraq, and the upper classes exiled there. But they returned 50 years later to Jerusalem. Then there was a desperate attempt to reunite all 12 tribes with a capital in Jerusalem, and much of the Old Testament was written or rewritten at this time to argue that Israel and Judah ought never to have been divided. It was mostly xenophobic; they thought that God was only interested in his Chosen People, and did not care about the idolatrous Gentiles. But one anonymous author, whose writings occupy the second portion of the book of Isaiah, declared that the Jews had been chosen, only so that they should share what they had learnt about God with all the nations on earth. He represented God as saying to Israel:

> It is too light a thing that you should be my servant to raise up the tribes of Jacob and to restore the survivors of Israel; I will give you as a light to the nations, that my salvation may reach to the end of the earth.

Sepphoris

This call to international mission is transferred in the New Testament to Jesus, God's Suffering Servant. Simeon sang, when baby Jesus was first brought to the Temple, 'you shall be a light to lighten the Gentiles'. Jesus praised the Roman centurion, saying, 'I tell you, not even in Israel have I found such faith.' In fact, the Galileans may have had much more contact with foreigners than the nationalists of Jerusalem. Only a short distance from Nazareth, on the next hilltop, stood the city of Sepphoris. Built by the Assyrians, it became an administrative centre for each successive invading army, until when Jesus was a child it was burnt down by the Romans, following a revolt led by the Jews who lived there. Jesus will have seen the 2,000 citizens of Sepphoris who were crucified, and then the firm of Joseph and Sons, Carpenters of Nazareth, probably worked on the rebuilding programme. That was the last time that Sepphoris revolted; its mixed population learned to live tolerantly together. Jesus may well have watched Greek dramas in the large Roman theatre there, and recent excavations revealed synagogues cheek-by-jowl with pagan temples and bath houses. Beautiful mosaics, such as the so-called 'Mona Lisa of Sepphoris', which would have been regarded by strict Jews as idolatrous, were found on the floors of the houses. When the Romans destroyed Jerusalem in AD 70, Sepphoris remained standing, becoming a centre for tolerant international Judaism.

Internationalism

All this explains why Jesus was so hated by the narrow nationalistic Pharisees of Jerusalem. The Galilean Messiah represented a far too unprejudiced and inter-racial religion for their taste, and refused to fight the Romans. There was no time while Jesus was alive to expand his mission beyond the boundaries of Judaea, but he told his disciples at his ascension to be his 'witnesses in Jerusalem, in all Judea and Samaria, and to the ends of the earth'. The same command applies to us. The task of evangelism must begin with our own families and near neighbours, but then we must broaden our horizons, not stopping until all nations are drawn into one, liberal, inclusive family of believers. Then, we shall be pretty close to the kingdom of God on earth that Jesus taught us to pray for.

All-age worship

Enlarge the map on en.wikipedia.org/wiki/Christianity_by_country, *marking in the names of the larger countries. Pray for the church in countries with a low proportion of Christians.*

Suggested hymns

God is working his purpose out; God's Spirit is in my heart; Jesus shall reign, where'er the sun; We have a gospel to proclaim.

Second Sunday of Epiphany   15 January
Second Service   **Christianity in Russia**
Ps. 96 Among the nations; Ezek. 2.1—3.4 Eating the scroll; Gal. 1.11–24 Proclaiming God's Son to the Gentiles; *Gospel at Holy Communion*: John 1.43–51 The call of Nathanael

> *'God, who had set me apart before I was born and called me through his grace, was pleased to reveal his Son to me, so that I might proclaim him among the Gentiles.' Galatians 1.15–16*

Mission

The Magi who visited the infant Christ in Bethlehem were non-Jews, from Persia. Thus from the very beginning the good news which Jesus brought has been shared with people of other nations. We celebrate the visit of the wise men on 6 January, the feast of the Epiphany; the word means to reveal. So on the Sundays after the Epiphany we rejoice in the way Christianity has spread to and grown in different nations, and face the challenge of helping it to spread more and more widely. Today I want to think about Christianity in Russia, and what we can learn from Russian Christians.

Beginnings

St Paul planted churches along the Mediterranean coast of Turkey and Greece. He planned that they should spread inland, but when they reached the boundaries of the Roman Empire it was too dangerous to travel. There is a legend that St Andrew the Apostle visited Scythia and the Greek colonies along the north coast of the Black Sea, and even the future site of the city of Kiev. But the earliest recorded missions are from the Greek Orthodox Church of Constantinople, in the ninth century, to the south of Russia, known as the Rus [rhymes with 'loose'], which includes the modern states of Ukraine, Belarus, and the area of Russia around Kiev. In 863–869, St Cyril and St Methodius translated parts of the Bible into the Old Church-Slavonic language, making the evangelization of the Slavs possible. This ancient language is still used in the worship of the Russian Orthodox Church, but not for any other purpose. The Church had spread up to Kiev by the tenth century, where it was adopted by the local nobility, who imposed it on their subjects. Princess Olga converted to Christianity, and her grandson Vladimir I chose the Byzantine rite of the Greek Orthodox Church as the model for the Russian Church. So Russian Orthodox worship contains much of the ceremonial and robes borrowed from the royal court of the emperors of Byzantium, later called Constantinople and now Istanbul. In the nineteenth century beautiful chanting and operatic solos were introduced. The word 'orthodox' means 'right worship'; any other way of worshipping is considered to be heretical. Under threat from the Mongol invasion, the headquarters of the Russian Church was moved from Kiev to Moscow.

Monasteries

As in Europe, the spread of the Russian Church was largely powered by the monasteries. It is a vast country, with many tribes, languages and religions, but the travelling monks brought a vigorous faith even to the remotest areas. The silent meditation of the

Cappadocian Fathers, with the use of the Jesus Prayer – 'Lord Jesus Christ, Son of God, have mercy on me a sinner' – has been influential in and outside Russia – see the book *The Way of a Pilgrim*. And the 'Holy Fools', living in poverty and taking St Paul's saying 'We are fools for Christ's sake' as their motto, are fascinating.

Church and State

The Mongol invaders and after them the Ottomans believed it was against Islamic law to persecute people for their religion. So the Russian Church achieved a degree of independence from the State, in return for praying for their rulers. But under the Tsars this developed into a dangerous collusion between Church and State. After the communist revolution the party swore to follow Lenin's instruction to bring an end to religion, and under Stalin millions of Christians died. Russian Orthodox Christians living outside Russia formed an independent Russian Church. But, following the end of communism, the State rebuilt, very beautifully, many of the churches they had previously destroyed. Yet there have been demonstrations protesting that the Church is now getting too cosy with the politicians.

Other denominations

Approximately 83 per cent of those who live in Russia describe themselves as Orthodox, though many do not visit their churches regularly. There are between half a million and a million 'Old Believers', who do not accept reforms made in the seventeenth century. The Russian Baptist Church has become an indigenous fellowship, lustily singing Russian words to western tunes; and there is a multitude of other Protestant Churches. The Roman Catholics reckon they have between half a million and one and a half million members, but the official figure is 140,000. Yet even under communism, observers had the feeling that the Russians are a naturally religious people, and nothing will ever make them change that.

Suggested hymns

Give rest, O Lord, to thy servant with thy saints (Russian Contakion); God the Omnipotent (Lvov); Hills of the north, rejoice; O worship the Lord in the beauty of holiness.

Third Sunday of Epiphany   22 January

See also 'Week of Prayer for Christian Unity' p. 297.

Principal Service   **Unity through Baptism**

Isa. 9.1–4 The people who walked in darkness have seen light; Ps. 27.1, 4–12 The Lord is my light and my salvation; 1 Cor. 1.10–18 Unity through Baptism; Matt. 4.12–23 Call of the fishermen

> *'I appeal to you, brothers and sisters, by the name of our Lord Jesus Christ, that all of you should be in agreement and that there should be no divisions among you, but that you should be united in the same mind and the same purpose . . . Has Christ been divided? Was Paul crucified for you? Or were you baptized in the name of Paul?' 1 Corinthians 1.10, 13*

Disagreements

Wherever people meet together, disagreements arise. This is true between the nations of the world, in the political life of each nation, between the denominations of the international Church, and in most congregations. It also occurs in most families, from time to time. Often, through God's grace, people who differ can meet together, have a friendly discussion, and either find a compromise or agree to differ. If this is done in friendliness and love, that is fine. If voices are raised, the harm can be undone if both parties apologize and shake hands. But where disagreements become satanically evil is when one party criticizes the other behind their backs, implying that the truth is all on one side, namely their own. That causes lasting damage to the nation, the Church, or the family, that God is trying to use to spread his love in the world by demonstrating their unity. Gossiping and backbiting cause scars which take years to heal.

Local churches

St Paul wrote a letter to his friends in Corinth. His good friend Chloe had written to tell him that the Corinthian church was deeply divided. They disagreed on matters which were important, but not important enough to split the church, the Body of Christ, about. Some of them claimed to be representing Paul's point of view, but everybody claimed they were right and everybody else was wrong.

47

Thank God that never happens in this church! So Paul said that they should be united, because they had all been baptized in the name of Christ, and Christ cannot be divided.

Denominations

In most areas in this country the churches are split into different denominations: Roman Catholic, Anglican, Methodist, Baptist, URC and several others. This is the Week of Prayer for Christian Unity, and in many places joint services are held to pray for the unity of the Church; and then we go away, and do ... what? Nothing much, but carry on in the same old way. Well, that's not quite true. In many places the different denominations undertake together acts of witness, care for the needy, and service to the local community. People look at us amazed, saying, 'I always thought you lot hated each other and would never ever speak.' I wonder where they got that idea from? In about AD 200 a Christian called Tertullian remarked that the pagans hate each other, but when they see a group of us together they are astonished, exclaiming, 'See how these Christians love one another!' They ought to be able to say that today, if we are really witnessing to the presence of Christ within us.

Do nothing separately

So each of us needs to take a fresh look at church unity. Go to united services, not as a tourist to laugh at what different tribes of Christians do in church, which *we* would never ever do, but to look and see what we can learn from each other. When any act of evangelism or social service is proposed, don't think for a moment that you can do it on your own, but plan it as a joint activity of all the local churches. Have joint publicity leaflets, maybe a joint magazine. Have a joint carol service. Together, give out free pancakes on Shrove Tuesday and free hot cross buns on Good Friday. When people ask you why on earth you do this, it is a perfect opportunity to talk about the love of God for each of his children. Have combined Bible study, at which everyone is free to say why they believe what they do.

Relating

One local ecumenical magazine asked how you treat other people. I quote:

When we encounter Christians who are different from us, we can relate in different ways:
stand shoulder to shoulder by doing things together,
carry those who are weak or helpless,
face each other in open-hearted sharing,
hold hands in prayer and praise,
or *walk* by on the other side.

Which will you do?

All-age worship

Find out at what time a local church of a different denomination has its Sunday service, and attend it together. Then invite some of its members to your service and ask what they thought of it.

Suggested hymns

A new commandment I give unto you; Great shepherd of thy people, hear; Pray that Jerusalem may have; There's a quiet understanding.

Third Sunday of Epiphany   22 January

See also 'Week of Prayer for Christian Unity' p. 297.

Second Service   Singing to God a New Song

Ps. 33 Sing a new song; Eccles. 3.1–11 A time for everything; 1 Peter 1.3–12 Living hope; *Gospel at Holy Communion:* Luke 4.14–21 Beginning his ministry

> *Rejoice in the Lord, O you righteous,*
> *for it is good for the just to sing praises . . .*
> *Sing for him a new song;*
> *play skilfully, with shouts of praise.'*
> Psalm 33.1, 3 (Common Worship)

Church music

For many Christians, the musical part of the service gives them the greatest joy. Hymns, anthems, worship songs, psalms or choruses, everyone has a favourite type of music to add joy and beauty to the worship. Even those who think they cannot sing like listening to the others doing their best. It is a good thing if you enjoy it, but that is not why we do it. We make music to praise God. Music is more than an entertainment or an interlude. There are a few atheist church musicians; and yes, many Christians sing and play in church for the pure enjoyment of it, and are too busy getting it right to think much about God. Some people, however, come to church for the music and there realize that they owe their whole being to God the life-giver, who created in us a love of beauty. So we may become strong believers through the blessings of music. Yet it is pure self-indulgence to enjoy the music with never a thought about what the words mean. Our enjoyment of the music is irrelevant; what matters is whether God enjoys it. Of course, God is not troubled which type of music we perform, only that we should do our very best for God's sake. If we enjoy it ourselves at the same time, that is a gift from God.

Blessings of music

Music brings many blessings. It fills our minds with deep thoughts, and our hearts with profound emotion, granting to us the means of expressing those feelings. We wonder how the whole of life comes to be so full of rhythm and harmony, and how God inspires some people to compose and perform with a more than human talent, which seems to come from somewhere outside them. We can believe then that life is not just a story of material molecules, but has a spiritual side to it. Our hearts tell us that music can fill marching soldiers with courage and determination; fill romantics with love; and hold us back from destroying the irreplaceable beauty which is all around us. So church music inspires us to defend the weak, to share God's love with the needy; and stirs our consciences to do right. It widens our view of the world with its wonders, and gives us a new vision of God at work still on his creation. Music makes us dance and sing when we are happy, and comforts us when we are sad. The Spirit of God, like the wind, fills our sails and takes us to places and situations where God can use us to continue his work of love. Singing with others sweeps us off our feet with emotion – think of a football crowd enthusiastically singing 'Abide with me'. Singing God's praise in a congregation of believers enables us and inspires us to glorify God, lament our loss, or commit ourselves to service, and sometimes all three at once.

Change

So we have no right to limit the music in our church to the old familiar tunes and the dignified words. We need music to constantly stir us up to new thoughts and fresh challenges. That is why the psalms constantly call us to 'sing a new song to the Lord'. A life in music is a constant exploration of new styles, new territory, new rhythms in our life that we had never thought of before. Then we are ready for anything that God may send to us, and able to praise him even from the pit of despair.

True story

The mother of a talented professional musician suffered from Alzheimer's. She had not spoken a word for months, and seemed not to recognize any of her relations. Then at Christmas time her children and grandchildren gathered around her bed and sang Christmas carols. To their astonishment, her lips began to move, and quietly she joined in the singing. Then she seemed to wake up after a long sleep, and spoke to them happily for half an hour, telling them how much she loved them. Then, as though it was the most natural thing in the world, she turned over, closed her eyes, and died with a smile on her face. Believers will say that she had gone to enjoy the music of heaven. Her son, the musician, commented, 'Such is the power of music.'

Suggested hymns

Angels from the realms of glory; Brightest and best of the sons of the morning; Sing to God new songs of worship (Beethoven); Songs of thankfulness and praise.

Fourth Sunday of Epiphany   29 January

(or Candlemas; see p. 302)

Principal Service   **Gallons of Guilt and Gallons of Grace**

1 Kings 17.8–16 The widow's oil jug; Ps. 36.5–10 God's steadfast love; 1 Cor. 1.18–31 Christ the wisdom of God; John 2.1–11 Water into wine

> *'Standing there were six stone water-jars for the Jewish rites of purification, each holding twenty or thirty gallons. Jesus said to them, "Fill the jars with water." And they filled them up to the brim. He said to them, "Now draw some out, and take it to the chief steward." . . . the steward tasted the water that had become wine . . .' John 2.6–9*

51

Wedding

Jesus was invited to a wedding, and the wine ran out. He called the waiters to fill the huge jars with water, totalling up to 180 gallons. Next, Jesus turned all that water into top-quality wine. St John's Gospel tells us that this was a sign, meaning an indicator, drawing the disciples' attention to something significant. No ordinary man can perform a miracle like that, so they realized that Jesus must be somebody quite extraordinary. Each year, God turns gallons of ground-water into wine through the grapevines. So perhaps what Jesus had done pointed to some special relationship between Jesus and the God whom he called 'Father'. But surely he could have done that with one glassful of water; why did he change so much?

Guilt

To answer that, you have to look at what the water was there for. St John tells us it was for 'the Jewish rites of purification'. Water was used to cleanse the guests' hands and feet. The roads of Palestine were dusty in summer and muddy in the wintertime, so the host called one of the slaves to wash the feet of the guests. Then the hands were washed before the meal began, originally to get rid of any dirt or germs that might cause food poisoning. Such rules of hygiene are very commendable, and as important today as they were then. But it didn't stop there. Everybody's hands had to be washed again before each course. That was not for hygiene: that was because it was a religious ritual. Each hand in turn was held upright and the water poured down to the wrists, then held downwards so that it ran to the fingertips; then each palm was washed by rubbing it with the fist of the other hand. If this was not done before each course, the hand was regarded as unclean, not in a hygienic but in a religious sense. Pardon? Yes, for the Jews, the idea of cleanliness had got mixed up with holiness. God is pure, he has no 'dirty thoughts' and never does anything 'dirty'. In one sense that is true, as God has no evil in him, but is pure love. But the priests thought they must not approach God's Temple without making themselves holy – they imagined they could wash away their sinful thoughts and selfish habits by purifying themselves with water. God had said 'Be holy, as I am holy'; so the rabbis had thought up all sorts of rules about every Jew washing on every conceivable occasion, because God is everywhere. There are hundreds of laws in the Old Testament, and each of us must have broken at least one of them every day, possibly without realizing it. So they were filled with guilt; Jews do guilt in a big way. Therefore they needed gallons of water to wash all this guilt away, otherwise God would not listen to them. There are still some poor souls today whose religion consists in pointing out how guilty and unworthy everybody is, and even they themselves are.

Grace

But this was not how Jesus thought. He taught that God is like a loving father, only waiting for us to say sorry so that he can immediately forgive us. Yes, I know that Jesus gave us baptism as a sign of God's forgiveness, but you only need to be baptized once, not between every course of your dinner! God forgives us for everything, generously and graciously; the word for God's forgiveness is his 'grace'. Religion for Christians is no longer a matter of hunting out every little stain of guilt on our characters; but of rejoicing as in one big happy family party of forgiven sinners.

Gallons

So Jesus has turned our relationship with God from gallons and gallons of grim and ghastly guilt, into gallons and gallons and *gallons* of glorious, generous grace! *That* is why he performed the miracle on the water that was there for the rites of purification, to show that religion, for a Christian, is a question of being as happy as the guests at a wedding reception. For happiness is infectious, whereas telling other people how guilty they are just puts them clean off!

All-age worship

Wear party hats and badges saying 'Church is like a happy party'.

Suggested hymns

God forgave my sin; Hail to the Lord's anointed; Songs of thankfulness and praise; There's a wideness in God's mercy.

Fourth Sunday of Epiphany   29 January

(or Candlemas; see p. 302)

Second Service   **The Lord Hears Them?**

Ps. 34 O taste and see; Gen. 28.10–22 Jacob's ladder;
Philemon 1–16 The runaway slave; *Gospel at Holy Communion*:
Mark 1.21–28 Casting out an unclean spirit

> *'The righteous cry and the Lord hears them*
> *and delivers them out of all their troubles.'*
> *Psalm 34.17 (Common Worship)*

Is God deaf?

Is God deaf? Psalm 34 is full of wonderful phrases, like 'O taste and see that the Lord is gracious'. Yet over and over it repeats that God answers our prayers, and it just isn't true:

> I sought the Lord and he answered me . . .
> This poor soul cried, and the Lord heard me
> and saved me from all my troubles.
> The angel of the Lord . . . delivers them . . .
> those who fear him lack nothing . . .
> those who seek the Lord lack nothing that is good . . .

All I can say to the Psalmist is: 'Nonsense. Try saying that to those who pray that their loved one should not die. Or to those in war-torn countries who pray for peace to come soon. Or to the workers praying that they may not be made redundant'. None of those had their prayers answered, or at least not in the way they had hoped for. And if you tell them that this was because they didn't have enough faith, when they had screwed up every ounce of faith they were capable of, they will probably give up on God altogether.

Unanswered prayer

The problem of unanswered prayer goes back at least as far as the book of Job. But there is a prayer in the Book of Common Prayer which may hold a clue on this subject. It is in the order for Morning Prayer, or Matins, and that for Evening Prayer or Evensong, and comes just before 'the Grace'. It is called the Prayer of St Chrysostom. He was the Bishop of Constantinople, now Istanbul, and died in AD 407. He was a brilliant preacher, so was given the nickname of Chrysostom, which means 'golden-tongued'. In his time the Liturgy of the Greek Orthodox Church was revised, so that it is now known as the Liturgy of St John Chrysostom. Archbishop Cranmer, who compiled the English Prayer Book, was a great admirer of the Eastern Church, and made a beautiful translation of this prayer. It begins by thanking God for bringing us to worship him together:

> Almighty God, who hast given us grace at this time with one accord to make our common supplications unto thee . . .

Then it reminds us of one of the most misunderstood promises of Jesus:

> And dost promise that when two or three are gathered in thy name thou wilt grant their requests . . .

Which raises the question, why did Jesus promise this, when so often he does not give to good people, who meet to pray to him, what they had asked him for?

Expedient

The answer comes in one little word, 'expedient'. The prayer continues:

> Fulfil now, O Lord, the desires and petitions of thy servants, as may be most expedient for them; granting us in this world knowledge of thy truth, and in the world to come life everlasting.

It is a beautiful prayer, and well worth learning by heart; but what does that word mean? 'Expedient' is more than 'convenient'; it means to our greatest advantage. It may be *desirable* that the sick person should be kept alive a few months more, but it would only add to their agony. We may wish they could be restored to full health and strength, but the doctors will tell us that the process of decline has gone too far to be reversed. Except of course by a miracle. God does sometimes work miracles, but it would not be to our advantage if he was constantly interfering with the processes of nature which he himself created. These ensure that everybody dies some time, to make room for new generations to be born and grow. Or God may decide that now is not the right moment to give us what we ask for. Better that we should learn to be patient in adversity, to find new cures, to work for reconciliation between warring factions – these are the truths we ask to be given knowledge of in this world. Then we must release the dying into the loving arms of Jesus, who will lead them to, 'in the world to come, life everlasting'.

God knows best

Of course we don't like it when things go wrong, and when God doesn't give us exactly what we ask him for. But God sees everything in proportion, from the perspective of eternity, and we cannot expect to understand everything he does. We must still pray in faith and patience, and learn that 'God knows best'.

Suggested hymns

God moves in a mysterious way; I cannot tell why he whom angels worship; In heavenly love abiding; Through all the changing scenes of life.

Fourth Sunday before Lent (Proper 1) 5 February
Principal Service **Law of Moses or Law of Love?**
Isa. 58.1–9a [9b–12] The fast God wants; Ps. 112.1–9 [10] Happy are those who do good works; 1 Cor. 2.1–12 [13–16] The Spirit of wisdom; Matt. 5.13–20 salt, light, law and righteousness

> '[Jesus said to the crowd,] "Do not think that I have come to abolish the law or the prophets; I have come not to abolish but to fulfil."' Matthew 5.17

Jesus or Moses?

'The law indeed was given through Moses; grace and truth came through Jesus Christ.' That is what St John wrote. Moses was a law-giver, and was regarded by Jews as the founder of their religion. Sometimes Jesus was called the new Moses; and indeed he did found a new religion – Christianity. But he did not ignore everything which had gone before; he had a high respect for Moses, and based his teaching on what Moses had achieved. But he went beyond it, because, he said, he *fulfilled* the Law of Moses. According to St Matthew, Jesus said in the Sermon on the Mount: 'Do not think that I have come to abolish the law or the prophets; I have come not to abolish but to fulfil. For truly I tell you, until heaven and earth pass away, not one letter, not one stroke of a letter, will pass from the law until all is accomplished.' We all need to begin with law, so that we know that what we are doing is wrong. When children are growing up, they need rules and discipline, to stop them harming themselves or other people. But that is not enough. Children do not realize how much they are wounding other people by the selfish things they do, until someone sets them an example of unselfish and considerate love. This is what St John called 'grace and truth'; St Matthew filled the Sermon on the Mount with the teaching of Jesus on the law of love.

Law or love?

The Law of Moses was given to the human race in its adolescence, like the rules of behaviour we give to teenagers. Jesus was speaking to Jews, and he did not want them to become irreligious. But they must be more law-abiding even than the experts, the scribes and the Pharisees. These men spent their lives arguing about the meaning of each word in the five so-called 'Books of Moses', the first five books in the Old Testament. Yet Jesus does not call us to keep every pernickety detail of the Sabbath regulations, for instance, but to the inner spirit of love which lies behind the laws. The aim of the Pharisees was to achieve 'righteousness', a word which to them meant being law-abiding. If they were righteous, they thought, that would earn them a place in the kingdom of God. But to Jesus 'righteousness' meant having a right relationship with God our heavenly Father. Nobody can earn a place in heaven; it is God's free gift to the deserving and undeserving alike. But it is only possible if we have a loving relationship with the God who offers it to us free, gratis and for nothing. So Jesus called us to avoid sin, and live a moral life, yet not as the Pharisees tried to achieve by obeying precise regulations, rather, by filling our lives with universal love for everybody we meet. And this can only flow from accepting the all-inclusive love of God into our hearts. This is the 'grace and truth' which St John referred to. Once the word of God is written down, we can argue about it and misuse it. If we remember that the Word is a person, Jesus, we can live by the Spirit of love which he pours into us.

Casuistry

If the intention is good, occasional breaches of the written law, such as healing people on the Sabbath day, may occasionally, but very rarely, be justified. Sometimes keeping one law involves breaking another, and we have to choose 'the lesser of two evils'. This process of applying ancient laws to changed circumstances is called 'casuistry'. It means applying the basic principles which lie behind the moral law to particular cases. We can pray, read the Bible, ask advice and discuss our moral dilemmas with our friends. But the Bible does not tell us exactly what to do in all circumstances. Ultimately the decision is ours and ours alone – we must work out what to do to achieve righteousness according to the law of love.

All-age worship

Make bookmarks to put in your Bible. Write on the one to go in the Old Testament 'Old Law of Moses' and on the one for the New Testament 'New Law of Love'.

Suggested hymns

Blest are the pure in heart; Dearest Jesus, we are here; Lord, thy word abideth; The kingdom of God is justice and joy.

Fourth Sunday before Lent (Proper 1)   5 February
Second Service   **The Old Life and the New Life**
Ps. [1 Righteousness, 3 Trust] 4 Answer me; Amos 2.4–16 God judges his people; Eph. 4.17–32 The old and new ways; *Gospel at Holy Communion*: Mark 1.29–39 Healing and preaching

'You were taught to put away your former way of life, your old self, corrupt and deluded by its lusts, and to be renewed in the spirit of your minds, and to clothe yourselves with the new self, created according to the likeness of God in true righteousness and holiness.' Ephesians 4.22–24

Theology

When I am preaching to you, do you ever sigh and think to yourself, 'Oh no, not more theology'? I thought so. Sometimes I think that myself. But a sermon must be like St Paul's letters. If they seem dull, that is probably the fault of the translation. But a good modern translation will show you that most of his letters are divided into two parts. The first part discusses what Jesus taught us about God. And that is theology, which literally means 'thinking logically about God'. The second part of Paul's letters, usually linked to the first part by the word 'therefore', tells us what we should do about it. But you cannot have the second part without the first: you cannot know how God wants you to behave, without thinking logically who God is. A group of denominations have joined together to suggest which chapters of the Bible we should read in church, to cover all the most interesting bits in the course of three years. Today we heard from Paul's letter to the Ephesians, and you will be relieved to hear that this was from the second part, so there will be no theology this week; just down-to-earth advice on living! Chapter 4 begins, 'I *therefore*, the prisoner in the Lord, beg you to lead a life worthy of the calling to which you have been called.' Paul, writing from his prison in Rome, has told us, in the first three chapters, who God is, according to Jesus; now he is going to tell us what, *therefore*, we should be.

Old and new

Paul keeps on contrasting the old and the new: how we used to behave, and how we ought to live now. There must be no more of the old lies, but we must speak the truth. No more uncontrolled anger, but live together tolerantly. No bitterness, no shouting or insults; but kindness to everyone. In a word, we must treat others as Jesus has treated us. What a contrast between the old way of living, and the new, Christian, behaviour! You may think that you have never done any of those terrible things which are described here as the old way of life. That is just possible, if you were brought up in a very loving family, and never met anyone who annoyed you. More likely you are deceiving yourself, and have forgotten how often you yielded to the dark side of your personality. But there is hope for us all, if we believe that our heavenly Father loves us, and Jesus died to make us change our ways. And it never stops; Oscar Wilde said 'I can resist anything except temptation', and you are tempted to be selfish and crotchety right up to your dying day. But Jesus gives us the power to overcome.

Lying

Finally, let us look at each of those bad habits that Paul points to in our old way of life. First: lying. 'Putting away falsehood,' he writes, 'let all of us speak the truth to our neighbours.' You can deliberately mislead others when you speak, or when you wrongly keep silent. This breaks the bonds of fellowship and trust.

Anger

It is right to be angry in some circumstances: on behalf of the oppressed, as Jesus was with the money-changers; but if it is because you cannot have your own way, anger is sin. 'Do not let the sun go down on your anger,' Paul writes; always make it up with the folk you rowed with before going to bed.

Bitterness

Bitter words tear down our relationships; kind words build them up again. Say things that will make others feel better about themselves.

Insults

There should be no insults in the new life. Paul writes, 'Put away from you all bitterness and wrath and anger and wrangling and slander, together with all malice.' So don't insult anyone to their face; and it is even worse to spread unkind gossip about others behind their backs.

Kindness

Finally, says St Paul, 'be kind to one another, tender hearted, forgiving one another, as God in Christ has forgiven you.' Which echoes what Jesus said. We cannot say the Lord's Prayer until we forgive those who have wronged us. Our attitude towards everyone, in the new Christian life, must be one of unremitting kindness.

Suggested hymns

Alleluia, sing to Jesus; Make me a channel of your peace; O for a closer walk with God; When a knight won his spurs.

Third Sunday before Lent (Proper 2) 12 February
Principal Service **Adultery**

Deut. 30.15–20 *or* Ecclus. (Ben Sira) 15.15–20 Choose life; Ps. 119.1–8 Walk in the law of the Lord; 1 Cor. 3.1–9 Unity between followers of Paul and Apollos; Matt. 5.21–37 Judgement and forgiveness

> *'[Jesus said,] "You have heard that it was said, 'You shall not commit adultery.' But I say to you that everyone who looks at a woman with lust has already committed adultery with her in his heart."'*
> *Matthew 5.27–28*

Sin

The Old Testament lays down the law in no uncertain terms: 'You *must* not commit adultery.' Adultery means when someone who is married makes love to someone other than the person they are married to. Jesus was confronted with a woman who was caught committing adultery. But this was a special case, because both the adulterer and the adulteress were supposed to be stoned to death, and the first stone was supposed to be thrown by the innocent husband who had been cuckolded. Yet neither man appeared in this case, so it was obviously a set-up. Jesus protected the woman from those who had entrapped her. In the Sermon on the Mount he pointed out that what is wrong when adultery is committed is not the act, but the thinking that lay behind it, and nobody's conscience is completely clear of immoral thoughts. He did not condemn the woman, but said to her, 'go and sin no more', so that nobody should have any doubt that adultery is *always* contrary to the will of God.

Betrayal

What is so wrong, then, about a 'casual liaison', 'having a brief affair', or even 'sleeping around a bit'? We make these euphemisms to pretend that it doesn't really matter. But it does, whether you are married or just living together, because of what goes on in your brain. No partnership will ever be really happy unless both parties decide that the most important thing in their lives from now on will be making the other one contented. The emotions which are aroused when you make love are so powerful that you can never feel the same about your previous partnership ever again. There is no use kidding yourself that your partner will never know; sooner or later they always find out. And then they feel betrayed. They may decide to be unfaithful themselves, in revenge, and that is the end of the respect and security which is at the heart of any relationship, and both will feel miserable. Or the one who has been sinned against decides, for the sake of their future happiness, to forgive their partner 'just this once', but they will never feel truly happy ever again. So even a single act of unfaithfulness is absolutely guaranteed to make two, three or even four people miserable in the long run.

Temptation

When Jesus said that lustful thoughts are as bad as the act of adultery, he was warning us not to condemn other people because we think we are better than them. Temptation comes to all of us. It is what you do with temptation that matters. If you make up your mind firmly to resist it, God will help you to if you ask him. But if you allow temptation to build its nest in your heart, turning your selfish thoughts over and over, without considering what the results would be, then that is the opposite of the love which Jesus commanded us to show to everybody. It is no use pleading that you were drunk when it happened; if inebriation makes you unable to resist temptation, then that is another reason never to get drunk.

Addiction

For some people sex is an addiction, just like hard drugs. If so, you need to seek counselling, medical assistance, or something equivalent to the Twelve Steps process used by Alcoholics Anonymous. If adultery has caused guilt or anger in you or your partner, you should speak in confidence to a minister of religion – the Church has many centuries of experience in dealing with temptation, sin and forgiveness. Maybe the difficulty of continuing a partnership when one partner has been unfaithful is why so many people live together without marrying – the solemnity of making marriage vows in God's house is one more weapon in the fight against temptation. We should always be firm with ourselves, but we should never judge other people; we just don't know how hard it was to 'Just say no!' In the end, God will forgive us all our selfish acts; but God cannot prevent us causing a great deal of pain to ourselves and to those we love in the meantime.

All-age worship

Colour a card reading 'Just say no!' Discuss what it means, then hang it up in your bedroom.

Suggested hymns

Be thou my guardian and my guide; The kingdom of God is justice and joy; Soldiers of Christ arise; To God be the glory.

Third Sunday before Lent (Proper 2)   12 February
Second Service   **Reasons to Believe**
Ps. [7 Rise up] 13 How long?; Amos 3.1–8 God has his reasons; Eph. 5.1–17 Imitate God; *Gospel at Holy Communion*: Mark 1.40–45 Healing a leper

> *'Does a snare spring up from the ground, when it has taken nothing? . . . Surely the Lord God does nothing, without revealing his secret to his servants the prophets.' Amos 3.5, 7*

Logic

The prophet Amos lived more than 2,000 years before the emergence of modern science, yet he proclaimed a message which lies at the heart of scientific reasoning: nothing ever happens without a cause. Only, the scientists limit themselves to talking about physical causes, whereas the prophet also included spiritual causes. A snare is a device for trapping a wild animal, which snaps shut when any creature steps on it. It would be unreasonable to think it could spring into the air unless something had trodden on it. In the same way, says the prophet, it would be unreasonable to suggest that a civilization could fall without God being involved it its collapse. God has his reasons for everything that he does; unbelievers may not understand, but he reveals why things happen to those who trust him. We often do not recognize the logic of religion, but God is never irrational.

Rabbi

This comes as a shock to those who have been brought up to a religion of simple stories. Rabbi Louis Jacobs was born in 1920 to an Orthodox Jewish family in Manchester. During his rabbinical training, he was dismayed to discover that some Jewish scholars accepted the discoveries of archaeology and the evidence of writings by nearby civilizations, which showed that many things could not possibly have happened exactly as the naive scriptural accounts said they did. He devoted the rest of his life to comparing the scientific, critical view of the Scriptures with the traditional literal way of interpreting them. In 1957 he wrote a book, entitled *We have reason to believe*, which tried to reconcile these views. This split the English Jewish community into a dispute which echoed all through the 1960s, and saw Rabbi Jacobs forbidden to take up a position he had been appointed to, in a college for training other rabbis.

Modernism

A similar story happened among Christians. Some students from either of the traditional wings of the faith go to university to study science. There they find scientists who reject Christianity, because they imagine that all Christians deny the discoveries of modern science. A central faction, sometimes called modernists or liberals, try to keep the peace between these two groups, and evolve a logical, rational interpretation of the Bible, which rejects neither the spiritual truths of revelation, nor the historical discoveries of science. As another rabbi put it, 'Many people want the protective clarity of being told who they are, what to do, whom they are for and whom against. Hence, perhaps, the revival of Islamic, Christian and Jewish fundamentalism.'

Change

All religions have to change, and keep changing. The only things which never change are dead things. If we refuse the logic of recent empirical discoveries, we shall be rejected by the growing number of people who have had a basic scientific education. How can we say we worship the God who created the laws of science, which enabled the universe to be formed, and to survive, and in his Son, who is called the Word or *logos* – and then reject the *logic* of those

64

who have found irrefutable proof that history happened in a different way than the ancient legends say it did?

Peace

Jesus prayed that his followers might be united, so that the world should believe in their message of love and tolerance. The Church needs to embrace the discoveries of archaeology and science, to convince this materialistic age that we are not a coven of illogical bigots. The world needs a body of rational, realistic religious believers, to correct the descent into materialism which endangers the compassionate side of human nature, and to counteract the fundamentalist forms of religious extremism which lie behind many of the bloody wars of recent years. The teaching of the Bible was not a once-and-for-all revelation of a complete corpus of faith and morals, but the product of centuries of listening to God by varied communities. These groups applied what God had told them to the various differing environments in which they lived, philosophical, cultural and economic. And the different religions in the modern world need to dialogue with each other, learning to disagree without fighting, and to appreciate what the One God has revealed to those of different cultural traditions. We cannot afford to go on resisting the reasonableness of God. As the prophet Amos said, every effect has its own cause or causes, in the spiritual world as well as the material one.

Suggested hymns

Above the moon earth rises; Lord of the boundless curves of space; O Lord my God! When I in awesome wonder; The spacious firmament on high.

Second Sunday before Lent   19 February
Principal Service   **Giving to God**
Gen. 1.1—2.3 The creation; Ps. 136, or Ps. 136.1–9, 23–26 Creation, salvation; Rom. 8.18–25 The creation waits for salvation; Matt. 6.25–34 Lilies of the field

'God saw everything that he had made, and indeed, it was very good.' Genesis 1.31

Creation

The first chapter of Genesis tells us that everything we have comes from God. The sources of our food were made by God, not by us. The strength in our arms and the cleverness of our brains comes from him – and these earn us money to buy food, clothing and accommodation. But such things are not our possessions; they are God's property, which he has kindly loaned to us for a few years.

Time

So when we give some of our time to God, we are not being generous; we are returning a little of what God has made back to its creator. It is God's time, lent to us to use as God wishes us to. That will include time to sleep, and time to enjoy ourselves; but it should also include some time spent helping other people; and time spent praying to God, worshipping in his church, encouraging others to join us there, and making sure that everything runs smoothly.

Talents

You may think you are not very talented. You are wrong. God has placed all sorts of skills in your brain, some of which you use regularly, which you should thank him for, and some which you didn't even know were there. So think: are you good at cooking? Couldn't you spend a few hours a week cooking for your needy neighbours, or catering at church functions? You have a friendly disposition; could you spend an hour once a month or so welcoming people as they come into church? You have experience maintaining property; could you mend your neighbours' fence when it blows down, or organize the maintenance of the church? Work out how many hours a month you could spend putting your talents at God's disposal. You probably know what tasks are needed for the smooth running of this church.

Money

Now I'm going to make myself unpopular by talking about money. But it must be said sometime. Many people think the Church is very wealthy. The opposite is the case. It owns land and buildings which it cannot sell, because people gave them in trust years ago, on condition they were used for church activities. Most of the money each local church has to contribute to central funds goes on paying the ministers and housing them. The state has ruled that the pensions of the growing number of retired clergy should be paid out of a large pension fund, which we have only just begun to build, so whatever interest the Church does gain on its investments all goes to paying clergy pensions. The repair of the buildings has to be paid out of the collections; the State gives nothing to the Church, and even charges VAT on what we spend on repairs. Fewer come to church than used to, and we have to ask those few to pay the total expense of their building and minister.

Tithing

So I appeal to you to work out what percentage of your income you can give back to God. It is no use putting in a few pence when you feel like it; a few years of that and the church will fall down. For a start, work out what your after-tax income is, and give 1 per cent of that to your church, whether you are in church on Sunday or not, and 1 per cent to other charities. Next year make it 4 per cent in total, and go on increasing it each year as long as you can without starving! In the Bible it suggests a total of 10 per cent of your after-tax income given back to God. Make that your eventual target. You may think that is impossible, but the advantage of a percentage is that it goes up and down with your income. So poor people have to give much less than rich people. Surprisingly, the poor are much more generous, percentage-wise, than the rich. I'm not rich, and I have been giving 5 per cent of my income to the church and 5 per cent to other charities for several years now; if I can do it, why not you? After all, it's not your money; it's God's money which he has lent you. If you want to stone me to death for my impertinence, please wait till we get outside!

All-age worship

Ask your parents for a fixed amount of pocket money each week, and try to buy all the toys you want out of that. Thank God that he has lent them enough to be so generous. Work out what one-twentieth of that is, and put it in the church collection each week.

Suggested hymns

Angel voices ever singing; Give thanks with a grateful heart; O Lord of heaven and earth and sea; Take my life, and let it be.

Second Sunday before Lent   19 February
Second Service   **The Blessed Damozel**

Ps. 148 Praise God, you angels; Prov. 8.1, 22–31 Wisdom;
Rev. 4 Worship in heaven; *Gospel at Holy Communion*:
Luke 12.16–31 The rich fool

> *'At once I was in the spirit, and there in heaven stood a throne,
> with one seated on the throne!' Revelation 4.2*

Rossetti

The poet Dante Gabriel Rossetti was born in London in 1828 to
Italian émigré parents; he was the brother of another poet, Christina
Rossetti, who wrote 'In the bleak midwinter'. He was also an artist,
and one of the founders of the Pre-Raphaelite Brotherhood. He often
painted scenes from his or his sister's poems. They called themselves
that because they thought art deteriorated when Raphael brought
in the viewpoint of the Romantic Movement, so their subjects were
often set in the Middle Ages; nonetheless they were deeply sensual.

Poem

One of his best-known poems is entitled *The Blessed Damozel*, and
he also painted a ravishing painting with the same title. His medi-
evalism is shown by his choice of the word 'Damozel' for a damsel
or young woman. He was inspired by Edgar Alan Poe's poem *The
Raven*, about a lover grieving for his loved one, who has died. But
Rossetti turned the idea around, and his poem depicts the grief of
the girl in heaven as she waits for her lover to come and join her
there. What is particularly moving is the description of heaven. It
is a long poem, so I will only read you the first two and the last
two verses:

The Blessed Damozel

> The blessed damozel leaned out
>   from the gold bar of Heaven;
> her eyes were deeper than the depth
>   of waters stilled at even;
> she had three lilies in her hand,
>   and the stars in her hair were seven.

Her robe, ungirt from clasp to hem,
    no wrought flowers did adorn,
but a white rose of Mary's gift,
    for service meetly worn;
her hair that lay along her back
    was yellow like ripe corn.

Herseemed she scarce had been a day
    one of God's choristers;
the wonder was not yet quite gone
    from that still look of hers;
albeit, to them she left, her day
    had counted as ten years.

[Then the lover, on earth, sings:]
(To one, it is ten years of years.
    . . . yet now, and in this place,
surely she leaned o'er me – her hair
    fell all about my face . . .
Nothing: the autumn-fall of leaves.
    The whole year sets apace.)

Middle

Then the centre of the poem describes heaven as like a castle built in space:

It was the rampart of God's house
    that she was standing on;
by God built over the sheer depth
    the which is Space begun;
so high, that looking downward thence
    she scarce could see the sun.
It lies in Heaven, across the flood
    of ether, as a bridge.

She senses the pulse of time throughout the universe, but in heaven all is still, as the prayers of those on earth, and the souls of those who have died, pass by on their way to God. She looks forward to when she will be reunited with her lover, and the poem ends:

Ending

'All this is when he comes.' She ceased.
The light thrilled towards her, fill'd
with angels in strong level flight.
Her eyes prayed, and she smil'd.

(I saw her smile.) But soon their path
was vague in distant spheres:
and then she cast her arms along
the golden barriers,
and laid her face between her hands,
and wept. (I heard her tears.)

Heaven

There are no words to describe the afterlife, so the poet uses a dream of a medieval castle as a metaphor, and his recollection of his own grief when the one loved unexpectedly died. The book of Revelation in the Bible also has a description of heaven in terms of a royal court, but it is no less metaphorical:

> ... there in heaven ... the first voice ... said, 'Come up here, and I will show you what must take place after this.' At once I was in the spirit, and there in heaven stood a throne, with one seated on the throne! And the one seated there looks like jasper and carnelian, and around the throne is a rainbow that looks like an emerald. Around the throne are twenty-four thrones, and seated on the thrones are twenty-four elders, dressed in white robes, with golden crowns on their heads.

So this is a vision, describing the indescribable in poetic words which resonated in the first century AD. You may choose different words for now; perhaps metaphors about other dimensions and alterative universes. But the object is to give hope to those who grieve, helping them to imagine 'what must take place', not at the end of the world, but when we die; and our joy at being reunited with God, and with those we love.

Suggested hymns

Blessed city, heavenly Salem; Give me the wings of faith to rise; God, whose city's sure foundation; Lord, it belongs not to my care.

Sunday next before Lent   26 February
Principal Service   **The Law and the Prophets**

Ex. 24.12–18 God appears to Moses on Mount Sinai; Ps. 2
You are my son, *or* Ps. 99 A pillar of cloud; 2 Peter 1.16–21
We ourselves heard this voice; Matt. 17.1–9 The transfiguration

'Jesus . . . was transfigured before them . . . Suddenly there appeared to them Moses and Elijah, talking with him.' Matthew 17.1–3

The Hebrew Bible

When our Jewish friends are talking about what we call the Old Testament, but which to them is the whole of the Scriptures, they may just call it 'the Law', with a capital 'L', or they may be more specific and call it 'the Law and the prophets'. The first five books are about Moses – not *by* him, because they describe his death – and they are the Law; then come the history books, Joshua, Judges, 1 and 2 Samuel, 1 and 2 Kings, which the Jews call the former prophets, and they tell the story of Elijah, Elisha and several other early prophetic figures. Next come the later prophets: Isaiah, Jeremiah, Ezekiel, and the twelve minor prophets; and finally the Psalms, Proverbs, and other books of poetry.

Transfiguration

So when Jesus went up the mountain with Peter, James and John, where they saw him talking to Moses and Elijah, that symbolized the whole of the Holy Scriptures: the Law and the prophets. As he said himself, Jesus had not come to supersede the Jewish religion, but to fulfil the promises to which it had been pointing. The disciples had come to know him as their dear friend; now they realized that he was far more than that: Jesus was the climax of the process of revelation which began with the creation, but was incomplete until he came to show what the laws and the prophecies really meant.

Discipline

When you are bringing up children, you must start with a little simple discipline. 'Don't do that, darling, you'll hurt yourself if you go on like that.' Of course they don't listen, and carry on misbehaving regardless, and you try to catch them before they have wounded themselves too badly. Then they cry, and you comfort them, and gradually they learn that it is advisable to pay some attention to what their parents say. It was like that when the human race was young; God revealed his laws to us, to stop us harming each other. In the early days, it was the job of the tribal chief to keep his tribesmen in order. Sometimes he or she would do this by inflicting very harsh punishments on the disobedient. So they started to write the laws down, so that there should be a uniform standard of justice across the whole country, with only limited vengeance allowed. Your neighbour knocked out your eye-tooth and put out one of your eyes, did he? That is serious, the tribe can't ignore that. If you insist, you can do to him what he did to you; but no more than that: only one eye for one eye, no more than one tooth in revenge for one tooth – any more than that would lead to a vendetta.

Justice

Even in the modern world we cannot manage without a justice system. Those who work as lawyers are often inspired by an ideal of creating a more just society. It is important to remember that the accused must always be treated as innocent until they are proved guilty, and for that reason many suspects cannot be punished because there is not enough evidence; but that is preferable to imprisoning the innocent.

Prophets

But if you develop a rigid legalistic code, with every possible offence covered, many acts which are deeply immoral, but not illegal, will be ignored. So God also sent prophets, to dig beneath the surface of the Law, and bring out the principles on which it is based. They called kings and judges to account, and warned them to treat the poor folk fairly, avoiding corruption and violence. Elijah's contest on Mount Carmel with the immoral prophets of Baal was as a symbol of the task of the prophet, just as Moses on Mount Sinai receiving the tablets of stone represented the role of the Law. But a just society needs both. Jesus met Moses and Elijah on yet another mountain, the Mount of Transfiguration, to show that the teachings of the Law and the prophets are both overridden by the law of love. Observe the basic principles of love God and love your neighbour, said Jesus, even if it means healing on the Sabbath day; seek justice for the oppressed, even if it means being a lone prophetic voice crying in the wilderness. Both the Law and the prophets are subsumed in the teaching of the transfigured Christ.

All-age worship

Make cardboard 'tablets' with commandments for parents on one, and commandments for children on the other.

Suggested hymns

Jesus, these eyes have never seen; Long ago, prophets knew; Lord, the light of your love is shining; 'Tis good Lord to be here.

Sunday next before Lent 26 February
Second Service One Day in Your Courts
Ps. 84 How lovely is your dwelling; Ecclus. (Ben Sira) 48.1–10 Elijah's work, *or* 2 Kings 2.1–12 Elijah ascends into heaven; Matt. 17.9–23 (*or* 1–23) Elijah will come first

> *'One day in your courts is better than a thousand.'*
> *Psalm 84.9 (Common Worship)*

High point

For some people, going to church is a duty, an obligation which they fulfil grudgingly. All praise to them if they keep on attending. Particularly if you don't like the style of worship or the choice of music, but you keep coming because your family want to, or you want to support your local community. In that case, what the Bible calls 'the sacrifice of praise' may be a real sacrifice for you, but one which God accepts because it's a way of showing that he's important. We're in church to worship God, not to enjoy ourselves. But if you *are* enjoying yourself it helps a lot! For many people, I'm glad to say, coming to church is the high point of the week. Many people like meeting their friends, or enjoy the beauty of the building and the music, or singing, or mental stimulation, or like being told that God loves them, or even in some cases all of the above. So much so that if circumstances prevent them being in church one Sunday, the week seems to get off on the wrong foot and they feel something important is missing from their lives. Like the Psalmist, who with pardonable poetic exaggeration said that one day in God's house is better than a thousand days spent somewhere else, many people actually prefer the time they spend in church to anything else. If you haven't reached that point yet, examine your attitude when you come to church, make up your mind to enjoy the service and the socializing and to ignore the minor irritations, and the pleasure of church-going will grow on you.

Pottering

It's not only during Sunday services that this pleasure's to be found. Many people go into church at other times, arranging the flowers, dusting the pews, practising the organ, or visiting old churches while they're on holiday, and find an atmosphere of indescribable peace. More than the fun which the characters in *The Wind in the Willows* found in 'messing about in boats', there is a real satisfaction to be found in pottering about in church. Logic tells us that if God exists, he must be everywhere. But it's easy to forget that. In church, the beauty and the calm, or the inspiring worship, remind you of the presence of God. Whatever logic says, it's above all in church that you can *feel* the presence of God close to you. Some people when they step through the church door say, silently or aloud, 'Hello, Jesus!'

The presence of God

The advantage of going into a church, and feeling that God is near you, is that you can take him with you when you leave. Having once become aware of the presence of God, it only needs something to jog your memory later in the week to bring home vividly to you that though we may forget God, he never forgets us and never leaves us. Gradually you become more and more aware that every moment of every day you are living in the presence of God. This isn't anything solemn; God likes to watch you enjoying yourself in many different ways. Knowing that God is with you and loves you increases the enjoyment. Going to church once a week or more can transform your whole life.

The presence of the saints

When somebody dies we say they have gone to be with Jesus. Where's Jesus? In heaven, certainly, but he is everywhere. He is very especially present in God's house, the church. So when you feel the presence of Jesus in church, you're also especially close to those you love who have died. That is why church-going is such a comfort to the bereaved. But it is not only people you know; the long list of famous Christians that you have read about are also with Jesus; so they, too, are close to us when you're in church. We call this 'the communion of saints'.

Family

For the Church is God's family. The communion of all the saints, in heaven and on earth, is our family life. It's not hard to imagine a husband or a wife saying to their spouse, 'I love you, and nothing will stop me loving you, but it's not much of a relationship because you're hardly ever here with the rest of your family.' I hope God never has cause to say to you, 'I love you, my child, and nothing will stop me loving you, because I'm your Father; but it is not much of a relationship, because you are hardly ever in my house with the rest of my family.'

Suggested hymns:

Blessèd city, heavenly Salem; Sometimes a light surprises; The Church's one foundation; We love the place, O God.

This is a season of preparation for the great festivals of Holy Week and Easter. Lent is a time to repent for our sins, which were the cause of Christ's death, and learn discipline of life, so that we may resist temptation whenever it comes. And yet the church music should not be too solemn, lest worshippers are deterred by the thought of a gloomy and unmerciful God. There must also be an underlying note of hope for God's forgiveness. So we do not sing the 'Glory to God in the highest' during Lent. And we chose hymns like: 'Be thou my guardian and my guide'; 'Come, my soul, thy suit prepare'; 'Dear Lord and Father of mankind'; 'Forgive our sins as we forgive'; 'Forty days and forty nights'; 'Jesu, grant me this, I pray'; 'Jesu, lover of my soul'; 'Just as I am, without one plea'; 'Lift up your hearts! We lift them, Lord, to thee'; 'Lord Jesus, think on me'; 'Lord, teach us how to pray aright'; 'My spirit longs for thee'; 'O for a closer walk with God'; 'O for a heart to praise my God'; 'Oft in danger, oft in woe'; 'Soldiers of Christ, arise'; and 'Take up thy cross, the Saviour said'.

Ash Wednesday   1 March
Miserable Sinners
Joel 2.1–2, 12–17 Rend your hearts, *or* Isa. 58.1–12 Care for the needy; Ps. 51.1–18 Cleanse me from my sin; 2 Cor. 5.20b—6.10 Suffering of an apostle; Matt. 6.1–6, 16–21 Secret fasting, *or* John 8.1–11 Adultery and forgiveness

> *'Rend your hearts and not your clothing. Return to the LORD, your God, for he is gracious and merciful, slow to anger, and abounding in steadfast love, and relents from punishing.'* Joel 2.13

Litany

A Litany is a form of intercession, in which whoever is leading it utters a short prayer, and all the congregation say or sing an even shorter response. The Litany in the 1662 Book of Common Prayer is very beautiful, but the language seems very old-fashioned today; worse still, some words can be completely misunderstood. One of the responses was 'have mercy upon us, miserable sinners'. When that prayer was translated into English, 'miserable' meant 'deserving of pity'. Nowadays, many people assume it means 'downhearted, unhappy, sad and gloomy'.

Misunderstanding

Because of this misunderstanding, those who are not regular church-goers often assume that Christians are a miserable lot, downcast of features and pessimistic in personality. Even some who go to church regularly assume that they *ought* to be like that, even if they came into the building feeling quite cheerful! So they put all happy thoughts out of their mind, and start making a mental list of all the things that will make them sad.

Sinners

There is no doubt that we *are* all sinners. Not that we have ever murdered anybody; though we may have hated a few, which Jesus said is as bad. We have gossiped, criticizing others, forgetting that the Bible calls this, too, a sin. We need to say sorry to God, because we have wounded his loving heart by hurting another of his children. So we ask him to have mercy on us, or in other words to forgive us. But God is more eager to pardon us than we are to ask him to. So our apology opens the sluice gate to the flood of love which he is waiting to pour into our hearts. Never doubt God's promises. He has promised to forgive us as soon as we repent. Maybe there is a look of misery on our faces when we remember the hurtful things we have said and done to others; but it ought not to stay there longer than a nanosecond, giving place to an expression of joy and gratitude that God is so ready to forgive. We need God's pity; but we ought never to be gloomy.

Ashes

This is Ash Wednesday. It takes its name from the ashes which people who were sorry for what they had done used to pour over their heads, as they tore off their smart clothes, and put on garments made from shabby old sackcloth. Certainly we should be solemn through the 40 days of Lent, as we approach Good Friday and think of the awful suffering that Jesus went through because of his love for us. But that does not mean we should be outwardly miserable. In fact, any outward display is condemned by Jesus, who said 'whenever you pray, go into your room and shut the door and pray to your Father who is in secret; and your Father who sees in secret will reward you.'

Joel

One of the two possible Old Testament readings today was taken from the book of the prophet Joel. Joel prophesied in Jerusalem soon after the Jews had returned from exile in Babylon. Their fields had recently been stripped bare by a plague of locusts, grasshopper-like insects which fly along in huge black swarms, devouring on their way every single thing which is edible. The Jerusalemites concluded that the locusts were sent by God as a punishment for their sins, and held a very public display of mourning, tearing their clothes into shreds. But Joel told them, 'Rend your hearts and not your clothing. Return to the LORD, your God, for he is gracious and merciful, slow to anger, and abounding in steadfast love, and relents from punishing.'

Penitence

I think we should all take that to heart. Take some time in Lent to look critically at your way of life, and tell God that you are sorry. But do it in private, where nobody can see you. Then come out with a broad grin on your face. If anyone asks you what you are so happy about, answer that it is because our God is a loving heavenly Father, and he is so quick to forgive us when we say sorry. We must be pitiable, but not miserable, sinners.

Suggested hymns

Forty days and forty nights; Just as I am, without one plea; Lord Jesus, think on me; O for a heart to praise my God.

78

First Sunday of Lent   5 March
Principal Service   **Personality**

Gen. 2.15–17; 3.1–7 The Fall; Ps. 32 Happy are those who know
God's forgiveness; Rom. 5.12–19 Christ's obedience cancels
Adam's disobedience; Matt. 4.1–11 The temptation of Christ

> *'Then Jesus was led up by the Spirit into the wilderness to be
> tempted by the devil.' Matthew 4.1*

Personal God?

Sometimes people say to me, 'I believe that there is a spiritual world
as well as the material one; and I believe there is a guiding force
behind everything that happens. But I don't believe in a personal
God.' Then I like to shock them by replying, 'No, neither do I.'
When they have got over their astonishment, I say something like
this: If you mean, is God a person like you and me, then of course
not. God is not an old man sitting on a cloud. He has no body, and
he is invisible. God is not limited by time and space, he can be anywhere he chooses at any time of day. He doesn't get into a paddy or
lose his temper, like we do. God is omnipotent and omniscient. God
is altogether greater than we are, in every possible way. C. S. Lewis
wrote a book called *Beyond Personality*, arguing that God is too
great to be thought of in human terms, such as describing God as
'personal'. A respectable Christian teaching, called 'negative theology', suggests that we cannot even say that God is love, because his
love is so much greater than ours that words cannot describe it.

Personal relationships

So all you can say about the infinite God is what God is not: God
is not ignorant; God is not evil; God is not created; God cannot
be defined in terms of time and space. But – and here comes the
crunch – God wants to have a relationship with each one of us
which resembles nothing so much as the truly personal relationship
that exists between two people who are in love with each other.
So God *reveals* himself to us as a person, so that we can grasp
who it is that we are dealing with. And then he actually *became* a
human person for a few years, in the person of Jesus Christ. In the
ancient Roman theatres, the actors were so far away that the audience could not see the subtle changes of expression on their faces.

So they wore a mask, adopting the character of a hero or a villain, a king or a slave. This mask was called a *persona*; it showed what role they were playing. So Christians teach that there is only one God, but he reveals his character to us by wearing three masks: as the Creator of the beauties of nature; as Jesus who sacrifices his life for others; and as the Holy Spirit bringing love to our hearts.

A personal devil?

In today's Gospel, we read that 'Jesus was led up by the Spirit into the wilderness to be tempted by the devil.' So who is this devil that Jesus talked about? A person, or just a character in fiction – a little green cartoon character with horns, hooves and a tail? The Bible nowhere describes him like that. But the Scriptures certainly want us to take the power of evil seriously. In the story of the temptation of Jesus in the wilderness, Jesus shows us that, when God became human, he found temptation as hard to resist as you or I do. When St Peter tried to stop Jesus going up to Jerusalem to be crucified, Jesus said, 'Get behind me, *Satan!*' The word means 'tempter'; sometimes advice from our friends can tempt us to take the easy path.

Resist

So if you find yourself tempted to do something thoughtless or unkind, resist it. Always take the power of evil seriously. Yet the devil is not equal and opposite to God. If God is 'beyond personality', a superhuman being, then Satan is subhuman, a sneaky little rat. Neither God nor the devil is truly personal; God, because he is so good that he is beyond personality, and the devil because he is beneath contempt. But if it helps you to love God by thinking of him as a person like us, then that is OK. And if it helps you to resist temptation to think of the devil as a person, then go ahead, and do battle with the evil forces in the world with all your strength. Fight the good fight, and God's grace be with you.

All-age worship

In which situation do you feel tempted. Promise Jesus that you will try to say no. Would you like to role play saying no to that temptation?

Suggested hymns

Be thou my guardian and my guide; Christian, dost thou see them; Fight the good fight; Oft in danger, oft in woe.

First Sunday of Lent 5 March
Second Service **A Sacrifice of Thanksgiving**

Ps. 50.1–15 A sacrifice of thanksgiving; Deut. 6.4–9, 16–25 Keeping God's commandments; Luke 15.1–10 Lost sheep, lost coin

> *'Offer to God a sacrifice of thanksgiving,*
> *and fulfil your vows to God Most High.'*
> *Psalm 50.14 (Common Worship)*

Thank-you presents

After somebody has invited you to a meal at their house, or given you a treat, it is nice to give them a thank-you present – a box of chocolates, for instance. It pleases your hosts because it was not expected. It was not a condition of what they did for you that you should give them anything in return. Your gift is not intended to be equal to what they did for you – it is the thought that counts – yet it cost you something, even if it was only taking the trouble to go down to the shops to buy it. A thank-you present is a gesture of gratitude, making your thankfulness visible. It creates a warm feeling in both your hearts, and deepens your relationship immeasurably.

Sacrifices

Whenever we come across the word 'sacrifice', I suggest we should replace it, silently in our minds, with the words 'thank-you present':

> 'Gosh, you made a real sacrifice of your time to hunt for exactly the right size of slipper to buy for me!'
> 'Not at all, it was just a little thank-you present to show my gratitude for all that *you* have done for *me*.'

And in the Bible, when people went up to the Temple to sacrifice an animal, it was not really a bribe, because God does not need anything that we can give him. What God has done for us, and what he has given us in this incredibly beautiful world, could never be paid for, even in the currency of animal carcases, no matter how costly they are. So in Psalm 50 God says:

'I will not reprove you for your sacrifices,
for your burnt offerings are always before me.
I will take no bull out of your house,
nor he-goat out of your folds,
For all the beasts of the forest are mine,
the cattle upon a thousand hills . . .
If I were hungry, I would not tell you,
for the whole world is mine and all that fills it . . .
Offer to God a sacrifice of thanksgiving,
and fulfil your vows to God Most High.'

Worship

In other words, our worship is not offered as a payment to God – it is to give us an opportunity to express our gratitude. Thank you, God, for my astonishing body; that I have enough food to eat and liquid to drink; that I have people who love me and whom I can love in return; a house to live in and work to do; the skills to make other people happy. Above all, thank you God for loving me, though I have done nothing to deserve it. And I am giving up an hour of my time, and singing some songs to you, not because you need it, but because I can think of no other way of saying thank you!

Forgiveness

In the Old Testament, there was a special day each year called the Day of Atonement. The priest took an animal outside the city and offered it as a sacrifice to atone for the sins of all the people – it was known as the 'scapegoat'. Then they all went home happy, knowing that God had forgiven them. But of course you can never *buy* forgiveness; it is far too costly. God forgives us as soon as we say sorry. Any sacrifice we make, such as giving up something for Lent, is a thank-you present to the God who has *already* forgiven us. We do something visible, so that we can express our gratitude, and as a visible reminder of God's forgiveness.

Jesus

Sometimes a hero will sacrifice their own life while they are saving other people from danger. But if you could ask them why, they would answer, 'I couldn't do anything else. I've had a wonderful life, and I wanted these other people to have the same chances I've had.' So when Jesus died on the cross, we describe it as an atoning sacrifice. God has already forgiven us when we confessed our sins. The death of Jesus is a way of showing that God will forgive us, no matter how much it costs him. When we realize that, it makes us eternally grateful.

Communion

We use the language of sacrifice often in the Communion service, which we call 'a sacrifice of praise'. It is a sacrament: a way of making God's forgiveness visible, and expressing visibly our thankfulness. Communion is a thank-you present to God for all he has done. It is the least we could do. It makes the relationship between God and us all warm and cosy. And that makes everybody happy.

Suggested hymns

Alleluia, alleluia, give thanks to the risen Lord; Now thank we all our God; Thank you, Jesus; Thank you, O my Father.

Second Sunday of Lent   12 March
Principal Service   **Born-again Christians**
Gen. 12.1–4a Abram begins his journey of faith; Ps. 121 I lift my eyes to the hills; Rom. 4.1–5, 13–17 Abraham was justified by faith; John 3.1–17 Born again

> *'Jesus answered [Nicodemus], "Very truly, I tell you, no one can see the kingdom of God without being born anew . . . For God so loved the world that he gave his only Son, so that everyone who believes in him may not perish but may have eternal life. Indeed, God did not send the Son into the world to condemn the world, but in order that the world might be saved through him."'*
> *John 3.3 (margin), 16–17*

83

Offered

What do you most want out of life? Most people would answer that question with words like 'love, long life and happiness'. Those three things are offered to every Christian in our Gospel reading today, though in slightly different words. In St John's Gospel are some of the best-known words in the Bible:

God so *loved* the world that he gave his only Son, so that every-one who believes in him may not perish but may have eternal *life*. Indeed, God did not send the Son into the world to condemn the world, but in order that the world might be *saved* through him.

There God offers us the chance to be loved; to have a very long life – as long as eternity; and salvation. 'To be saved' has a range of meanings, but at the very least it means being set free from fear, guilt, despair and all the other things which make us unhappy. So you are being offered love, long life and happiness; but how much do you have to pay to get these things?

Pharisees

Jesus offered them to a Jew called Nicodemus who belonged to the Pharisees, the most narrow-minded, moralistic sect of the Jewish religion. Nicodemus thought that to please God you must read every law in the Old Testament, then apply them strictly in your own life. Then this would earn you entry into something called 'the kingdom of God', which most Jews believed would be a new era in earthly history, beginning in their lifetime, when Jews would rule the world through a new king called 'the Messiah'. But this could only happen when *every* Jew had obeyed *every* law in the Scriptures for 24 hours. That is why they hated this dangerous liberal called Jesus, who seemed to be saying, 'Forget the details; just learn to love God and love your neighbour.'

Born again

Jesus said, 'You can't even see the kingdom of God when it's under-neath your nose,' which left Nicodemus flabbergasted. The entry-ticket depends not on strict morality, but on *rebirth*. The word Jesus used is translated differently in different Bibles: most give it as 'born again'; the New Revised Standard Version puts 'born from above' in the text and 'born anew' in the footnote. To enter the kingdom of God you need a fresh start, entirely dependent on God. Don't boast of your achievements, says Jesus, but begin your life all over again. Just as a newborn child is totally dependent on its parents, you must rely entirely on God's grace. Then you will receive love and happiness as you build God's earthly kingdom of justice and peace; and after you die, your life in God's heavenly kingdom will be not just long, but eternal.

Decision

This is the good news, the gospel. Some eager Christians ask you out of the blue, 'Are you born again?' If they mean, have you had a particularly emotional conversion experience, you can safely answer, 'No. St Paul himself spoke in tongues, but he accepted that there are many good Christians who don't (1 Corinthians 12.30).' But if you mean, 'Have you given your whole life to Jesus', your answer should be, 'Yes! I am born again every day!' Stop relying on your own achievements, and start your life all over again, trusting only in God's love. Make living a life of unselfish love, as Jesus told us to, the most important thing in your life. Then depend on God's forgiveness to bring you to heaven, not your own virtues. You want love, long life and happiness, do you? Easy! Just be born again: make a fresh start, and give your whole life to Jesus. If you haven't done it before, or if you are slipping a bit, do it right now: say 'Amen' to this prayer:

> Dear Jesus, I want to be born again, giving my whole life to you, doing what you want to me to, and trusting in your forgiveness, not what I have done, to get me to heaven. **Amen.**

All-age worship

Make a sign for the church door: 'Come here to make a fresh start', then add Sticky Notes with words like 'Love', 'Forgiveness', etc.

Suggested hymns

And can it be that I should gain? God forgave my sin in Jesus' name; O happy day! That fixed my choice; There's a wideness in God's mercy.

Second Sunday of Lent   12 March
Second Service   **Grumbling**

Ps. 135 God is good; Num. 21.4–9 The bronze serpent; Luke
14.27–33 Counting the cost

> 'The people spoke against God and against Moses, "Why have
> you brought us up out of Egypt to die in the wilderness? For there
> is no food and no water, and we detest this miserable food." Then
> the Lord sent poisonous serpents among the people, and they
> bit the people, so that many Israelites died. The people came to
> Moses and said, "We have sinned by speaking against the Lord
> and against you; pray to the Lord to take away the serpents from
> us."' Numbers 21.5–7

Grumbling

God had brought the people of Israel out of their slavery in Egypt.
He spared them from the plagues and the death of the firstborn;
he parted the waters so that they could walk across; he guided
them through the wilderness; fed them with manna when they
were hungry; and gave them fresh water to drink when Moses
struck the rock with his staff. Were they grateful? Not at all; all
they did was to grumble. Then they were infested with poisonous
snakes in the desert. I think they were wrong to assume that God
had sent the snakes especially to punish them for their grumbling;
snakes live in a desert environment, because they are about the
only creatures that can. Instead of complaining about God, they
would have done better to pray for his help. But they did eventually confess their ingratitude, and apologized. Then God forgave
them, giving Moses a bronze snake to heal them by a sort of sympathetic magic.

Ungrateful

Why are we human beings such ungrateful creatures? God pours his
blessings on us, and we forget to thank him. Our life is less than perfect, and we whine and moan as though nothing good had ever happened to us. It becomes a habit, until some people appear to enjoy
grumbling. W. S. Gilbert wrote a song about 'The Disagreeable
Man', who sings, 'Oh, wouldn't the world seem dull and flat with
nothing whatever to grumble at?' We all know people who, when

you ask them how they are, reply, 'Well, I mustn't grumble,' and then detain you for the next 40 minutes doing just that!

Blame

Worse still, we always look for somebody to blame. The media are particularly naughty at this, and no report of any bad happening can appear in the newspapers without them immediately howling on the hunt for somebody to be held responsible for it. Instead we should be looking to see what we can do to put it right. If we have time to whine and complain about something then we have the time to do something about it. Very often it may be our own fault: the German poet Goethe wrote, 'I will not be as those who spend the day in complaining of headache, and the night in drinking the wine that gives it.' Why should we always complain to God, when he has given us free will to disobey him, and we use it to cause suffering to other people and ourselves? Mind you, it is better to complain to God than to bottle up your anger. God has broad shoulders and can take our unjustified criticisms, and then forgive us when we apologize for them later.

Miserable

But the trouble with people who are always complaining is that they start to make everybody else miserable, too. Everyone starts complaining about the person who is grumbling, and then they all become bad tempered as well. It is almost a disease. The best cure is to find a sympathetic ear, and then warn the owner of it that you are going to have a good old gripe. Then your friend must listen to you in silence, with an occasional, 'Oh, how terrible for you . . . I do sympathize.' Then you should slowly accept that some of the blame is yours, and that many of the things you complain about were inevitable and nobody could have prevented them anyway. Finally, thank your friend for listening, and say that you feel much better now. Just the chance to talk may be in itself a healing.

Positive attitude

The Israelites in the wilderness forgot that they had much to be thankful for. It is a question of attitude. If you decide to take a more positive approach to life, you will always see the good things that are happening, and give thanks for them, even as you suffer the 'slings and arrows of outrageous fortune.' My final quotation occurs in many places, but the most convincing attribution is to Benjamin Franklin. It is reported that he once said, 'The sentence which has most influenced my life is, "Some persons grumble because God placed thorns among roses. Why not thank God because He placed roses among thorns?"'

Suggested hymns

Awake, our souls, away, our fears; In the Lord I'll be ever thankful (Taizé); Jesu, lover of my soul; O for a closer walk with God.

Third Sunday of Lent   19 March
Principal Service   **Reconciliation**
Ex. 17.1–7 Water from the rock; Ps. 95 Testing God; Rom. 5.1–11 Reconciliation to God; John 4.5–42 The Samaritan woman at the well

> *'If, while we were enemies, we were reconciled to God through the death of his Son, much more surely, having been reconciled, will we be saved by his life.' Romans 5.10*

Quarrels

Two of your friends have had a blazing row, and are not speaking to each other. When they simmer down, both of them realize that this is no good, but they can't see how to be reconciled to each other. How can you advise them to end their quarrel? They need you to be a mediator, carrying messages from one to the other, assuring each that the other feels as they do, and wants to bring their enmity to an end. Then you can suggest to both of them that the only way is if both say 'Sorry!' That word always sticks in the throat, but there is no use in apportioning blame; each of us is at least partially at fault when there is a breakdown of relationships. But we may be unwilling to apologize unless we are sure that the other is going to do the same, and that is where you come in, as the go-between to tell each what the other is feeling. Then, of course, both of them should say, 'I forgive you.' Forgiveness does *not* mean that what you have done doesn't matter, or that I can easily forget it. But it does mean that your friendship is more important to me than your unkind words or actions, and I am not willing to ruin the rest of my life in bearing a grudge against you.

Sacrifice

So reconciliation requires repentance and forgiveness. But how do you know that your estranged friend means what they say when they offer you their repentance and forgiveness? Could it perhaps be make-believe, pretending to an attitude which you don't, in truth, actually feel? After all, you cannot see repentance and forgiveness. You cannot touch them with your hands, or taste them with your tongue. So you would be wise to bring with you something that you can see, touch, and taste: some sort of a present. It can be a small thing, and need not be expensive, but it helps if your offering has cost you time and trouble in finding it or making it. In other words it must be a symbolic sacrifice. *Repentance plus forgiveness plus sacrifice equals reconciliation.*

With God

Now apply that to our relationship with God. You and I have each quarrelled *with God*; individually and in the communities we belong to. Maybe nobody heard us shouting at him, but in our hearts we complained bitterly that God is so unfair, and why wasn't he around to help when those terrible things happened to us? What had we done to deserve it? Then, when we calmed down, perhaps we realized that maybe we were partly to blame, ourselves. God can't always give us what we want without taking away our freedom to disobey him. So how can we be reconciled to God? Only by repentance, forgiveness and sacrifice.

Mediators

For that we need a mediator. How can we know that God will accept our repentance? Well, he sent prophets to assure us of that. Then God sent Jesus so that we could see God's forgiveness in action; and Jesus died on the cross as a costly sacrifice – costly to the triune God himself – leading towards our reconciliation with God. St Paul wrote, 'If, while we were enemies, we were reconciled to God through the death of his Son, much more surely, having been reconciled, will we be saved by his life.' *Repentance plus forgiveness plus sacrifice equals reconciliation.*

Jesus

The death of his Son is an enormous sacrifice for God to make. But we shall not feel comfortable in his company unless we can give God a small sacrifice in return. Well, a few hours of our time spent in prayer and worship is a start; then we shall make up our quarrel with God. But mainly we need to prove our genuineness by offering the rest of our lives to God in sacrificial love for our neighbours. The best way to do that is helping them to make up their quarrels with each other, and with God, by sharing with them the good news of God's love. St Paul said in another place,

> God . . . reconciled us to himself through Christ, and has given us the ministry of reconciliation.

The recipe is always the same: *repentance plus forgiveness plus sacrifice equals reconciliation.*

All-age worship

Decorate cream buns with the word 'sorry'. Pairs of children can represent people or nations in the news who have hurt each other. Give each other a bun, shake hands, say 'I forgive you', then eat the buns together.

Suggested hymns

And can it be that I should gain?; Dear Lord and Father of mankind; 'Forgive our sins as we forgive'; God moves in a mysterious way.

Third Sunday of Lent   19 March
Second Service   Be Bold, Be Strong
Ps. 40 Deliver me; Joshua 1.1–9 Be courageous; Eph. 6.10–20
The armour of God; *Gospel at Holy Communion*: John 2.13–22
Cleansing the Temple

> 'The LORD spoke to Joshua son of Nun . . . saying . . . "Be strong
> and very courageous, being careful to act in accordance with all
> the law that my servant Moses commanded you; do not turn from
> it to the right hand or to the left, so that you may be successful
> wherever you go."' Joshua 1.1, 7

Joshua

The book of Joshua is largely fiction. Some of the battles it describes were fought over cities which archaeology shows to have been uninhabited at the time the book describes. Wikipedia says:

> Almost all scholars agree that the book of Joshua holds little historical value for early Israel and most likely reflects a much later period. Rather than being written as history . . . [it] was intended to illustrate a theological scheme in which Israel and her leaders are judged by their obedience to the teachings and laws . . . set down in the book of Deuteronomy.

This quotation may shock you. But many Christians believe that it is those who insist on a literal interpretation of the Bible who are disrespectful to Scripture, because they misdirect readers to the surface meaning, and away from the deep spiritual truths which only fiction can reveal. The historical books of the Old Testament contain very old traditions from different times and places, but they were probably edited soon after the remnants of the 10 northern tribes of Ephraim had been decimated by their deportation to Assyria, in an attempt to show that only when all 12 tribes, including the southern tribes based in Jerusalem, are united as brothers can they hope to survive. The first chapter of Joshua, taken literally, must be responsible for more bloodshed than any other part of Scripture, because it suggests that God had given to the Israelites all the land from the Mediterranean to Iraq and from Lebanon to Beersheba. Yet at the heart of it is a verse which sums up the whole moral message of the Old Testament.

Be strong

God says to Joshua, 'Be strong and very courageous, being careful to act in accordance with all the law that my servant Moses commanded you; do not turn from it to the right hand or to the left, so that you may be successful wherever you go.' Substitute for the Law of Moses the law of love, which Jesus said sums up the whole of the Law and the prophets, and you have a message which every Christian would agree with. All life is a battle, not fought with physical weapons against human enemies, but using God's grace to resist the temptations of the forces of evil. This message is reinforced in the Letter to the Ephesians, where we are told to put on the armour of God:

Be strong in the Lord and in the strength of his power. Put on the whole armour of God, so that you may be able to stand ... against the spiritual forces of evil ... take up the whole armour of God ... truth ... righteousness ... peace ... faith ... salvation, and ... word of God.

Choruses

The words from Joshua are also quoted in a modern chorus, 'Be bold, be strong'. Some Christians hate these repetitive verses sung over and over to what they call a banal tune. Others, with no experience of classical music, find the rhythmic melodies preferable to what they call the dull old hymn tunes; and repeated words can be easily memorized by slow readers and those who want to wave their arms in the air. One of the greatest challenges to the Church today is to help these two groups to respect, love and tolerate each other. The worship song I am referring to exhorts us to

Be bold, be strong,
for the Lord your God is with you.

Battling evil

It is a mistake to underestimate the power of temptation, and this chorus forbids you to. Take, for example, the temptation to overeat, leading to obesity. This may have a physical cause, and like most addictions is better treated as a medical problem requiring medical treatment than as a crime to be punished judicially. But together with that must go an effort of the will to resist it. It will be a hard struggle, and needs a determined act of the will. Be bold, be strong. Then there is the temptation to the misuse of power, at all levels of society from the family to the Government. It is not easy to put the needs of others before your own personal benefit. Be strong and very courageous. It is a good message for Lent, and shows that a moral message for today can often be found in ancient Bible stories of doubtful historicity.

Suggested hymns

Be bold, be strong; Jesu, grant me this, I pray; Lead us, heavenly Father, lead us; Soldiers of Christ, arise.

Fourth Sunday of Lent   26 March

(For Mothering Sunday, see the Second Service.)

Principal Service   **Milton's 'Ode on His Blindness'**

1 Sam. 16.1–13 Samuel anoints David as king; Ps. 23 The
Lord is my shepherd; Eph. 5.8–14 Live as children of light;
John 9.1–41 The light of the world

> *'Once you were darkness, but now in the Lord you are light. Live as children of light.' Ephesians 5.8*

Milton

John Milton lived from 1608 to 1674, during the English Civil War,
the author of *Paradise Lost*. By 1654 he had gone completely blind,
and was frustrated that his talent for writing was now no use to
him; he had to dictate his poems to others, who wrote them down;
a frustrating process. He wrote an 'Ode on his blindness', which is
quite short, but it is full of deep reflection.

Darkness

Milton compares a blind person to someone who has been carrying
a lamp, which has gradually gone out, leaving them in complete
darkness. He was only 46 years old, and imagined, wrongly as it
turned out, that he had another half of his life ahead of him which
would be totally wasted:

> When I consider how my light is spent
> e're half my days, in this dark world and wide . . .

Talent

He regarded his ability to write poetry as a talent which God had
given him, and which he could use in the service of God. Without
the ability to write, he felt he was as good as dead, and he was
afraid God would come, as in the parable, to ask what use he had
made of his talents:

> and that one talent which is death to hide,
> lodged with me useless, though my soul more bent
> to serve my Maker, and present
> my true account, lest he returning chide . . .

Without becoming angry with God, Milton felt it was unfair to expect him to work for God when it was too dark to do so:

'Doth God exact day-labour, light denied?',
I fondly ask . . .

Patience

The remainder of the poem is written by a personification of the virtue of Patience, who tries to help him to see his misfortune from God's point of view. God doesn't *need* any of the things that we offer him – either our work, or the talents which he himself has given to us in the first place:

But Patience, to prevent
that murmur, soon replies, 'God doth not need
either man's work, or his own gifts . . .'

Yokes

Jesus said:

Come to me, all you that are weary, and are carrying heavy burdens, and I will give you rest. Take my yoke upon you, and learn from me; for I am gentle and humble in heart, and you will find rest for your souls. For my yoke is easy, and my burden is light.

The carpenter of Nazareth must have known all about shaping a wooden yoke to fit comfortably on the shoulders of a beast who pulls the plough. There is no virtue in unnecessary pain and stress. So Milton reflects that it is not necessary to work hard to please God – just to do what he asks us to in a relaxed way; it is not your achievement, but your intention, which counts:

who best
bear his mild yoke, they serve him best.

Angels

God also rules over thousands of angels who travel as fast as the horse which carried letters all, round the globe; they will do his will, whether we do or not:

> His state
> is kingly – thousands at his bidding speed
> and post o'er land and ocean without rest . . .

So Milton's blindness is not a total disaster; from it he can learn to be patient, and offer that patience to God instead of his poetry. If his earthly light has gone out, Jesus is himself the Light of the World. The final line of the poem is one of the most famous in the whole of English poetry – but what a profound lesson for us in patience it carries:

> they also serve who only stand and wait.

Complete

So now let me read the whole poem:

> When I consider how my light is spent
> e're half my days, in this dark world and wide,
> and that one talent which is death to hide,
> lodged with me useless, though my soul more bent
> to serve my Maker, and present
> my true account, lest he returning chide,
> 'Doth God exact day-labour, light denied?',
> I fondly ask. But Patience, to prevent
> that murmur, soon replies, 'God doth not need
> either man's work, or his own gifts; who best
> bear his mild yoke, they serve him best; his state
> is kingly. Thousands at his bidding speed
> and post o'er land and ocean without rest:
> they also serve who only stand and wait.'

All-age worship

How long can you sit still, thinking about Jesus?

Suggested hymns

Give me oil in my lamp; In a world where people walk in darkness; Lead, kindly light; Lord, the light of your love is shining.

Mothering Sunday   26 March
Motherliness

(Common Worship *gives two Old and New Testament readings,*
Psalms and Gospels, either of which may be used in any year.
The Canterbury Preacher's Companion *will set the first of each*
for year B and the second for year C, and offer a new set of
readings for Year A.)

Tob. 4.1–5 Honour your mother, *or* Prov. 31.10–31 A good wife;
Ps. 113 The joyous mother of children; Eph. 5.21; 6.1–4 Mutual
submission of parents and children; Luke 2.41–52 Jesus at 12

> *'That same day Tobit remembered the money that he had left*
> *in trust with Gabael at Rages in Media, and he said to himself,*
> *"Now I have asked for death. Why do I not call my son Tobias and*
> *explain to him about the money before I die?" Then he called his*
> *son Tobias, and when he came to him he said, "My son, when*
> *I die, give me a proper burial. Honour your mother and do not*
> *abandon her all the days of her life. Do whatever pleases her, and*
> *do not grieve her in anything. Remember her, my son, because*
> *she faced many dangers for you while you were in her womb.*
> *And when she dies, bury her beside me in the same grave. Revere*
> *the Lord all your days, my son, and refuse to sin or to transgress*
> *his commandments. Live uprightly all the days of your life, and do*
> *not walk in the ways of wrongdoing.' Tobit 4.1–5*

Tobit

The book of Tobit is a lovely story, but it is not in the Hebrew Bible so
it is not in most Protestant Bibles. But it *is* in the Greek Bible, so Roman
Catholics include it in their Bibles, and some other Bibles place it in a
section between the Old and New Testaments called the Apocrypha.
Our lectionaries provide two sets of readings for Mothering Sunday,
so some of us have decided to select a third set for Year A in the three-
year cycle, which is why you heard today Tobit's wonderful instructions to his son, Tobias, to honour his mother in gratitude for the
sufferings she endured while giving birth to her children.

Childbirth

Most men did not know anything about that, nor many children, but
thanks to television, it is much more widely understood nowadays.

And I think that is a good thing. As Jesus said, 'A woman suffers pain when she is in labour, but as soon as the child is born, she forgets all about it because of her new happiness.' How did Jesus know? I expect the walls of their houses then were so thin that everybody in the village could hear the exclamations that come from a mother's mouth when she is giving birth. It increases everyone's love for our mothers when we think what they were willing to suffer to bring us into the world.

Mothering Sunday

Mothering Sunday is the Fourth Sunday of Lent, and has nothing to do with the American invention of Mother's Day, observed on the second Sunday in May. This year Mothering Sunday is the day after Lady Day, or the feast of the Annunciation, when we remember the angel Gabriel's visit to the Virgin Mary, telling her that God wanted her to have a baby. Not just any baby, but Jesus, the Son of God. Mary must have known what giving birth would involve, and yet without hesitation she agreed to do what God wanted her to.

Motherliness

But it is not only our mothers' willingness to take on the pain of childbirth that we should be thankful for today; it is the many sacrifices, great or small, that they make for us in the rest of our lives when we are growing up. They don't usually complain, unless their children or their partner are being particularly difficult! But it is not just motherhood that we want to thank them for, but their wonderful *motherliness*. And we must remember that there may be stepmothers here today, or adoptive parents, grandparents and aunts and many other wonderful women who have blessed us by their motherly care, and show our gratitude to them, too. A family is not just a structure of people who have a physical status with regard to each other, but a living web of caring relationships. Let us thank God today for our mothers, for the sacrifices they have made for us, but above all for their motherliness; and include in that all the others who have shown their loving care towards us – and yes, that includes fathers. And don't keep this gratitude bottled up, but tell them how thankful we are for them, and what they have done, and give them gifts, however small, to show our gratitude.

All-age worship

Make a collage of pictures illustrating the theme of motherliness.

Suggested hymns

For the beauty of the earth; Jesus, good above all other; Lord of the home, your only son; Ye who own the faith of Jesus.

Fifth Sunday of Lent   2 April
Principal Service   Wake Up and Smell the Coffee

Ezek. 37.1–14 The valley of dry bones; Ps. 130 Out of the depths; Rom. 8.6–11 The Spirit gives life; John 11.1–45 The raising of Lazarus

> *'Jesus said to [Martha], "I am the resurrection and the life. Those who believe in me, even though they die, will live, and everyone who lives and believes in me will never die. Do you believe this?"'*
> *John 11.25–26*

Wake up

There is an expression which has been going around for a while now. If somebody seems to be missing the point, wandering off in the discussion to talk about irrelevant and trivial details, you say to them, 'Wake up and smell the coffee!' Nobody is sure where the phrase originated, but obviously it implies that the one you are talking to is half-asleep, and completely missing what is going on in the real world. In other words you are telling them to 'Get real!'

Lazarus

His disciples were missing the point when Jesus spoke to them about new life. So he performed perhaps the most dramatic of all his miracles. His friend Lazarus was ill, and his sisters Martha and Mary sent a message to ask Jesus to heal him. But he did nothing until after Lazarus had died and was buried. Then Jesus said to his disciples, 'Lazarus is asleep, but I am going to wake him up.' He came to Bethany, where they lived, and Martha met him. She couldn't understand what was happening, but she trusted Jesus to bring good out of the terrible thing which had occurred. Jesus said to her, 'I am the resurrection and the

98

life. Those who believe in me, even though they die, will live, and everyone who lives and believes in me will never die. Do you believe this?' Then she began to wake up to what was going on. Jesus said to her, 'Didn't I tell you that if you believed, you would see the glory of God?' So they rolled away the stone from the cave where they had buried Lazarus. Jesus called him, and he came out, still wrapped in a shroud. Jesus did not say anything about waking up and smelling the coffee – what he cried was 'Release him – let him go!'

Salvation

Jesus healed Lazarus from the worst sickness of all – that is, from death. It was as though Jesus had found Lazarus a captive, tied down by his shroud, and had set him free. That is what salvation means: setting us free from sickness, guilt, loneliness and death – free to return to the real world of freedom, love and joy. When Jesus healed sick people, he always said to them, 'Your *faith* has *saved* you!' Death is sleep, said Jesus; but when you rise again, you achieve reality. Many of the Jews therefore, who had come with Mary and had seen what Jesus did, believed in him. The raising of Lazarus was a one-off miracle; but it was also a symbol for all time. Without Jesus we are all sleep-walking; when we have faith in him, we return to the real world – we wake up, and smell the coffee. The raising of Lazarus symbolizes new life. When we discover the joy of Jesus living in our hearts, we can turn and say to each other, 'This is what I call really living!'

Mary of Bethany

Yet Jesus wept when his friend died, just as we all do when we are bereaved. And Mary wept when Jesus came to their home at Bethany later, on his way to be crucified. Because pain and loss are real; but they are not the ultimate reality. Mary filled the house with a most wonderful smell: not coffee, but an alabaster jar of precious ointment, because she had woken up to the final reality: that Jesus can save us from death, by giving us a new fullness of life in this world, and eternal life in the world to come.

Life

That is the pattern of life for each one of us: pain, leading to tears; then waking up to the reality of Christ our Saviour. Next follows the joy of knowing that we are loved and precious to God. Finally we enter into the bliss of eternal life with Jesus in the afterlife. But to enjoy all this you have to have faith – by which I don't mean signing your name to a lot of incomprehensible doctrines, but a deep trust that Jesus would never mislead us. So get real! Wake up and smell the coffee!

All-age worship

Make an Easter card with an open gate and a sunrise beyond it. Write 'Jesus says death is the gateway to life'. Check with (for example) parents whether somebody would appreciate receiving it; or put it up in your own home at Easter.

Suggested hymns

Drop, drop, slow tears; I danced in the morning; It is a thing most wonderful; Take up thy cross, the Saviour said.

Fifth Sunday of Lent 2 April
Second Service **Everybody's Slave**
Ps. 30 Mourning turned to dancing; Lam. 3.19–33 New every morning; Matt. 20.17–34 Jesus foretells his death and resurrection

> '[Jesus said,] "Whoever wishes to be great among you must be your servant, and whoever wishes to be first among you must be your slave; just as the Son of Man came not to be served but to serve, and to give his life a ransom for many."' Matthew 20.26–28

Slaves

Jesus said that anyone who wants to be a Christian must be everybody's slave. Yes, that's right – he didn't say 'servant', he said 'slave'. People in those days knew all about the misery of slavery. A rich man who owned a large home, or a farm, or a business, would go to the slave-market and *buy* another human being, as though they were an object, a piece of property; and from then on they had to work hard – to 'slave' – for their owner, receiving a meagre allowance of food and drink, but not allowed to own anything. Slaves had to obey their owners without question, day or night. You can guess what that meant for the female slaves. Slavery was not quite as common in Palestine as in the rest of the Roman Empire, but it existed there, and the economy of the Empire depended entirely on unpaid slave labour. So nobody wanted to be a slave; it was their worst nightmare; and here was Jesus telling them they must be everybody's slave! Not the way to win friends and influence people, you would think.

Jesus

But Jesus acted out what he meant when he washed the disciples' feet at the Last Supper. That was the job of the humblest slave, yet it was being performed by the host who had invited them to the meal. 'I am among you as one who serves,' he said. Some households had a few servants. Unlike the slaves, servants were free men and women, paid a wage, owning property, and able to hand in their notice when they wished to. Older translations of the Bible muddled the two words; but in either case servants or slaves did what they were told and aimed above all things to please their master. So the whole life and death of Jesus fulfilled Isaiah's prophecy of the Suffering Servant.

Us

Then that is what Jesus is calling us to be, is he? Yes. He warns us about the cost of discipleship. It means accepting gratefully all the freedoms that God gives us, then fighting tooth and nail for the freedom of the oppressed; but never demanding to have our own way where it interferes with the freedom of others. 'Following in the footsteps of Jesus' means making our main aim in life to improve the lives of others; sacrificing our own time and our own wants for the needs of other people; putting others first and ourselves second. In a word, we are called to 'altruism', which means living in the interest of others.

Redeemer

But one hope was left for a slave. Some benefactor might buy the slaves from their owner and set them free. The money paid to buy someone's freedom is called a 'ransom', and the process is known as the 'redemption'. Jesus said he gave his life to pay the ransom for many. The benefactor is called the redeemer; Jesus Christ is our Redeemer. He has set us free from all the appalling slaveries we suffered under before we met him: slavery to temptation, sin and guilt, to fear, to bad habits, to addiction and false reasoning. For delivering us from these cruel masters we are so grateful that we want to do something to repay him; yet there is nothing that Jesus needs from us, except our loving hearts. So we show our gratitude by worshipping him, Sunday by Sunday, and loving our neighbours as much as we love ourselves.

Evolution

And that is why Jesus came to earth. Indeed it is why God created the world and started the long history of evolution, leading to thinking creatures, able to respond to God's love. There are rare examples of altruism in the animal kingdom, mostly in those creatures which live in tribes or swarms, who are willing to sacrifice their own needs, or even their lives, for the sake of the whole tribe. Among humans, the need for altruism has increased as we move from tribe to nation to an international society. So making yourself the slave of others is the true goal of evolution; quite the opposite of the 'selfish gene' theory. It is also what we pray for, when we ask that God's kingdom may come 'on earth as it is in heaven'. As we move thankfully away from the societies in which human beings could be the slaves of cruel masters, we seek the kingdom of God, when absolutely everyone lives as everybody else's slaves.

Suggested hymns

Brother, sister, let me serve you; From heaven you came, helpless babe; There is a Redeemer; Ye servants of God.

HOLY WEEK

In Holy Week we celebrate the last week of Christ's life: the triumphal entry on Palm Sunday; Christ's teaching in the Temple on the Monday, Tuesday and Wednesday; the Last Supper on Maundy Thursday; and the trial, crucifixion and burial on Good Friday. Hymns, or American spirituals, proclaiming the salvation which Jesus won for us by his willing self-sacrifice are suitable for any day this week. *The Canterbury Preacher's Companion 2015* suggested hymns for Good Friday and Passiontide; also for Maundy Thursday and Holy Communion. There is a wealth of beautiful choral music for this season, from J. S. Bach's *St Matthew Passion* and *St John Passion*, to Stainer's *Crucifixion*. The many settings of the Requiem Mass are also suitable for this time of year. Then there are some heart-breaking choral anthems, including 'Drop, drop slow tears', by Orlando Gibbons, and many others. Any Christian who finds themselves jaded by the annual repetition of the Holy Week ceremonies is advised to go to a concert of Passiontide music, even if it is in a style which is not normally to their taste; I would be surprised if your eyes are not moist at the end of it.

Palm Sunday   9 April
Principal Service   Illegal Legalities

Liturgy of the Palms: Matt. 21.1–11 Triumphal entry; Ps. 118.1–2, 19–29 Blessed is he who comes; *Liturgy of the Passion*: Isa. 50.4–9a God's suffering servant; Ps. 31.9–16 Assurance in suffering; Phil. 2.5–11 Jesus' obedience unto death; Matt. 26.14—27.66 The Last Supper to the burial, *or* Matt. 27.11–54 The trial to the death on the cross

> 'Jesus stood before the governor; and the governor asked him, "Are you the King of the Jews?" Jesus said, "You say so." But when he was accused by the chief priests and elders, he did not answer.' Matthew 27.11–12

Farce

The trial of Jesus was a farce, except that it wasn't in the least bit funny. In no other legal process have so many people been behaving illegally. It finished up in such a tragic mess, because everyone had mixed motives. We could ask why the disciples behaved so cravenly, and Judas Iscariot so traitorously. But let's just concentrate on the motives of the priests and of Pontius Pilate.

Last chance

Jesus wanted to give the people of Jerusalem one last chance. He claimed to be King of the Jews, but what sort of king? They wanted a military Messiah, who would lead them into battle and defeat the Romans. But Jesus understood that you can never defeat violence with violence. So instead of riding into their capital city on a warhorse, he paraded on a rather ridiculous donkey, showing that he was the Prince of Peace, ushering in the Kingdom of Universal Love. At first the crowd welcomed him, because they wanted a revolution against the cruel Roman dictatorship. That made the priests panic, because a revolt would mean the Romans would take away the priests' authority. But the crowd's euphoria vanished like the morning mist, when they realized that Jesus did not want what they did.

Priests

The priests were more interested in maintaining their own cosy positions than working towards a just society. So they looked for a way to get rid of Jesus. Yet if they arrested him publicly, they feared the crowds would take his side. Then Judas Iscariot told them where Jesus went to pray. And so they had Jesus seized in Gethsemane, without a shred of evidence against him. Then they arranged a parody of a trial. Yet their assembly was illegal if it met after dark. Second, they wanted the death penalty, yet had no power under Roman law to impose it. They bribed some witnesses to tell lies; but there was too much discrepancy between their accounts to satisfy even a corrupt judge. Then two witnesses made the same accusation. They had heard Jesus say something like, 'I will destroy the authority of the priests in the Temple to make oppressive laws, and in just a few days I will remove the Temple's claim to be the only place where God can be met, and replace it with myself.' Which they deliberately misinterpreted as a threat to demolish the building.

Jesus refused to answer their accusations. But when the priests put him under a solemn oath before God to tell them whether he was the Messiah, the Son of God, he spoke out. His reply quoted from the book of Daniel, about a superhuman figure who nonetheless looked human, 'one like a son of man', coming *to* God on the clouds for God to appoint him to bring justice to all peoples. That was too much; the chief priests threw a hissy fit, and they remanded Jesus to appear before Pilate in the morning.

Pilate

Pilate was already in trouble for starting a riot by building a much-needed water channel through the holiest parts of Jerusalem. Any more dissent and he would lose his job. But when he asked Jesus whether he was a king, Jesus redefined what kingship meant, talking about the need for those in authority to speak the truth. But Pilate still needed some evidence before he could convict. So he asked the crowd to request the release of Jesus. But when they refused, the corrupt legal process reached its inevitable tragic conclusion.

Bonhoeffer

Today happens to be the seventy-seventh anniversary of the execution of Dietrich Bonhoeffer, one of the brave German Christians who plotted the assassination of Adolph Hitler. In an unjust society, to stand up for truth often leads to the death of the protester, as it did in the case of Jesus. Yet we shall never achieve an equitable society unless some are prepared to be whistle-blowers, at whatever cost to themselves. And can any of us here swear that they have never done something slightly illegal because it was to our own advantage? We shall never live in peace until selfishness and corruption are clamped down on in the name of the God of truth.

All-age worship

Study the working of your nearest magistrates' court.

Suggested hymns

All glory, laud and honour; Make way, make way, for Christ the King; Ride on, ride on in majesty; You are the King of glory.

Palm Sunday 9 April
Second Service **Vineyard Religion**

Ps. 80 Come to save us; Isa. 5.1–7 The song of the vineyard;
Matt. 21.33–46 The parable of the wicked tenants

*'Let me sing for my beloved my love-song concerning his vineyard:
My beloved had a vineyard on a very fertile hill. He dug it and
cleared it of stones, and planted it with choice vines; he built a
watch-tower in the midst of it, and hewed out a wine vat in it; he
expected it to yield grapes, but it yielded wild grapes. And now,
inhabitants of Jerusalem and people of Judah, judge between me
and my vineyard.' Isaiah 5.1–3*

Pastoralists

All the evidence suggests that Israel was at first made up of migrant
tribes of pastoralists, shepherds leading their flocks from one pasture to another, but owning no land. In these circumstances they will
have been very aware of their total dependence on God. Psalm 23
comes from that type of background. But later they settled down as
agriculturalists, becoming permanent occupiers of particular fields
on which they grew wheat, and, especially in that sunny climate,
grapevines. But one of the temptations when you settle down is
to become money-grubbing and greedy, thinking that you own
the land. And forgetting that both the land and those who farm it
belong entirely to God, and depend on him.

Prophets

Therefore God sent many prophets, to call the children of Israel
back to their original priorities; to stop oppressing those who
worked for them, and adopt a more generous, sharing attitude
to their possessions. The prophet Amos, for instance, rebuked his
fellow countrymen for adopting corrupt city ways instead of the
mutual dependence of the desert:

Thus says the LORD: For three transgressions of Israel, and for
four, I will not revoke the punishment; because they sell the
righteous for silver, and the needy for a pair of sandals – they
who trample the head of the poor into the dust of the earth, and
push the afflicted out of the way; father and son go in to the

same girl, so that my holy name is profaned; they lay themselves down beside every altar on garments taken in pledge; and in the house of their God they drink wine bought with fines they imposed.

Amos represented wilderness religion protesting against what happened to morality in vineyard religion. The religion of the wandering tribes was not without its faults, but it was the lesser of two evils. Yet the tension between wilderness and vineyard religions was creative, teaching the people a new understanding of their duty to God and their neighbour.

Isaiah

The prophet Isaiah appeared at first to rejoice in the love of the owner for his vineyard. But the vineyard was a disappointment. Isaiah wrote:

> Let me sing for my beloved
>   my love-song concerning his vineyard:
> My beloved had a vineyard on a very fertile hill.
> He dug it and cleared it of stones,
>   and planted it with choice vines;
> he built a watchtower in the midst of it,
>   and hewed out a wine vat in it;
> he expected it to yield grapes,
>   but it yielded wild grapes.
> And now, inhabitants of Jerusalem and people of Judah,
> judge between me and my vineyard.

Parable

Jesus was echoing Isaiah's sentiments when he told the people of Jerusalem the parable of the wicked tenants. Speaking of the tenants killing the son of the vineyard's owner challenged them to look at what they were planning to do to Jesus in Holy Week. Jesus said:

> There was a landowner who planted a vineyard, put a fence around it, dug a wine press in it, and built a watch-tower. Then he leased it to tenants and went to another country. When the harvest time

had come, he sent his slaves to the tenants to collect his produce. But the tenants seized his slaves and beat one, killed another, and stoned another . . . Finally he sent his son to them, saying, 'They will respect my son.' But when the tenants saw the son, they said to themselves . . . 'come, let us kill him and get his inheritance.' So they seized him, threw him out of the vineyard, and killed him. Now [asked Jesus,] when the owner of the vineyard comes, what will he do to those tenants? [The people of Jerusalem predicted their own fate when they replied:] 'He will put those wretches to a miserable death, and lease the vineyard to other tenants who will give him the produce at the harvest time.'

Christians

Now we Christians have no right to gloat complacently, imagining that God has taken away the promises he first made to the Jews and transferred them to us. We dare not adopt the city's selfish ways of materialism, corruption and dishonesty. What we have has been lent to us by God, and God expects us to use it generously to help the poor, in gratitude for God's generosity to us.

Suggested hymns

Give me oil in my lamp; My song is love unknown Thou didst leave thy throne; You are the vine, we are the branches.

First Three Days in Holy Week   10–12 April
The Court of All Nations

(Following are the Tuesday readings, but this sermon may be used on any day.)
Isa. 49.1–7 The servant a light to the nations; Ps. 71.1–14 Rescue me from the wicked; 1 Cor. 1.18–31 The cross is the wisdom of God; John 12.20–36 The death of a seed yields a great harvest

> *'It is too light a thing that you should be my servant to raise up the tribes of Jacob and to restore the survivors of Israel; I will give you as a light to the nations, that my salvation may reach to the end of the earth.' Isaiah 49.6*

Anger

According to St Luke, Jesus rode into Jerusalem on a donkey, and the following day drove the traders out of the Temple. So it makes sense to think about this event in Holy Week. What happened when Jesus entered the Temple? Imagine one of the friends of Jesus, out of breath with excitement, trying to tell the story just after it occurred. She or he would say something like this:

> I saw him – I saw him with my own eyes – though I could hardly believe what I was seeing – a man we respected for his great compassion and understanding, positively steeped in the love of God – actually resorting to – (gasp) – violence! Positively enflamed with anger, he drove out *all* who were selling and buying in the outer courts of the Temple! He overturned the tables of the money-changers – all the coins cascaded to the floor – the seats of the pigeon-sellers were tipped over, and people were tripping over them, trying to pick up coins mostly, I think – a scene of total chaos and confusion – a great bellowing and shouting, screaming and raging! Animals charging about, the air filled with the sound of beating wings, doves and pigeons flying everywhere. Suddenly above all the noise and mayhem could be heard the thunder of Christ's angry voice – raised in *fury* – how his Father's house was a house of prayer, and it was becoming a bandits' cave – you know? Those bits from the prophets Isaiah and Jeremiah, I think, totally incredible! [Pant! Pant!] Phew!

Gentiles

That imaginary account conveys the atmosphere well. You may not realize, however, that the trading and money-changing all happened in what was called the Court of the Gentiles, the only place where non-Jews were admitted to pray. Only Mark gives in full the quotation from Isaiah: 'my house shall be called a house of prayer for *all peoples*.' But this was what infuriated Jesus. He believed the Jews *are* God's Chosen People, but not chosen to relax while other nations waited on them, but to spread what God had told them, to every other nation on earth. The first part of the message they were entrusted with was this: there is only one God. Not a different god for every nation, willing them to fight each other. All countries worship the same God, so we are all brothers and sisters. When sibling fights with sibling, the result is always disaster for both. As St Paul the Jew said to the Greeks in Athens, 'What . . . you worship as unknown, this I proclaim to you.' By denying non-Jews the right to worship in their Temple, the Jews were nullifying the purpose they had been chosen for.

Love

The second part of the message the Jews were chosen to spread was this: God is a God of love, and he cares how we treat each other. God even wants us to treat with compassion and respect our neighbours of a different race. The Law, originally intended to control our selfish behaviour, had become a hindrance to love, because it forbad even healing sick people on the Sabbath day, and had so many rules that no non-Jew could be bothered with it. It was the way Jesus opposed this narrow interpretation of the Law that led the priests to call for his crucifixion. Remember that as we read the stories of Holy Week.

Prayer

Finally, a prayer:

> We imagine, dear Lord, in our pride and arrogance, that we can live in our own strength, and do it all alone. We *cannot* – Christ's words must have so enflamed the priests and religious leaders who imagined they led exemplary lives – though probably, in their heart of hearts, they were only too aware of their shortcomings and failures! They must have *hated* hearing words which effectively blew their cover, and made them feel bad about themselves – but we, with the benefit of hindsight, have taken to ourselves the words of Jesus in the gospel, and understand that we lack his perfect, wholehearted love for us all, without exception. Help us to put this into practice. **Amen.**

Suggested hymns

Inspired by love and anger; Jesus shall reign where'er the sun; Love divine, all loves excelling; We love the place, O God.

Maundy Thursday 13 April
Where's the Body?

Ex. 12.1–4 [5–10] 11–14 The Passover; Ps. 116.1, 10–17
The cup of salvation; 1 Cor. 11.23–26 The Last Supper; John
13.1–17, 31b–35 Foot-washing

> *'The Lord Jesus on the night when he was betrayed took a loaf*
> *of bread, and when he had given thanks, he broke it and said,*
> *"This is my body that is for you. Do this in remembrance of me."'*
> *1 Corinthians 11.23–24*

Empty tomb

Jesus could not have helped us, if he had not become truly human like we are; a ghost would be no use. Jesus really died on the cross. Yet on the third day the tomb where the body of Jesus had been buried was found to be empty. So, as in some excellent detective stories, the question arises: where's the body? Maundy Thursday may give us the answer.

Pilate

The priests had warned Pontius Pilate that Jesus had assured his friends that he would rise again. So Pilate authorized them to set a troop of soldiers to guard the tomb, so that that his disciples should not steal the body, claiming that Jesus had come back to life. So when the soldiers found that the tomb was empty, they ran back into the city and told the chief priests what had happened. 'Where's the body?' they asked. So the priests devised a plan to bribe the soldiers to say, 'His disciples came by night and stole him away while we were asleep.' 'If the governor asks us, "Where's the body?"', they added, 'we will satisfy him and keep you out of trouble.' St Matthew's Gospel adds that this story was still being told among the Jews. But when each of the 12 disciples was later arrested and questioned about where the body was, they all denied having taken it. They could easily have saved their lives by admitting the theft and pointing out where it had been reburied, but all of them accepted martyrdom instead. Why should they have done that unless they knew the accusation was untrue? The only possible answer was that the disappearance of the body was a miracle.

Appearances

That afternoon, Jesus appeared to two disciples on the road to Emmaus, yet they failed to recognize him. So something had changed in his body. Then when they sat down to a meal, they recognized him when he broke bread together with them. They must have been at the Last Supper, and recognized the words he used then, 'This is my body.' Suddenly, he disappeared. They rushed back to Jerusalem to tell the other disciples, and that same evening Jesus appeared to the disciples gathered in the upper room where the Last Supper had been held. But it wasn't an ordinary physical body, as the doors were locked, yet he could pass through them. A week later he invited Thomas to touch him, and later still he was cooking breakfast for them; so it was not just an apparition. The mystery deepens.

Physical?

Some Christians insist until they are blue in the face that it was a physical resurrection. But physical bodies don't appear and disappear. Then, they say, the physical body of Jesus ascended into heaven. So where is heaven, then? Astronomers will tell you that heaven is nowhere in the physical universe. The problem arises because, when Jesus lived, most Jews were waiting for a physical resurrection of all the dead, on earth, after the last battle. So when Jesus rose, the disciples at first thought that Jesus had been resuscitated ahead of time, and that in their lifetime, all the dead would come back to earth to be judged. But the years passed, and it didn't happen.

Spiritual body

Then they remembered Jesus spoke to them about eternal life – something different from but better than physical life. St Paul eventually called this a spiritual body; something more real and lasting than a merely physical body. So, then, they remembered that Jesus at the Last Supper, when his disciples met to eat bread together, he looked around him, smiling, and said '*This* is my body'. He still says it, every Sunday when you and I come to the Holy Communion; Jesus looks at us and says, 'You, my dears, *you* are my body.' We have taken the place of his physical body. Through us the presence of Jesus is recognized; through us he speaks to the world; and through us he wants to make the world a better place for people to live in. The bread is not his physical body; but it is here to remind us that we are. So the answer to the question, 'Where's the body?' is *here*! Maundy Thursday gives the true answer to Pilate's question: Christ's body is here, in you and me.

Suggested hymns

Come, risen Lord, and deign to be our guest; God is here! As we his people (Blaenwern); Hands that have been handling; Now let us from this table rise.

Good Friday 14 April
Suffering

Isa. 52.13—53.12 The Suffering Servant; Ps. 22 Why have you forsaken me?; Heb. 10.16–25, *or* Heb. 4.14–16; 5.7–9 Jesus the priest; John 18.1—19.42 The blood of the covenant

> *'My God, my God, why have you forsaken me? Why are you so far from helping me, from the words of my groaning? O my God, I cry by day, but you do not answer; and by night, but find no rest.'*
> *Psalm 22.1–2*

Abandoned

Is suffering a punishment for sin, a test, or simply the way things are? Jesus was quoting from Psalm 22 when he cried out, as he hung on the cross, 'My God, my God, why have you forsaken me?' It was an expression of deepest despair, when Jesus, who had spoken of feeling so close to God that he called him 'Daddy', now felt that his Father had abandoned him. It shows us that when Jesus left heaven to come to earth, he became completely human, and knew all the agonies we feel when we have been rejected by others and are in pain. He even put aside his feeling of being one with God, so that we should never say, 'It was easy for him, because he was the Son of God.' His willingness to identify with us, when we feel at our lowest, moves us to feel that God understands, because we know that Jesus was the Son of God, and suffers with us.

Types of pain

I think every one of us, at some time or another, has felt that God is being unfair, and doesn't understand how awful is our physical pain or mental anguish. 'Why does a God of love allow us to suffer like this?' we cry. Yet some sorts of pain are unavoidable. For instance, road accidents can be caused by

- speed (which could be avoided); or
- thoughtlessness and wandering attention; or
- sinful carelessness, such as alcohol, competitiveness or bad workmanship; or
- natural mishap, such as rain or ice on the road.

The first three are human error, and do not raise the problem of pain. Natural mishaps, however, simply show that we live in the real world, with real consequences. God would be a bad father if he was constantly interfering and saving us from the consequences of our folly; that way we should never learn. God wants freely chosen obedience, so we must be free to choose to disobey, and to suffer for it. It seems unfair that innocent children should suffer from the sins of the drunken motorist, but we are made dependent on each other; if we wish to benefit from other people's good deeds, we must suffer for their bad ones. It is a good thing that life isn't fair: if we all received justice for our deeds, most of us would lack the undeserved blessings which we now receive.

Evolution

Similarly disease can be put into classes due to:

- foolish habits, like lung cancer resulting from smoking, or a weak heart in consequence of over-eating; or
- ignorance, resulting in tetanus, cholera or sepsis; or
- factors beyond our control, such as cancer.

Only in the last case is there any problem in seeing why God allows it. Yet pain and death are essential to the progress of evolution. Without pain, species would not have to evolve the characteristics which help us to avoid dangerous situations. Without death, the world would be so overcrowded that no new individuals could be born. Also, for humans, death is the gateway to a better life. There is an Arab proverb which says, 'If our life were all sunshine and no rain, it would soon become a desert.' If we will only trust God, and pray for his grace to help us to endure it patiently, suffering may actually be a cause for our growth in character.

Whether or not pain can be explained, it must be borne. Before the good Samaritan came by, there was a problem why God allowed the suffering of the victim. Afterwards, though he had not solved the intellectual problem, God had done something about the practical one, and revealed a goodness which, if there had been no suffering, would never have been seen. Similarly, when Jesus suffered, by not retaliating or causing his followers to do so, he absorbed the evil, but was not conquered by it. Christianity shows how, with love, suffering can be made use of for good.

Overcoming suffering

Jesus did not explain suffering; he began the process of overcoming it. If we pray to Jesus, he will give us the grace to bear our pain with patience, which will deepen our own sense of total dependence on God, and by our example, we may encourage others to do the same.

Suggested hymns

I danced in the morning; Morning glory, starlit sky; O sacred head, sore wounded; There is a green hill far away.

EASTER

After the solemn 40 days of Lent, the Easter Season is full of joyful music. The fact that Jesus, who was dead, is now alive for evermore, brings us the happy certainty that those who ask him for it will receive eternal life. In the concert hall and on CD we can listen again to Handel's *Messiah*, or Bach's Easter Oratorio; in church we can sing the Exultet at the Easter Vigil. Here are a few of the many glorious Easter hymns; check out that you are singing most of them at least once in Eastertide: 'A brighter dawn is breaking'; 'Alleluia, O sons and daughters'; 'Alleluia, alleluia, give thanks to the risen Lord'; 'Alleluia, sing to Jesus'; 'At the Lamb's high feast we sing'; 'Christ the Lord is risen again'; 'Christ triumphant, ever reigning'; 'Come, ye faithful, raise the strain'; 'Good Christians all, rejoice and sing'; 'Good Joseph had a garden'; 'He is Lord, he is Lord'; 'I am the bread of life'; 'I serve a risen Saviour'; 'Jesus Christ is risen today'; 'Jesus is Lord'; 'Jesus lives! Thy terrors now'; 'Light's glittering morn'; 'Love's redeeming work is done'; 'Now is eternal life'; 'Now the green blade riseth'; 'See, what a morning, gloriously bright'; 'The day of resurrection'; 'The strife is o'er, the battle done'; 'Thine be the glory'; 'This is the day the Lord has made'; 'This is the day, this is the day'; 'This joyful Eastertide'; 'Through the night of doubt and sorrow'; 'Ye choirs of new Jerusalem'; 'You shall go out with joy'.

EASTER
Easter Vigil   15–16 April
The Exultet

(*A minimum of three Old Testament readings should be chosen. The reading from Exodus 14 should always be used.*) Gen. 1.1—2.4a Creation, Ps. 136.1–9, 23–26; Gen. 7.1–5, 11–18; 8.6–18; 9.8–13 Noah, Ps. 46 Our refuge and strength; Gen. 22.1–18 Sacrifice of Isaac, Ps. 16 The path of life; Ex. 14.10–31; 15.20–21 The Exodus, *Canticle*: Ex. 15.1b–13, 17–18 The song of Moses; Isa. 55.1–11 Come to the waters, *Canticle*: Isa. 12.2–6 Great in your midst; Bar. 3.9–15, 32—4.4 God gives the light of wisdom, *or* Prov. 8.1–8, 19–21; 9.4b–6 Wisdom,

Ps. 19 The heavens declare God's glory; Ezek. 36.24–28 I will sprinkle clean water on you, Ps. 42 and 43 Faith and hope; Ezek. 37.1–14 The valley of dry bones, Ps. 143 A prayer for deliverance; Zeph. 3.14–20 I will bring you home, Ps. 98 Salvation and justice; Rom. 6.3–11 Baptism, death and resurrection, Ps. 114 The Exodus; Matt. 28.1–10 The resurrection

> *'I will sing to the L*ORD, *for he has triumphed gloriously; horse and rider he has thrown into the sea. The L*ORD *is my strength and my might, and he has become my salvation; this is my God, and I will praise him, my father's God, and I will exalt him.'*
> *Exodus 15.1–2*

Song

The Easter Vigil is a time of celebration and thanksgiving for the resurrection of Jesus, which happened sometime between his burial at Passover time, and the third day when his grave was found empty. In those days they counted inclusively, so 'Friday, Saturday, Sunday' makes Easter Day the third day. Probably the resurrection happened not long before the women came to the tomb at sunrise; in other words during the Saturday night. So a very moving service is held in some churches after sunset on the Saturday evening or around sunrise on Sunday. One of the memorable features of this service is when a very ancient song is often sung, known, from the first word in the original Latin, as 'the Exultet'. There are several different ways of organizing the Vigil service; [you have already heard the Exultet read/sung / we have not used the Exultet here today, but you can find the full text in books of liturgy or by searching the internet]. I have no time to read it in full in this sermon, but I will quote a few memorable phrases – in English of course – in the hope that they will lead you to deeper thanksgiving to God for raising his Son.

Rejoice

The Exultet is first found in missals of the seventh century, and may have been composed as far back as the fifth century AD. The song begins by calling on heaven and earth to praise God:

Rejoice, heavenly powers! Sing, choirs of angels . . .

It climaxes by calling upon the Church, our mother, to join them in shouting with joy. Then follow the traditional responses – 'Lift up your hearts . . .' – which may go back to the time of Jesus. Next come a rapid succession of phrases each beginning with the words 'This is the night – or day – when . . .', linking the resurrection of Jesus to the Passover in the Old Testament, when the Jews were saved from death by the blood of a lamb, for in this night – or on this day – Jesus vanquished hell, broke the chains of death, and rose triumphant from the grave. Then in a supreme paradox, it describes our own sin as a 'happy fault' because it resulted in Jesus coming to earth to save us and give us immortality; 'evil and hatred are put to flight and sin is washed away, lost innocence regained, and mourning turned to joy.'

Beeswax

Because this song is often sung, by a deacon if possible, during the lighting of the Paschal Candle, some versions compare it to the pillar of fire which led the Israelites through the wilderness, and end by offering the candle to God as a 'burnt sacrifice':

> this wax, the work of bees and the hands of your servants.
> As we gaze upon the splendour of this flame,
> fed by melting wax conceived by Mother bee,
> grant that this Easter Candle may make our darkness light.
> For Christ, the morning star, has risen in glory;
> Christ is risen from the dead and his flame of love still burns
>   within us!
> Christ sheds his peaceful light on all the world!
> Christ lives and reigns for ever and ever!

Truly the Exultet is one of the most beautiful poems in the whole of our liturgy; it brings us close to tears to think of what Jesus did, to bring eternal life to you and me.

Suggested hymns

A brighter dawn is breaking; Sing choirs of heaven! Let saints and angels sing!; This is the night of new beginnings; Within our darkest night (Taizé).

See www.churchofengland.org/media/41157/tseasterlit.pdf.

Easter Day   16 April
Principal Service   **Is Anyone There?**

Acts 10.34–43 Peter and other witnesses to the resurrection, *or* Jer. 31.1–6 An everlasting love; Ps. 118.1–2, 14–24 I shall not die but live; Col. 3.1–4 Resurrection with Christ, *or* Acts 10.34–43 Peter and other witnesses to the resurrection; John 20.1–18 Magdalene at the tomb, *or* Matt. 28.1–10 The women see Jesus

> *'Joyful shouts of salvation*
> *sound from the tents of the righteous:*
> *"The right hand of the Lord does mighty deeds;*
> *   the right hand of the Lord raises up;*
> *the right hand of the Lord does mighty deeds."*
> *I shall not die, but live,*
> *and declare the works of the Lord.'*
> *   Psalm 118.15–17 (Common Worship)*

Telephones

'Hello. Hello? Is anyone there? Hello? Oh, bother these telephones. Complete silence. Hello, I say. Hello? Is anyone there? Speak up! If there's anybody on the other end of this wretched line, would you please do something to prove that you're still alive. I give up!' Have you ever felt like that when you are on the phone? Isn't it frustrating? But now I have another question for you: have you ever felt like that when you were saying your prayers? Frustrated, because you cannot hear any voice in reply to your requests. Is it worth going on, you wonder. Well, let me tell you straight away, it is worth it. Jesus *is* there, and he *is* listening to what you say, even though you cannot hear any sounds. And Jesus does answer your prayers. And I'll tell you how we know.

Orthodox

A recent traveller to Russia described a Russian Orthodox priest leading his congregation out of the church. They have shared with him the grief of Good Friday. Now, in the hush of Easter Eve, all is dark. In their imagination, they pretend that their little church is the tomb where the body of Jesus has been laid. At midnight, the priest stoops down and looks in. The congregation are all holding their breath in suspense. The question they are all asking themselves is, 'Is anyone there?' The priest stands up straight, turns to his people, and shouts, 'Christ is risen!' And they all shout back, at the top of their voices, 'He is risen indeed. Alleluia!' They have faith that Jesus is really there, in the silence, though they cannot hear him.

Only with God

You cannot understand Easter until you have seen that merely human plans will always be defeated. But when you have laid your dead hopes in the hands of Almighty God, for him to breathe new life into them, then all things are possible.

Not just human

The merely human Jesus, whose teaching on how we should live is admired by so many people, is dead and buried. But his tomb is now empty. Just because Jesus is more than merely human, his work and teaching was indeed a great success. The human Jesus is no longer there in the tomb; the superhuman Jesus is with us wherever we go. When you talk to him, he is right there listening to you, and giving you the strength you ask for. When a Christian congregation surrounds you with love, Jesus is living in your fellow Christians.

What answer?

Prayer is much like a one-way telephone conversation. You keep talking into the machine, and you hear nothing in reply. But there *is* an answer, though it may not be the one you are expecting. You ask for great riches and an easy life. Jesus hears your request, and gives you what you need, which is not necessarily what you are asking for. Often, he gives you a hard life, but the inner strength and wisdom to make of it something terrific, which will be an inspiration to other people and a comfort to your family. You ask for a change in your circumstances; Jesus, because he knows you better than you know yourself, gives you a change in your attitudes. But you have to persevere. If you give up as soon as you have started to pray, because you didn't get the miraculous results you asked for, you will never succeed with anything. And you have to be self-critical, trying to discover what God wants, from you and for you; then comparing that with what you are asking for, and trying to reconcile the two. Hello. Hello? Is anyone there? Oh yes! Because we know from our own experience of prayer that 'Christ is risen!' 'He is risen indeed. Alleluia!' And if Jesus died and is alive again, then you know that you shall do the same. As the Psalmist said, I shall not die, but live. Happy Easter!

All-age worship

Bring a mobile phone, and pretend that it is a direct line to Jesus. What would you say to him?

Suggested hymns

Come, my soul, thy suit prepare; I serve a risen Saviour (He lives); Jesus Christ is risen today; Thine be the glory.

Easter Day   16 April
Second Service   Love and Death

Morning Ps. 114 The Exodus, 117 God's love for all nations; Evening Ps. 105 The Exodus, *or* 66.1–11 God holds our souls in life; S. of Sol. 3.2–5; 8.6–7 Love is strong as death; John 20.11–18 Mary Magdalene *if not read at the Principal Service,* or Rev. 1.12–18 I was dead and am alive

> 'Set me as a seal upon your heart, as a seal upon your arm; for love is strong as death, passion fierce as the grave.' Song of Solomon 8.6

Love

Many people become atheists because they say that you cannot prove that anything exists unless you can weigh and measure it. In other words, they are materialists: they believe nothing exists except the material world. This point of view was presented to a distinguished scientist; he replied, 'Any scientist who says that has never been in love!' Of course you can measure the pheromones, the smell of which attracts members of the other sex; and many species, as well as *Homo sapiens*, have evolved genes which give us a strong desire for sexual intercourse, because that prevents the species from dying out. But that is lust, not love. There is nothing materialistic about the human emotion of being deeply in love with somebody, so that your strongest desire is to make them happy, even at the cost of sacrificing your own wishes and to share many other experiences with your beloved as well as sleeping together. And this suggests that there may be many other things which we feel, do and say which do not have a material origin. One of these may be the strong conviction that many people have that there is a life after death.

Death

Of course, if there is an afterlife, it is not material. The days have long gone when people believed that heaven was a place above the clouds. But if we enter an immeasurably splendid non-material spiritual existence when we die, you could never prove by scientific means whether or not that is true. Yet there is plenty of evidence that the spiritual world really does exist. One scientist described the spiritual world as the fifth dimension. You can see and measure space and time, but there is a real probability that there are other dimensions, just as real as the ones we live in now, the truth of which we can deduce but never see, any more than we can see dark matter. The existence of heaven is exactly parallel to the existence of love; and the Song of Songs in the Bible says that 'Love is stronger than death.' The evidence we have for life after death takes three forms:

1 the teaching of Jesus;
2 the experience that bereaved people have of the nearness of their loved ones; and
3 the reports that many people give of having been in a coma and almost dying.

Let me say a few words about each of those pointers:

Jesus

First, Jesus taught that God created us because he wanted creatures to love, who are capable of returning his love. But the eternal God is not satisfied with loving us for a few score years; so he promised that those who love him will be able to share his experience of eternal life. The Son of God came to earth, to share our human lot for 30 years, then died and rose again to show us that it is love for God and love for our fellow humans that enables us to inherit eternal life; for love is stronger than death.

Bereaved

Second, many bereaved people report having visions or dreams of those who have died, after which they feel an enduring sense of their invisible presence near them. This is not just wishful thinking; they find the experience strengthens and transforms them.

Near-death

Finally, there have been many reports of near-death experiences. They often share features such as travelling down a dark tunnel towards a bright light; and other descriptions of the world-to-come depend on the culture in which the patient had been brought up. But the experience of meeting again with people who have died, and even of meeting some divine figure, shows that is their loving relationships which gives them their certainty of an afterlife. Dr Eben Alexander is a neurosurgeon at Harvard in the USA. His 15-year study of brain function had led him to be sceptical about life after death, until he suffered a coma caused by meningitis. Like many others, he described a vision of bright colours, with a sense of peace and the love of God. Someone told him he would have to return to earth, but would long to return to the afterlife when he dies. He is sure there is no neurological explanation for his experience, and is dedicating the rest of his life to a study of consciousness. The material world is not everything, and truly, love *is* stronger than death. Happy Easter!

Suggested hymns

Alleluia, alleluia, hearts to heaven and voices raise; Give us the wings of faith to rise; Jesus lives! Thy terrors now; This is the day the Lord has made.

Second Sunday of Easter   23 April
Principal Service   **Resurrection in John's Gospel**
Ex. 14.10–31; 15.20–21 The Exodus (*if used, the reading from Acts must be used as the second reading*), or Acts 2.14a, 22–32 Peter and other witnesses to the resurrection; Ps. 16 You show me the path of life; 1 Peter 1.3–9 Hope from the resurrection; John 20.19–31 The upper room, Thomas' doubt and faith

> *'Jesus said to [his disciples], "Peace be with you. As the Father has sent me, so I send you." When he had said this, he breathed on them and said to them, "Receive the Holy Spirit. If you forgive the sins of any, they are forgiven them."' John 20.21–23*

Synoptics

Matthew, Mark and Luke are known as the Synoptic Gospels, because they all come from the same viewpoint. But John is quite different. Not that he contradicts the others, although he occasionally disagrees with them on the order in which events happened. But the Gospel is based on the account of an eyewitness, called the Beloved Disciple; and he develops the teaching of Jesus not as short parables but as long discourses. Today we heard John's slant of the resurrection of Jesus.

Frontier

After his resurrection, Jesus stood on a frontier between the past and the future. As he hung on the cross, he spoke of the task which God had given him in his earthly life, saying, 'It is finished.' That surely means 'Phase 1', for the task of bringing in the kingdom of God was not yet completed; the message of Jesus had to be spread to people all round the world. So the risen Christ appeared to his disciples in the upper room and said, 'Peace be with you. As the Father has sent me, so I send you.' He gave farewell instructions to his disciples before he left them. The continuation of the story is up to us.

Bodies

Jesus joined his disciples in the upper room. They had locked the doors, so that they should not be attacked by what John calls 'the

Jews' – yet this is not anti-Semitic; people like John, who came from Galilee or other places outside Jerusalem, used this term to describe the people from Judaea, around Jerusalem, whom they rightly considered to be under the thumb of the priests and Levites. Jesus appeared to them in the locked room – but ordinary bodies cannot pass through locked doors, so, already, Jesus must have acquired what St Paul calls a 'spiritual body'. Jesus himself said to the Sadducees, 'In the resurrection they neither marry nor are given in marriage, but are like angels in heaven.' So we do not expect to come back to earth in quite the same way that Jesus did. All we can say for sure is that the resurrection body which we shall inherit when we die has far more powers than a merely physical body; in fact the resuscitation of a physical body would be no use to us in the world of eternity.

Farewell discourse

Jesus came and stood among them and said, 'Peace be with you.' This is not a promise that they will have no more pain and trouble; as we know, most of them were martyred. But we, like the apostles, shall have a deep inner calm until the day when God calls us, because we know that he intends us to enjoy another world, far superior to this one.

Peace

'As the Father has sent me,' continued Jesus, 'so I send you.' So we, like them, are given clear instructions to continue Christ's mission of spreading the good news of God's love, and building his kingdom here on earth as it is in heaven. We do not have to do this on our own: we are blessed by being part of a community, the Christian Church, who work together on the task of evangelism, and we have the power of the Holy Spirit, God's love working in our hearts, to help us find the right words. However, far more important than our words is the example of our loving behaviour, until people say, 'I wish I was like that!'

Holy Spirit

Then Jesus breathed on them and said, 'Receive the Holy Spirit. If you forgive the sins of any, they are forgiven them.' The purpose of the Spirit of God within us is to enable us to speak God's words to those who hear us. Most importantly, God wants us to tell everybody that God forgives them. First we must feel convinced that God has forgiven us. Can you carry on the mission of the Son of God in that way, if God our Father gives you his Holy Spirit?

All-age worship

Learn to do mouth-to-mouth artificial respiration. Does that help you understand how God gives us life?

Suggested hymns

Alleluia, alleluia, give thanks to the risen Lord; Alleluia, sing to Jesus; Jesus is Lord, creation's voice proclaims it; He is Lord, he is Lord;

Second Sunday of Easter   23 April
Second Service   Resurrection in Daily Life
Ps. 30.1–5 You restored me to life; Dan. 6.1–23 *or* 6.6–23
The lions' den; Mark 15.46—16.8 They were afraid

> 'You brought me up, O Lord, from the dead,
> You restored me to life from among those that go down to the Pit.'
> Psalm 30.3 (Common Worship)

Belief

There is a world of difference between 'believing that something happened in the past', and 'trusting that it is still happening now'. Then again there is 'believing that something will happen in the future'. Christians believe in the resurrection in all three senses. St Paul wrote that more than 500 people had seen the risen Christ, in the 40 days between when his tomb was found to be empty and his ascension into heaven, and many of them were still alive when Paul wrote, so that any disbeliever could challenge them. To reject that amount of eyewitness evidence is very perverse; it would certainly convince a jury in a law court, and is far greater than the evidence for many other historical events which we accept without question to have occurred. But exactly what the witnesses saw we cannot be certain: was it physical molecules of flesh and blood, or, what Paul called a 'spiritual body', such as we shall all receive after we die? We may never be able to answer that question, but in either case, Jesus was persuading us that we shall be more alive after we die than we are now.

Experience

But Paul went on to describe how he himself had seen the risen Christ, on the road to Damascus. Since this was after the ascension, it must have been a vision. Now some people claim to have seen a vision, when actually they had an hallucination, which is a derangement of their mind causing people to see something that isn't there. The difference between that and a true vision is that an hallucination is caused by the brain of the person who sees it, whereas a vision is caused by the person who wants to appear to them. The way to tell the difference is by the effect it has upon somebody's life. An hallucination makes them do crazier and crazier things – a true vision makes them better people. Paul had the evidence of his own changed life to prove that his vision had been caused by Jesus.

Daily life

We can produce that evidence, too. We may never have had a vision of the risen Christ, but our belief that he is alive now and answers our prayers has turned us into better human beings than we were when we first believed, and continues to make daily improvements in our character. Our changed lives now are clear evidence that we shall enjoy a far better life in the future, after we die. We call this 'resurrection in daily life'. The old, selfish 'you' has died; the new generous Christian 'you' has been reborn, given fresh life by God's Holy Spirit. Your old personality considered itself to be the centre of the universe; the new resurrected you is focused on serving others, in the hope that we shall all be raised to a better life beyond the grave. Self-absorption is sin, which is a living death; the risen life which we experience here and now has proved that when we pray for God's grace, all sorts of good deeds are possible to us, which the old self-centred 'me' could never have coped with. That's what I call really living, and this leads us to eternal life.

Thanksgiving

The way to this new life is by thanksgiving. You will experience daily resurrection, if you spend every day thanking God:

- for the beauty of the world around you
- for the joys of art and music
- for the love which you receive from your family
- for the love which arises in your heart for those around you
- for the revelation of God's love for you in the Bible
- and in the grace which he gives you to achieve impossible things for God's sake.

Proof

So this is the real proof of the resurrection of Jesus, and of proving that we shall live to enjoy a new life after death. No amount of quibbling about the historical details of what happened after the dead body of Jesus was buried will get you there. The evidence which will convince you that Jesus is alive is that he gives you so many wonderful gifts. The risen life you now live, full of joy, gratitude, faith, hope and love, is the evidence that will convince you, and those who see the changes for good in your character, that the resurrection is true, in the past, today and in the future. Alleluia! Christ is risen! He is risen indeed. Alleluia!

Suggested hymns

All heaven declares the glory of the risen Lord; Christ the Lord is risen again; Now is eternal life; This is the day, this is the day.

Third Sunday of Easter   30 April
Principal Service   **Sunset to Sunrise**
Zeph. 3.14–20 The Lord is in your midst (*if used, the reading from Acts must be used as the second reading*), or Acts 2.14a, 36–41 The response to Peter's preaching; Ps. 116.1–3, 10–17 The cup of salvation; 1 Peter 1.17–23 Born anew through the resurrection; Luke 24.13–35 The road to Emmaus

> *'While they were talking and discussing, Jesus himself came near and went with them, but their eyes were kept from recognizing him.' Luke 24.15–16*

Cleopas

Two disciples were walking from Jerusalem towards Emmaus, on the evening of the day when Jesus came alive again. They met he risen Jesus, but they did not recognize him. This has been described as 'one of the immortal short stories of the world'. But unlike most other short stories, this one is absolutely true. St Luke tells us that one of the two disciples on the road was called Cleopas; the other one is not named. They had been present when the women returned from the tomb where Jesus had been buried. Cleopas is not mentioned anywhere else in the Bible, but in St John's account of the crucifixion we read that 'standing near the cross of Jesus were his mother, and his mother's sister, Mary the wife of Clopas, and Mary Magdalene'. So we may speculate that Cleopas and Clopas were the same person, and that the other disciple on the road with him was his wife Mary. It is even possible that this Mary was the sister, or half-sister, of the Virgin Mary, and therefore the Aunt of Jesus.

Emmaus

They were walking from Jerusalem to Emmaus, and all the documents, contemporary with the New Testament, that mention this town, agree that it was west of Jerusalem. But there are four towns or villages west of Jerusalem that have been suggested as the site of the original Emmaus, and nobody is quite sure which is correct. Emmaus means 'warm wells', and the small town of Amwas, which sounds a little like it, does have some warm wells. But it is much further from Jerusalem than the seven Roman miles that St Luke mentions. But if the disciples were walking towards the west, and, as Luke says, 'it [was] almost evening and the day [was] now nearly over', they were walking towards the setting sun, and may have been dazzled by the brightness of the sunset. This could explain why they did not recognize Jesus.

Barclay

William Barclay, the great twentieth-century Scots commentator on the Bible, calls this section of St Luke, rather romantically, 'the sunset road that turned to dawn'. As he points out, the gloomy disciples had not understood the implications of the empty tomb, and thought that the sun of their life was now setting; the good times were gone, they thought, never to return. But when they recognized Jesus, and realized that he had been dead, but was now alive again, they understood that his death was not an end, but a beginning. Now Jesus would not come and go, as he had done before, but would be with them always; now he would give them the strength of character to face suffering as bravely as he had; now he would pour his love into their hearts, enabling them to love their neighbours – and even their enemies – for his sake and through the power of his Holy Spirit. So they were not sinking into a gloomy sunset, but rising anew into a beautiful dawn. 'The Christian goes onward,' writes Barclay, 'not to a night which falls, but to a dawn which breaks.'

Making sense

Because of this, Jesus makes sense of our lives for us. The disappointed disciples complained about their dead Messiah, 'We had hoped that he was the one to redeem Israel.' 'Redemption' is the word they used when a payment was made to set free a slave. As they saw it, Israel was a slave to the Roman Empire. They gained financial benefits from Roman colonialism; but they were not free to make their own decisions. So they hoped Jesus would be a violent rebel, bringing about the downfall of Rome by killing Roman soldiers. There are people today who think that physical force and bloody murder can bring about freedom; and they always find that 'the last state is worse than the first'. Jesus revealed that submitting to your oppressor, while speaking up for the oppressed and keeping your moral integrity clean, is the only way to build a kingdom of love.

Sunrise

So when we are puzzling why everything seems to be going wrong in our lives, Jesus shows us that it is learning to face adversity bravely which helps our characters to grow, 'for only they who bear the cross may hope to wear the glorious crown'.

All-age worship

Learn to sing from memory as much as you can of the hymn, 'Abide with me'.

Suggested hymns

Abide with me; Light's glittering morn; Now the green blade riseth; The day of resurrection.

Third Sunday of Easter   30 April

Second Service   Herod's Temple

Ps. 48 In the midst of your Temple; Hag. 1.13—2.9 Rebuilding the Temple; 1 Cor. 3.10–17 You are God's temple; *Gospel at Holy Communion*: John 2.13–22 Cleansing the Temple

> *'The latter splendour of this house shall be greater than the former, says the LORD of hosts; and in this place I will give prosperity, says the LORD of hosts.' Haggai 2.9*

You are God's temple

St Paul wrote, 'Do you not know that you are God's temple and that God's Spirit dwells in you? If anyone destroys God's temple, God will destroy that person. For God's temple is holy, and you are that temple.' The temple, of course, was where people went to meet God; Paul said you meet God in the Christian community. The Temple which Paul and Jesus knew was the one built by King Herod.

Herod's Temple

King Herod the Great was not Jewish by race. His father and grandfather were nobles from Idumea, who converted to the Jewish faith in the period in which the descendants of the Greek king Alexander the Great ruled most of the Middle East. It was a turbulent time, and Herod became King of Judaea after laying siege to Jerusalem, with help from the forces of the Roman Empire, in 37 BC. He hoped to make himself popular by rebuilding what was still known as the Second Temple in Jerusalem, though it had been destroyed and rebuilt several times since it was originally built by Solomon. It was one of the finest buildings in the Roman Empire.

The great builder

Herod was an ambitious builder. Down in the wilderness by the Dead Sea he built the fortress of Masada, a steep hill with a flat top, on which he built barracks for the soldiers, while he himself lived in a magnificent palace balanced on rock ledges on the side of the cliff; inaccessible from the ground, and entered only through hidden tunnels chiselled in the rock. He was notoriously nervous, with perpetual paranoia, and executed several of his close relatives, whom he suspected of plotting against him. Masada was a bolt-hole; yet by his lavish building schemes he increased the respect in which his country was held. Finally Herod built himself a tomb, an artificial mountain outside Jerusalem called 'the Herodium'. Recent excavations have revealed that this, also, had a network of secret tunnels.

Stones

But his greatest work was the Jerusalem Temple. The disciples of Jesus drew his attention to it: 'See what big stone,' they exclaimed. For centuries the only part of this Temple visible to tourists was the Western Wall, known as the Wailing Wall because there, Jewish people would lament the destruction of the place where they met God. Stones are visible there, still in place from when they formed the walls of Herod's Temple. More recently, restricted access has been given to the tunnels which run underneath the Temple Mount. Most of the stones were about two and a half feet deep, three and a half feet high and 15 feet long, and weighed about 28 tons. The biggest foundation stones weigh around 600 tons, and are 44 feet long, 11 feet deep and 16 feet high.

The Church

But Jesus grew angry over the misuse of the Temple, which was meant to be a place where all nations could meet God, yet the Court of the Gentiles was full of money-changers. St Paul said that the fellowship of Christians, worshipping together, is where we now meet God in action; and the solid foundation stone on which it is built is Jesus Christ himself. Each of us, in our own small way, should be a place where our friends and neighbours meet God; but it is especially when we act together as a community that people recognize in us the power of God and the love of God.

Zionists

Yet a small minority of extremist Jews in Jerusalem plan to rebuild the Temple there one day. In this they are supported by some fundamentalist Christians in the USA. They think they are fulfilling the commands of God in the Old Testament, but actually they are doing the exact opposite. St Paul stood before the Acropolis in Athens and declared, 'The God who made the world and everything in it, he who is Lord of heaven and earth, does not live in shrines made by human hands.' Humans need buildings to remind them that God is always present; but to imagine that he is limited to only one place on earth is to make the Creator of the vastness of inter-stellar space too small. The best place to meet God these days is in the heart of Jesus, the mediator between God and humans. And since he cannot be seen on earth now, God's presence is found right here, in his body, the Christian Church.

Suggested hymns

Christ is made the sure foundation; Christ is our corner-stone; The Church of God a kingdom is; The Church's one foundation.

Fourth Sunday of Easter   7 May
Principal Service   **A Popular Shepherd**
Gen. 7 Noah goes into the ark (*if used, the reading from Acts must be used as the second reading*), *or* Acts 2.42–47 Life in the early Church; Ps. 23 The Lord my shepherd; 1 Peter 2.19–25 Christ the shepherd of your souls; John 10.1–10 I am the good shepherd

> *'You were going astray like sheep, but now you have returned to the shepherd and guardian of your souls.' 1 Peter 2.25*

Catacombs

During the Roman Empire, most people in Rome were buried in the tunnels called 'catacombs'. At first, followers of all faiths were bur-ied side by side; then they developed catacombs which were espe-cially reserved for the burial of Christians. Their surviving relatives would go there to pray, just as people do in churchyards today. Occasionally, in times of persecution, groups of Christians might hide there, but the legend that they were regular places of Christian worship is just that – a legend.

Good Shepherd

Out of respect for the deceased, families liked to have pictures painted on the walls behind the tombs, and this was the begin-ning of Christian art. One of the favourite images in the catacombs was of Jesus the Good Shepherd, carrying the lost sheep across his shoulders. There was a simple economic reason why this was such a common subject, and this was that, before the Christians came along, the local artists were accustomed to painting the pagan god Hermes with a ram round his neck, which he was supposed to be bringing for a sacrifice. So the artists could copy an image which was already in their portfolio, and had no need to start from scratch!

Popular

But there was another, more serious reason why this image was popular. Many of the words that the first Christians used were based on stories or ideas from the Jewish Scriptures, which meant nothing to most non-Jews. But everybody, from whatever culture, knew what shepherds were, and what a lot of trouble they had to take looking after their flock. Psalm 23 says that the Lord God is my Shepherd; and in St John's Gospel Jesus says he is the Good Shepherd. So when the First Letter of St Peter was written, probably from Rome, everybody knew what he was on about when he wrote, 'You were going astray like sheep, but now you have returned to the shepherd and guardian of your souls.'

Teaching

Psalm 23 teaches us these things about God. I am quoting the version in the Book of Common Prayer:

- Verse 1: 'The Lord is my shepherd' teaches us about our relationship with God. God is not, as most people thought when this psalm was written, remote and uncaring; God cares for us individually, as a shepherd searches for the lost sheep.
- 'Therefore can I lack nothing' tells us how God supplies all our needs.
- 'He shall feed me in a green pasture,' sang the Psalmist, so we can relax when we know that God loves us.
- 'And lead me forth beside the waters of comfort' promises that God will refresh us when we are weary.
- 'He shall convert my soul' speaks of God healing our spiritual lives, giving us the power to carry on bravely when we seem to be losing the battle.
- God guides us when we are confused and lost, as we learn from the words, 'And bring me forth in the paths of righteousness, for his name's sake.'

- 'Yea, though I walk through the valley of the shadow of death, I will fear no evil' shows how God gives us strength in the testing times of life, and promises us new life beyond the grave.
- Protection is promised by 'For thou art with me, thy rod and thy staff comfort me'
- Hope is brought to us by 'Thou shalt prepare a table before me against them that trouble me'.
- 'Thou hast anointed my head with oil, and my cup shall be full' tells us that we are consecrated in his service.
- 'But thy loving-kindness and mercy shall follow me all the days of my life' teaches us of the abundance of God's blessings.
- 'And I will dwell in the house of the Lord for ever' promises a secure future for us throughout all eternity.

Favourite

So the psalm promises fellowship; answers to prayer; rest; spiritual strength; guidance; protection; hope; consecration; blessings and eternal life. No wonder the image of the Good Shepherd was popular in the catacombs, and still is now.

All-age worship

Learn one verse each of Psalm 23. Recite it while passing a woolly lamb toy from person to person.

Suggested hymns

Faithful Shepherd, feed me; Loving Shepherd of thy sheep; The king of love my shepherd is; The Lord's my shepherd.

Fourth Sunday of Easter   7 May
Second Service   **A Contract with Everyone**
Ps. 29.1–10 God in the storm; Ezra 3.1–13 Foundations
of the Temple; Eph. 2.11–22 Jew and Gentile united; *Gospel
at Holy Communion*: Luke 19.37–48 Cleansing the Temple

> *'Now in Christ Jesus you who once were far off have been brought near by the blood of Christ. For he is our peace; in his flesh he has made both groups into one and has broken down the dividing wall, that is, the hostility between us.' Ephesians 2.13–14*

Families

Our early human ancestors soon realized that they would never survive as individuals; they were too vulnerable to predators, and too inefficient at hunting for food. So the first social unit was the family. If the children were obedient to their parents, and the parents caring to their children, they stood a better chance of survival. So they made a solemn promise to look after each other. King David's best friend was Jonathan. They were not related, but they swore to behave as though they were brothers; the Bible says that 'Jonathan made a covenant with David, because he loved him as his own soul.' It was the same when two people got married; we read that 'a man leaves his father and his mother and clings to his wife, and they become one flesh.' They are not *physically* related, but they become closer due to the marriage contract even than they were to their own parents beforehand. Adoption of a child, also, was a way of creating a blood relationship where there was none before.

Tribes

But even families are not strong enough to defend themselves, so the next step was for two or more families to covenant together to become a tribe. The covenant was not a written document at first, but it was a solemn ceremony. The blood of an animal was sprinkled over both tribes, so that they might become 'blood brothers'. You owed the same obligations to members of the other tribe as you would to your own blood relations. Then several tribes might covenant together to become a nation; and at each stage it becomes clearer that God is involved in the contract; you all agree to obey the same God as the father of the family; God and the people signed the covenant by the sprinkling of blood, only in God's case it was sprinkled over the altar. We see examples in the covenant which the Israelites signed at Mount Sinai, with the terms of the contract written on tablets of stone; and when Joshua renewed this contract with the 12 tribes at Shechem.

Nations

Nations are still held together by a covenant: it may be a written constitution, or a document like the Magna Carta; or a history of common law defining the duties of the citizens to each other.

Whether they admit it or not, each nation depends on having the same god, or at the very least a set of inherited cultural traditions. Do you see the direction I am moving? The next step up in the progress of civilization is when two or more nations sign a solemn league or alliance, not to fight each other, and to defend each other from a common enemy. Perhaps the most successful of these was the British Commonwealth of nations: a voluntary union, based not on force, but on a shared heritage of culture, law and respect.

Unity

What is so exciting is that I believe you can see the hand of God in the whole covenanting process. Jesus established a new covenant, or New Testament, to be based not on law, but on love, and it would lead eventually to the kingdom of love, when love would rule over the whole world. But alliances in our own day have been more controversial, from the United Kingdom, to NATO, to the European Union, to the United Nations. Yet I believe that, with all their faults, these agreements have been steps along the way towards a world of tolerance and mutual understanding. God intends we should replace the old way of settling our disagreements by fighting with a deeper universal covenant in which everybody has a contract with everyone else, sealed by the blood of Christ. In his day, Jew and Gentile hated each other; the Romans were regarded as enemies because they were not party to the Jewish covenant with God. All the more astonishing was it, then, that St Paul argued:

> In Christ Jesus you who once were far off have been brought near by the blood of Christ. For he is our peace; in his flesh he has made both groups into one and has broken down the dividing wall, that is, the hostility between us.

When we pray 'thy kingdom come', we ask God to help us establish a world civilization, covenanted on love, peace and justice.

Suggested hymns

Peace is flowing like a river; Peace, perfect peace, in this dark world of sin?; The kingdom of God is justice and joy; Thy kingdom come, O God.

Fifth Sunday of Easter   14 May
Principal Service   **Living Stones**

Gen. 8.1–19 Noah comes out of the ark (*if used, the reading from Acts must be used as the second reading*), or Acts 7.55–60 The death and faith of Stephen; Ps. 31.1–5, 15–16 Deliver me; 1 Peter 2.2–10 Living stones in God's Temple; John 14.1–14 I will prepare a place for you: the way, truth and life

> *'Come to him, a living stone, though rejected by mortals yet chosen and precious in God's sight, and like living stones, let yourselves be built into a spiritual house, to be a holy priesthood, to offer spiritual sacrifices acceptable to God through Jesus Christ.'*
> *1 Peter 2.4–5*

Building site

Picture in your mind's eye a site where a large building is being erected. Only imagine that is before the time of reinforced concrete, so that great heavy stones are being laid one on top of another, squared off and flattened so that they fit snugly and can together bear the weight of whatever is being built on top of them. Now imagine that it is a cartoon film. Through the magic of computer graphics, each stone is made to look like a living person. Because each stone is a human being they are bring uncooperative. They struggle and rebel, and have no wish to cooperate with each other. So the master-builder comes round, points at one of the living stones, and says to the foreman, 'That one will need to have a few rough corners knocked off, if it is to remain there. No stone can bear the weight that will be laid on it unless it is willing to cooperate with its neighbours.' It is an amazing image, and you may think it could only have been dreamt up by one of the way-out modernist film directors. But actually it originates in a letter which was written by St Peter around 2,000 years ago. Peter wrote about Jesus being the foundation stone in God's new Temple. He imagines that in this cartoon, Jesus is the foundation stone, and he quotes from the book of Isaiah, in which God is represented as saying:

See, I am laying in Zion a stone,
a cornerstone chosen and precious;
and whoever believes in him will not be put to shame.

Then on this foundation, God builds those who believe in Jesus into a wonderful new temple, the place where people come to meet with God:

> Like living stones, let yourselves be built into a spiritual house, to be a holy priesthood, to offer spiritual sacrifices acceptable to God through Jesus Christ.

Living stones

'Living stones'! It is an amazing thought, and the mind boggles. But no stone is any use when it is lying around loose on the building site. So Christians are weak and powerless while they work as individuals, but can resist all the attacks of the powers of evil when they are built together into a living community. In the process we shall all get our rough corners knocked off us: the prickly personality, our individualistic unwillingness to cooperate with others or with the master-builder; our tendency to criticize and judge other people, and to get angry when others refuse to do what we think they should! But that is all part of the polishing process by which God makes us beautiful and strong.

Crumbling

A guidebook in Thailand once described a ruined city as 'falling into crumbles'! The church, the family of God, can easily crumble if just one member is missing from worship even one Sunday. My absence, unless because of sickness, is another weak spot in God's magnificent building work. God will never allow the community he built to tumble down; though occasionally a local church may have to be closed due to lack of support. But if you don't cooperate with the other believers, and won't show up among the worshippers as often as you possibly can, then God can always find a new stone to take your place. But you don't want the shame of becoming a rejected piece of rubble around the building site of God's Church; after all, the community is not only for this life, but carries on together in eternity after we rise again.

Unbelievers

St Peter warns us that

To you then who believe, he is precious; but for those who do not believe, 'The stone that the builders rejected has become the very head of the corner,' . . . But you are a chosen race, a royal priesthood, a holy nation, God's own people, in order that you may proclaim the mighty acts of him who called you out of darkness into his marvellous light.

All-age worship

Each writes their name on a brick, preferably of lightweight plastic, then builds them together (with adhesive?) into a wall labelled 'God's family, here and hereafter'.

Suggested hymns

Christ is made the sure foundation/Blessed city, heavenly Salem; Christ is our corner-stone; The Church's one foundation; Ye that know the Lord is gracious.

Fifth Sunday of Easter   14 May
Second Service   Old Jerusalem and New
Ps. 147.1–12 God heals the broken-hearted; Zech. 4.1–10
Not by might, nor by power, but by my spirit; Rev. 21.1–14
The new Jerusalem; *Gospel at Holy Communion*: Luke 2.25–32
[33–38] Simeon's song

> *'I saw a new heaven and a new earth; for the first heaven and the first earth had passed away . . . And I saw the holy city, the new Jerusalem, coming down out of heaven from God.'*
> *Revelation 21.1–2*

Jerusalem

Jerusalem is a real city in the Middle East, inhabited by real people. Yet when Christians talk about Jerusalem, they tend either to idealize it, as though it was as clean as the pictures in the Sunday school books, or else to demonize it as a corrupt city which has failed to live up to the intentions which God had for it. Both images are partly right, and both are in another sense totally wrong. When King David captured it from the Jebusites – the original inhabitants – he hoped it would become the focus of unity for the 12 scattered tribes; and King Solomon built a Temple on Mount Zion to be the place where they could all meet with the one true God. Yet it was soon corrupted, and the prophet Jeremiah sat in the precincts of the Temple proclaiming its downfall, at a time when the kings of Judah hoped to show that it was strong enough to resist the rising power of Babylon. Jesus followed this critical tradition when he wept over Jerusalem, and drove the traders out of the Temple. He predicted its destruction by the Romans, which followed a mere 40 years later.

New Jerusalem

So Jerusalem became once again the dream of the idealist, and St John in the book of Revelation pictured what he called 'the *new* Jerusalem' coming down from heaven to earth. What did he mean by this? It is a mistake to try and give a single simple meaning to the words of a mystic, but many people think that he was talking about two things: the first, a physical human society which would be formed on earth; and the second, a spiritual realm to which we can pass when we die, and which has no connection with the physical universe.

Progress

So under the guise of a physical city, whose dimensions he reports, but which could never contain the bodies of all the Christians who have died over the past 2,000 years, and which would be far too heavy to descend from somewhere up among the clouds to the surface of this gravitational planet, John raises our hopes of forming an ideal human society in the real world. This new Jerusalem would be a world in which nation lived at peace with nation; in which individuals were inspired by universal love and mutual self-sacrifice; in which greed and corruption were no more, and in which wealth was principally used to meet the needs of others. Could this dream ever become a reality? I don't know, but I do know we should all devote ourselves to working towards it by spreading love around us wherever we go. Will God create such a society by means of a miracle? The book of Revelation suggests that this might happen. But William Blake in his poem called 'Jerusalem' seems to be suggesting that it is up to us:

> Bring me my Bow of burning gold;
> Bring me my Arrows of desire:
> Bring me my Spear: O clouds unfold!
> Bring me my Chariot of fire!
>
> I will not cease from Mental Fight,
> Nor shall my Sword sleep in my hand:
> Till *we* have built Jerusalem,
> In England's green and pleasant land.

Heaven

Or is the new Jerusalem an attempt to describe that for which we have no adequate words – the spiritual life with which a loving God endows those who return his love, in a non-physical alternative universe? St Paul wrote that 'flesh and blood cannot inherit the kingdom of God, nor does the perishable inherit the imperishable.' So there must be a new society, timeless or measured by an entirely different dimension, where we shall meet 'the spirits of forgiven people made perfect', and share in a world of love of which the descriptions of angels and harps can only be a pale attempt at a metaphor. We shall know the answer to these questions one day; in the meantime, we can prepare ourselves for whatever is going to happen by trying to live lives of unselfish altruism.

> Then I saw a new heaven and a new earth; for the first heaven and the first earth had passed away . . . And I saw the holy city, the new Jerusalem, coming down out of heaven from God . . . Death will be no more; mourning and crying and pain will be no more, for the first things have passed away.

Suggested hymns

And did those feet?; Glorious things of thee are spoken; Jerusalem the golden; There is a land of pure delight.

Sixth Sunday of Easter (Rogation Sunday)   21 May
Principal Service   **Spirits in Prison**

Gen. 8.20—9.17 God's covenant with Noah (*if used, the reading from Acts must be used as the second reading*), or Acts 17.22–31 Paul witnesses to the resurrection in Athens; Ps. 66.7–18 God brought us out; 1 Peter 3.13–22 Christ preached to the spirits in prison; John 14.15–21 The promise of the Holy Spirit, the Advocate

'[Christ] made a proclamation to the spirits in prison.' 1 Peter 3.19

Creeds

The Nicene Creed, dating from AD 325, which is used by many churches at Holy Communion services, is based on the earlier Apostles' Creed; though not written by them, it summarizes what the apostles taught, about the birth, death, and resurrection of Jesus. But it includes the puzzling phrase, 'he descended into hell'. This is drawn from today's reading from the First Letter of St Peter: 'he went and made a proclamation to the spirits in prison' must be one of the hardest verses to understand in the whole New Testament. But it contains some precious truths, so it is worth the effort.

Hell

The word 'hell' is misleading. Modern versions of the Apostles' Creed says 'he descended to the dead'. Two words are translated into English as 'hell': one is the name of the Jerusalem municipal rubbish tip, where 'the flames never go out, and the maggots always have something to eat'. Jesus, like other prophets, told his sceptical listeners that they were rubbish, only fit to be, metaphorically, thrown on the tip and permanently destroyed. But this is not meant to be taken literally. In his days, most people believed that everybody, when they die, goes to a massive subterranean antechamber, called 'Hades' in Greek, or 'Sheol' in Hebrew. Maybe rewards and punishments would be allotted at the Last Judgement. In the meantime they kicked their heels in a place which, like any other waiting room, was cold, gloomy and 'dead boring'. St Peter had spent many days in prison in his long life, and he must often have thought, 'I'll bet this is what Hades is like.' So Hades is what he meant when he said that Jesus preached to the souls in prison.

Noah

Peter said that Jesus spent the hours between his death and resurrection among the dead, especially those 'who in former times did not obey, when God waited patiently in the days of Noah, during the building of the ark, in which a few, that is, eight persons, were saved through water'. The story of a great flood was told in many versions in the Middle East, always as the act of an angry god in a fit of pique. By contrast, the Jewish version of the legend emphasizes the patience of a loving Creator. It resonates today because everybody then, as now, was busy destroying the beautiful environment which God had made for them. If there was any justice in the world, God would have given all of us the punishment we deserve long ago, which means there would not be much hope for me and you. But our God is not a god of punishment, but the Lord of forgiveness. So instead of drowning the whole human race and starting again, which would have been logical, God saves eight humans, and two of each of the other species, in the ark, with instructions to rebuild and care for the world of nature their ancestors had destroyed. Those who had been drowned in the flood were sent to the gloomy anteroom to wait for their judgement.

Eternity

The difference between St Peter and us is that we have a new understanding of time. In another universe, outside this space–time continuum, time is very different. We can believe that in the very nanosecond that we die, we are judged, and, if we repent, forgiven and welcomed into the eternal universe of love. St Peter would never have understood that, so in his terms he emphasized that Jesus shared our human experience of death, and, with his new spiritual body, he went to where every human being who had ever lived was waiting for him, and told them that, provided they had repented, they were discharged from prison. No corner of this universe or the next is beyond the reach of the gospel of God's love. And that really is good news, for us and for everyone else. As St Peter wrote:

[Christ] suffered . . . for the unrighteous, in order to bring you to God. He was put to death in the flesh, but made alive in the spirit, in which also he went and made a proclamation to the spirits in prison, who . . . did not obey, when God waited patiently in the days of Noah, during the building of the ark.

All-age worship

Read parts of the funeral service, and discuss how you would comfort somebody who is bereaved.

Suggested hymns

Alleluia (x3) O sons and daughters; At the Lamb's high feast we sing; Finished the strife of battle now; This joyful Eastertide.

Sixth Sunday of Easter (Rogation Sunday) 21 May
Second Service   Old Age
Ps. 87 Glorious things, 36.5–10 The fountain of life; Zech. 8.1–13 The faithful city; Rev. 21.22—22.5 The river of life; *Gospel at Holy Communion*: John 21.1–14 The lakeside

> 'Thus says the LORD of hosts: Old men and old women shall again sit in the streets of Jerusalem, each with staff in hand because of their great age.' Zechariah 8.4

Ageing

People are living so much longer these days, on the whole. Tragically, many people still die young, leaving their family shattered by their unexpected bereavement. But apparently one-third of the babies born this year are expected to live until their hundredth birthday. For this increasing longevity we must be profoundly grateful. The prophet Zechariah looked forward to long life as a gift from God. He wrote:

> Thus says the LORD of hosts: Old men and old women shall again sit in the streets of Jerusalem, each with staff in hand because of their great age.

Problems

But ageing brings problems. Dementia makes many elderly people unable to think clearly, or to look after themselves, or vulnerable to other diseases. And even people whose mind is blessedly clear need looking after because of physical weakness. This all costs money, and has to be paid for out of the taxes on people who are still of working age: it is a delusion to think that we have saved up enough in our National Insurance contributions to pay for our own care. There is no reserve fund; our contributions were used to pay for those who at that time needed care. Some elderly people become obstinate and hard to care for. And although our lives are getting longer, we still have to face the certainty that all of us will die sometime.

Death

In past ages, most people accepted, in theory at least, the Christian teaching that after we die we shall be raised to a new and more enjoyable life in heaven. In the Victorian era, people talked endlessly about death, and sex was a taboo subject; now the position has been reversed. Because of this, many people are terrified of dying, yet neither they nor their family know how to talk about it. Some people with no religious faith can face death calmly, and some worshipping Christians still find it frightening; but on the whole, those who have a belief in the resurrection take a more positive attitude.

Encouraging

So how are we to encourage people to talk about death? First we must pray with them and for them, that they may have the determination to cooperate with the medical profession, as they seek to keep elderly people alive as long as they can. Nevertheless, when the pain is unending, and their life doesn't seem to be bringing any benefits for themselves or anybody else, their families may have to give them permission to die. We should not force the terminally ill, by artificial feeding or any other means, to go on living longer than they wish to. Palliative care is very good these days at giving people a pain-free death. Bur when the right time comes, we should be willing to talk about looking forward to meeting again those we love in heaven.

Eternal life

We believe in eternal life, because Jesus believed in it, and talked about it, and gave his disciples hope by what he said. Jesus was not the sort of person to deliberately mislead us, or to share irrational delusions. So if the best man who ever lived believed in resurrection, his own and that of those who believe in him, who am I to disagree? Also, many bereaved people have a strong feeling that their loved ones are as close to them now they are dead as they were when they were alive. Some of these experiences are too intimate to talk about, and of course none of them can be proved. But the cumulative evidence of so many people down the ages is surely a reason for describing eternal life as a strong possibility.

Ministry

Talk positively about death as you grow older, and encourage others to do the same. Offer to pray with the dying, those in the 'departure lounge' of life. If you are too nervous to do this, suggest that they see the hospital chaplain or a minister of their own choice. Most of us in the ministry have seen an expression of calm hope come on to the face of someone who has never been able to speak about it before, when the minister prays that they may enjoy eternal life with those they love in heaven. Often they subsequently die wearing an expression of calm peace. Who would deny them that, just because we are too shy to talk about it?

Suggested hymns

Christ triumphant, ever reigning; Give us the wings of faith to rise; Through the night of doubt and sorrow; Ye choirs of new Jerusalem.

ASCENSION, PENTECOST AND TRINITY

Music bridges the gap between literal history and metaphor. When we talk about Jesus 'ascending into heaven', about God's Holy Spirit entering our hearts, and about three Persons in one God, are we talking about measurable physical facts, or about spiritual experiences which our mere human words are insufficient to describe? When the words are sung, there is no need to answer that question, for it is the emotions which the words arouse in our hearts, and the loving behaviour which they motivate, which matter. Here are some suggested hymns for these festivals:

Ascension Day and the Sunday after: 'A man there lived in Galilee'; 'All hail the power of Jesus's name'; 'At the name of Jesus'; 'Christ triumphant, ever reigning'; 'Crown him with many crowns'; 'Hail the day that sees him rise'; 'Hail, thou once despised Jesus'; 'Hail to the Lord's anointed'; 'How lovely on the mountains'; 'Jesus is Lord! Creation's voice proclaims it'; 'Jesus shall reign'; 'Lord, enthroned in heavenly splendour'; 'Our eyes have seen the glory'; 'Rejoice, the Lord is King'; 'The head that once was crowned'; 'We hail thy presence glorious'; 'We see the Lord'.

Pentecost: 'Be still, for the presence of the Lord'; 'Breathe on me, breath of God'; 'Come down O Love Divine'; 'Come, Holy Ghost, our souls inspire'; 'Dear Lord and Father of mankind'; 'Fear not, rejoice and be glad'; 'God's Spirit is in my heart'; 'Gracious Spirit, Holy Ghost'; 'Like the murmur of the dove's song'; 'O King enthroned on high'; 'O thou who camest from above'; 'Our blest Redeemer, ere he breathed'; 'Spirit of God, unseen as the wind'; 'Spirit of holiness'; 'Spirit of the living God'; 'Spirit of mercy, truth, and love'; 'The Spirit lives to set us free'; 'There's a quiet understanding'; 'Wind, wind, blow on me'.

Trinity Sunday: 'Bright the vision that delighted'; 'Father of heaven, whose love profound'; 'Father, Lord of all creation'; 'Father, we adore you'; 'Father, we love you'; 'Firmly I believe and truly'; 'Holy holy, holy holy'; 'Holy, holy, holy is the Lord'; 'Holy, holy, holy! Lord God Almighty!'; 'I bind unto myself today'; 'Immortal, invisible, God only wise'; 'Majesty, worship his majesty'; 'O worship the king'; 'Thank you, O my Father'; 'The God of Abraham praise'; 'There is a Redeemer'; 'Thy hand, O God, has guided'.

Ascension Day   25 May
Thrones

Acts 1.1–11 The ascension (*must be used as either the first or second reading*), *or* Dan. 7.9–14 The Son of Man; Ps. 47 God has gone up, *or* Ps. 93 The Lord is king; Eph. 1.15–23 Christ is seated beside God; Luke 24.44–53 The ascension

> *'God put this power to work in Christ when he raised him from the dead and seated him at his right hand in the heavenly places, far above all rule and authority and power and dominion, and above every name that is named, not only in this age but also in the age to come.' Ephesians 1.20–21*

> *Or: 'When [Jesus] had said this, as they were watching, he was lifted up, and a cloud took him out of their sight.' Acts 1.9*

Up

If you meet someone from humble origins who has moved to a position of importance, you congratulate them, saying, 'My! You have gone up in the world!' To which they may reply with a grin, 'No, my office is still on the ground floor, I am still at the same altitude as I always was before.' And you laugh together, because you both know that a higher position in the organization is nothing to do with your height above sea level. So let us take the same attitude towards the ascension of Jesus into heaven. In those days, many people believed that heaven was a place above the clouds, so to explain to his disciples that he was being given a new position of authority, he gave them a vision of himself rising up. But of course after the resurrection he had a spiritual body, not a physical one, and he could appear and disappear at will, and pass through locked doors. So it was no problem for him to appear to be rising into heaven, to take a seat in the heavenly court of God.

Monarchies

For most nations and empires in those days were monarchies. The king or emperor, queen or prince, was the absolute ruler. All other authority was devolved from the monarch: everybody had to obey the orders of the subordinates, because otherwise you would be disobeying the supreme governor, who could expel you from ever appearing in his kingdom again. The king would 'hold court' in a large room in his palace, seated on a large throne up several steps, and his subordinates would sit around him on smaller and lower thrones. The second-in-command had the throne on the right-hand side of the monarch; this was the place of honour. But very rarely a monarch might share his throne with somebody else, so that they two had equal authority.

Heaven

Since this was the only image of authority that they had, that was how they pictured God, seated on a throne in the court of heaven. Since God is invisible, and cannot be described in human words, this imagery has to be symbolic, rather than a literal description of what heaven looks like. But the symbolism is important enough for the Jerusalem Temple to be described in the psalms as 'God's courts', and for the book of Job to begin with a debate in the heavenly court, reminding us that courts are places where legal cases are heard.

Jesus

So as the followers of Jesus began to realize that, although he was completely human, he was no ordinary human being, they began to use regal language to describe him: the Messiah, meaning the anointed king; the Son of God, meaning the first in succession to the royal throne – though of course there was no question of God dying and passing on his throne to his Son! This imagery had already been used in the book of Daniel, where 'one like a son of man' – which is the Hebrew way of saying 'a completely human figure', a representative of the human race – came to God on the clouds, and

> to him was given dominion and glory and kingship, that all peoples, nations, and languages should serve him. His dominion is an everlasting dominion that shall not pass away, and his kingship is one that shall never be destroyed.

There is no actual mention of thrones in this passage, but it explains why Jesus chose the title 'Son of Man' for himself, and why the longer ending of Mark's Gospel, and many other places, say that 'the Lord Jesus . . . was taken up into heaven and sat down at the right hand of God.' Ascension Day is all about God the Father and Jesus the Son of God sharing absolute authority over everything that happens in the whole universe. In Jesus we have a friend at court; in the ascended Son of Man, we see that heaven is an essentially human place.

Suggested hymns

Crown him with many crowns; Hail the day that sees him rise; Jesus shall reign; Rejoice, the Lord is King.

Seventh Sunday of Easter (Sunday after Ascension Day)   28 May
Principal Service   **Celebrity**
Ezek. 36.24–28 I will put my Spirit in you (*if used, the reading from Acts must be used as the second reading*), or Acts 1.6–14 The ascension; Ps. 68.1–10, 32–35 Let God arise; 1 Peter 4.12–14; 5.6–11 Share Christ's suffering and his glory; John 17.1–11 Father, glorify your Son

> '[Jesus prayed,] "So now, Father, glorify me in your own presence with the glory that I had in your presence before the world existed."' John 17.5

Celebrities

Some of us may once have had a few seconds' conversation with a film star, or other celebrity, and boast about it still. Others, who have never had this experience, sometimes feel very envious of that, as though some of the glory of the famous person has brushed off on to those who met them. Others, still, have no time at all for the cult of celebrity. I think it all depends on what the person is famous for. If they have put on a brilliant performance, or created a work of art, if they have been kind and generous to others, or done anything else which makes the world a better place to live in, then they deserve their fame. But if they are simply famous for being famous, then they will soon be forgotten. Yet if we have a positive attitude to greatness, that is a good thing. Our praise does not help the glitterati: in fact I suspect that many of them find that being surrounded by adoring fans and the paparazzi is a perishing nuisance. But becoming a fan of someone who is talented will spur us to work at developing our own talents; admiring people who are generous encourages us to be generous ourselves; hero-worshipping those who are wise will help us, too, to grow in wisdom. Praising those we respect leads us into developing their good qualities within our own personalities.

Glory

I want to suggest to you today that there is a connection between celebrity and the word we find so often in the Bible: 'glory'. Of course, there is a great deal more to glory than mere celebrity. We often speak today of a glorious view or a glorious victory, but less frequently about glorious human beings. Glory is the innate quality which turns good people into celebrities; and the Scriptures refer over and over again to the glory of God. God does not need to be praised; but adoration and worship of the Almighty does us a power of good. Now you may think that mere humans cannot hope to imitate the qualities which they admire in God; but all that changed when Jesus came to earth. He showed that it *is* possible for human beings to have those qualities of love, forgiveness, benevolence and generosity which we respect in the Divine nature. So to be members of God's fan club turns us into better people.

Jesus

Yet Jesus gave a whole new range of meanings to the word 'glory'. He prayed:

Father, the hour has come; glorify your Son so that the Son may glorify you . . . I glorified you on earth by finishing the work that you gave me to do. So now, Father, glorify me in your own presence with the glory that I had in your presence before the world existed. I have made your name known to those whom you gave me from the world . . . All mine are yours, and yours are mine; and I have been glorified in them.

So Jesus prays that he may be glorified; but this is not mere celebrity that he asks for. Jesus had come to the moment when he would be crucified, and he describes willing self-sacrifice for the sake of others as the true character of glory, which he shares with God, and has done since the world began. When he ascended into glory, he returned to

152

the fellowship of mutual love which characterizes the life of the Holy Trinity. And it is for this that we worship him. He says that he is willing to share his glory with us who follow him; but it is not celebrity which he offers us, but the same path of suffering gladly born that he himself walked. *That* is glory; suffering for others' sake is the most glorious thing we can do, and is far better than mere celebrity.

Praised by God

Yet though we may never gain the fame of a celebrity on this earth, if we share Christ's suffering here on earth, we shall share his glory hereafter. The praise of other humans is nothing, compared with the praise we receive from Jesus if we live a life like his. This is the true glory, to be celebrated for our self-sacrifice by God himself.

All-age worship

Learn to sing a modern version of the 'Gloria in excelsis'.

Suggested hymns

Christ triumphant, ever reigning; Jesus is Lord! Creation's voice proclaims it; Our eyes have seen the glory; The head that once was crowned with thorns.

Seventh Sunday of Easter (Sunday after Ascension Day)   28 May
Second Service   **All the Earth**
Ps. 47 God has gone up; 2 Sam. 23.1–5 The Spirit of the Lord speaks through David; Eph. 1.15–23 Seated at the right hand of God; *Gospel at Holy Communion*: Mark 16.14–20 The ascension of Jesus

> [At a Communion Service]: '[Jesus] said . . . to [his disciples], "Go into all the world and proclaim the good news to the whole creation."' Mark 16.15

> [At other services]: 'For God is the King of all the earth; sing praises with all your skill.'
> Psalm 47.7 (Common Worship)

Last words

The last words which Jesus spoke on earth, before he ascended into heaven, were to command his followers to go into all the world and proclaim the good news [of God's love] to the whole creation. That is the version in St Matthew's Gospel and the longer ending of St Mark's. In the Acts of the Apostles, Jesus says, 'you will be my witnesses in Jerusalem . . . and to the ends of the earth.' This teaches clearly that the purpose of Jesus in coming to earth was not just to make his fellow Jews into Christians, or even the people of Western Europe and America, but that we should bring the whole human race to believe in him. This sounds rather intolerant to modern ears, but of course he did not mean us to force other faiths to convert, but to show them, by our words and our lives, that the love which Jesus taught has something of value to offer, which they may not yet have found in their own faith.

Old Testament

Though the worship of Jehovah may have begun in the Old Testament as a narrow religion for those born of Jewish parents only, the psalms and many of the prophets say that 'God is the King of all the earth'. They soon realized that if they were worshipping the one true God, then he must be one with all the gods which the other nations were worshipping. As St Paul said in Athens, 'I found . . . an altar with the inscription, "To an unknown god." [That same God which] you worship as unknown, this I proclaim to you.'

Multi-faith community

An English comedian back in the 1980s said that you can easily recognize an Englishman by the shamrock in his turban and the leek in his buttonhole! Already then we were beginning to build a multi-faith community, yet there is still discrimination. It shocks us to share with friends of minority races the pain that comes from receiving inferior treatment and hurtful words. This should make us particularly sensitive to our loving Christian duty to protect our neighbours from any trace of racism. We cannot hope to convert anyone to the Christian gospel, as we are commanded by Christ to do, while a so-called Christian country shows such unloving behaviour.

Learning

A successful missionary said, 'Never try to teach anybody anything, until you have learnt something from them.' Study the other religions, and you will be filled with admiration, especially for the deep prayer life of many adherents of other faiths. After all, Jesus chose as the hero of his parable a good Samaritan, a member of a different race and a different faith from his own. Being a Christian means understanding and learning to approach God in Jesus Christ. All religions are not the same. Christianity has given us a unique path to salvation, which we would like to share with the whole human race; but that does not mean that we cannot learn from other religions truths about God which we have under-emphasized.

Elephant

A Hindu poet long ago wrote about some blind men and an elephant. One caught hold of a leg and said it was a tree; one held its trunk and said it was a snake. The one with the tail said it was a whip, and another holding its ear said it was a sail. There was only one elephant, and there is only one God; yet we fail to grasp that others may have discovered other aspects of the one God than the one we know. When Jesus said, 'No one comes to the Father except by me,' he meant that no other religion had realized that God relates to us with a father-like love. He also told us to 'Go therefore and make disciples' – meaning 'learners' – 'of all nations, baptizing them . . . and teaching them to obey everything that I have commanded you.' Yet as Bishop Kenneth Cragg, author of *Sandals at the Mosque*, used to say, the first step may not be to convert people, but to encourage followers of other faiths to 'take Jesus into their own religion'. Then they can continue the process that St Paul described as seeking God and eventually finding him – even though he is close to each one of us.

Suggested hymns

At the name of Jesus; Christ is the King, O friends rejoice; In Christ there is no east or west; How lovely on the mountains.

Day of Pentecost (Whit Sunday)   4 June
Principal Service   Gifts of the Spirit

Acts 2.1–21 The day of Pentecost (*must be used as either the first or second reading*), *or* Num. 11.24–30 The elders receive the Spirit; Ps. 104.26–36, 37b The Spirit in creation; 1 Cor. 12.3b–13 Different gifts, one Spirit; John 20.19–23 Jesus breathes the Holy Spirit, *or* John 7.37–39 Living water of the Spirit

'There are varieties of gifts, but the same Spirit.' 1 Corinthians 12.4

Distortions

What's all this about the Holy Spirit?

- Is it some complicated theological idea thought up by people who are too clever for their own good?
- Or is it some emotional happy-clappy version of Christianity which only comes to privileged semi-hysterical Christians, and anyone who does not experience such emotions is not really a Christian?
- Or is it some mystical pie-in-the-sky form of faith invented by those who are so heavenly minded they are no earthly use?

Unsurprisingly, I think all three pictures of the Holy Spirit are distortions of the truth. Or rather, I think that all are true, when taken together, but none is true on its own. What the Bible means, when it speaks about the Spirit of God, is both far bigger than any of these misconceptions, and at the same time far more down to earth.

Gifts

So imagine you are thinking about some problem, and you say, exasperated, 'Somebody ought to do something about that! Why does God allow it?' It can be any problem, from the international to the local, a problem in your own family or among your close friends. 'Somebody ought to deal with it,' you say. Next time that happens, stop for a moment and ask yourself, 'Does God, perhaps, want *me* to do something about it?' Possibly you are too busy doing other things which are just as important to God. What you mustn't say is, 'I couldn't do that. I'm not clever enough, or strong enough, or caring enough, or good enough.' Because, although any of those things may be true of you *now*, you are forgetting what God can do with you. God won't make you an intellectual genius overnight, a superman or superwoman. But you never know till you try how much you can achieve if you ask God to help you. God will give you just enough intelligence, after consulting your friends, to see what needs doing, and what even you could do to put it right. Or God fills you with a wave of compassion for some underprivileged person. You are moved to pray for them for an hour, and then talk it through till you agree what you can both do to put things right. You may be moved to stand up in a meeting, and speak words which persuade many of those present to see the matter from God's point of view. Afterwards you gasp, 'I don't know who put those words into my mouth, but I certainly couldn't have thought them up by myself.' Do you see what is happening? God is making you a present of some qualities or skills to enable you to do things that you never dreamt were possible for you. We call those the gifts of the Spirit, and they are often mentioned in the Bible:

- 1 Corinthians 12: 'There are varieties of gifts, but the same Spirit; and there are varieties of services, but the same Lord; and there are varieties of activities, but it is the same God who activates all of them in everyone.'
- 1 Peter 4: 'Like good stewards of the manifold grace of God, serve one another with whatever gift each of you has received. Whoever speaks must do so as one speaking the very words of God; whoever serves must do so with the strength that God supplies.'
- And so on.

Unity

Notice that none of these gifts is exclusive to just one group of Christians; all are open to everyone. The Greek word for presents is *charismata*. In which case, every Christian is a charismatic. The Bible says it is wicked to argue about what sort of worship you prefer – you don't come to church to do what you want, but what God wants. But God promises to give you whatever qualities of character or personality you need, to be successful in whatever task God sets you today. That's what Pentecost means; that's what the

Holy Spirit is all about; and the Spirit is available to you anytime you need help. If ever one of my sermons moves you, don't thank me – well, you can if you want to – but remember the words are not mine, but what the Holy Spirit gives me to say.

All-age worship

List the gifts of the Spirit in 1 Corinthians 12.8–10 and Romans 12.6–8. Pray for those you will need today.

Suggested hymns

Gracious Spirit, Holy Ghost; O thou who camest from above; Our blest Redeemer, ere he breathed; Wind, wind, blow on me.

Day of Pentecost (Whit Sunday)   4 June
Second Service   Visions and Dreams
Morning Ps. 87 As they dance; Evening Ps. 67 God bless us, 133 Anointing; Joel 2.21–32 I will pour out my Spirit; Acts 2.14–21 [22–38] Fulfilment of prophecy; *Gospel at Holy Communion*: Luke 24.44–53 Power from on high

'In the last days it will be, God declares, that I will pour out my Spirit upon all flesh, and your sons and your daughters shall prophesy, and your young men shall see visions, and your old men shall dream dreams. Even upon my slaves, both men and women, in those days I will pour out my Spirit; and they shall prophesy.' Acts 2.17–18

Marginalized

We have a tendency, these days, to listen only to people who think like we do. That means that we marginalize many people from whose ideas we could learn a lot. 'Oh, he's too young,' we say. 'He hasn't lived; he has no experience.' And we ignore the views of the elderly, because they are 'past it'. Thereby we miss the opportunity to hear some imaginative new ideas, or to learn from people who have long years of experience behind them. We also tend to ignore the working class, and the uneducated. Men hardly notice the opinions of women, and, to a lesser extent, vice versa.

Pentecost

But the Day of Pentecost has put an end to all that. On that day, St Peter addressed a crowd of 3,000 people – quite an experience for a Galilean fisherman who had never spoken in public before – and told them that the experience of the Holy Spirit, which they have all enjoyed, is a fulfilment of the prophecy of Joel. Notice that Joel foresees what will happen 'in the last days', and they have just experienced it. So *these* days are the last days: not sometime in the distant future, but the period of history which began with the resurrection of Jesus, and in which we live today. Then, observe that the prophet promises that the Holy Spirit will be poured out 'upon all flesh'. Not just the Jews, not a select few, not just on people like us. The Spirit speaks for God through the mouths of people we have hitherto ignored and despised. Some examples are given: God will speak through young people, old people, uneducated, working-class people, who in those days were usually slaves, and through '*both* men *and* women'.

Young

Actually, Joel promised that 'your sons and daughters shall prophesy . . . and your young men shall see visions'. St Peter ran those two phrases into one. The meaning is clear, though: young, inexperienced people, whose opinions we have so far ignored, will speak with a new insight, giving us a picture of what the future ought to be. Prophets very rarely have a magical certainty about what *will* happen; usually they hold up for us a vision of what the future *ought* to hold for us, if we will only listen to what God is saying through his Spirit in our hearts, and *act upon* it. Young people, whose minds are not cluttered up with ancient prejudices, can often catch a glimpse of the ideal society, which their elders have been blind to for years. Go to it, youngsters! Show us your vision of what the future should hold, and inspire us to help you build it, if not in our lifetime, then if possible when you have taken charge of things, and we, the elders, are dead and gone.

Old

But the older generation have something to teach us, too. They can dream dreams, from which we all can learn. They can dream of happy times gone by, and warn us what we have lost when we gave up the values with which they grew up. They can dream of a society where all is compassion, caring and love, and urge us to keep pressing on towards that goal.

Poor

There is a widespread delusion that the only people who can tell us how the country should be run are the rich. Whereas all that many of them are interested in is how to make themselves even richer. It is the poor, who suffer from the wide inequality of society, who should set the priorities for a fairer distribution of wealth. And it is the women who still suffer from lower pay, the glass ceiling and sexual abuse who can advise us on equality and protection. The Bible is a remarkably feminist document for its time.

Empowerment

So it is the Holy Spirit, given at Pentecost, which can bring power to the powerless, and causes us to listen to the marginalized. Young and old, rich and poor, male and female, we all need to listen to each other, and hear the Spirit of God speaking through the mouths of those we had never listened to before.

Suggested hymns

Breathe on me, breath of God; Come down, O Love Divine; Spirit of God, unseen as the wind; Spirit of holiness (Blow the wind southerly).

Trinity Sunday   11 June
Principal Service   Fellowship
Isa. 40.12–17, 27–31 The greatness of God; Ps. 8 Stewardship of nature; 2 Cor. 13.11–13 God, Jesus and the Holy Spirit; Matt. 28.16–20 Baptism in the name of the Trinity

> *'Agree with one another, live in peace; and the God of love and peace will be with you . . . The grace of the Lord Jesus Christ, the love of God, and the communion of the Holy Spirit be with all of you.' 2 Corinthians 13.11, 13*

Yeats

The Irish poet W. B. Yeats wrote a poem called 'The Indian upon God', suggesting that just as human beings imagine God as a human being, so other animals may imagine God as being like them. The poem reads like this:

I passed along the water's edge below the humid trees,
My spirit rocked in evening light, the rushes round my knees,
My spirit rocked in sleep and sighs; and saw the moor-fowl pace
All dripping on a grassy slope, and saw them cease to chase
Each other round in circles, and heard the eldest speak:
Who holds the world between His bill and made us strong or weak
Is an undying moorfowl, and He lives beyond the sky.
The rains are from His dripping wing, the moonbeams from
His eye.
I passed a little further on and heard a lotus talk:
Who made the world and ruleth it, He hangeth on a stalk,
For I am in His image made, and all this tinkling tide
Is but a sliding drop of rain between His petals wide.
A little way within the gloom a roebuck raised his eyes
Brimful of starlight, and he said: *The Stamper of the Skies,*
He is a gentle roebuck; for how else, I pray, could He
Conceive a thing so sad and soft, a gentle thing like me?
I passed a little further on and heard a peacock say:
Who made the grass and made the worms and made my
feathers gay,
He is a monstrous peacock, and He waveth all the night
His languid tail above us, lit with myriad spots of light.

Fellowship

I think that is very beautiful. But – although thinking of God as a human being, like us, may be the beginning of a relationship between us – in fact, God is much greater than that, and Christians teach in our creeds that God is three Persons in one God. So God is not a man, or even a woman, but much more like a community, a group of people living together in fellowship.

Trinity

Today is Trinity Sunday. The doctrine of the Holy Trinity is not just dry theology and word-twisting. If God resembles three Persons joined together in a loving relationship, and we are made in God's image, then as long as we remain isolated individuals, too proud to speak to anyone else, we are missing our vocation and failing to achieve our potential. God made us to live together with other human beings as families, fellowships and communities. Perhaps what God wants of us is for all the world to live together as one happy family – that is what we mean when we pray that God's kingdom may come on earth, as it is in heaven. Communities are more effective than individuals; the Old Testament book of Ecclesiastes says that 'though one might prevail against another, two will withstand one. A threefold cord is not quickly broken.' So the three-in-one God is an image for human community.

St Paul

St Paul ends his second letter to the Christians in Corinth with an appeal for the squabbling church members in that city to learn to live together in harmony: 'Agree with one another, live in peace; and the God of love and peace will be with you.' He sums it up with the words we know as 'the Grace', which, although the word 'Trinity' is not found in the Bible, are as perfect an enunciation of that doctrine as you could ask for. I shall say it alone first:

The grace of [our] Lord Jesus Christ, [and] the love of God, and the [fellowship] of the Holy Spirit be with [us] all, [evermore. Amen.]

Then will you please stand, and repeat it together, with your eyes open, turning your head and smiling at as many people as you can, so as to deepen our sense of being a fellowship, just as God the Trinity is:

Together: **The grace of our Lord Jesus Christ, and the love of God, and the fellowship of the Holy Spirit be with us all, ever-more. Amen.**

All-age worship

Tie each end of a short length of knitting wool to a stick for a handle, and pull till it breaks. Repeat with three lengths twisted together. Which is harder to break? Learn the Grace by heart.

Suggested hymns

Father of heaven, whose love profound; Firmly I believe and truly; Holy, holy, holy! Lord God Almighty!; Majesty, worship his majesty.

Trinity Sunday   11 June

(*For Corpus Christi, the Thursday after Trinity Sunday, see page 329.*)

Second Service   **Incomprehensible**

Morning Ps. 86.8–13 No God like you; Evening Ps. 93 God's majesty, 150 Praise God in his sanctuary; Isa. 6.1–8 Holy, holy, holy; John 16.5–15 The Father, Jesus and the Advocate

> *'[Jesus said,] "Now I am going to him who sent me; yet none of you asks me, 'Where are you going?' . . . Nevertheless I tell you the truth: it is to your advantage that I go away, for if I do not go away, the Advocate will not come to you; but if I go, I will send him to you."' John 16.5, 7*

Athanasian Creed

In the Book of Common Prayer, Common Worship and many of the service books of the Roman Catholic, Lutheran and many of the other 'Liturgical Protestant' Churches, there occurs a document known as the Athanasian Creed. You probably did not know that, as it is very rarely used in public worship. It is a very long exposition of the doctrine of the Holy Trinity, and the Book of Common Prayer version contains the words:

> The Father incomprehensible, the Son incomprehensible: and the Holy Ghost incomprehensible.

Many an unwilling student of theology, forced to read this boring work, has exploded, saying, 'The whole blooming thing is incomprehensible', or words to that effect! But in fact the *Quicunque vult*, to give it its Latin name, does not mean that the doctrine is impossible to understand. To 'comprehend' something originally meant to contain that thing within a particular space. So the document is saying that the nature of God is too great to be contained within our little brains.

Negative theology

Some teachers say that God is so great, and we are so small, that all we can say about God is the sort of negative statement like 'God is not weak', 'God does not hate us', and so on. So we can never expect to understand the positive doctrine of the Trinity, God the Father, Jesus God's Son, and the Holy Spirit of God in our hearts. Nevertheless, it is an important teaching, and we need to have a rough idea of what it is all about.

Bible

Although the word 'Trinity' never appears in the Bible, Jesus often spoke of God as his Father, saying 'I and the Father are one', and promised to send us the Holy Spirit of God, whom he calls 'the Advocate'. An Advocate is a lawyer called to your side, to help you to defend yourself against false accusations, and to help you present a powerful case when you are trying to persuade others of what you believe in. So God the Creator is God; Jesus, whose story is told in the Gospels, is God; and the Spirit of God in our hearts, who inspires us, is God. Yet there are not three Gods, but only one God. So 'three Persons in one God' is the only way we can describe our experience of the Divine.

Essence

Before Abraham, and in some places still today, there were people who believed that every tribe had its own god, who could be at loggerheads with the god of another tribe, and would expect his own tribe to fight together with him against the followers of the other god. You would pray to the god of love on Tuesdays and the god of war on Fridays, so there was no absolute standard of morality. But the Jews were chosen to teach the rest of the world that there is only one God for everybody, who wants us all to be kind to each other; though they never really grasped this till Jesus came. The Christian teaching that we experience God in three ways, as our Maker, Friend and Inspirer, could undermine this, unless we emphasize that nonetheless there is only one God.

Cultures

Jesus explained this in a Jewish way, calling himself the Messiah, the Son of God. When the Church spread into the Roman Empire, they had to try to translate this into words which philosophers would understand. Aristotle had said that everything has its accidental appearance, but also an underlying nature which it shared with all objects of the same type; he called these the 'accidents' and the 'substance'. But those words mean nothing to us today, when Aristotle is almost forgotten, so we have to retranslate them into words which people of today will understand. I suggest that to talk about the one God for everybody, who shows his or her love for us in three different ways, God the creator, God in Jesus, God in our hearts, will have to do, to be going on with. Even those who know nothing about philosophy shouldn't find that completely 'incomprehensible'.

Suggested hymns

Bright the vision that delighted; Immortal, invisible, God only wise; O worship the king; There is a Redeemer.

ORDINARY TIME

There is no such thing as ordinary time! Although the Sundays after Trinity, and occasionally a couple of those of Epiphany, bear that title, each Sunday is in its own way unique. If the Old Testament reading and psalm at the Principal Service are marked '(Related)', they reflect the same theme as the New Testament reading and Gospel. If they are marked '(Continuous)', they follow a book of the Old Testament chapter by chapter, Sunday by Sunday. At the Second Service, too, there are themes running through the readings each week, and the congregation will be helped to meditate on what God is telling us through the readings if the sermon and the hymns are on the same subject.

Each of the sermons in each annual volume of *The Canterbury Preacher's Companion* is followed by a list of four suggested hymns, based on the theme of the sermon, which is of course on the theme of at least one of the readings. They are drawn from a variety of traditions and hymnals, so you may find that the congregation is not familiar with all of them. One new hymn in a service, repeated a few weeks later, and again after that until it has become familiar, is all right; any more than that, or new hymns every Sunday, and people will become fed up; they feed on familiarity. Most hymnals have an index of Sundays, an index of readings and an index of themes, or at least one of these. You can start by looking to see what hymns are suggested for the services on one particular Sunday, at the Principal Service. But not all of them are appropriate to the reading on which the sermon is based. So then look up that reading in the Scripture index, to find hymns which are relevant. Or your hymnal may have an index of themes, so that you can see all the hymns about love, or forgiveness, or whatever. It is good to buy a copy of *Sing God's Glory* (Canterbury Press), giving suggested hymns from many hymnbooks for the Principal Service on each Sunday of the year in the Revised Common Lectionary, and *Sunday by Sunday* (Canterbury Press) which does the same for the Second Service. Then none of your services, even in Ordinary Time, will be commonplace, but each will be a fascinating exploration of some new aspect of God's love.

First Sunday after Trinity (Proper 6)   18 June
Principal Service   **There Could Be Trouble Ahead**

(*Continuous*): Gen. 18.1–15 [21.1–7] Abraham entertains the strangers, Ps. 116.1, 10–17 (*or* 116.9–17) Thanks *or* (*Related*): Ex. 19.2–8a A kingdom of priests, Ps. 100 Worship in the Temple; Rom. 5.1–8 While we were sinners, Matt. 9.35—10.8 [9–23] Witness to the kingdom

> '*Jesus went about all the cities and villages, teaching in their synagogues, and proclaiming the good news of the kingdom, and curing every disease and every sickness. When he saw the crowds, he had compassion for them, because they were harassed and helpless, like sheep without a shepherd.' Matthew 9.35–36*

Kingdom

Jesus went round proclaiming the good news about the kingdom of God. The Jews he was talking to knew what that meant. Their first king had been King David. He led them into battle, and drove out all the enemies who were invading their country. But during the exile of the Jews in Babylon, the last descendant of David was killed, and the royal line died out. When they returned to their homeland, it was invaded and ruled, first by the Greeks, then by the Romans, and they were no longer a free and independent people. They hated this, and dreamt that one day a new monarch would arise, a military genius who would call them to arms and drive their enemies out of their country. So when Jesus told them that the kingdom of God would arrive any day now, they raised a cheer, confident that he was about to start a bloody revolution.

Enemies

But he didn't. Instead, he wasted his time, as they saw it, in healing the sick, cheering up the depressed, and waffling on about love. That was never going to drive the Romans out of their land. Meanwhile, the Romans were becoming thoroughly scared. If this Jesus fellow claimed he would bring in a new kingdom, he must be a dangerous revolutionary. If the people listened to him, they would soon have a riot on their hands, and Palestine would become a battle zone. Jesus had to be silenced; but if they arrested him, their empire would fall apart. But the priests were also scared, because if there was a revolution, they would lose their positions of power. As Nat King Cole sang, 'There could be trouble ahead!'

Love

But they completely misunderstood what sort of revolution Jesus was talking about. It was to an overturning of people's attitudes and beliefs. He demonstrated a strategy of care for the weak, and healing of the ills of society. The Jews thought the Romans were their enemies, did they? Then they must learn to love their enemies, said the Prince of Peace. It was the most world-shatteringly political statement that he or anybody else had ever made. If put into practice, it really would turn the world upside down. Which is why most people ignored it then, and still do today. 'Love your enemies, indeed? What nonsense! If you are weak, they will defeat you, and take away everything you possess.' That's what most people think. But it all depends on what you mean by love. Love is not weak; it is the most powerful force on earth. If you actively seek the well-being of everybody, whether you like them or not, and however you hate their policies, they will be baffled. We can tolerate their different opinions, without allowing them to hurt others. The kingdom of God will be a kingdom of love. Because of this teaching, his followers did not raise a riot when he died, but tried to bring Jew and Gentile together in love.

Reconciliation

Whom do you regard as your enemies today? On a personal level, on a community level, a national and an international level? What could you do to show that you care for them as human beings, just like us underneath all their aggression? Would that also have the effect of showing them that we, too, are human beings, just like they are. What is needed is a strategy of reconciliation, and a kingdom of love. We need to work towards that, otherwise there certainly will be trouble ahead. Most people don't believe such policies would work, because they have never been tried. But Jesus told his disciples:

> Proclaim the good news, 'The kingdom of heaven has come near. Cure the sick, raise the dead, cleanse the lepers, cast out demons. You received without payment; give without payment.'

I think he meant us to heal those with sick attitudes, bring those in whom all compassion has died back to life, bring the outcasts back into society, drive the demonic forces of selfishness from people's hearts, and share what we have with the needy. That really would be heaven on earth!

All-age worship

Make paper crowns. Write on them 'A prince (or princess) in the kingdom of love'.

Suggested hymns

O Lord, all the world belongs to you; The Church of God a kingdom is; The kingdom is upon you; Thy kingdom come! On bended knee.

First Sunday after Trinity (Proper 6)   18 June
Second Service   The Return of the Demon
Ps. [42 Like a deer] 43 The altar of God; 1 Sam. 21.1–15
Feigning madness; Luke 11.14–28 The return of the demon

> '[Jesus said,] "When the unclean spirit has gone out of a person, it wanders through waterless regions looking for a resting-place, but not finding any, it says, 'I will return to my house from which I came.' When it comes, it finds it swept and put in order. Then it goes and brings seven other spirits more evil than itself, and they enter and live there; and the last state of that person is worse than the first."' Luke 11.24–26

Demons

In the time of Jesus, most people believed in demons. If somebody was angry, aggressive and violent, that person might claim to be blameless, because it was the fault of a demon that possessed them. Jesus accepted this, and authoritatively instructed the demons to depart. Then a great calm came over the person who had claimed to be possessed, who believed the demons had now left them. Thus Jesus became famous as a successful exorcist.

Language

In the Old Testament, the same word covered both good and evil spirits; we translate it 'angel', and the belief grew that bad spirits were fallen angels. In the book of Genesis, divine beings come to earth to mate with human women. But in Greek thought, good angels and evil demons were quite different, and the word 'demon', which had meant a minor god, was transferred to evil spirits. When Jesus came to earth, he used the language which people around him spoke, without wasting time by questioning their assumptions. So it may be true that evil spirits exist, because Jesus said so. Or alternatively, when the Son of God took human form, he may have described what we now call psychological illness as demon possession, because that was the only terminology the people he met could understand. He could not tell a sick man, 'You have severe bipolar disorder,' because they would not have understood him. The doctor must always use words which the patient can grasp. Psychiatry or demonology? Maybe we can never say that one is true and the other is false; they are just alternative languages. If God calls us to heal a person who believes they are possessed, we had better explain to them that the power of Jesus is stronger than any other power, and then call for an experienced and trustworthy person to perform an exorcism.

Science

Many people with limited education probably still believe in demons. But in the developed world, most probably reject that way of speaking as laughably outmoded. God calls us Christians to minister to both types of people. So we should not argue with either group, but speak to each of them in their own tongue. It is no use trying to convince conservative Christians that the words Jesus used were merely figurative; but we shall never persuade people who use psycho-speak of the truth of Christianity if we use demon language in speaking to them. The first thing we need to persuade everyone of, is to take evil seriously. For a while, philosophers taught that there is no difference between good and evil; but none of them speak that way now. There are processes in our brains, and forces which seek to influence our minds, which are definitely harmful, and we must all pray in the words of Jesus, 'Do not allow us to give way to temptation, but deliver us from evil.'

Something in its place

Jesus told a story, which we have just heard in our reading, about somebody who *had* been demon-possessed, but who was exorcised. But – and this is the crux of the story – nothing was put into his mind to fill the vacuum which the departing demon had left. The demon, finding no resting place in the outside world, decided to return to its former home in the patient's head. But rather than go there alone, he recommended the patient's brain – and remember that this is fiction with a moral – to seven of his devilish friends as a desirable residence for demons, and they moved in together. Then, in the memorable words of the Gospel, 'the last state of that person was worse than the first'. That is a warning which we should all heed. When you are cured of a bad habit, an addiction, a psychosis or neurosis, you must always *put something in it's place*! Something positive, calming and therapeutic. The best thing, of course, is faith in the abundant love of God. That is stronger than any evil force that has ever attacked anyone.

Suggested hymns

A mighty fortress is our God; Christ triumphant, ever reigning; Do not be afraid, for I have redeemed you; God moves in a mysterious way.

Second Sunday after Trinity (Proper 7)   25 June
Principal Service   **Do Not Be Afraid**
(*Continuous*): Gen. 21.8–21 Hagar, Ps. 86.1–10, 16–17 All nations; or (*Related*): Jer. 20.7–13 Jeremiah's prayer, Ps. 69.8–11 [12–17] 18–20 Zeal for the Temple; Rom. 6.1b–11 Dead to sin and alive to God; Matt. 10.24–39 His eye on the sparrow

> '[Jesus said to his disciples,] "Are not two sparrows sold for a penny? Yet not one of them will fall to the ground unperceived by your Father . . . So do not be afraid; you are of more value than many sparrows."' Matthew 10.29, 31

Fear

What are you most afraid of? Now come on, everybody is afraid of something, and the first step to overcoming that fear is to admit to yourself that you are scared. Your fears may be quite insignificant; or else what the psychologists call 'phobias'; yet in either case there is a path to dealing with them, and I am going to lead you along that path today. So what are your particular fears? Fear of water? Spiders? Public speaking? Heights? Criticism? Mockery? Making a fool of yourself? Pain? I'll let you into a secret: there is at least one of those that I am subject to – but I shan't tell you which one it is!

Admit it

The first step in dealing with any fear is to admit to yourself that you are afraid. Don't bury your fears down in the subconscious, they will only come back later and bite you. But if you face up to them, you can deal with them. Yes, really! Fears are like addictions in that respect; you cannot deal with them until you accept that you have a problem, and decide that you want to be rid of it.

Step by step

Then you have to face up to the thing you fear very gently, step by step. Look at a dead spider in a museum. Try speaking a sentence or two to a small group of your family and friends. Try jumping off a low stool – that sort of thing. Then, very gradually, increase the challenge: step into the shallow end of the pool, then each day go a foot deeper. By facing up to your phobias and being gentle with yourself, you will find you have a courage you never knew existed.

Sharing

The final step is to share your problem with somebody you can trust to be sympathetic. Someone you know has confidence in you, and will encourage you by being sympathetic. Best of all, share it with Jesus. In today's Gospel reading, he told his friends not to be afraid of anything, because God our heavenly Father loves each one of us.

Sparrows

He reassured us of that by talking about sparrows. In those days people ate almost anything if they were hungry enough. But of all the meat sources sold in the market, the sparrow was the cheapest. In modern translations they are two-a-penny; the Authorized King James Version talked about farthings. So nobody bothered when a creature as worthless as that died – except that God did. Jesus tells us that, although millions of birds, animals and fish die every day as part of the food chain, the infinite God cares for every single one of them. They, like us, when they are attacked, have to choose between fight or flight. The only difference with human beings is that we can worry about the pain in advance, and complain about how unfair it is. But that only makes the all-loving God love us more.

Recipe

The epitaph of the Scottish reformer John Knox read: 'Here lies one who feared God so much that he never feared the face of any man.' So the ultimate answer to the problem of fear is to trust God. 'Put your hand in the hand of the man who ruled the water.' Believe that you are precious to God, like everything he has made, but more than the rest precisely because you can have a conversation with God and ask for his help. Believe in God; remember that God believes in you. God knows more about you than you know about yourself, even to the number of hairs on your head. God knows that he has put in you the courage to grit your teeth, hold his hand, and go ahead to do the thing you were so frightened of before. That was then; now is now; and now you have the Holy Spirit in you to give you exactly as much courage as you need. What a wonderful God he is!

All-age worship

Compare an old teddy bear with a new one. Which is worth more at an auction? Which is worth more to the child who loves it? How much are you worth to the God who loves you?

Suggested hymns

Awake, our souls, away our fears; Do not be afraid, for I have redeemed you; Fear not, rejoice and be glad; Take up thy cross, the Saviour said.

173

Second Sunday after Trinity (Proper 7) 25 June
Second Service Too Busy

Ps. 46 God makes wars cease [48 Walk about Zion]; 1 Sam. 24.1–17 David spares Saul; Luke 14.12–24 Dinner guests, excuses

'But they all alike began to make excuses.' Luke 14.18

Silence

Archbishop Justin Welby has written that he starts the day with prayerful meditation on the Scriptures: reading a passage slowly and thinking about what it prompts him to pray about. That is very different from what many Christians call prayer, which is gabbling off a series of requests with hardly time to draw breath, and then complaining when they don't get what they ask for. But many people think they are too busy to spend time in silence with God. Like the people invited to a party in the parable, they all make excuses.

Shopping list

There is a place in our prayers for asking God to supply the needs of those worse off than us, and for requesting our daily bread. But prayer must never become a shopping list, telling God what we want him to do. Instead we should be waiting on God patiently, until God tells us what *he* wants *us* to do. Prayer is volunteering for God's agenda, not dictating yours to God. We must sit in silence until God tells us what he wants from us. This needs patience, courage and strength – doing nothing can actually be quite hard work!

Psalms

Psalm 46 is a song for troubled times. The nations are in an uproar, and the kingdoms are shaken. Whither can God's people flee? 'Only to God', answers the Psalmist. 'God is our refuge and strength,' the song begins – 'a very present help in trouble.' Martin Luther, when he was weary of the turmoil of the Reformation, sought refuge in the castle called the Wartburg [vahtboorg], and while he was there paraphrased Psalm 46 into the great hymn which we know in English as 'A safe stronghold our God is still'.

Entering

But if God is the refuge to which we can escape the trials and tribulations of this weary world, where is the entrance? How do we find our way into 'the peace of God, which passes all understanding'? The only way into the stillness is to learn the art of silent prayer. We feel desperate, and want God to take immediate action against the things which are troubling us. We beat our fists against heaven's gate in our agonized praying. But God very wisely does nothing until we calm down, stop shouting, and leave everything to him. Then, as we learn to control our clamouring, God comes to us in the silence and pours his peace into our hearts. Then, as we look at our worries again in the stillness, God shows us that our agitation is not the answer to our problems, but may be part of the cause. When we calm down, then God's peace can enter into our hearts, and he will give us the inner strength to cope with our dilemmas in his way, not our own.

Intentions

It is not easy to find a silent place to pray. In the days when women wore large aprons, the mother of a big family used to sit down and pull her apron over her head; then all the family knew she was praying and they had to keep quiet. But the problem is that many of us are not very good at being quiet. We shut the noise out, and think of God, and before long our mind has gone down all sorts of irrelevant sidetracks. We have to learn to be silent. A woman visiting New York told the taxi-driver she was a cellist, and, wanting to be in the audience for a concert, she asked him, 'How do I get into the Carnegie Hall?' Thinking that she wanted to perform, he replied, 'Practice, lady, lots of practice!' And to be successful in the use of silence, too, we need practice, lots of practice. A wise spiritual director, though, once told someone who complained of wandering thoughts in worship, 'Perhaps God is telling you to pray for whatever you started thinking of. So do that, and then gently bring your thoughts back to what you should have been thinking of. God rewards you for your intention to do something good, and he is ready to forgive you if you do not achieve what you intended to immediately.'

Peace

Amid all the seething turmoil of the world, remember that God said, 'I will be exalted among the nations; I will be exalted in the earth.' All we have to do is 'Be still and know that I am God.'

Suggested hymns

A safe stronghold our God is still; Be still, for the presence of the Lord; Be still my soul (Finlandia); Prayer is the soul's sincere desire.

Third Sunday after Trinity (Proper 8)   2 July
Principal Service   **A Cup of Cold Water**

(*Continuous*): Gen. 22.1–14 The sacrifice of Isaac, Ps. 13 How long? or (*Related*): Jer. 28.5–9 True prophecy, Ps. 89.1–4, 15–18 Covenant with David; Rom. 6.12–23 Freed from sin; Matt. 10.40–42 A cup of cold water

> *'[Jesus said,] "Whoever welcomes you welcomes me; and whoever welcomes me welcomes the one who sent me. Whoever welcomes God's messenger because he is God's messenger, will share in his reward. And whoever welcomes a good man because he is good, will share in his reward. You can be sure that whoever gives even a drink of cold water to one of the least of these my followers because he is my follower, will certainly receive a reward."'*
> Matthew 10.40–42, Good News Bible

Translation

I read today's Gospel from a modern translation, because the New Revised Standard Version is a fairly literal translation of the words which Jesus spoke. To Jesus, the words 'in the name of a prophet' meant 'because they are a prophet', and 'prophet' was a common word for anyone who proclaims the words of God.

Messenger

Jesus referred to a common attitude in his day: if anybody brings you a message from the king, you should treat the messenger as respectfully as you would treat the king. Honouring the messenger is honouring the one who sent them. So in this passage, Jesus is calling on the people to respect his 12 apostles, who preached his message, with the honour due to Jesus himself. In fact any preacher, any Christian who speaks about Jesus to their friends, is acting as a messenger for Jesus, and should be treated with respect. The words in the older translations, 'one of these little ones', seems to have meant 'any follower of Jesus, however humble and insignificant'. So he is telling us we should each treat other Christians as though Jesus himself had come to visit us. Of course, that *does* include small children; if we give any child a drink of cold water, for Jesus's sake, because Jesus loves us all equally, then that act of kindness is as praiseworthy as if we had given the water to Jesus himself.

Kindness

Jesus said that any kind deed, no matter if it is done to somebody quite ordinary and insignificant, will receive a reward. Now if you expect to receive a reward here on earth for the kind things you have done, you will probably be disappointed. No, he was probably referring to 'rewards in heaven', after we die, when we are all together again and together with Jesus, our Saviour and our loving friend. So this is a direct statement from Jesus that each of us, if we repent of our sins, will live in a much better universe than the one we live in now. And if there is a judgement before we get there, it is to forgive us our unloving actions, and reward us for every little kindness we have given.

Chaplain

A retired priest was acting as Visitors' Chaplain in an English cathedral, when a visitor asked him, 'Do you know who is taking the mid day Communion service? If it's a woman priest I'm not staying!' The chaplain replied sternly, 'I don't know and I don't care – I have no problem with women priests.' Then, when he had just got out his lunchtime sandwiches, the vergers told him that the priest who was supposed to come had been delayed, and asked the chaplain to take the service instead. He did this, and returned to the back of the church, only to find that his sandwiches had disappeared – a homeless man had eaten them! The Dean, when she was told this story, assured him that he would be rewarded for three kind deeds: taking the service, giving the homeless man his lunch, and . . . not being a woman priest!

Rewards

In fact, we do good deeds not in hope of a reward, but in gratitude to Jesus for his kindness to us. The promise of a reward is an added bonus. We shall certainly be rewarded if we make grand plans which make the world a better place; but equally, we shall have a reward even for giving a drink to somebody who was thirsty. A loving disposition, in a Christian, witnesses to unbelievers that we believe in a God of love, and are returning God's love in the only way we know how. We must also learn how to receive kindnesses graciously. As the hymn says: 'Pray that I may have the grace to let you be my servant, too.' Take the cup of cold water if it is offered to you, for that will ensure your benefactor a reward in heaven. Simple gifts are best.

All-age worship

At the end of the sermon, offer a cup of cold water to everyone in church.

Suggested hymns

Brother, sister, let me serve you; Our Saviour's infant cries were heard; Strengthen for service, Lord, the hands; Where cross the crowded ways of life.

Third Sunday after Trinity (Proper 8)   2 July
Second Service   **Punishment**
Ps. 50 A sacrifice of thanksgiving; 1 Sam. 28.3–19 The witch of Endor; Luke 17.20–37 The coming of the kingdom

> '[Jesus said,] "Those who try to make their life secure will lose it, but those who lose their life will keep it. I tell you, on that night there will be two in one bed; one will be taken and the other left. There will be two women grinding meal together; one will be taken and the other left."' Luke 17.33–36

Deadheading

This is the time of year when, if the British climate is not having one of its hissy-fits, those of you lucky enough to have a garden with roses in it should be out there doing what we call 'deadheading' the roses. This involves recognizing those blossoms which are now effectually dead, and nipping off the dead bits with secateurs or with your fingers. Now if the rose plant was a human being you would describe that as cruel and heartless. Fancy cutting off a person's hope for the future, just because they are a bit unsightly. But roses do not have feelings; so those reservations need not bother us. If you left the dead buds on the plant, they would absorb some of the energy which is flowing up in the sap, and use it for making seeds. But nobody grows roses from seeds these days, it is always from a cutting. So leaving the useless dead parts still on the rose bush is hindering the growth of new flowers, and next year's sprouts. You could say it was cruel not to deadhead a rosebush.

Punishment

That illuminates what we mean by punishment. When somebody does something wrong it usually harms either their own body or that of somebody else. Of course the harm may be mental or spiritual rather than physical, but it is nonetheless destructive. Religious people are supposed to be compassionate and forgiving. But if we pay no attention when somebody harms other people, that would be cruel, because it would appear that we didn't care about the harm the bad person has done. So we ask the offender to say they are sorry and make restitution to those whom they have hurt. We give them as light a punishment as we dare, not to seek revenge, but

- to deter the criminal and others from ever doing that crime again,
- to give them a chance to learn how to live better lives, and
- to bring closure to their own feelings of guilt.

So compassionate punishment is a bit like deadheading the roses: it gives them a better chance of growing and flourishing in the future.

God

The same applies when we complain that God is punishing us. The loving God gets no pleasure out of causing us pain. But if he totally ignored the bad things we do, we would say that God was

179

unjust and cruel, as though he did not care about those who suffer because of other people's cruelty. God must deter people from doing bad things again, or from starting to do bad things in the first place, because we see that it brings the wrongdoer nothing but pain and distress. God is not cruel, but he has to protect other people from the harm we might do them and express his displeasure when we do things he has warned us, for our own sake, not to do.

Readings

Today's readings seem to be full of God's punishment. Psalm 50 is about God calling to the heavens above and to the earth, that he may judge his people. In the story of the witch of Endor, King Saul asks a spiritualist medium to give him hope that he will not be punished for his crimes, but the ghost of the prophet Samuel, whom she summons, tells him he *must* be punished. As with most of us, God does not cause us to suffer as a punishment for our selfish deeds; we are capable of hurting ourselves by our own actions. But he may deny us some pleasure we had been looking forward to, just to show us how seriously God takes our misdoings. And in the Gospel, Jesus tells us that when the kingdom of God comes, 'on that night there will be two in one bed; one will be taken and the other left. There will be two women grinding meal together; one will be taken and the other left.'

Self-punishment

All these readings at one service might give the impression of a very harsh God. But remember, these sufferings are a judgement we bring upon ourselves, and a severe warning of the danger of our wrongdoing. God is only deadheading the roses he loves, to make them grow better.

Suggested hymns

Hark, what a sound, and too divine for hearing; Soon and very soon; The kingdom of God is justice and joy; Thy kingdom come, O God.

Fourth Sunday after Trinity (Proper 9)   9 July
Principal Service   **Restless Without God**

(*Continuous*): Gen. 24.34–38, 42–49, 58–67 Rebecca betrothed, Ps. 45.10–17 A royal wedding, *or Canticle*: S. of Sol. 2.8–13, Love and springtime; *or* (*Related*): Zech. 9.9–12 Rejoice, Ps. 145.8–15 God's kingdom and love; Rom. 7.15–25a Judgement and the law of God; Matt. 11.16–19, 25–30 John the Baptist

> '[Jesus said,] "Come to me, all you that are weary and are carrying heavy burdens, and I will give you rest."' Matthew 11.28

Augustine

He spent his youth, like so many other young people, in the restless pursuit of pleasure. He studied at university, went to parties, he got drunk, he chased women. He had a long-term mistress, who cleaned and cooked for him, and even bore him a son, but he never married her. Yet in spite of all this self-indulgence he was never satisfied. 'There must be more to life than this,' he thought. So he read the philosophers, and learnt that life was a struggle between light and darkness. The whole material world and the desires of the flesh were the realm of darkness, and we must have nothing to do with it. So he ditched his mistress without providing for her, and set off on a teaching career. His name was Augustine, and he was born in North Africa during the Roman Empire. He went to lecture in Rome, and then Milan, but there was still this inner struggle. The oriental religion of Manichaeism, from which he had learnt his ideas, did not tell him how to put them into practice. He listened to the sermons of Bishop Ambrose of Milan, and wondered whether Christianity was the answer. One day he heard a child singing, 'Take up and read, take up and read!' He picked up a copy of the Bible, and it fell open at the words, 'not in reveling and drunkenness, not in debauchery and licentiousness, not in quarreling and jealousy. Instead, put on the Lord Jesus Christ, and make no provision for the flesh, to gratify its desires.' He and his son were baptized, to the relief of his Christian mother Monica who never stopped praying for him. Eventually he went home to North Africa, where he was made bishop of a town called 'Hippo', which means 'horse'.

Confessions

Ten years after his conversion, he wrote an autobiography, which concentrated on his feelings, and took the form of a long prayer to God. A famous phrase lies at the heart of the story, when he says to God: 'You have made us for yourself, and our hearts are restless, until they find rest in you.'

Restlessness

I wonder whether you sometimes have feelings of restlessness? Maybe you are depressed. Or perhaps you are normally happy, but questions keep crossing your mind like, 'What am I here for?' 'What is the meaning of life?' 'Is there anything beyond this life?' These are good questions to ask – because Jesus has the answer.

'Come'

Jesus looks you in the face when you are at your lowest, and says to you:

Come to me, all you that are weary and are carrying heavy burdens, and I will give you rest. Take my yoke upon you, and learn from me; for I am gentle and humble in heart, and you will find rest for your souls. For my yoke is easy, and my burden is light.

It is not easy being a Christian. But it is a far lighter burden to carry than that of being an unbeliever, with all the uncertainties and doubt that go with agnosticism. If you know that Jesus loves you, you are never alone. The purpose of your life is to love Jesus in return, and love everybody else for his sake; and at the end of the road lies a life of joy and happiness, free from worry, with Jesus and all those whom you love in the unimaginable life we call 'heaven'. So respond to the invitation which Jesus offers you, come to him and throw down that sackful of restless worries you have been carrying on your back all these years. Say 'Amen' to this prayer, which is an amalgam of the sayings of St Augustine of Hippo:

Almighty God, in whom we live and move and have our being, you have made us for yourself, so that our hearts are restless till they rest in you; grant us purity of heart and strength of purpose, that no passion may hinder us from knowing your will, no weakness from doing it; but in your light may we see light clearly, and in your service find perfect freedom; through Jesus Christ our Lord. **Amen.**

All-age worship

Carrying a sack, act as though you were all itchy. Then throw the sack down at the feet of a picture of Jesus, and become very, very calm.

Suggested hymns

All ye who seek for sure relief; 'Come to me' says Jesus; I heard the voice of Jesus say; O love that wilt not let me go.

Fourth Sunday after Trinity (Proper 9) 9 July
Second Service Blindness
Ps. 56 In God I trust [57 Steadfast love]; 2 Sam. 2.1–11; 3.1
David anointed king; Luke 18.31—19.10 Jericho

> *'[Jesus said to the blind man,] "What do you want me to do for you?" He said, "Lord, let me see again." Jesus said to him, "Receive your sight; your faith has saved you."' Luke 18.41–42*

Miracles

Jesus healed a blind man. That is called a *miracle*, because it makes us *admire* God. Most people would say that it is scientifically impossible to heal blindness, because there has been an irreversible change to the eye and the nerves. But there are some exceptions: if there is an hysterical or psychosomatic illness, which meant that the blind man was not physically ill, but for some reason would not face up to the fact that he could see. Or maybe a small physical problem could be healed by a sudden shock. Science cannot say, 'This could never happen'; only, 'This happens very rarely, and we cannot yet explain what happened in this case.' So perhaps it is best to say it was a miracle, and as yet we cannot explain it.

Metaphor

The word 'blindness' is often used in the Bible as a metaphor for being unable to see the truth when it is staring us in the face.

Many people could not see, meaning could not understand, that Jesus was the Messiah, and Jesus describes them as spiritually blind. But we must be careful about using that metaphor, if there are physically blind people present, as it could be seen as insulting. Blind people were outcasts from society when Jesus was alive, so I doubt if the opportunity for this type of misunderstanding could have arisen then. Jesus was always careful to treat sick people with dignity and respect. But he may have performed a few miracles so as to convince people that spiritual blindness, too, can be cured.

Respect

It would be a tragic mistake for us to promise healing to a blind person these days, unless we were absolutely sure their physical condition was curable, or we might break their hearts with disappointment if it didn't work. Instead, Jesus would want us to treat people with disabilities in a caring way that builds up their self-respect. We must speak to blind people often, having first told them who we are, instead of ignoring them as though they were not really there. Simply getting from one place to another presents many challenges to the blind, so we should praise them for the way they manage it, and offer gentle help in getting about if they say they need it. Many blind people have a high level of intelligence and skills, so we should help them to find suitable work, and be sure the employer makes necessary changes to the working conditions so that they are not looked down on by their colleagues. And finally, if they have a guide dog, we should help the animal, too, and praise them for the wonderful job they do.

Church

A blind professor of theology, Dr John Hull, said in the *Church Times* a few years ago that 'On the whole, the Church doesn't cope very well with disability.' He reprimanded those who imagine that the imitation of Christ involves working miracles as Jesus did. He continued, 'The true miracle . . . is when disabled people are fully integrated into Church life and accepted exactly as they are.' He was right. So I want to ask you: is this church building as disabled-friendly as it could be? With large-print hymn sheets for the partially sighted; a good amplifier and a hearing loop for the deaf, ramps for those in wheelchairs and those with Zimmer-frames, and somewhere on the seats for people with walking sticks to hang them up? Have you provided accessible disabled toilets in accordance with the current regulations? The respect and care which we have recognized that the blind deserve, people with other disabilities are entitled to as well.

Fellowship

Above all, is your fellowship inviting to people with disabilities? Do people go up to them and show them that they are welcome? Are you friendly, so that folk with disabilities can feel they have a group of people they can chat with, whatever the weather, without travelling too far to specialized facilities dedicated to such people. If we are to follow the example of Jesus, the least we can do is to care for people who struggle in the way they would wish us to. If we don't see the necessity of that, perhaps it is we who are spiritually blind, and the ones with disabilities are those who can see the truth which is hidden from us.

Suggested hymns

Amazing grace; Make way, make way, for Christ the King; Sometimes a light surprises; You, living Christ, our eyes behold.

Fifth Sunday after Trinity (Proper 10)   16 July
Principal Service   **Shallow**
(*Continuous*): Gen. 25.19–34 Esau sells his birthright, Ps. 119.105–112 Your word a lamp; *or* (*Related*): Isa. 55.10–13 God's word brings joy, Ps. 65.[1–7] 8–13 Joy of harvest; Rom. 8.1–11 Flesh, law and Spirit; Matt. 13.1–9, 18–23 Parable of the sower

> '[Jesus said,] "As for [the seed which] was sown on rocky ground, this is the one who hears the word and immediately receives it with joy; yet such a person has no root, but endures only for a while, and when trouble or persecution arises on account of the word, that person immediately falls away."' *Matthew 13.20–21*

Shakespeare

In Shakespeare's play *King Henry IV Part 2* he introduces a judge called Sir Robert Shallow, who says of himself: 'I am Robert Shallow, sir, a poor esquire of this county, and one of the King's justices of the peace.' He always says everything twice, and is determined that everybody should know about his rank in society. Later he says, 'A good varlet, a good varlet, a very good varlet, Sir John. By the mass, I have drunk too much sack at supper. A good varlet. Now sit down, now sit down.' From this you conclude that the depth of his thinking is like his name: shallow. The audiences found him so funny that he reappears in *The Merry Wives of Windsor*, boasting that his family has had a coat of arms for '300 years'!

Superficial

There are many superficial people like that still today, with no depth. This is not just a question of failing to use their brain, though many people have depths to their thinking which they hardly ever use in daily life. Shallowness is also a matter of not using their heart. They see other people as caricatures, slotting them into a box of a type of character they dislike, without recognizing that everyone is unique. They are always judging others, but are blind to their own failings. You know the sort of people I mean? I am sure that you yourself are not at all like that!

Parable

Jesus spoke of shallow people in the parable of the sower. A farmer goes out to toss seeds randomly on his field, and it lands on different types of soil. In one area the bedrock is very close to the surface, so that the earth is very shallow. Jesus said that this represents a common personality type, with their reaction when they hear the good news of the Christian message:

> As for [the seed which] was sown on rocky ground, this is the [sort of person] who hears the word and immediately receives it with joy; yet such a person has no root, but endures only for a while, and when trouble or persecution arises on account of the word, that person immediately falls away.

Love

As with all the parables, you start off laughing at the characters it describes, then suddenly get the uncomfortable feeling that you yourself are a bit like that. Jesus is the farmer scattering the seeds; but they are seeds of love. He teaches us about loving our neighbours as much as we love ourselves, and doing for them what we would like them to do for us. Then he sets us an example by his death on the cross, showing he loves each of us enough to die for us. As Jesus said, 'There is no greater love than this, to lay down one's life for one's friends.' He shows us that he loves us, and tells us what we should do about it. The seed of love which he sows in our hearts springs up, growing bigger and bigger . . . until we meet with some discouragement or disappointment, when we say, 'I can't believe in a God who would let me suffer like that,' and we stop going to church altogether. As I have already said, I am sure none of you is shallow like that, or you wouldn't be here. But maybe the temptation to think along those lines crosses your mind occasionally. If the love for others which is planted in your heart doesn't grow deep roots, it will soon wither and die.

Love never dies

Remember, the love-seed which Jesus planted within you when you first realized that he loves you, is meant to grow till it is a strong plant, producing the fruit of love in your heart. When we learn that God loves us, we are enabled to love others, and that love will never die, now or in eternity. There is nothing shallow about love like that.

All-age worship

Buy seeds and study the instructions on the packet. Plant two pots, following all the instructions with one, and none of them with the other. Which grows stronger? What instructions did Jesus give us, to grow love in us and in others?

Suggested hymns

Come, ye thankful people, come; Now the green blade riseth; We have a gospel to proclaim; Ye servants of God, your Master proclaim.

Fifth Sunday after Trinity (Proper 10) 16 July
Second Service **Authority**

Ps. 60 Prayer for victory [63 The king rejoices]; 2 Sam. 7.18–29
David's prayer; Luke 19.41—20.8 The time of visitation

> 'One day, as [Jesus] was teaching the people in the temple and
> telling the good news, the chief priests and the scribes came
> with the elders and said to him, "Tell us, by what authority are
> you doing these things? Who is it who gave you this authority?"'
> Luke 20.1–2

Headship

A few years ago, a letter in the *Church Times* caused unintended
hilarity at many vicarage breakfast tables. The writer suggested that
the Queen, as head of state, could not be forced by synod to sign
legislation to appoint women bishops, which would go against the
long-standing Christian tradition that women cannot have headship over men! Indeed, up to the time of Queen Elizabeth I it was
believed that women have not the strength of will to control oppos-
ing groups of squabbling men, but she soon proved them wrong.
The period of greatest British power was when Queen Victoria was
on the throne. So attitudes towards authority and leadership can
change with changing circumstances.

Kings

In today's Old Testament reading, we heard King David's prayer,
thanking God for giving authority to 'the house of David', meaning his male descendants. This line died out soon after the Jews
returned from exile in Babylon, and although hope remained strong
that it would be restored by the birth of a Messiah, in fact the
authority God had given to the monarch now passed to the whole
Jewish nation, God's Chosen People. They were chosen to pass on
the tradition of belief in one God only, which they had inherited, to
the rest of the world.

Authority

The chief priests asked Jesus by what authority he taught and
healed the people, claiming the right to reinterpret some of the old

laws about healing on the Sabbath. Jesus answered their question by asking another question. Knowing that the rulers dared not challenge the very popular ministry of John the Baptist, Jesus asked them who had given John the authority to break the tradition that baptism was required only by non-Jewish converts. John said that even people who were born as Jews needed to repent and be baptized. By what right did he do this? The unspoken answer was that God gives authority to those individuals whom God has chosen. They can reveal new developments in understanding God's will for today.

Leadership

But that disturbs a hornets' nest of problems which we have still not solved today. How do we know whether an individual is chosen by God, or is a victim of their own delusions? Who chooses the leaders, and gives them the authority to depart from tradition? What is the connection between authority and leadership? In some countries, leaders are appointed by the power of the army, and then turn into dictators, with many people dying for daring to resist them. Then the dictators are overthrown, only to be replaced by a coalition of oligarchs who are even worse. In the West we argue that democracy is a fairer form of government, when the leaders are authorized to break with tradition by the majority vote of the whole people, and can be removed without the need for assassination. Yet even in democracies, the votes of the selfish majority can cause undreamt-of distress to the needy minorities.

Answers

For the answer to the authority-leadership dilemma we must return to King David and Jesus, who asserted that only God has the right to appoint leaders. But in the modern world, we have changed the tradition about how God's will is to be discerned. We now say that God speaks through the votes of the people, *provided that* the people pray and think about what is the most loving and responsible way to cast their votes, and the leaders enter on their task as an opportunity for public service, not for private enrichment. If that is so, then those who serve under them must obey their orders, to maintain a stable society, until they have found a peaceful way of changing the leadership for one which is more in line with the will of God.

All forms

That goes for all forms of leadership. The authority of parents over their children, teachers over their pupils, employers over their workforce and managers over their assistants must be earned, not snatched. Leadership must be looked on as a vocation to humble service for those whom you lead, not as a way of becoming rich and powerful at the expense of others. It all comes back to what King David and Jesus said: authority to lead is given by God alone, and then only for as long as the leaders regard their position as an opportunity for loving care towards those whom they are called to serve.

Suggested hymns

Brother, sister, let me serve you; Judge eternal, throned in splendour; Lord of Lords and King eternal; O God of earth and altar.

Sixth Sunday after Trinity (Proper 11)   23 July
Principal Service   **God Knows Best**
(*Continuous*): Gen. 28.10–19a Jacob's ladder, Ps. 139.1–11, 23–24 Ascension into heaven; *or* (*Related*): Wisd. 12.13, 16–19 Righteousness and love, *or* Isa. 44.6–8 Witnesses to the one God, Ps. 86.11–17 God's grace; Rom. 8.12–25 Children of God; Matt. 13.24–30, 36–43 Parable of the weeds

> *'I consider that the sufferings of this present time are not worth comparing with the glory about to be revealed to us.'* Romans 8.18

Suffering

This sermon begins in gloom and ends in joy. Many people look around this world and agree with the English philosopher Thomas Hobbes, that 'the life of man [is] solitary, poor, nasty, brutish and short'. We seem to be surrounded by suffering, and very few can say that they have never known pain in their lives at some time or other. The novelist H. G. Wells once wrote that the human race, 'who began in a cave behind a windbreak, will end in the disease-soaked ruins of a slum'.

Explanation?

Many people have sought to provide an explanation of this, without, it must be admitted, a great deal of success. We know now that we have emerged as a species by a process which we call evolution. This depends on each individual competing with others for the means to live long enough to have offspring, and avoiding the things which threaten our survival because they give us pain. Without pain, neither we nor our evolutionary ancestors would have realized the need to avoid predators, disease, fire and drowning. But, you object, if there is a loving Creator, couldn't he have kept *my* life, at least, free of undeserved suffering? Well yes, he could, but to achieve that he would have had to take away your freedom to walk into dangerous situations, and to destroy your health by addiction to harmful foods, if you so choose; and he would have had to remove your enemies' free will, when they choose to oppress you. The parable of the weeds addresses this dilemma: if the farmer dug up all the harmful plants, he would have had to dig up the good ones too, because they are all intertwined. And if God destroyed everyone in the world who has ever done anything hurtful or selfish, very few of us would survive, because good and evil grow intertwined in everybody's heart.

God knows best

The final answer to those who complain how unfair the world has become is to ask them, had they been in God's place as creator, could they have done anything better, without destroying the whole purpose of the project, which is to produce human beings capable of choosing to love? Of course not. None of us deserves to suffer as we do. But then none of us deserves all the good things which happen to us, either. When children are told to do this and not that, they always ask why; and after a while, their frustrated parents always say, 'Because I say so, and Mummy knows best.' Which means, there is an answer, but it would be impossible to put it into words which a child could understand. Similarly, the reply to those who criticize God is that God cannot put the answer into words which humans could understand, so you must do what God commands, because God tells you to, and God knows best.

Coping

Yet if you give that answer to somebody who is in acute agony, you will be accused of being unsympathetic, to say the least. As Alister McGrath points out in his book *Mere Theology*, for Martin Luther, who began the Reformation, 'the question was not primarily how can we explain suffering – which is there, whether we like it or not – but how can we cope with it, and how can God use it to enable us to grow into stronger, better people.' If we trust God, and pray, he will give us the moral strength to endure even the worst pain for as long as we need to; and, although we may not be aware of it at the time, looking back over our lives, we always find that the times of our worst suffering were also the times when we matured as human beings.

Hope of heaven

St Paul wrote to the Christians in Rome:

I consider that the sufferings of this present time are not worth comparing with the glory about to be revealed to us.

Maybe you could only just hang on to your faith in God by your fingertips when you were suffering, but if you did, then you will receive your reward in heaven. So we shall all travel from gloom to joy.

All-age worship

Write a prayer to say to God when you are in pain. Learn it by heart.

Suggested hymns

Abide with me; All ye who seek for sure relief; Christ triumphant, ever reigning; Lead, kindly light.

Sixth Sunday after Trinity (Proper 11)   23 July
Second Service   Other Faiths

Ps. 67 Let the peoples praise you [70 God is great]; 1 Kings 2.10–12; 3.16–28 The judgement of Solomon; Acts 4.1–22 Whom to obey?; *Gospel at Holy Communion*: Mark 6.30–34, 53–56 Feeding and healing

> 'Let the peoples praise you, O God,
> let all the peoples praise you.'
>   Psalm 67.5 (Common Worship)

Gentiles

When you consider the exclusiveness shown by many Jews in the Old Testament about their religion, Psalm 67 comes as quite a shock. Many believed that Israel alone was the Chosen People, and all the 'Gentiles', or 'nations', were idol-worshippers whom God is called upon to destroy. Yet here, 'all people' are called upon to worship the same God whom the Jews worship:

> O let the nations rejoice and be glad,
> for you will judge the peoples righteously
>   and govern the nations upon earth.

There is no mention here of the prejudice which St Paul found himself up against, which taught that any Gentile who wished to worship the Jewish God must first be circumcised, and promise to obey all the Old Testament laws.

Other faiths

We Christians have a similar problem. We assume that followers of other faiths must be converted and baptized before God is even interested in them. Yet Jesus healed a Roman centurion's boy and a Syrian woman's daughter without question, and said of the centurion:

> Truly I tell you, in no one in Israel have I found such faith. I tell you, many will come from east and west and will eat with Abraham and Isaac and Jacob in the kingdom of heaven, while the heirs of the kingdom will be thrown into the outer darkness.

193

You seldom hear such tolerant remarks from a Christian pulpit. In fact, you seldom hear a sermon about other faiths at all, as it is such a touchy subject. So I want to refer you to some words from David Sheppard's autobiography, *Steps along Hope Street*. As well as being a famous England cricketer, he was a respected Bishop of Liverpool, and a leading evangelical.

Jews

He found that some Jews were very offended about the Year of Evangelism, and especially by attempts to pressure Jews to convert to Christianity. So he set up a discussion group of Jews and Christians, who met 'with no holds barred'. At first, both sides were suspicious, but gradually they came to respect each other and learn from each other. Bishop David made a public statement, affirming his belief that Jesus 'is in an altogether unique way the Saviour of the world', and his death on the cross made a sacrifice 'to atone . . . for the sins of the whole world'. This, he said, was 'not to colonise Jewish people', and he recognized that there may be people living by faith who belong to other faith communities.

Muslims

Some Muslims asked if they could join in, and a new group of Muslims, Jews and Christians was formed. He was invited to meet people of all faiths in Southall, and they discovered that even blessing food in the name of the Trinity could be acceptable if it was done in a way which showed mutual respect. Some Christians objected to inter-faith dialogue, saying it 'betrayed the uniqueness of Christ'; but Bishop David said it was a method which St Paul had used. Back in Liverpool he found that in dealing with refugees and immigrants, he could not ignore the influence of religion on their behaviour; but the varieties in their beliefs meant they could not all be lumped together under one label. They discussed terrorism, agreeing that building a 'secular society' would only make the situation worse.

Inter-faith

Relations with other minorities, such as Sikhs and Hindus, seem to be getting better, too. But I want to end by referring to another bishop who moved on the cutting edge between faiths, and that was Bishop Kenneth Cragg, an assistant bishop in Egypt, and author of *Sandals at the Mosque* and other books about Islam. He frequently said that asking a Muslim to convert would cut off all their ties to their family and friends, and might even cost them their life. But by discussing the personality of Jesus – who is mentioned under the name of 'Prophet Isa [EE-sah]' in the Qur'an more times even than Muhammad – and what Jesus taught us about the one God who is worshipped by all religions, we might help them to 'take Jesus into their religion' without the trauma of an open conversion. I should be interested to hear your views, and whether you would like me to preach some more about the different religions. The psalm ends with these words:

> Then shall the earth bring forth her increase,
> and God, our own God, will bless us.
> God will bless us,
> and all the ends of the earth shall fear him.

Suggested hymns

In Christ there is no east or west; Jesus shall reign, where'er the sun; They shall come from the east; We three kings of orient are.

Seventh Sunday after Trinity (Proper 12)   30 July
Principal Service   **Destined to Grow**
(*Continuous*): Gen. 29.15–28 Jacob loves Rachel, Ps. 105.1–11, 45b Authority and thanksgiving, *or* Ps. 128 Family and possessions; *or* (*Related*): 1 Kings 3.5–12 Solomon's prayer for wisdom, Ps. 119.129–136 God's word is light; Rom. 8.26–39 All things work together for good; Matt. 13.31–33, 44–52 Parables of the kingdom

> '[Jesus] put before them another parable: "The kingdom of heaven is like a mustard seed that someone took and sowed in his field; it is the smallest of all the seeds, but when it has grown it is the greatest of shrubs and becomes a tree, so that the birds of the air come and make nests in its branches."'
> Matthew 13.31–32

Parables of the kingdom

People who attended church last Sunday, today and next Sunday will hear seven 'parables of the kingdom' which Jesus told. St Matthew was very careful not to take the name of God in vain. So when he wrote 'the kingdom of heaven,' he did not mean 'the place where we go when we die'; he was using a euphemism for 'the kingdom of God', which is wherever people obey God as their king. They are parables of growth. The first is about Christians who tell their neighbours about Jesus, who are likened to a farmer sowing seeds. Though most show little long-term growth, it is worth it for the few who yield a rich harvest. The second parable is about wheat and weeds growing together: God does not remove the weeds until the harvest. Third, the mustard seed is tiny, but it is destined to grow into a great tree, where the birds, representing the nations of the world, may roost. The next two are about hidden treasure and the pearl without price; the finder is willing to sell everything to exchange for the treasure, which holds so much future promise. Lastly, the kingdom is like a dragnet which scoops up all sorts of fish, leaving them to be sorted later. All these stories promise us that the Christian Church is destined to grow and grow.

Church growth

Is this promise being fulfilled? Well, Jesus began with 12 disciples; on the day of Pentecost 3,000 new believers were baptized; and soon the message had spread all over the Roman Empire. The next rapid expansion was in the eighteenth and nineteenth centuries, when the gospel was taken to Asia and Africa. In 1910, Christians amounted to one-third of the world population; it is the same now, but the population of the world has mushroomed, so the statistics hide the fact that the Christian Church is still growing at a fantastic rate. In Britain and Western Europe, the number of believers appears to be declining. But the figures are affected by other factors, such as social upheavals, wars, industrialization, and demographic shifts, leading to changing patterns of work and leisure. According to the last UK census, well over half claim to be Christians, even though many are not regular church-attenders. The kingdom continues to grow, though we have failed to make 'church' an attractive way of growing in faith. Even so, alongside decline in some areas, substantial church growth has taken place in Britain in recent decades. In London, the largest Anglican diocese in the country, electoral rolls have grown by 70 per cent since 1990. Most cathedrals show growth in their congregations; and many multiracial churches enjoy 'reverse mission' from the Global South. There are now more than half a million worshipping in black-majority churches in Britain, which are often ignored in official statistics. The promises of Jesus about the growth of seeds are being fulfilled.

Why not Western Europe?

Why, then, is church growth less rapid in Western Europe than in the rest of the world? I suggest it is a matter of language. When Christian missionaries enter a new country, the first thing they do is to translate parts of the Bible into the language of the people. This involves not just replacing one word with another, but an attempt to understand the idioms, metaphors and philosophical concepts through which they communicate. In twenty-first-century Europe, that language is the language of science. Yet Christians persist in talking and worshipping in words which were current hundreds of years ago, but are completely unknown today. No wonder those who hear us are baffled.

Evangelism

Christians are called to re-evangelize the world afresh in every generation. If every Christian realizes that this is what God is calling us to, and uses up-to-date terminology to do so, then the predictions of Jesus about mustard seeds growing into mighty trees will be fulfilled in our own nation in our time.

All-age worship

Search Wikipedia for 'Christianity_by_country'. On your own map of the world, mark significant countries with the percentage of Christians.

Suggested hymns

Jesu, priceless treasure; The kingdom is upon you!'; The kingdom of God is justice and joy; The sower went forth sowing (www.hymntime.com).

Seventh Sunday after Trinity (Proper 12) 30 July
Second Service **Solomon's Temple**

Ps. 75 God executes judgement [76 Judge of the earth]; 1 Kings 6.11–14, 23–38 Solomon builds the Temple; Acts 12.1–17 Peter and Rhoda; *Gospel at Holy Communion*: John 6.1–21 Feeding 5,000, walking on water

> 'The word of the LORD came to Solomon, "Concerning this house that you are building, if you will walk in my statutes . . . then I will establish my promise with you, which I made to your father David."' 1 Kings 6.11–12

The Exodus

When Israel came out of Egypt, they believed that God dwelt in the tabernacle, or tent of meeting. A plague was spreading towards Jerusalem, so King David prayed to the Lord, who sent an angel to stop it at a place called 'the threshing floor of Araunah'. To thresh wheat, you need a wind to blow the chaff away. Jerusalem lies in the wide valley between the Mount of Olives and the Western Hill; King David's headquarters were on a low rise between the Kidron Valley and the Valley of the Cheese-makers. But the land rises to the north, where there was a flat rock, close to David's City, which would be very suitable for threshing. A prophet came to David and said, 'Go up and erect an altar to the LORD on the threshing-floor of Araunah.' So David planned to build a Temple there, but God said 'No; that must wait for your son Solomon to do instead.' Very few pottery fragments from David's time have been found in Jerusalem, so probably it was only a small hill-town.

Solomon's Temple

They would not have been able to afford much; nevertheless Solomon erected a temple that was 60 cubits long, 20 cubits wide, and 30 cubits high. The short cubit was about 17.5 inches, so that makes Solomon's Temple around 87 feet long by 29 feet wide and 44 feet high. It was divided into three parts: the porch, the nave and the Holy of Holies. Our Old Testament reading today listed its elaborate furnishing, meant to reproduce the appearance of the

Temple in heaven where God's permanent dwelling was, though he could also be contacted in the Jerusalem Temple. This was the first of at least four buildings on the site. Solomon put the ark of the covenant in the holy of holies, so that the priests could meet God there. The Psalmist sang the praises of Mount Sion, where they could meet with God:

We have waited on your loving-kindness, O God,
in the midst of your Temple.

Zerubbabel

Solomon's Temple was destroyed by Nebuchadnezzar the King of Babylon. After the Jews returned from their exile in Babylon, the Jewish king Zerubbabel built the Second Temple. The prophet Haggai predicted: 'The latter splendour of this house shall be greater than the former, says the LORD of hosts.' Yet the people wept because the Second Temple was not as grand as the first. But King Herod built a grand new Temple on the site.

Cleansing

Jesus drove out the money-changers, who were occupying the Court of the Gentiles, the only place where non-Jews could worship, and said that if the Temple was destroyed, its function as a place to meet God would be replaced by his own body. This prophecy was fulfilled when the Roman army, fed up with Jewish rebelliousness, destroyed the Temple and the whole city in AD 70, leaving it as an open space. The Crusaders built several buildings, but not the Temple itself.

Dome of the Rock

Then the Muslim invaders built what we now call the Dome of the Rock. Their interest was that they believed that this was where Muhammad made his night-journey to heaven on a winged horse. The rock from which he is supposed to have taken off is exposed under the dome, and it has several markings which could have been the foundations of earlier buildings. Many people believe that this was the threshing-floor of Araunah, and the site of the holy of holies in the Jewish temples.

You

But St Paul gave a spiritual interpretation to the idea of the temple as a place to meet God, when he wrote to the Corinthians:

> Do you not know that you are God's temple and that God's Spirit dwells in you? If anyone destroys God's temple, God will destroy that person. For God's temple is holy, and you are that temple . . . Or do you not know that your body is a temple of the Holy Spirit within you, which you have from God, and that you are not your own? For you were bought with a price; therefore glorify God in your body.

That means that when other people see you, they should see the love, generosity and approachableness of God revealed.

Suggested hymns

Blest are the pure in heart; Lift up your heads, ye mighty gates; Our blest Redeemer, ere he breathed; Ye that know the Lord is gracious.

The Transfiguration of Our Lord   Sunday 6 August
God's Will, Not Mine
Dan. 7.9–10, 13–14 The Son of Man; Ps. 97 Clouds are around him; 2 Peter 1.16–19 We saw; Luke 9.28–36 The transfiguration

> *'About eight days after these sayings Jesus took with him Peter and John and James, and went up on the mountain to pray.'* Luke 9.28

Who?

Jesus had questioned his disciples, near to a town called Caesarea Philippi, as to *who* they thought he was. Various suggestions were put forward by his little circle of close friends: was Jesus perhaps Elijah returned to earth? Or was he John the Baptist, who had recently been beheaded by King Herod Antipas – was Jesus a sort of reincarnation of his cousin? So far they had been thinking of Jesus as a speaker, but not a doer. Then Peter came up with a dramatic suggestion: was Jesus the promised Messiah, a great leader who by his actions would save his people from their oppressors? Jesus congratulated Peter, who recognized that it was what Jesus was going to do that counted; his words explained his actions. He told his disciples that he was going to Jerusalem to be crucified. But then Peter tried to stop him; he wanted a triumphant conqueror, not a wounded healer. It sounds as though Jesus had decided by this stage that he was going to be crucified; but he needed to pray for the strength to go through with it; and he needed the disciples with him, so that they should begin to understand.

Where?

So Jesus, with his intimate best friends Peter, James and John, went up a mountain to pray. *Where* was this? Pilgrims to the Holy Land are taken on a dramatic drive up a winding road to the top of Mount Tabor, and told that this was the site of the transfiguration. The problem with this is that, at the time of Jesus, Mount Tabor was a fortress. A mountain swarming with soldiers was not a good place to go for a silent retreat. So probably it was much further to the north, at Mount Hermon, which rises to 9,400 feet above sea level, or 11,000 feet above the level of the Jordan Valley. It is so high that it is hard to breathe in the rarefied atmosphere on the summit, so Jesus and the disciples may have spent the night in prayer on one of the upper slopes.

Why?

So the answer to the question, '*Why* did Jesus climb the mountain?' is, 'In order to get away from the busy world and spend a night in prayer with his heavenly Father.' Here we come up against the mystery of the Trinity. There is only one God. But although the Son of God was one with the Father, he laid aside his omniscience when he became human at Bethlehem, and still had to question the Father as to whether he, Jesus, had got it right. Was offering his life as a symbol of self-sacrificing love really what his loving Father required of his Beloved Son?

What?

Most of us spend our time asking ourselves, 'What do *I* want to do.' Jesus did not ask that question; instead all he asked was 'What does

God my Father want me to do?' We should follow his example. When you are uncertain which path to follow, ask advice from a few wise friends. But then go on to spend some time in prayer, asking God what he wants you to do with the life which he has lent you. You may hear a voice, as Jesus did on the mountain-top; more likely you will form a deep inner certainty that you are doing what God requires of you. There is an old hymn by Horatius Bonar, not included in many of the modern hymnals, which sums up exactly what Jesus was asking on the Mount of Transfiguration, and what we should be saying in our own prayers:

Thy way, not mine, O Lord,
however dark it be!
Lead me by thine own hand;
choose out the path for me.

I dare not choose my lot,
I would not if I might;
choose thou for me, my God,
so shall I walk aright.

Not mine, not mine the choice
in things both great or small;
be thou my guide, my strength,
my wisdom and my all.

Who? Where? Why? What? Those are the questions which Jesus asked on the mountain-top, and which we should be asking about our own lives; and those are also the answers we should give. Who? Someone who lays down their life for their friends. Where? Somewhere away from life's hustle and bustle. Why? To spend time in prayer with our heavenly Father. What? To follow God's will, not our own.

All-age worship

Play 'follow my leader' using things which Jesus might have done.

Suggested hymns

God of mercy, God of grace; Immortal, invisible, God only wise; 'Lift up your hearts!'; 'Tis good Lord to be here.

Eighth Sunday after Trinity (Proper 13) 6 August
Second Service **What We Owe to the Jews**
Ps. 80 The Vine; 1 Kings 10.1–13 The Queen of Sheba;
Acts 13.1–13 Paul and Barnabas in Cyprus; *Gospel at Holy
Communion*: John 6.24–35 I am the bread

> '*[Paul and Barnabas] proclaimed the word of God in the syna-
> gogues of the Jews.*' Acts 13.5

Patriotism

Patriotism is a good and healthy emotion. Everyone should love
the land where they were born. We need to be proud of the good
qualities we have, and the opportunities we have to help others. But
this is not an uncritical admiration. We should be fully aware of the
faults of our ancestors, and ready to admit to their failings. But if
you agree with what I have said, an important conclusion follows:
the *only* people entitled to criticize the faults of a nation are those
who belong to that nation. For example: the only people entitled
to be anti-Semitic are the Jews! Many of them *are* highly critical of
their own race, especially of the policies of the State of Israel. The
intensity of their criticism arises from the depth of their love.

Paul

St Paul was proud to have been born a Jew. He continued to observe
the Jewish Law, with the exception that he rejected the food laws
when he was dining with his non-Jewish friends, as that would have
prevented them from enjoying table fellowship. But reading behind
the lines, you can see that at the beginning of his ministry he was
deeply frustrated and torn. He had been sent to Antioch to preach
to the Hellenists. Now that is a word with two meanings. It can
mean either Jews who were brought up speaking Greek and are not
very fluent at Hebrew. Or it can mean non-Jews who, like many
in the Roman Empire, were brought up speaking Greek but found
themselves fascinated by the Jewish religion. They hung around the
synagogue doors listening to the parts of the worship which were
in Greek, admiring what was, in those days, the only monotheistic
faith; and attracted by the Jewish moral teaching. But they were
blowed if they were going to learn Hebrew, be circumcised, and
obey all the laws of the Torah. Paul was fluent in both languages, so

he was successful in interesting both types of Hellenists in Antioch. Then Paul and Barnabas were sent to Cyprus to get rid of them . . . sorry, to see if they would have any success there. Barnabas was delighted to meet up with all his friends in the synagogues where he had grown up; Paul was furious to see there were no Greek-born converts in any of them. 'Well, we always leave the door open for them,' was the reply. 'The sermon is usually in Greek. They could always ask for a series of lessons in the Jewish Law.' The same answers everywhere. Then they met the Greek Governor, and from then on Paul's mission was principally to non-Jews.

Messengers

Recently, two singers were performing in a Christian oratorio. The Jewish singer said to her Christian friend, 'These words sound more Jewish than Christian.' To which the Christian replied, 'Nearly everything in Christianity is borrowed from the Jews.' 'Just tell everybody that,' urged the Jew. If it were not for the Jews, you and I would never have arrived at the idea that there is one God for everyone, who cares how we treat each other, and saves us when we get into a mess. The message of Jesus came to us through the Jews; otherwise we would never have known that God loves all his children, and wants us to love each other for his sake. Also – and it was at this point that Paul's heart broke – God had chosen the Jews to tell the rest of the world all about him.

God's plan

God's plan was to create a world in which beings would evolve who could think, choose and love. Then he chose one nation to learn this lesson; but, with the exception of Paul and people like him, for the most part they failed to pass the message on. But, as I say, we must not be anti-Semitic. God has admitted us to his chosen people, even though we were not born Jews. Yet we Christians too have failed to pass the message on, by word and example. Thank God there are exceptions; and pray God that we may build the kingdom of love in our own nation, and pass it on to others.

All-age worship

Draw a heart broken down the middle, and label it 'God's heart'. Discuss the things we do, and fail to do, which break God's heart.

Suggested hymns

God is working his purpose out; Guide me, O thou great Redeemer/ Jehovah; The Church of God a kingdom is; The God of Abraham praise.

Ninth Sunday after Trinity (Proper 14)   13 August
Principal Service   **Impossible Miracles**
(*Continuous*): Gen. 37.1–4, 12–28 Joseph and his family, Ps. 105.1–6, 16–22, 45b Joseph in authority; *or* (*Related*): 1 Kings 19.9–18 A still small voice, Ps. 85.8–13 Love, works, peace, faith; Rom. 10.5–15 Justification by faith, not by works of the Law; Matt. 14.22–33 Walking on water

> *'The boat, battered by the waves, was far from the land, for the wind was against them. And early in the morning [Jesus] came walking toward them on the lake.' Matthew 14.24–25*

Scientific laws

Many people think that scientific laws are incontrovertible statements of what must always happen, which have been proved by measurable, material tests. But any scientist will tell you that is not true. Take the law of gravity. Sir Isaac Newton, watching an apple fall from a tree, guessed that there might be a force of attraction between any two objects proportionate to the product of the their masses divided by the square of their distance apart. He called this his Law of Universal Gravitation. This law dealt with visible physical objects. But Newton was not satisfied until he had correctly predicted the time the moon would take to orbit around the earth. Bingo! Newton's prediction was confirmed, so the law was immutably true. Except that it isn't. Sir Albert Einstein pointed out that Newton had not included one other factor: velocity. Einstein's Law of General Relativity says the force of attraction between two objects depends on how fast they are travelling relative to each other. On this basis, for instance, black holes, while not themselves observable, are the best explanation for the observable facts. So we had better say that scientific laws are predictions of material observations, yet valid only until we discover what other factors must be taken into account.

Miracles

This matters to Christians because many sceptics say that science proves that miracles cannot happen, because they break the laws of science. But that is a misunderstanding of the nature of science. These so-called laws are only provisional, until we discover that another factor is present which needs to be included in the calculation. Christians say that the unconsidered factor is the presence of God. Just as Newton's law had to be changed when velocity was included, so many other laws may have to be modified if God's will is taken into account. But frequent miracles would make the whole world unpredictable, which would be very difficult to live in. For that reason, God does not often cause miracles to happen, certainly not as often as we ask him for them. But maybe he *is* intervening, all the time, at the subatomic level, which causes unpredictable mutations in our genes. You could define scientific laws as descriptions of how God *normally* behaves, to show us he is reliable; miracles are how he behaves when he wants to persuade us of his love.

Healing miracles

Actually, *healing* miracles are not hard to explain. Medicine is not an exact science; it predicts the *probability* of your being healed, but cannot say for certain that you will be. God has put into our bodies remarkable powers of self-healing, which are hindered if the patient is depressed, but helped if the patient has hope, faith and knows they are loved. Jesus said, 'Your faith has healed you.' But he didn't heal every sick person in Palestine during his lifetime, for he said that death is God's greatest blessing.

Walking on the water

But it is much harder to explain the *nature* miracles, such as that described in today's reading when Jesus walked on the water. It *may* have been a vision; or it *may* have been that he was walking on a sand bank just below the surface. But when Jesus said to the disciples, 'Take heart, it is I; do not be afraid', the literal translation of 'it is I' is 'I am', and 'I am' is the name of God. The disciples replied, 'Truly *you are* the Son of God.' Maybe the miracle was specially performed to convince them of that. The missing factor we forgot about when we alleged that science says, 'human beings cannot walk on water', is that this may not apply when the human being in question is the incarnate Son of God. The presence of God changes everything. When we talk about the infinite, our normal human laws of science may not apply.

Controversial

Now this is all very controversial, and you may not agree with what I have said. All I ask is that you are modest about the powers of human logic, and admit that we are dealing with matters far deeper that our reasoning can fully cope with. And praise God, whatever conclusion you come to.

All-age worship

Make a list of Jesus' miracles. Suggest explanations.

Suggested hymns

Eternal Father, strong to save; From thee all skill and science flow; Sometimes a light surprises; Thine arm, O Lord, in days of old.

Ninth Sunday after Trinity (Proper 14)   13 August
Second Service   Two Kingdoms

Ps. 86 Show me a sign; 1 Kings 11.41—12.20 Two kingdoms; Acts 14.8–20 Paul and Barnabas mistaken for gods; *Gospel at Holy Communion:* John 6.35, 41–51. The one who is from God

> 'When all Israel saw that [King Jeroboam] would not listen to them, the people answered the king, "What share do we have in David? ... To your tents, O Israel! ..." So Israel went away to their tents. But Rehoboam reigned over the Israelites who were living in the towns of Judah.' 1 Kings 12.16–17

Two kingdoms

The Old Testament claims that the 12 sons of Jacob were each the ancestor of one of the 12 tribes of Israel, but their descendants all came out of Egypt at the Exodus as one nation in about 1250 BC, and that King David in about 1000 BC, followed by his son King Solomon, made Jerusalem the capital city of the whole people. But then, following the death of Solomon, King Jeroboam formed a schismatic movement, taking ten of the tribes to form a separate state, known as Ephraim, then as Israel, with its capital in Samaria. This left Rehoboam as king of the two southern tribes of Judah and Benjamin, with their capital in Jerusalem. I will repeat that, because it will help you to understand much of the Old Testament:

*Jer*oboam, king of Ephraim or Israel, the ten northern tribes, in Samaria; and
*Reh*oboam, king of Judah, the two southern tribes, in Jerusalem.

But many scholars believe this may not have been literally true – it may have been invented as a piece of political propaganda to emphasize to the tribes that 'divided we fall, united we stand'. The alternative theory is that only two tribes came out of Egypt and settled in Jerusalem; the other ten entered Israel separately from the east across the river Jordan, and later were united to form the kingdom of Israel.

Next

Following this, the two kingdoms of Israel in the north and Judah in the south went their separate ways, until both of them came under attack from armies based in Mesopotamia – present-day Syria and Iraq. First to fall was Israel, in 722 BC. Most of the population was deported by their Assyrian captors to their capital in Ashur, where they intermarried with the local population and were no longer distinguishable as a distinct nation. At the same time, many people emigrated from Assyria to take the place of the deportees in the area around Samaria. This forms the origin of the myth of the ten lost tribes, and explains the Jewish hatred of the Samaritans in the time of Jesus, who were not racially pure, and only accepted the first five books of the Jewish Scriptures. In fact the area north of Samaria where Jesus came from was suspect to the Jerusalem authorities, and known as 'Galilee of the Gentiles', which you could interpret as 'the land full of immigrants'! The two southern tribes were defeated by King Nebuchadnezzar and exiled, in 587 BC, to his capital in Babylon. At first they thought the Lord had deserted them, but in 538 they were allowed to return home and rebuild Jerusalem.

Two Scriptures

Determined that they should never be defeated again, the southern tribes tried to attract the mixed-race people of Samaria to form one nation with them, and actually merged the holy books of the northern and southern peoples into one Scripture. Any passage of the Old Testament which refers to the Lord or Jehovah probably comes from the south, and those which call him God or El come from the northern tribes. That is why there are two different accounts of the Creation, for instance, in Genesis 1 and Genesis 2.

Lessons

All very interesting, you may say, and helps us put the Bible into its context. But what difference does it make to us today? Well, I told you it was political propaganda. The two kingdoms collapsed because they were divided, and neither was strong enough to defend itself. They were divided because they imagined they were different races. So the stories of both nations were adjusted to argue that they were all related. From then on, the Jews tried to keep themselves racially pure. It took Jesus, followed by St Paul, to teach that race does not matter. All the people who live in one area must unite, not on the basis of genetics but of their shared culture and beliefs. In fact we are all related, because we are all members of the human race. I will leave you to work out the implications of that for our divided denominations, for England and Scotland, the European Union, and the United Nations. But remember what the editors of the Old Testament were trying to teach their readers: divided we fall, united we stand!

Suggested hymns

All hail the power of Jesus' name; O God of earth and altar; O God our help in ages past; Thy hand, O God, has guided.

Tenth Sunday after Trinity (Proper 15)   20 August
Principal Service   **Humour and Holiness**

(*Continuous*): Gen. 45.1–15 Joseph and his family, Ps. 133
Victory; *or* (*Related*): Isa. 56.1, 6–8 The Temple a house of
prayer for all nations, Ps. 67 Let all the peoples praise you;
Rom. 11.1–2a, 29–32 God and Israel; Matt. 15.[10–20] 21–28
Hypocrisy and faith

> *'[Jesus said,] "Let [the Pharisees] alone; they are blind guides of
> the blind. And if one blind person guides another, both will fall
> into a pit."' Matthew 15.14*

Blind guides

We have the option of leaving out verses 10–20 in today's Gospel
reading, but I have chosen to preach on verse 14, where St Matthew
tells us about Jesus cracking a joke. A joke? Jesus? Most people
never think of our Saviour as a comedian. But that's because we
always read the Gospels in a solemn voice from a book with a black
cover. In fact, if you look at the parables, many of them, if not most,
must have made those who first heard them roll around laughing.
Until, of course, they realized that the joke was on them. Jesus used
satirical humour to burst the balloon of people's pomposity. For
instance, his parable about the blind leading the blind is a witty barb
aimed at the Pharisees, who were very self-righteous people, and
thought they were much more holy than anybody else. They gave
their fellow Jews opinionated guidance about how to follow God's
laws in the way they lived But Jesus said the most important laws
are to love God and love your neighbour. The Pharisees despised
their neighbours and believed God owed them a reward for being
so law-abiding. 'Ha,' said Jesus. 'Imagine one blind man offering to
show another blind man how to walk home, when neither of them
can see the ditch by the roadside. And you know what happens
then? They both finish up in the muddy water at the bottom of the
ditch! Well, the Pharisees are just like that. They're blind to what
love means. They think they can show other people the way to live,
but they can't even follow the road which God has mapped out for
us, the way of compassion and encouragement.' Hilarious, isn't it?
Then ask yourself, how often have you offered others unasked-for
advice? Are you really so wise that you invariably know better than
them? Or are you being just a little pompous? If the joke made

you look at yourself a little more humbly, it has done what Jesus intended.

Parables

Look at some of the jokes in the other parables that Jesus told.

- A big camel wanted to climb through the tiny eye of a needle, but it couldn't even get started. That's like a rich man trying to be generous.
- Sulky children in the marketplace wouldn't join the others in playing at weddings or funerals. Some people are never satisfied.
- A visitor calls on you and you have no food to offer him, so you knock on your neighbour's door asking to borrow some. The neighbour protests: 'It's midnight, go away.' You give up too easily, so you miss what he would have given you if you had persisted. It's like that with prayer.
- You are invited to a wedding reception, and take a seat at the top table. A VIP arrives, and everyone laughs as you are thrown out of your seat and have to sit among the lower classes. Pride goes before a fall.

And so on and so on. Jesus softens us up with humour, before pricking the bubble of our pomposity.

Respect

But isn't it disrespectful to laugh at religion? Not if their religion makes people narrow and judgemental; it may be the only way of turning them back to the way of love. From Chaucer's *Canterbury Tales* down to *The Life of Brian*, satire has been the best way of turning people from self-centred religiosity to God's kingdom of love. Some people won't like it; but then many squirmed at the jokes that Jesus told.

Laughter

Although Jesus was named the Man of Sorrows, there was space in his life for parties and laughter with friends. His life ended in the triumphant joy of the resurrection and ascension. Just as loving human parents rejoice to see their children chuckling together, so surely our

211

loving heavenly Father must be delighted when he hears us his children having a good laugh. Martin Luther, the German Reformer, said, 'If you are not allowed to laugh in heaven, I don't want to go there.' In fact some have described heaven as echoing with divine laughter from one horizon to the other. We may as well prepare for it by having a good laugh at our own folly here and now!

All-age worship

Write down a few of your favourite jokes. Do you know any about religion?

Suggested hymns

Give me joy in my heart; Lord of all hopefulness; The kingdom of God is justice and joy; You shall go out with joy.

Tenth Sunday after Trinity (Proper 15) 20 August
Second Service   A Letter to Paul from Philippi
Ps. 90 Our everlasting refuge; 2 Kings 4.1–37 Widow's jar, widow's dead son; Acts 16.1–15 Troas and Philippi; Gospel at Holy Communion: John 6.51–58 Eating flesh

> 'A certain woman named Lydia, a worshipper of God, was listening to us; she was from the city of Thyatira and a dealer in purple cloth.' Acts 16.14

My dear friend Paul,
Here's a letter from your old lady-friend Lydia, one of the bishops of the church in Philippi. We do miss you. We are, after all, the first church you founded west of the Hellespont. But we heard that you'd been arrested in Jerusalem, and were all worried about you; but we didn't know how to contact you. Next we heard you were in Caesarea-on-Sea, and a couple of years later that you'd been shipwrecked on the way to Rome. I'm surprised at dear Doctor Luke allowing you to travel; was he with you? Poor thing, he always hated the sea. And still we heard nothing from you, not even a short letter.

Mamertine? My business takes me all over the Eastern part of the Empire, selling purple-dyed cloth, but never up to Rome. A few firms have got a monopoly on the purple trade there, and tried to keep me away.

Please tell me which prison you're in. Then I'll leave my overseers and servants to run the business, and the church, and come to Rome at my own expense. I've worked hard for my money since my dear husband died, and what's the point of being a wealthy woman if you can't spend it on visiting your friends when they're in need?

The church in my house is growing all the time. We used to worship in the atrium, but last year we moved into the stock-room of the shop, because it's bigger. But there's such a demand for purple cloth here that it's full of bales. Emperor Nero tried to limit the wearing of purple to members of the Emperor's household. But you can't regulate that sort of thing outside Rome. Most Philippians are children or grandchildren of the soldiers to whom Augustus gave their citizenship after the Battle of Philippi. So they claim the right to wear the purple too. Which is all good business for me. But I think maybe I shall build another room soon, just for worship.

All your old friends are still worshipping with us: Clement, and Epaphroditus – and dear old Apollonius, the jailer, and all his family whom you baptized in prison after the earthquake. He never stops talking about how you and Silas were singing hymns in prison! He keeps trying to sing the one you sang then, and forgets the words. Could you send them to us when you write, beginning 'Let this mind be in you . . .'.

There still aren't enough Jewish men in Philippi to form a synagogue, and those who haven't joined the church still worship down by the river where you baptized me. But you remember Sybil, the slave girl who used to be a fortune-teller? Her owners threw her out after you healed her. She's had a relapse – keeps going into a trance and seeing visions. Some Jews passing through persuaded her that Gentiles cannot be in the People of God unless we keep every letter of the law. So that's what she prophesies these days. Surely the food laws aren't as important as knowing God? Just think how my business would suffer, if I told my Greek staff never to work on the Sabbath?

And Euodia and Syntyche are still with us. I wish they weren't. They never agree about anything – always needling one another. When any newcomer joins our worship meetings, the first thing they hear is one of these ladies saying something bitchy about the other. Nobody wants to join a spiteful fellowship like that, and they never come again.

When I think of all the work you and I put into building up this congregation in love, it breaks my heart. Your 'yoke-fellow', you used to call me, as though we were a cow and a bull pulling together on the same yoke! And now these two seem to be pulling apart everything we'd built up. Please write, giving me authority to rebuke them, or expel them from the congregation.

Farewell, Paul, or Rejoice, as we Greeks say. Epaphroditus will bring you some money from me and some of my friends who have interests in the gold-mines on Mount Pangeion. We can easily afford it. Could you buy yourself out of prison and rent a house till your trial comes up?

Your sincere friend (and the old cow who shared the same yoke with you!)

Lydia

Suggested hymns

All praise to thee, for thou, O King divine; At the name of Jesus; Lord, it belongs not to my care; May the mind of Christ my Saviour.

Eleventh Sunday after Trinity (Proper 16) 27 August
Principal Service   **The Church is the Body of Christ**
(*Continuous*): Ex. 1.8—2.10 Moses in the bulrushes, Ps. 124 Salvation and providence; *or* (*Related*): Isa. 51.1–6 The servant, a light to the peoples, Ps. 138 Temple and prayer; Rom. 12.1–8 Be transformed by the Holy Spirit; Matt. 16.13–20 Peter recognizes the Messiah

'For as in one body we have many members, and not all the members have the same function, so we, who are many, are one body in Christ, and individually we are members one of another.' Romans 12.4–5

Bodies

St Paul writes to the Christians in Rome, who were deeply divided into two camps: those who were born as Jews, and those who were not. He describes the Christian Church as the Body of Christ, which must not be torn apart. It is a strange metaphor, which, as far as I know, had never been used for a group of people before. So we need to ask ourselves exactly what he meant by a body. Some people these days are very body-conscious. They spend a lot of time and money making their bodies stronger or more beautiful. Others think that this is going to extremes. The body, they say, is a useful tool, given to us by God, and we should keep it in good running order; but we are not our bodies, and in the end they are disposable, like the bodies of the animals and birds. The truth may lie between these two positions. But we must take the debate deeper, and ask what our bodies are used for?

Nametag

A preacher asked a group of children 'What is my body?' 'That thing dangling from your neck,' they replied. 'No, I mean what is it for?' 'So we can recognize that you're not Marilyn Monroe, because you've got a different shaped body than hers.' 'You mean my body is like the nametag you tie to your suitcase,' he told them, 'to enable you to spot it at the airport. I am not my body, but my body is a tag by which I can be recognized.'

Telephone

The discussion continued. They decided that, second, my body enables me to communicate. Some serious ailments leave patients literally speechless, and they have to develop other means, such as blinking, to get their opinions across. Either way, I am using my body as a means of communication, like a telephone.

Tool

Third, my body is a tool for me to work with. I use it in a hundred ways to change the world I live in, and hopefully to make it a better place. So I use my body in three ways: to be recognized, to communicate, and to work. Or in a brief, alliterative phrase, my body is a tag, a telephone and a tool. 'What's alliterative?' asked the children. 'Never mind,' replied the preacher.

Resurrection

St Paul uses this image in 1 Corinthians 15 to describe what happens to us after we die. Our physical body does not return to life on earth: 'Flesh and blood cannot inherit the kingdom of God.' But we shall have what he calls a 'spiritual body': we shall still be able to recognize each other, communicate and praise God after we die.

Eucharist

This also clarifies what Jesus meant at the Last Supper. When he took bread and said, 'This is my body,' he was not performing a magic trick, turning bread into flesh – it wouldn't do us any good if he did – he was saying that in the bread and wine his presence can be recognized, he can tell us how much he loves us, and he can change us into better people – a tag, telephone and tool.

Church

Finally, returning to where we started, the Christian Church is the Body of Christ, because when believers meet together in love, Jesus uses us as his tag, telephone and tool: through us, people can recognize his presence; he can tell them how he wants them to live; and he can change the world until it becomes more like the kingdom of God. That means that you as an individual, and all of us here as a community, are given a tremendous privilege: to act as Christ's spokespeople. But it is also a colossal responsibility: we must overcome our differences, and grow together in love; we may tolerate disagreements, but if we stop loving each other and go our separate ways, we are literally tearing the Body of Christ limb from limb.

All-age worship

Draw a cross, and superimpose on it a sketch of your church from above. Label it: 'The Church, the body of Christ'.

Suggested hymns

O thou who at thy Eucharist didst pray; Onward Christian soldiers; The Church's one foundation; Thy hand, O God, has guided.

Eleventh Sunday after Trinity (Proper 16) 27 August
Second Service **Islam**

Ps. 95 Venite; 2 Kings 6.8–23 Elisha's mercy; Acts 17.15–34
Paul in Athens; *Gospel at Holy Communion*: John 6.56–69 Spirit
gives life, flesh is useless

> *'Paul . . . said, "Athenians, I see how extremely religious you are
> in every way . . . I found . . . an altar with the inscription, 'To an
> unknown god.' What therefore you worship as unknown, this I
> proclaim to you."' Acts 17.22–23*

Idolaters?

Some Christians allege that ours is the only true religion; all others
are idolatry. Some passages in the Bible support this; it sounds as
though there was an underlying conflict between intolerant narrow-
minded believers and tolerant broad-minded Christians in those
days, just as now. In the passage we heard read today about St Paul
in Athens, he clearly falls into the second camp, saying that outwardly Athenians worshipped idols, but one inscription showed
that we all worship the same God; yet Christians had some ideas to
offer humbly to their opponents about their God, which they had
not yet realized. This is a struggle in all religious; it has become
crucial in our own generation, where certain Christians and some
Muslims claim we have a duty to kill the infidels who follow other
religions.

Islam

From AD 325 when the Emperor Constantine made Christianity
legal, many Christians made the pilgrimage to Jerusalem, praying
in the holy places without opposition from the local Arab population. In the seventh century the Prophet Muhammad received
from God through an angel the revelations which form the Holy
Qur'an. At that time Arabs, Jews and Christians lived harmoni-
ously together, though the Jewish Scriptures were in Hebrew and
the Christian Bible was in Greek, so the Arabs felt left out until they
had their own Scriptures in Arabic. But the Qur'an tells Muslims
to respect the 'People of the Book', which is what it calls the other
two monotheistic religions. The following quotations demonstrate

this. Chapters in the Qur'an are called 'surahs'; from Book 2 Surahs 53–58 we read:

> . . . you will find the nearest in love to the believers (Muslims) those who say: 'We are Christians.' That is because amongst them are priests and monks, and they are not proud . . .

> And when they (who call themselves Christians) listen to what has been sent down to the Messenger (Muhammad (peace be upon him)) you see their eyes overflowing with tears because of the truth they have recognized. They say: 'Our Lord! We believe; so write us down among the witnesses . . .

> 'And why should we not believe in Allah and in that which has come to us of the truth (Islamic Monotheism)? And we wish that our Lord will admit us (in Paradise on the Day of Resurrection) along with the righteous people (Prophet Muhammad (peace be upon him) and his Companions (may Allah be pleased with them))' . . .

> So because of what they said, Allah rewarded them Gardens under which rivers flow (in Paradise), they will abide therein forever. Such is the reward of (the good-doers).

The Qur'an refers more often to Jesus (prophet Isa [EE-sah]) than it does to Muhammad; he was the second greatest prophet, and will come again to judge the earth. The Qur'an also says, 'Let there be no compulsion in religion; truth stands out clearly from error.' And Muhammad also wrote: 'The true Muslim is the one who hurts no one by word or deed.' Muslims worship 'Allah, the compassionate, the merciful', and some say that all the world's religions share an emphasis on the virtue of compassion.

Warfare

Unfortunately Muhammad was attacked by fellow Arabs on his way to Mecca, and so arose the idea of holy Jihad, the duty to fight in self-defence. His friend Abu-Bakr claimed the title of Caliph and the right to rule all Muslims; his followers became the Sunnis, and those who would not obey were the Shia. Syrian Saracens, taking control of the Holy Land from the original Arabs, attacked Christian pilgrims on the way to Jerusalem. The first Crusaders went with the aim of protecting the pilgrim routes, but could not resist the temptation to loot and kill all the Muslims, Jews and even fellow-Christians they met on the way. The Saracens counter-attacked, reaching the gates of Vienna before they were defeated. Arabs supported Lawrence of Arabia during the Great War; but afterwards the Allies made an arbitrary boundary between Syria and Iraq, and encouraged the Jews to resettle in Israel.

Reconciliation

After this sorry history, some are attempting Christian–Muslim reconciliation; but it is hard. Some people remain practising Muslims while believing fully in the core doctrines of both religions. Christians emphasize that we do not mean by the doctrine of the Trinity what Muslims think we do. A professor from Yale Divinity School teaches that two faiths, worshipping the same God, can work together under a single government.

Suggested hymns

In Christ there is no east or west; Let all the world in every corner sing; They shall come from the east; We three kings of orient are.

Twelfth Sunday after Trinity (Proper 17)
3 September
Principal Service   **Pain and Hope**
(*Continuous*): Ex. 3.1–15 The burning bush, Ps. 105.1–6,
23–26, 45b Moses; or (*Related*): Jer. 15.15–21 Jeremiah's call,
Ps. 26.1–8 Temple thanksgiving; Rom. 12.9–21 Love in action;
Matt. 16.21–28 Take up your cross

'Rejoice in hope, be patient in suffering, persevere in prayer.'
Romans 12.12

Interconnected

St Paul wrote to the Christians in Rome about hope, suffering and prayer. The three are interconnected: you cannot endure suffering unless you hope that there is something better in the afterlife; and you cannot hope unless you remain connected to God through prayer. Yet you cannot pray unless you hope that there is something better beyond this world of suffering.

Pain

So what is pain? Is it the same as suffering? Is it good or bad? How can a loving God allow us to endure pain? Well, looking first at the wider picture, Charles Darwin showed how this complex and beautiful world could only have evolved if minor changes in one individual could be inherited by that creature's descendants, and that useful changes could be prioritized over harmful ones by natural selection. The main feature of the harmful changes is that they cause the creature to suffer more. So if there were no pain, there would be no evolution, and human beings would never have appeared on the earth. Of course, if you are a fundamentalist, you can say that pain is God's punishment for sin. But if God had created the whole human race from two progenitors, it is hard to see how there could be the glorious diversity that we see around us; we should all be identical. So pain and death are necessary for the process of learning from our mistakes, which makes us human.

Pain and sacrifice

Pain is also a good thing on the individual level: I can learn lessons from my agonies which I could learn in no other way. I learn to admit my total dependence on God. I learn that strength to endure comes as a result of prayer, and in no other way. I learn to long for the pain-free existence of the world to come. A sick woman was urged to offer her pain as a sacrifice to God; 'but surely he doesn't want it,' she said. 'But God is sharing your pain already,' came the reply. 'Offering pain to God is a way of making you aware of that. So offer your courage to God instead.' She thought about this for a while, then asked, 'Didn't Jesus say that self-sacrifice is the highest form of love? I wish God would take this pain away; but if that is not possible, I shall offer it to God with a prayer that he will give me grace to remain brave.'

The broken God

Jesus showed us on the cross that even God suffers from the way we reject him, and even he felt at one point that God had abandoned him. Extreme pain reduces us to complete helplessness. Sometimes non-religious people say that belief is a kind of a crutch; but leaning on God does not take away the pain – only it casts us back on to him, by the awareness that he is there, suffering with us, and will take the pain away, by healing or else by death, when he thinks the time is right. We cannot summon up God to do our bidding; the medieval mystic Meister Eckhart said, 'To use God is to kill him.' God often seems to remain hidden from us until we feel absolutely broken. This is a God stripped of all sentimentality, unreachable by our attempts at manipulation; yet a God who has known pain on the cross, leading to death, and then on through death to resurrection. Jesus, then, tells us to become like him: 'If any want to become my followers, let them deny themselves and take up their cross and follow me.'

Hope

So pain and suffering show us our need for hope. We must be prepared to risk all, hoping that at the end God will save us. The Brazilian Roman Catholic Archbishop and social reformer Helder Camara said that 'Hope without risk is not hope.' Yet it is the times when God has saved us by giving us the grace to endure which fill us with hope for the future. St Paul was giving very down-to-earth advice when he told the Christians in Rome, and through them each one of us, to 'Rejoice in hope, be patient in suffering, persevere in prayer.'

All-age worship

Play doctors and nurses. What would you, as a Christian, do when one of your patients died?

Suggested hymns

All my hope on God is founded; Jesu, the very thought of thee; Lord of all hopefulness; Lord, teach us how to pray aright.

Twelfth Sunday after Trinity (Proper 17)
3 September
Second Service **Sharing Good News**
Ps. 105.1–15 Mindful of his covenant; 2 Kings 6.24–25; 7.3–20
The siege of Samaria; Acts 18.1–16 Paul in Corinth; Gospel at
Holy Communion: Mark 7.1–8, 14–15, 21–23 Tradition

> *'[The lepers] said to one another, "What we are doing is wrong.
> This is a day of good news; if we are silent and wait until the
> morning light, we will be found guilty; therefore let us go and tell
> the king's household."' 2 Kings 7.9*

Samaria

The news today is full of stories of how people all round the world
are starving. Most of us in this country have never seen anybody
who has had too little to eat for a long period, but a little imagination will point us to what an agonizing experience this must be. So
we can imagine what the inhabitants of Samaria felt like in the story
we just heard read from the Old Testament, when the Assyrians
besieged them in their city with no access to food or water. It is a
gripping story, and has all the trademarks of an account written
down soon after the events by an eye-witness. Particularly graphic
is the story of the four men suffering from leprosy, who were not
admitted into the city for fear of infection. So they decided to desert,
and change sides. They went to the enemy camp to hand themselves
in, only to find it empty. They stuffed themselves with the food that
had been left behind, but suddenly realized it was selfish to keep
the story to themselves. So they hastened to tell those besieged in
Samaria, saying, 'What we are doing is wrong. This is a day of good
news . . . let us go and tell the king's household.' So they arrived at a
basic ethical principle: it is immoral to keep good news to yourself.

Gospel

Christians describe the story of what Jesus has done to bring us forgiveness for our sins as 'the gospel'; the word means 'good news'. If
we know that God loves us, and fail to tell other people, who need
our heavenly Father's forgiveness as much as we do, we are being das-
tardly selfish. The purpose of the Christian Church is to glorify God
in making the Christ of the Scriptures known through the love of God

in worship, word and action. So, the big question is 'What can each of us do to encourage our friends to grow in God's love and in their knowledge of Jesus Christ?' A good place to search for answers is to turn to the Bible and look at the ways the early Church grew.

- They worshipped God together – *praise*.
- They prayed together and God acted – *prayer*.
- They cared for any in need – *care*.
- They shared their faith in Christ – *share*.
- . . . And 'the Lord added to their number'.

Praise – prayer – care – share – a good theory, and it must have worked 2,000 years ago or none of us would be here, nor would we have a worldwide Church of 2,000 million souls. But how can you and I put it into practice, here and now?

Sharing

Well, ask yourself, how did *I* come to faith in Jesus? It may be that you were brought up by good Christian parents, had the usual teenage rebellion, but later came back to the Church. It may be that you saw Christians busily involved in caring for needy people, and wanted to know where they got their inspiration from. Probably you got into casual conversation with a Christian friend, who seemed an example you wanted to copy, and who quietly demolished the reasons why you were prejudiced against religion. Then your friend invited you to come to church, and you were impressed by the warm welcome, and the moving quality of the worship, and decided to keep coming.

Congregation

Your priest or minister can only do so much, and if you leave the task of promoting church growth to the professionals, very little will happen. So we as a congregation, and each of us as individuals, must check ourselves to see how good we are at attracting people by *praising* God together in our worship; by *praying* for the non-churchgoers; by *caring* for those in need; or by *sharing* our faith in Christ with anyone who is willing to listen. Everybody is different, so each needs a different approach. But all those who have not yet heard the good news are starving to death. So whether you have an opportunity this month for evangelizing one of your friends by *praise – prayer – care – share*, ask God to give you the right words to say. To keep the good news to yourself would be indescribably selfish.

Suggested hymns

God is working his purpose out; God's Spirit is in my heart (Go tell everyone); We have a gospel to proclaim; Will you come and follow me?

Thirteenth Sunday after Trinity (Proper 18)
10 September
Principal Service   **Do or Die**

(*Continuous*): Ex. 12.1–14 The Passover, Ps. 149 Praise and judgement; *or (Related)*: Ezek. 33.7–11 Turn back from evil, Ps. 119.33–40 Law and repentance; Rom. 13.8–14 Love fulfils the law; Matt. 18.15–20 Where two or three agree

> 'Love does no wrong to a neighbour; therefore, love is the fulfilling of the law.' Romans 13.10

Strategy

An individual or organization must have an overriding strategy, a plan for how they will achieve their objectives. Boring, but true. If we dare to guess at what *God's* strategy is in dealing with the human race, we might suggest that the divine plan began by persuading each primitive tribe that there is a spiritual power which is stronger than them, and will protect them if they worship him or her. Only later did God reveal that all these gods are really one God, who cares for all and does not take sides in our disputes. God chose the Jews to learn this lesson first, and to spread it to others. They believed that the one true God cares deeply about how we behave to each other; we call this 'ethical monotheism'.

Laws

The way that kings and tribal rulers kept control in those days often developed into a code of law. His subjects said, 'You want us to obey you, o king, but how can we do that if we do not know what you want us to do and not to do?' The monarch would then issue a set of instructions, and appoint group leaders or magistrates to put them into effect in their region. But this situation would collapse in confusion if each magistrate made a different interpretation of the ruler's orders, and imposed different punishments on those who disobeyed. So, following the reign of King Hammurabi in Babylon, in about 1800 BC, onwards, there emerged written codes of laws, instructing the magistrates what punishment to apply for which crime. The Old Testament tells us that God gave Moses the Ten Commandments as the small print on a contract or covenant between God and the people; God would guide them and protect them, on condition they avoided these ten sins. But there followed a proliferation of other laws, some containing errors of fact – you shall not eat the meat of the hare because it has cloven hoofs – and others inflicting harsh punishments such as stoning to death for acts of adultery.

Jesus

The Jews spent happy hours debating these laws, writing further details, until the broader vision of how we care for each other was lost. Jesus supported the idea of law – 'not a jot or tittle shall perish' – as showing that our heavenly Father cares how we behave. But he also broke the laws against any form of work, even healing, on the Sabbath day. People were making the detailed observation of rituals a distraction from the important issues of morality. Jesus said that the law of love overrides every other law: 'Love God and love your neighbour; on these two laws depend every other law in the book.' If you behave in a loving way, you can work out the detail for yourself, and let the written code go hang. That shocked many people, and still does today.

Practice

So Jesus put his teaching on love into practice in his own life. He made caring for the needy his priority, and when others attacked him he refused to retaliate. He made self-sacrifice his guiding principle, telling those who followed him to do the same. In this way he started to build the kingdom of love on earth, as it is in heaven. Just imagine what the world would be like if everyone fully practised these two basic laws!

Do or die

When someone makes a radical attempt to transform society, we say they have adopted a '*do or die*' philosophy. In the case of Jesus, it turned into 'do *and* die.' For if he once admitted that love doesn't *really* matter, we must be realistic . . . then his whole plan would collapse! If he tried to resist arrest, or lied to escape conviction, everyone would say he was a hopeless idealist, and nobody would continue to build the kingdom of love. But if he took self-sacrifice to the limit, laying down his life so that his friends would still believe in the importance of what he taught, then the high priests and Romans would have won the physical battle, but he would have won the spiritual, ethical struggle. Then he could leave his followers . . . us . . . you and me . . . to carry on building the kingdom of love, until God's strategy has been fulfilled, and a world of squabbling is transformed into an international community of mutual service and care. So let's just get on with it!

All-age worship

How many hymns about love can you think of? Learn one of them by heart.

Suggested hymns

A new commandment I give unto you; Gracious Spirit, Holy Ghost; My song is love unknown; Such love, pure as the whitest snow.

Thirteenth Sunday after Trinity (Proper 18)
10 September
Second Service   **Magic**
Ps. 108 Steadfast love [115 Not to us]; Ezek. 12.21—13.16 False prophets; Acts 19.1–20 Magic; *Gospel at Holy Communion*: Mark 7.24–37 Crumbs from the table

> '*A number of those who practised magic collected their books and burned them publicly; when the value of these books was calculated, it was found to come to fifty thousand silver coins.*' Acts 19.19

Paul

St Paul taught in the city of Corinth, and gained a reputation as a healer. Some of his healing miracles took place without any direct contact: people would touch a piece of cloth against his skin, and then lay it on the skin of a sick person, who would then recover. This is a very strange type of miracle, and sounds almost like magic. Yet the early Church was opposed to magic: when the local healers realized that Paul could achieve far more by his prayers than any of them could with their magical tricks, they renounced their wicked ways, and publicly burnt all their valuable books of magical spells in the marketplace. So what is the difference between miracles and magic? In magic, the one who does the deed is the magician, though they may be claiming to draw on powers outside of themselves. But with miracles, the healer prays to God, asking him to choose to use his own, God's power, to bring about the healing.

Sacraments

But then what about the sacraments? Christians say that the bread and wine in Holy Communion 'are' the body and blood of Jesus. Is this another magical trick, turning one thing into another? Or is it a miracle, in which we pray to God to perform magic for us? There has been much debate among Christians about these questions down the ages. One thing that Christians have been firm about is that the bread and wine continue to be still, in some sense, bread and wine; we are not committing cannibalism by eating actual flesh and drinking real blood. In the Middle Ages, the words used by the Greek philosopher Aristotle were very popular. He distinguished between the outward appearance of something: it's colour, texture, weight and so on, which are purely accidental, so he called them the 'accidents'; and the underlying nature of what the object 'really is'. The Latin for 'underlying' – or rather 'standing under' – is *substantia* which we translate as 'substance'. So Christians said that the sacrament has the outward appearance of bread, but the underlying nature of flesh. That suited medieval philosophers just fine, but it is hard to translate it into modern English. Although some have spoken of the priest performing a daily miracle on the altar, the Church of England Catechism defines a sacrament as 'an outward and visible sign of an inward and spiritual grace'. In other words, the bread and wine make God's invisible love visible to us. What *is* miraculous is not the bread, but God's love and its effect on us; for which the technical term is 'God's grace'.

Grace

But grace is something which most of us here have personal experience of in one way or another. It may have been a warm feeling of the presence of Jesus when we are praying or worshipping. Maybe you felt inspired to say or write something which you could never have possibly thought up for yourself without the help of God. Or perhaps you were able to do an act of kindness for somebody else which required a degree of devotion and determination, which, if you were doing it in your own strength would have exhausted you and made you give up much sooner. In each of these cases, and many others like them, you are experiencing the spiritual power of God made freely available to one of his creatures in response to prayer. And that is what grace is. This certainly is a miracle, because it is all done in God's power, and not by human efforts. And again, the miracle is not magical, because it is not a trick produced by *legerdemain*, in order to dazzle the observers and make money for the magician, which all healings and other wonders performed without any reference to God our loving heavenly Father certainly are. I am not talking about conjuring tricks, but so-called 'faith healings' performed by somebody with no religious faith.

Relationship

Acts done by the grace of God, including sacraments and healings, depend on the truth that God can do more to help you face life's challenges if you have a close-up and intimate relationship with him. Magic does not. So the magicians of Corinth did well to burn all their books of spells, even though they lost a lot of money in doing so.

Suggested hymns

Amazing grace, how sweet the sound; God moves in a mysterious way; God of mercy, God of grace; O gladsome light, O grace.

Fourteenth Sunday after Trinity (Proper 19)

17 September

Principal Service **Forgiveness**

(*Continuous*): Ex. 14.19–31 The Exodus, Ps. 114 The Exodus *or Canticle*: Ex. 15.1b–11, 20–21 The Exodus; *or (Related)*: Gen. 50.15–21 God turns evil to good, Ps. 103.[1–7] 8–13 God's love and fatherhood; Rom. 14.1–12 Tolerance and justice; Matt. 18.21–35 Forgiveness seventy times seven

> 'Peter came and said to [Jesus], "Lord, if another member of the church sins against me, how often should I forgive? As many as seven times?" Jesus said to him, "Not seven times, but, I tell you, seventy-seven times."' *Matthew 18.21–22*

Film

A documentary film was made a few years ago, by Lekha Singh and Roger Spottiswoode, called *Beyond Right and Wrong*. So, even before you have watched it any further than the title, it has stirred up a storm of controversy in your heart. Surely right and wrong is all there is? There is no middle ground; no considerations which can take you any further than common-sense morality. Or is there? The film doesn't answer the question. It simply tells a number of stories of people who met each other, in Northern Ireland, Rwanda and the Middle East, some years after one had caused life-shattering harm to the other. 'Some of it', wrote Giles Fraser in the *Church Times*, 'was almost unbearable to watch.'

Truth

All these, remember, are true stories:

- There was the story of the woman from Rwanda, in Africa, whose five children had all been killed, one after another, during an attack on a church by a fighter from one of the tribal wars which shattered that part of the world not long ago. A few years later, she was approached by their killer, who asked her to forgive him for murdering her children.
- An Irish schoolboy, who had been blinded by a rubber bullet, met the British soldier who fired the shot.

- Palestinian and Israeli families met on neutral territory, despite the fact that each of them had lost relatives during the seemingly never-ending war between the two nations, both of which believed they were fighting for what they considered their ancestral land.

Forgiveness

Each of these deeply wounded people knew that the injury which had been done to them was evil, and nothing could alter that. But does 'forgiveness' mean denying the wrongness of what had happened? St Peter asked Jesus how many times he should forgive somebody who had offended him? Should he aim, impossible as it sounds, to forgive them for as many as seven successive injuries? Peter held his breath. After a pause, Jesus answered simply, 'No,' and Peter breathed again. 'No,' Jesus continued. 'No, not seven times – forgive them for *seventy-seven* offences.' Collapse of stout Peter! Now saying, even once, that what you did doesn't matter a bit, I don't care about it at all, would make you choke, because it is a lie. Is that what Jesus meant? No, and again I answer 'No!' 'I forgive you' means that what happened was terrible, but that is in the past – what matters is our relationship in the future.

Proportionate

Our usual reaction to evil deeds is to say: 'Offenders must be punished, or they will think their crime doesn't matter.' Which is quite true; but what if the offender genuinely repents? And how do you decide what is a proportionate punishment? What sentence can balance in the scales of justice the loss of a child? Will imprisonment, or capital punishment, quench the thirst for retribution in the hearts of the bereaved? Nothing can alter the past; all we can do is to change the future in such a way that the hatred in our hearts gives way to hope. It feels like a betrayal to say 'I forgive you', and hatred cannot be turned off like a tap. But if you take out your anger in whipping up the cake mixture or beating out the hearth rug, anywhere in private, you may leave behind the dangers brought by the desire for revenge, and find a new hope in building a more peaceful future. Try it out sometime: think of something that makes you really angry, then say to yourself: 'I'll put that in a box marked "past", and concentrate on filling the box marked "future" with lovely things full of hope.' That is what forgiveness means. If you can do it once, Jesus assures you, then, with his help, you can do it 77 times! Then you can say sincerely, 'Forgive me my trespasses, as I forgive them theirs.'

All-age worship

Make two boxes marked 'past' and 'future'. Write things that make you angry on scraps of paper, scrumple them up, put them in the 'past' box and put it in a black bag to go out with the rubbish. In the 'future' box put a cake iced with the word 'hope', and share it round with everybody.

Suggested hymns

Come and see, come and see (Kendrick); 'Forgive our sins as we forgive'; O happy day! that fixed my choice; There's a wideness in God's mercy.

Fourteenth Sunday after Trinity (Proper 19)
17 September
Second Service   **Giving and Receiving**
Ps. 119.41–48 [49–64] An answer for mockers; Ezek. 20.1–8, 33–44 Judgement and restoration; Acts 20.17–38 Farewell to Ephesus; *Gospel at Holy Communion*: Mark 8.27–38 Take up your cross

> '*I coveted no one's silver or gold or clothing. You know for your-selves that I worked with my own hands to support myself and my companions. In all this I have given you an example that by such work we must support the weak, remembering the words of the Lord Jesus, for he himself said, "It is more blessed to give than to receive."' Acts 20.33–35*

Paul

St Paul spent from AD 52 to 54 building up the Christian congregations in Ephesus, a huge city on the west coast of what we now call Turkey. He gave his time to this voluntarily, meanwhile earning his living by tent-making. He was driven out, however, by an anti-Christian riot. Then he toured around Greece and some of the

Greek islands, evangelizing and teaching, before sailing down the Turkish coast on his way back to Jerusalem. He did not want to stop at Ephesus; not only would his own life be at risk, but he might endanger the Christian leaders there, whom he called 'elders'. So he arranged to meet them at the port of Miletus, about 25 miles further south down the coast.

Miletus

This is the only time that Miletus is mentioned in the Bible, apart from a brief reference in Paul's second letter to Timothy; but it was also a significant city, at the mouth of the River Meander. It was the first town in the world to lay out its streets in a grid pattern, intersecting at right angles. The foundations have been excavated there of a large theatre, roman baths, a gymnasium and a marketplace. A huge gateway from Miletus has been reconstructed in a museum in Berlin. In the theatre some seats are marked for 'Jews and God-fearers', which may be an early reference to Christians.

Speech

Paul's volunteer physician, St Luke, was with him on this journey, so we can be sure that his account in the Acts of the Apostles of Paul's speech to the Ephesian elders was very accurate. Paul emphasizes how hard he had worked for them, and warns them of persecution to come. Then he reminds them that he had been a volunteer, not wishing to be paid from anybody's gold. We are given money, he says, not to be extravagant in what we spend on ourselves, but to 'support the weak'. 'It is better to give than to get,' says the Apostle. This remark is the nub of the whole speech, which challenges:

- those who are 'strong', that is, able to help themselves and help others, which 'the weak' are not;
- those who imagine they have not enough money to share with anybody else;
- professionals; and
- those who think they have no time to volunteer.

Strong

We are all stronger than we think. When we meet someone in difficulties, we imagine we have no more mental, physical or moral strength than they have. But if we will stop and listen to them, discuss their options with them, and promise our presence and our encouragement in their present situation, they will thank us for sharing our strength, when we think we have done nothing at all. The reason is that we are all stronger than we imagine, if only we pray to God to share *his* strength with *us*.

Money

We also find it hard to make ends meet, or so we think. But you have only to look at how little your grandparents lived on in war-time, and how so very many people in the Third World manage to survive, to realize that compared with them, we are very well off. So if you meet somebody who could do with a fun day out at your expense, or someone appealing for charity, or your local church asks you for money to make ends meet, remember that 'it is happier to give than to get'.

Professionals

Professionals, in the Church as anywhere else, need to remember that they are paid servants, given just enough so that they can concentrate on the needs of those they serve, and administering the gifts of the other members so that they can work together for the benefit of the whole community.

Volunteers

But the professionals, in the Church as elsewhere, cannot do it all on their own. St Paul's remarks to the volunteers from Ephesus remind us how the Church today is still heavily dependent on the time and skills which unpaid volunteers give to the work of God. It makes you happier if you give your time, talents and money in serving others, than if you are always thinking of what you can get for yourself.

Suggested hymns

Brother, sister, let me serve you; Father, Lord of all creation; From heaven you came, helpless babe; Will you let me be your servant?

Fifteenth Sunday after Trinity (Proper 20)

24 September

Principal Service   **Work**

(*Continuous*): Ex. 16.2–15 Manna, Ps. 105.1–6, 37–45 Manna; or (*Related*): Jonah 3.10—4.11 Anger, love and prayer, Ps. 145.1–8 God's love; Phil. 1.21–30 Death and suffering; Matt. 20.1–16 Vineyard labourers

> '*The kingdom of heaven is like a landowner who went out early in the morning to hire labourers for his vineyard.*' *Matthew 20.1*

Puzzling

The parable of the labourers in the vineyard is a puzzling one. Strict justice requires that those who work long hours should be paid more; but Jesus said that the kingdom of God doesn't work like that. God calls you to do something for him; it may be to help a needy person, or to arrange the flowers in church, or any of the other voluntary tasks which are essential to the smooth running of its worship; or to be a lay preacher or a priest, to serve others as a supermarket assistant or a managing director or a politician, or to be a loving parent or helpful child. You do these for God, but not because you expect a reward; God *does* give rewards, but like the landowner in the parable, God gives you whatever he feels like. You cannot grumble because somebody else, who works less hard than you do, seems to have a more pleasant life than yours. None of us *deserves* a comfortable life; whereas we *all* deserve to be punished for our selfishness and our sins. So if God was completely just in his rewards and punishments, we should all be in the soup! Life is unfair, let's face it; but be grateful for all the undeserved mercies you receive.

Love

The payment God gives to us all for working in his vineyard is not a comfortable trouble-free life. No, the only currency God pays us in is that of his love. And there is no such thing as a little bit of love, as far as God is concerned – it's 'all or nothing'. That applies to humans, too. We are not talking about emotions or feelings which may vary; if you say to somebody that you love them, you have to show you care for them with all your being for ever and ever. For that is how God loves us.

Vocation

The parable also teaches us something about our daily work. Whatever our job is, we do it not just for the money, but as our response to God's call. You are a leading musician, or a cleaner of drains, not because you have chosen to do that job, but because it is your vocation, for the time being at least. Therefore you must do it well, for God's sake. As the seventeenth-century poet and clergyman George Herbert wrote:

> Teach me, my God and King,
> in all things thee to see,
> and what I do in anything
> to do it as for thee . . .
>
> All may of thee partake;
> nothing can be so mean,
> which with this tincture, 'for thy sake,'
> will not grow bright and clean.
>
> A servant with this clause
> makes drudgery divine:
> who sweeps a room, as for thy laws,
> makes that and the action fine.

Work and prayer

That means that all our work, from our daily employment to the latest project to make our church congregations grow, must be accompanied by prayer. St Ignatius of Loyola, in the sixteenth century, wrote:

> Pray as if everything depended on God;
> work as if everything depended on you.

Idleness

So we must never be idle in our work. In our school years and later, we must work hard to get the qualifications that will enable us to get a good job; and when we are employed, we must never slack off just because nobody is watching us. It is God whom we are disappointing if we do. It is said that one of the popes was asked, 'How many people work in the Vatican?' To which the pope replied, 'About one in ten.'

Unemployed

Finally, the parable of the labourers in the vineyard teaches us never to despise the unemployed. God, under the image of the landowner, takes a great deal of trouble to find work for those who have been 'standing all day idle in the marketplace'. If there are unemployed people in our country, and around the world, we should not blame them. It is our responsibility, by whatever means we can, to create as many job opportunities as we can.

All-age worship

What job would you most like to do? Play-act, if possible, doing it. What qualifications would you need? Pray about your work.

Suggested hymns

Father, hear the prayer we offer; Forth in thy name, O Lord, I go; Take my life, and let it be; Teach me, my God and King.

Fifteenth Sunday after Trinity (Proper 20)
24 September
Second Service   **God Speaks to Us**
Ps. 119.113–136 Unwilling to listen to the law; Ezek. 33.23, 30—34.10 Unwilling to listen to the prophet; Acts 26.1, 9–25 Agrippa unwilling to listen to Paul; *Gospel at Holy Communion*: Mark 9.30–37 The greatest like a child

> '*I was travelling to Damascus . . . when at midday . . . I saw a light from heaven . . . [and] I heard a voice saying to me in the Hebrew language, "Saul, Saul, why are you persecuting me?" . . . I asked, "Who are you, Lord?" The Lord answered, "I am Jesus whom you are persecuting."' Acts 26.12–15*

Paul

God wanted to speak to Saul of Tarsus, but Saul did not want to listen. So God spoke to him through a miraculous vision, a bright light and a voice. *What* God said was that he wanted Saul, later known as St Paul, to serve him as a travelling preacher, proclaiming the good news about Jesus Christ. *How* God spoke to Paul was in the Hebrew language, Paul's ancestral tongue.

Visions

God still speaks to us today. Occasionally he uses visions, like that which Paul saw and heard. If you see a vision or hear a voice, that is a great privilege. But it is a rare psychological phenomenon, and if God chooses that way to communicate with you, you have no choice to obey, even if it means handing over your whole life to God.

Agrippa

Then, in today's reading, God wanted to speak to King Agrippa, telling him to set St Paul free, and himself to become a Christian. God wanted to speak to Agrippa – but the King did not want to listen to God. He made fun of Paul: satirically he asked, 'Are you so quickly persuading me to become a Christian?' Agrippa was not the only one to whom God speaks, but who does not listen to God because they don't want to hear what God is trying to say. People were deaf to the Law and the prophets; and it still happens a million times a day in the modern world.

Nature

So, just as God spoke then in Hebrew, so God's word comes to us today in a familiar language which we can all understand, if we are willing. The first way is through beauty. Most of us have stood on a hilltop or beside the sea, and been overcome by awe. If we have been misled by the cynics, we dismiss it, saying to ourselves, 'That's all nonsense. I don't believe in the supernatural, it's just an unusual sequence of electrical happenings in my brain.' But if you are wise, you will accept that such beauty could not happen by accident, and must be the handiwork of a divine Creator, who wants us to become creative like him. The same applies when we hear lovely music or see a great work of art.

History

God also speaks through history. When you read about what people in other ages have thought or done, and the changes that have taken place in society in consequence, bringing, with many sad set-backs, a slow progress towards a better world, you realize that God must be in charge, however deaf people are to what God tells them. You read about the religious ideas and traditions of our ancestors, and realize they are far too precious to be thrown out in the name of modernity.

Conversation

God speaks to us in the day-to-day conversations we have with our family, friends and neighbours. They give us advice which, however reluctant we are to hear it, comes, often unwittingly, through them from God to us. Or you may be stirred by the courage with which they face the tough times of life, which gives you the strength to go forward, putting your entire trust in God's grace.

Imagination

Finally, God speaks to you through your imagination. Those trains of thought you have, waking or half-sleeping, about the meaning of life and the problems of being human – though they seldom rise to the level of prayer – are inspired by God, and may be God's phone messages, reminding you that he exists and he loves you.

Through us

So God speaks to us today through visions, nature, beauty, history and tradition, conversations and our imagination. But God can also speak through us to other people. Prepare yourself by thinking what you would say to someone in such-and-such a situation, acting as God's mouthpiece; listen carefully to what people say, and drop in the quiet sympathetic word, revealing what a difference God makes to your life. They may not be ready to listen, just as we ourselves often miss what God is trying to say. But if we open ourselves com-pletely to God, and talk lovingly to those we meet, sometimes God may speak through us, even when we are not aware. What a won-derful God he is!

Suggested hymns

Be thou my vision; God has spoken through his prophets; Rise and hear, the Lord is speaking; We sing the glorious conquest.

Sixteenth Sunday after Trinity (Proper 21)
(Alternatively the Dedication Festival)
1 October

Principal Service   **Humble**

(*Continuous*): Ex. 17.1–7 Water from the rock, Ps. 78.1–4,
12–16 Water from the rock; *or* (*Related*): Ezek. 18.1–4, 25–32
Individual responsibility, Ps. 25.1–8 Teach me your ways; Phil.
2.1–13 The mind of Christ; Matt. 21.23–32 The Baptist's
authority

> '[Jesus] emptied himself, taking the form of a slave, being born
> in human likeness. And being found in human form, he humbled
> himself and became obedient to the point of death – even death
> on a cross.' Philippians 2.7–8

The mind of Christ

One of the most poetic passages in the writings of St Paul, from his
Letter to the Philippians, begins: 'Let this mind be in you, which
was also in Christ Jesus . . .' That is from the old King James or
Authorized Version of the Bible. How could it be expressed in modern English, so that modern people can easily understand it? The
mind is the centre of our way of thinking, our attitude to the world
around us, and our basic patterns of behaviour. So the apostle was
calling us to adopt the same view of the world as Jesus had; to think
as he did, to share his values, and to pattern our lives on his. Crucial
to this teaching is the fact that Jesus was utterly humble in all that
he did. He dedicated himself to meeting the needs of others, and
never thought of considering his own needs at all.

Incarnation

So, says Paul, Jesus was living in heaven, sharing all the glories of
eternity with God his Father, in the most wonderful environment,
surrounded by saints and angels – for that is what heaven means,
absolute paradise. Then, in order to do his Father's will, he threw
the whole lot away – 'emptied himself' of his heavenly status and
glory, as the Bible puts it. This is about Paul's only reference to
the events at Bethlehem, though the teaching which underlies the
Christmas story is the basis of the whole apostolic message: that
Jesus, who was equally divine with God the Father, took flesh and

became completely human, equal in lowliness with you and me. A little bit of heaven came down to earth on Christmas night. We call that 'incarnation', which means entering into human flesh. Nothing so humble has ever been done before or since.

Humble

The incarnation and human life of Jesus defines the meaning of humility. It means not overestimating our own importance, and if we have any privileges due to our position in life, being willing to sacrifice them all in the service of others less fortunate than ourselves. Humility is the opposite of pride – humble is the converse of arrogant. St Paul is telling us that this is how we ought to be: thinking never of our own wishes, and always putting the needs of others first, as Jesus did. Proud people imagine they are more important than anyone else; Christ-like folk instinctively feel that others' needs are more important than their own.

False humility

Of course there is such a thing as false humility. It is characterized by Uriah Heep, a character in Charles Dickens' novel *David Copperfield*, who cringes to everyone, insisting that 'I'm a very *'umble* man, Mr Copperfield!' Yet he is the most self-important, proud man on the planet. This false humility is like a mask, put on when one wishes to impress other people, and slipped off in a second when nobody is looking. Uriah Heep is always trying to cheat somebody; he is the very opposite of true humility. Sadly, false humility like that is still found today.

Self-respect

Nor must the search for Christ-like humility rob us of our self-respect. To give us the self-confidence to undertake challenging projects we must believe that, even if we do not have the innate qualities which the task requires, God, through his 'amazing grace', will supply us with all the courage and skill we require, if we ask him to.

Self-sacrifice

So, says St Paul:

Let the same mind be in you that was in Christ Jesus, who, though he was in the form of God, did not regard equality with God as something to be exploited, but emptied himself, taking the form of a slave, being born in human likeness. And being found in human form, he humbled himself and became obedient to the point of death – even death on a cross. Therefore God also highly exalted him . . .

And God our Father will also exalt you, if you seek to imitate the genuine humility of Jesus, the incarnate Son of God, so that you may share with him all the glories and joys of heaven.

All-age worship

Make paper cut-outs, on sticks, of God and Jesus in heaven, Jesus coming down to earth and being crucified; several Christians bowing before him, and then being taken up to heaven with him.

Suggested hymns

And can it be?; From heaven you came; Meekness and majesty; Thou who wast rich beyond all splendour.

Sixteenth Sunday after Trinity (Proper 21)
1 October
Second Service   Heresies
Ps. [120 Lying lips, 123 As a handmaid] 124 The Lord on our side; Ezek. 37.15–28 Reuniting the nation; 1 John 2.22–29 Abide in him; *Gospel at Holy Communion*: Mark 9.38–50 Those not against are for

> *'Who is the liar but the one who denies that Jesus is the Christ? This is the antichrist, the one who denies the Father and the Son.'*
> *1 John 2.22*

Interpretation

Christianity did not come to earth as a fully worked-out philosophy. There were the teachings of Jesus, mostly in the form of parables;

accounts of his life, death and resurrection by those who claimed to be eyewitnesses; and the group of 12 disciples, chosen by Jesus to be the foundation of the Church. But within any group of people there are bound to be divergent opinions, and new converts became confused, asking which of the various teachings were to be accepted as the truth about Jesus and the salvation which he brought. Some people joined the young Church, full of their own importance; they had certain preconceived notions of their own, and tried to twist the Christian faith and force it to support their own beliefs, instead of letting the teachings of Jesus distinguish between true and false in the teachings of those who claimed to be Christians. The apostles were forced to define what true Christianity is, and to reject all false doctrines, before the Church could be harmed and its new members led astray.

Heresy

You may think, from reading the Fourth Gospel, that St John, its author, was a calm, peaceful sort of Christian. But in his first letter he becomes quite angry with those who are spreading false teaching about the nature of God and of Jesus, and their relationship to each other. He writes:

> Who is the liar but the one who denies that Jesus is the Christ? This is the antichrist, the one who denies the Father and the Son. No one who denies the Son has the Father; everyone who confesses the Son has the Father also.

There are similar explosions in other parts of the New Testament, and in the next century the number of divergent so-called Gospels was so great that many Christians wrote books attacking these false teachings. It is good to encourage people to think for themselves. But if they deny the possibility of Jesus saving us from sin and death, and reconciling us to his Father, they need to be stamped on before simple Christians are led dangerously astray. Christians are free to choose what to believe; but if it denies our salvation, it is a wrong choice. The Greek word for choice is 'heresy', so these false doctrines came to be called heresies. In AD 180 a Christian called Irenaeus wrote an influential book called *Against Heresies*, or *On the detection and overthrow of so-called knowledge*. The Greek word for 'knowledge' is *gnosis*, with a silent 'g' at the beginning, and the heretics were also known as *gnostics*. They threatened the survival of the true faith, but Christians are wrong to use violence to oppose heresy. The Emperor Constantine adopted Christianity because he thought it would unite his multi-faith empire, but when he found that Christians didn't agree on what Christian doctrine is, he locked the bishops in a church in Nicea, modern Isnik, saying he would not let them out until they could agree on a statement of doctrine. The result was what we call the Nicene Creed, used by many churches in their Holy Communion services.

Types

There are more types of heresy than anyone could remember, but I have divided them into six groups, which I will list for you with a few examples.

1   *Heresies which overemphasize one Person of the Trinity.*
    For example *Deism* taught that God the Father is not interested in his creation. *Montanism* taught that the Age of the Spirit had already arrived on earth.
2   *Heresies which deny the Unity of the three Persons.*
    For example *Arianism* viewed the Son as of a similar substance to the Father, but not the same.
3   *Heresies which deny the equality of the three Persons.*
    For example, *Adoptionism* viewed Jesus as a human, who was adopted by God as his son.
4   *Heresies which deny the separateness of the Persons.*
    Modalism teaches that the one God reveals himself in three modes.
5   *Heresies denying the divinity or humanity of the Son.*
    For example, *Socinianism* and *Docetism* respectively.
6   *Heresies which deny the need for grace in salvation.*
    Pelagius was alleged to teach that we can save ourselves by our own efforts.

Is that clear? I thought not! If you want to know more, ask me and I will give you the name of a pocket-sized book which gives a brief summary.* Finally, a poem by Edwin Markham:

He drew a circle to shut me out:
heretic, rebel, a thing to flout.
But Love and I had the wit to win
we drew a circle that took him in!

Suggested hymns

Firmly I believe and truly; Immortal, invisible, God only wise; Majesty, worship his majesty; Thy hand, O God, has guided.

*A Basic Christian Dictionary, by Michael Counsell, Canterbury Press, www.canterburypress.co.uk.

Seventeenth Sunday after Trinity (Proper 22)
8 October
Principal Service   **Perseverance of Athletes**
(*Continuous*): Ex. 20.1–4, 7–9, 12–20 The Ten Commandments, Ps. 19 The heavens declare the glory of God; *or* (*Related*): Isa. 5.1–7 Song of the vine, Ps. 80.9–17 The vine; Phil. 3.4b–14 Persevere; Matt. 21.33–46 The vine

> '*Not that I have already obtained this or have already reached the goal; but I press on . . . [and] this one thing I do: forgetting what lies behind and straining forward to what lies ahead, I press on towards the goal for the prize of the heavenly call of God in Christ Jesus.' Philippians 3.12–14*

Athletes

I think that if there had been newspapers in St Paul's day, the first thing he would have turned to after buying one would be the sports pages. Not that he ever tells us which team he supports, but there are an awful lot of mentions of athletics, and in particular running races, which were a feature of life in the first century AD in the Roman Empire, the running track often ending dramatically in the middle of the town square. But what appears to impress Paul most is the grit, determination and perseverance of the runners. As well as today's reading from Paul's letter to the Philippians, his first letter to the Corinthians encourages Christians to persevere like the athletes, when Paul writes:

Do you not know that in a race the runners all compete, but only one receives the prize? Run in such a way that you may win it. Athletes exercise self-control in all things; they do it to receive a perishable wreath, but we an imperishable one. So I do not run aimlessly, nor do I box as though beating the air; but I punish my body and enslave it, so that after proclaiming to others I myself should not be disqualified.

And in his letter to the Galatians, the apostle said:

I laid before [the leaders of the Church in Jerusalem] . . . the gospel that I proclaim among the Gentiles, in order to make sure that I was not running, or had not run, in vain.

Then, although the Letter to the Hebrews is not by St Paul, it contains the famous passage:

Since we are surrounded by so great a cloud of witnesses, let us also lay aside every weight and the sin that clings so closely, and let us run with perseverance the race that is set before us, looking to Jesus the pioneer and perfecter of our faith, who for the sake of the joy that was set before him endured the cross, disregarding its shame, and has taken his seat at the right hand of the throne of God.

Perseverance

The theme common to all these readings is perseverance. You may have heard the old joke about the three Christians called Luke, Mark and Percy: Luke Warm, Mark Time and Percy Vere! Although God is remarkably tolerant, it is presumptuous if we expect just to drift into heaven with no effort on our part. We cannot earn heaven, we never deserve it; but we really ought to work at being a Christian if we realize, like the athlete, how great a prize awaits us when we reach the finishing post. So we should pray when we don't feel like it; go to church when we would rather stay in bed; do odd jobs for any neighbours living with disabilities; take time to listen to those who are troubled; read a passage from the Bible carefully every day, and chat to our non-Christian friends about what it contains; and speak up on behalf of the oppressed. And then, when we are feeling exhausted and bored, to grit our teeth and pick up where we left off, until the job is finished. Not because God commands us to, but because we are so grateful for what God has done for us that we are desperate to find ways of saying thank you. Being a Christian and loving our neighbour is hard work, but somebody has to do it, and once we have started we have to persevere. We must pray in the words of Percy Dearmer's hymn:

Jesus, good above all other,
Gentle Child of Gentle Mother,
In a stable born our brother,
Give us grace to persevere.

Finally, I love these two typical quotations from Winston Churchill:

Never give in. Never give in. Never, never, never, never – in nothing, great or small, large or petty – never give in, except to convictions of honour and good sense. Never yield to force. Never yield to the apparently overwhelming weight of the enemy.

And:

If you are going through hell – keep going!

All-age worship

Have a running race. Give prizes, not to those who came first but those who persevered longest.

Suggested hymns

And now, O Father, mindful of the love; Fight the good fight; Gracious Spirit, Holy Ghost; Jesus, good above all other.

Seventeenth Sunday after Trinity (Proper 22)
8 October
Second Service **Harmful Sin**
Ps. 136 God's love lasts for ever; Prov. 2.1–11 Search for Wisdom; 1 John 2.1–17 Walk the way he walked; *Gospel at Holy Communion*: Mark 10.2–16 Divorce

'Whoever says, "I am in the light", while hating a brother or sister, is still in the darkness. Whoever loves a brother or sister lives in the light, and in such a person there is no cause for stumbling. But whoever hates another believer is in the darkness, walks in the darkness, and does not know the way to go.'
1 John 2.9–11

Morals

A man who was 'brought up as a traditional Roman Catholic', emailed a non-Catholic friend, suggesting that 'liberal Catholics generally reject RC doctrine not only on women priests but also on many moral issues including divorce, birth control – perhaps even abortion – and IVF. So there is a battle of ideologies across the board.' The friend found himself wondering whether, although these are undoubtedly important moral issues, they are important enough to split a church over. The next day being Sunday, he listened in church to Christ's summary of the law:

> Our Lord Jesus Christ said:
> The first commandment is this:
> > 'Hear, O Israel, the Lord our God is the only Lord.
> > You shall love the Lord your God with all your heart,
> > with all your soul, with all your mind,
> > and with all your strength.'
> The second is this:
> > 'Love your neighbour as yourself.'
> There is no other commandment greater than these.
> On these two commandments hang all the law and the prophets.

Although he had heard it many times, he suddenly realized he had never listened to it closely.

Love

Jesus was speaking to Pharisees, and experts in the interpretation of the fiendishly complicated laws of the Old Testament. Jesus had a high respect for these laws: 'not one jot or tittle of them shall pass away,' he said. But he said that the law of love, also quoted from the Old Testament, was the most important law of all: 'There is no other commandment greater than these.' That meant that any law, such as that against doing any work on the Sabbath day – even healing the sick – if it was in conflict with the law of love, was over-ridden by the higher law. Furthermore, every other law was dependent on – 'hangs on' – the law of love. Love is at the heart of what God expects of us; the other laws are only attempts to apply the law of love to particular situations. The society for which they were written was tribal, pastoral and agricultural, in which the patriarch of the tribe controlled the doings of every member, and needed written guidance on what offences he should punish, and how severely. When the young Christian Church tried to apply the Jewish commandments to a very different non-Jewish society in the Roman Empire, they ditched *all* the Jewish laws as inappropriate to the new situation, bar four, which they called 'essentials':

1 no meat which has been sacrificed to idols;
2 no blood – and nobody is quite sure what that means;
3 no meat of an animal which has been strangled to death;
4 no 'fornication', which probably means using prostitutes – see Acts 15.

These were important issues then; are they really crucial nowadays?

Hatred

So if the heart of the law is love, then the meaning of sin is hatred, or lovelessness. As St John said in his first letter:

> Whoever says, 'I am in the light', while hating a brother or sister, is still in the darkness. Whoever loves a brother or sister lives in the light, and in such a person there is no cause for stumbling. But whoever hates another believer is in the darkness, walks in the darkness, and does not know the way to go.

This means that if you are law-abiding but intolerant you are the worst sort of sinner; yet if you carefully work out the most loving way to behave, no matter how many so-called moral 'laws' you break, you are behaving in a moral way. Shock, horror!

Harm

Yet what is wrong about sin or selfishness is that it causes harm. It hurts your body, or that of your neighbour, or those of the animals and plants which make up the natural world. It harms your heart or those of others, their emotions, their freedom, and their power to love. And it causes harm to your soul, that part of you which can have a relationship with God. So when I say that only lovelessness is sinful, that does not mean you are free to behave as you choose. But it does mean you should not pay too much attention to laws and

248

traditions which were once relevant but are now outdated. Which category do you think intolerance of women priests, divorce, birth control, abortion or IVF fall into?

Suggested hymns

Come down, O love divine; Gracious Spirit, Holy Ghost; Let there be love shared among us; Love is his word, love is his way.

Eighteenth Sunday after Trinity (Proper 23)
15 October
Principal Service   **Man Friday**
(*Continuous*): Ex. 32.1–14 The golden calf, Ps. 106.1–6, 19–23 The golden calf; or (*Related*): Isa. 25.1–9 A refuge for the needy, Ps. 23 The Lord's my shepherd; Phil. 4.1–9 Rejoice in the Lord; Matt. 22.1–14 The wedding banquet

> *'Do not worry about anything, but in everything by prayer and supplication with thanksgiving let your requests be made known to God.' Philippians 4.6*

Crusoe

In Daniel Defoe's novel, Robinson Crusoe saved a man from assassination by his fellow cannibals. So grateful was the poor fellow that he became Crusoe's servant, his 'man'. He did not work for pay, but simply from gratitude to the man who had saved him. Not knowing his name, Crusoe called him, after the day on which he was saved, 'Man Friday'. In these politically correct days, that sounds rather patronizing, but if you look more closely at the story you realize that Defoe is describing a man who, although he has not experienced what westerners call 'civilization', has a nobler character than many who have. The story is told to illustrate the power of gratitude.

Gratitude

Scientific studies have shown that people who are grateful for what somebody else has given them, or to the world in general, or to God, are happier and more willing to help the donor, or even those who have given them nothing but are themselves in need of help, than those who have never learnt to be thankful. Gratitude has been said to mould and shape the entire Christian life. Martin Luther, the first Protestant, referred to gratitude as 'the basic Christian attitude'. Some Christians refer to gratitude as 'the heart of the gospel'. If you want to live a happy life, and overcome your fits of depression, learn to be thankful to God.

Love

Gratitude, springing from love, is what makes us human. Love is a powerful force which rules over every nation. The great power of love is what we call 'God', but it is not human. Yet what we learn from the Bible is that Love wants to have a relationship with each one of us which resembles that between two people who love each other. So we call this power 'God our Father'. There is no need to disbelieve in evolution to be a Christian; but it is much easier to explain why these apparently random but beneficial changes happened down through billions of years, if you believe that the power of love has been micromanaging the process all through. So we are grateful to this power, for causing us to evolve, and giving us such a wonderful world to live in, and caring for us when we get ourselves into trouble. As Louis Armstrong sang, or rather, croaked, 'It's a wonderful world.' So we are grateful to our Creator, and cannot help bubbling over with thankfulness to our God.

Selfless

Therefore Christians instinctively praise and give thanks to our heavenly Father. For Christians, God is seen as the selfless giver of all good things. Because of this, there is a great sense of indebtedness, which binds all Christians together, shaping every aspect of our life. Gratitude is an acknowledgement of God's generosity, which inspires Christians to shape their own thoughts and actions around the imitation of Christ. It is not just a sentimental feeling; gratitude is a virtue that shapes not only our emotions and thoughts, but our actions and deeds as well. Gratitude, and thankfulness towards God in particular, are among the signs of true religion.

Philippians

St Paul wrote to the Christians in Philippi, encouraging them to be kind to other people and to share the good news of God's love with their neighbours. To do this, they needed to be grateful. 'Rejoice in the Lord always,' Paul wrote. 'Again I will say, Rejoice. Let your gentleness be known to everyone. The Lord is near. Do not worry about anything, but in everything by prayer and supplication *with thanksgiving* let your requests be made known to God. And the peace of God, which surpasses all understanding, will guard your hearts and your minds in Christ Jesus.' Like Man Friday, our lives should be lived in response to gratitude.

Eucharist

In the Orthodox, Catholic and Anglican Churches, our weekly worship centres on commemoration of the Last Supper by sharing bread and wine. This most important rite is called the Eucharist. The name derives from the Greek word *eucharistia*, which means 'thanksgiving'. Gratitude for God's love is the very heart of our life as Christians, and the motivator of our love for others.

All-age worship

List what you should thank God for. Read it when you are feeling 'down'.

Suggested hymns

Fairest Lord Jesus; In the Lord I'll be ever thankful; Now thank we all our God; O Lord my God! When I in awesome wonder.

Eighteenth Sunday after Trinity (Proper 23)
15 October
Second Service   **See You in Heaven**
Ps. 139.1–18 God's omniscience; Prov. 3.1–18 God disciplines his children; 1 John 3.1–15 Children of God; *Gospel at Holy Communion*: Mark 10.17–31 Camels and needles

> *'Beloved, we are God's children now; what we will be has not yet been revealed. What we do know is this: when he is revealed, we will be like him, for we will see him as he is.' 1 John 3.2*

Transfiguration

Jesus took his close friends up a high mountain, and there, the Gospels tell us, he was 'transfigured before them'. The disciples interpreted this as a revelation of who Jesus really was. His face shone, like that of Moses when he had been with God receiving the Ten Commandments, revealing his glory. He entered a cloud, the symbol of the presence of God. Jesus spoke with Moses and Elijah, to show that he was the fulfilment of the Law and the prophets. And they heard the voice of God, saying, 'This is my Son, listen to him.'

Heaven

In these ways, Jesus gave them and us a foretaste of the glories of heaven. When we die, we shall be with Jesus in glory. We shall have a body, by which we may be recognized as we were by our earthly body. But it will be much more glorious than the body we have on earth. Words are not sufficient to describe the glory of heaven; it has to be conveyed in stories, images and metaphors.

Bodies

At first many of the friends of Jesus, as well as his enemies, thought he was promising to bring an earthly kingdom, a new Jewish empire. Yet this did not immediately happen. So St Paul began by promising a kingdom above the clouds. But even that did not arrive on cue, so Paul changed his wording again, in 1 Corinthians 15. There he wrote that 'flesh and blood cannot inherit the kingdom of heaven', but we shall have what he described as a 'spiritual body'. Whether this describes God's intervention in history or in another world after we die he was not quite clear. But many of the predictions of Jesus were fulfilled when the Roman army destroyed Jerusalem, so Christians turned their attention to the life after death. In most cases, Christians said we shall rise with a spiritual body, much like the body of Jesus which the disciples saw on the Mount of Transfiguration. The distinctive features of this spiritual body will be that we shall be able to recognize each other, communicate with each other, and work to fulfil God's purpose for the world.

Dimensions

But we are still trying to describe the indescribable. Perhaps the best approach in a scientific age is to say that after we die, it will be like entering another dimension. There will still be time and space after we die, but it will be very different from time and space as we know them. The important thing is that we shall still be able to recognize each other, and for the first time we shall see Jesus as he really is. What will he say to us then? Perhaps it will be something like, 'My friend, I love you now as I have always loved you. Why did you ever doubt it, you of little faith? Enter into the joy of your Lord.'

Our loved ones

Maybe we shall meet in heaven with people from a bygone age whom we have always admired. An elderly man came into a church, in a rather emotional state, and he said to the minister, 'My wife died last week, and I've come in here to say a prayer for her. Do you think she will know that's what I'm doing?' The minister replied without hesitation, 'Yes, I'm certain she will. I have been praying for years for people I loved, and I have felt them close to me as I did so. I am absolutely sure they know what's happening here on earth, and they too are praying for me.' But he wondered to himself, 'I wonder what happens to people who die young. My son died while he was still a child. I'm sure I shall see him again when I die. But will he still be a child, or will he have grown up?' To which the minister could only answer in the silence of his heart, 'Maybe we shall never know until we get there, and I suppose it doesn't really matter. If time is different in heaven, "a thousand years will be as yesterday", and it will only seem a moment to my son between when he died and when I shall join him. Never mind, what matters is that we shall meet again. When somebody dies we can say in our prayers, "See you one day in heaven, darling!"'

Suggested hymns

Blest are the pure in heart; Lord, it belongs not to my care; There is a land of pure delight; Who are these like stars appearing?

Nineteenth Sunday after Trinity (Proper 24)

22 October

Principal Service   **Church and State**

(*Continuous*): Ex. 33.12–23 Moses sees God's back, Ps. 99
Moses' Prayer; *or* (*Related*): Isa. 45.1–7 God uses Cyrus, Ps.
96.1–9 [10–13] Creation; 1 Thess. 1.1–10 Thanks for the Church;
Matt. 22.15–22 Give to those in authority what belongs to them

> '[His enemies asked Jesus,] "Should we pay taxes to the Emperor or
> not?" Jesus . . . said, ". . . Let me see one of the coins used for pay-
> ing taxes." They brought him a silver coin, and he asked, "Whose
> picture and name are on it?" "The Emperor's," they answered. Then
> Jesus told them, "Give the Emperor what belongs to him, and give
> God what belongs to God."' Matthew 22.17–21 (Contemporary
> English Version)

Taxes

In the time of Jesus, Israel was occupied by the soldiers of the Roman
Empire. This brought many blessings, including good roads, freedom
from tribal warfare, and a stable currency with coins which could
be used all over the known world. But this had to be paid for out of
their taxes, paid not in the local currency but only in coins which had
the Emperor's head and name on them. The Jews resented this bitterly, partly because they wanted to be free from having to obey the
Emperor, and partly because they thought the coins with the royal
head on it were idols. This broke the laws which said, 'You shall worship the Lord your God and him only shall you serve,' and also, 'You
shall not worship graven images.' So his enemies tried to trap Jesus,
by asking whether he thought it was lawful to pay taxes. If he said
'yes', he would lose the support of Jewish patriots, whereas if he said
'no', the Roman army would come down on him like a ton of bricks.

Ownership

Today we put our names on our books and our clothes to prove
that we own them. So Jesus said that the Roman coins, with the
Emperor's name on them, had only been lent to them by the Empire,
and paying taxes was simply giving the money back to its owner.
A brilliant answer to a deeply political question. Then, before they
could recover from the shock, Jesus pointed out that, according to

the Bible, you and I are made in the image of God. So our bodies belong to God, who has lent them to us, just so long as we use them to love and serve our neighbours, as God tells us to.

Politics

But this illustrates how tricky it is when the Church gets involved in politics. If we put a step wrong we make fools of ourselves, and lose the sympathy of the general public. But we have a duty to stand up for the oppressed and to cry out for justice. As we commemorate those who died in past wars, and at the same time urge caution about involvement in areas of strife today, we risk being accused of hypocrisy; but if we say nothing, we are guilty of not speaking up for what we believe. Yet anyone who tries to remain unbiased about war and peace, or helping the needy, is treading a very narrow line between hotly opposed opinions. Even if we keep midway between two bodies of opinion, we are bound to be accused by both sides of favouring the other.

Silence

Why don't Christians remain silent, then, on controversial matters? I believe this is impossible, if you truly love your neighbour. Vague religious benevolence won't do; it must be turned into practical action. Helping individuals won't do, if the structures of society prevent your neighbour developing as a person. Loving your neighbour involves trying to change the structures of society, and politics is the only way to do this.

Church and State

So the Church, and each individual Christian, has a duty to the State. First, to make the Church an example of a society in which people forgive each other, and sacrifice their own interests for the sake of others. It must be a truly tolerant society, in which we respect the right of others to disagree with us. Second, to criticize politicians when their policies are harmful. Third, to cooperate with them vigorously in practical love of our neighbours. When the time to vote comes round, pay no attention whatsoever to whether we like or dislike the party leaders, and concentrate on deciding which policies will be most beneficial to all levels of society, in this country and in every other land throughout the world.

All-age worship

Obtain the manifestos of the main parties. Try to explain them in simple terms. Discuss which policies (not parties) Jesus would like you to vote for.

Suggested hymns

For the healing of the nations; God is our strength and refuge (Dambusters); Judge eternal, throned in splendour; O God of earth and altar.

Nineteenth Sunday after Trinity (Proper 24)
22 October
Second Service   **Fathers' Wisdom**
Ps. 142 I cry to the Lord [143.1–11 None is righteous];
Prov. 4.1–18 A father's instruction; 1 John 3.16—4.6 Test
the spirits; *Gospel at Holy Communion*: Mark 10.35–45
A ransom for many

> *'Listen, children, to a father's instruction, and be attentive, that you may gain insight . . .Get wisdom; get insight: do not forget, nor turn away from the words of my mouth.' Proverbs 4.1,5*

Proverbs

The book of Proverbs in the Bible is just that: a collection of short sayings or aphorism, containing gems of wisdom, each of which can easily be learnt off by heart. They would be perfect for teaching young children to learn by heart, and as exercises for those who are learning to read and write, and were probably used for this purpose. The basis of each of them is wisdom: wise ways to behave and behaviour which it would be wise to avoid. Most of it is written as if for children, but in fact it applies to all of us: we should all be alert for wisdom in the speech of our elders, due to their longer experience. It may seem strange that a book in the Bible makes so little direct reference to God, but as I shall explain later, that is not really true.

Wisdom

There is a profound difference between wisdom and knowledge. Knowledge is awareness of material facts, which can be observed by those with their eyes open, and proved by experiment. Wisdom is spiritual awareness, about how to live and how not to, learnt by experience and shared by recounting what has happened to you. Knowledge can be learnt from books, but wisdom can usually be learnt from people older than you, who have more experience. Sometimes the book of Proverbs speaks quite generally about the importance of wisdom:

Hear, my child, and accept my words,
that the years of your life may be many.
I have taught you the way of wisdom;
I have led you in the paths of uprightness.
When you walk, your step will not be hampered;
and if you run, you will not stumble.
Keep hold of instruction; do not let go;
guard her, for she is your life.
Do not enter the path of the wicked,
and do not walk in the way of evildoers.
Avoid it; do not go on it;
turn away from it and pass on.

But at other times the advice is quite specific, as in the warning in the next chapter against being led astray by the words of the 'loose woman', or the advice against laziness which begins, 'go the ant, you lazybones; consider its ways and be wise'.

Young and old

But young people are frequently reluctant to ask older folk for advice. They say, 'I know more than those silly old codgers,' and, when it comes to operating computers, they are usually right. Mark Twain said something like this: 'When I was eight I thought my parents knew everything, and when I was twelve I thought they knew nothing. Then when I was sixteen I was amazed how much they had picked up in the meantime!' This is true of many children, because they confuse different types of knowledge. It is knowledge of material facts that young children admire in their parents. When they have grown a bit older, the children have themselves learnt knowledge in fields in which their parents are not interested. But as they approach maturity, they are beginning to appreciate the importance of wisdom, which their parents and other older friends will have acquired through their long experience. Of course there are exceptions: 'old codgers' indeed who learn nothing from their experiences and talk nonsense all the while. But they are few indeed, and we would all do well to listen carefully to the words of people older than ourselves, for gems of wisdom which they may not realize are of any particular value.

Wisdom

Wisdom is often mentioned in the Old Testament, especially in the books located just before and after the book of Psalms. It is spoken of as a property of God, or a person of the Trinity, almost like the Holy Spirit, except that Wisdom is always spoken of as feminine. When our friends and neighbours speak words of wisdom, though they may not realize it, they are speaking the words of God. Their experience of life is bound to be different from ours, so we would do well to listen alertly to what they say, because hidden in their conversation there may be words of wisdom, words of God.

Suggested hymns

God forgave my sin; God is working his purpose out; O for a closer walk with God; Spirit of holiness, wisdom and faithfulness.

Last Sunday after Trinity (Proper 25) 29 October
(Alternatively Bible Sunday or the Dedication Festival)
Principal Service   **Which Comes First?**
(*Continuous*): Deut. 34.1–12 The death of Moses, Ps. 90.1–6, 13–17 Prayer, providence and faith; *or* (*Related*): Leviticus 19.1–2, 15–18 Love for the needy, Ps. 1 Law and righteousness; 1 Thess. 2.1–8 Paul's love for the church; Matt. 22.34–46 Love God and love your neighbour

> '[Jesus said to the lawyer,] "'You shall love the Lord your God with all your heart, and with all your soul, and with all your mind.' This is the greatest and first commandment. And a second is like it: 'You shall love your neighbour as yourself.' On these two commandments hang all the law and the prophets."' Matthew 22.37–40

Important

A lawyer asked Jesus, 'Which is the most important command-ment in the Jewish Scriptures?' Jesus didn't choose any of the Ten Commandments, but instead told us to love God and love out neighbours. These, said Jesus, go to the heart of the matter. What God wants of us is that we should love; all the other rules in the Old Testament are simply attempts to work out what love means in practice. Jesus didn't hesitate to contradict all these lesser com-mandments, when the law of love overrides the outdated laws – 'It was said to them of old time . . . but *I* say to you . . .'

Loving God

To love the Lord God with all one's heart, soul and mind is the greatest and first commandment, he said. This was a heretical idea in the ancient world. People tried to obey their tribal gods, they were terrified of the god's punishment if they got anything wrong in the liturgy, and they begged their idol to help them kill their enemies. The Old Testament was the first book to describe God's feeling towards his people as amounting to love, and the idea that mere mortals should have the temerity to approach God close enough to love him was almost blasphemous. Yet Jesus brought the idea of God down to earth, and taught his disciples that the loving relationship he had with his friends was an image of the relationship our loving heavenly Father wants to have with us. When you fall in love with another human being, that wonderful relationship and overflowing emotion becomes the theme of every waking thought. That is how it should be when you fall in love with God, says Jesus.

Loving neighbours

The second commandment, he continues, is to love our neighbours as much as we love ourselves. If we don't love ourselves, that prob-ably flows from a low self-image, and can be overcome by remind-ing ourselves that, no matter how horridly we have behaved, God has declared us to be loveable. Everybody has ideas about how we would like other people to treat us; that, says Jesus, is how we should treat other people. Jesus taught us to love our neighbours, and to love our enemies: perhaps that is because our neighbours so often *are* our enemies! Their trees overhang our gardens, their dog frightens our visitors, and their cats eat our tame birds, yet God expects us to love those horrible people? Well, yes, if God loves you, whatever you do, you must show the same unconditional love to everyone you meet. And that means doing your best to make them happy, building up their self-respect, and making sure every physical and emotional need is met. You look at the people you dislike, and reflect that loving them is a tough job, but somebody has got to do it; and God says you are the one.

Which comes first?

So we have two commandments, love God and love your neighbour – which comes first? Now you may think that's like asking which comes first, the chicken or the egg? Without a chicken you can't have an egg, and without an egg you can't have a chicken. Similarly, you can't say you love God if you hate your neighbour, and you can't love your neighbour without first learning to love God. But Jesus says loving God comes first.

How to do the impossible

That is because loving your neighbour as much as you love yourself is an impossible task. No human being can come anywhere near to doing that on their own. But if you love God, God comes into your heart, and then God can love your neighbour *through* you. God can use your hands, your voice, your heart, to express his love for all the people around you who need somebody to love them. That sounds an impossible challenge; but if you love God, then all things are possible to you.

All-age worship

List the songs and books you know which mention love. Make up a prayer asking God to help you to go on loving people even when they seem unlovely.

Suggested hymns

Breathe on me, breath of God; Immortal love, for ever full; Make me a channel of your peace; When I needed a neighbour.

Last Sunday after Trinity (Proper 25) 29 October
Second Service **Youth and Age**

Ps. 119.89–104 How I love your law; Eccles. 11; 12 Youth
and age; 2 Tim. 2.1–7 Crowning an athlete; *Gospel at
Holy Communion*: Mark 12.28–34 Love God and love your
neighbour

> 'Light is sweet, and it is pleasant for the eyes to see the sun. Even
> those who live many years should rejoice in them all . . . Rejoice,
> young man, while you are young, and let your heart cheer you in
> the days of your youth.' Ecclesiastes 11.7–9

Optimism of youth

The eleventh chapter of the book we call 'Ecclesiastes' is full of the
optimism of youth, when life is pleasant, and you can dream of
what you are going to do with it. Chapter 12, by contrast, sounds
like the grouching of a grumpy old man. 'Remember your creator in
the days of your youth,' it begins – make the most of them, because
old age is terrible. The description of senility which follows groans
with pessimism. Yet the words are very beautiful, and you can
savour their sonority without even thinking about what they mean.
In fact, they are a string of metaphors for bodily decay, yet they
make it sound almost delightful.

> Rejoice, [it says,] before the days of trouble come, and the years
> draw near when you will say, 'I have no pleasure in them'.

Many old people enjoy a full and happy life up until the day they
die. Yet we must sympathize with old people who suffer. First, with
those whose sight is failing, and rheumy tears fall from their misty
eyes:

> [When] the sun and the light and the moon and the stars are
> darkened and the clouds return with the rain.

Did you realize that was what it means? What a poetic way to
describe the partially sighted! Then, if you are unfortunate, your
hands become shaky, your back is stooped, and your teeth fall out –
a terrible experience, but how beautifully it is painted:

In the day when the guards of the house tremble, and the strong men are bent, and the women who grind cease working because they are few.

Then your hearing goes – what did you say? Speak up, young man, I can't hear you:

When the doors on the street are shut, and the sound of the grinding is low, and one rises up at the sound of a bird, and all the daughters of song are brought low.

Not every elderly person suffers in this way, thank God – pray you will never have to endure these afflictions, and pray for those whose balance is unreliable:

When one is afraid of heights, and terrors are in the road.

So thank God for your health, before your hair turns white and nothing seems enjoyable any more:

The almond tree blossoms, the grasshopper drags itself along and desire fails.

Gloomy as these words seem, they are there in the Bible, alongside all the messages of hope, to remind us that we all have to die sometime. We don't like to think about that when we are young, but we should, so that we can see our own life in the perspective of eternity. Christians believe that death is the gateway to heaven, when we meet again those who have died before us, and are welcomed into our Saviour's arms. There is nothing to fear when the heart ceases to pound and the lungs to pant:

Because all must go to their eternal home, and the mourners will go about the streets; [when] the silver cord is snapped, and the golden bowl is broken, and the pitcher is broken at the fountain, and the wheel broken at the cistern, and the dust returns to the earth as it was, and the breath returns to God who gave it.

Youth and age

That is a beautiful description of death; yet it was penned by an old man, in quiet faith, long before Jesus brought the promise of resurrection. Young people have much to learn from the wisdom of age; yet so often we write-off older people as 'old-fashioned,' 'past their sell-by date', with nothing important to say to us. And the elderly should hush their grumbling, turn to the young, showing an interest in what they are doing, and encouraging them to enjoy life to the full while they have the chance. God loves us all, young and old – we need to listen to one another and learn from each other. *Pilgrim's Progress* leads him through many vicissitudes, and he learns something from each experience. That is what we are here for: the vaulting ambitions of youth, and the failing powers of age, are all part of our preparation for heaven. We must just accept them with faith in our Creator, who made us for himself, and who guides us throughout the long journey which leads at last to his eternal kingdom.

Suggested hymns

Abide with me; Awake, my soul, and with the sun; O God, our help in ages past; Will your anchor hold in the storms of life?

All Saints' Sunday   5 November
Principal Service   Saints Beyond Number
(These readings are used on the Sunday, or, if this is not kept as All Saints' Sunday, on 1 November itself; see pages 361 (All Saints' Day) and 265 (Fourth Sunday before Advent).)
Rev. 7.9–17 The crowd before God's throne; Ps. 34.1–10 Happy are those who find God; 1 John 3.1–3 We shall be like him; Matt. 5.1–12 The beatitudes

> *'I looked, and there was a great multitude that no one could count, from every nation, from all tribes and peoples and languages, standing before the throne and before the Lamb, robed in white, with palm branches in their hands. They cried out in a loud voice, saying, "Salvation belongs to our God who is seated on the throne, and to the Lamb!"' Revelation 7.9–10*

Infinity

How do you convey the idea of a very large number? Modern scientists talk about infinity, which means a quantity without end or limit, greater than any number that can be measured. It is a useful concept; yet we cannot imagine infinity, and it may not actually exist. Yet the idea of infinity had not been invented when the Bible was written, so it uses various metaphors to suggest that God is greater than the universe he created; and in the book of Revelation, St John the Divine writes of 144,000 Jews, who are admitted into the kingdom of heaven. Yet that is surely a symbolic figure, not meant to be taken literally. Then he describes the even larger number, drawn from all the other nations: 'a great multitude that no one could count, from every nation, from all tribes and peoples and languages, standing before the throne and before the Lamb'. In other words, an infinite number of saints. That is a poetic way of suggesting that, out of the much smaller number of human beings on earth in those days, nearly all will enter into bliss. Nowadays the population is much, much greater, but the symbolism remains the same: there are, or will be, an even greater number of people in heaven than we can possibly imagine.

Saints

Now, traditionally the inhabitants of heaven have been described as 'the saints'. Yet the number of saints which the Roman Catholic Church has canonized and whose names occur in *Butler's Lives of the Saints*, though very large, is clearly countable, and even if you add the heroes of the Protestant and Orthodox Churches it is nowhere near infinite. So Revelation must be using symbolic language to suggest a very great figure, and all of them saints. St Paul in his letters refers to all Christians as 'called to be saints'. This suggests that if we try to be kind, and confess our failures, God will forgive us our sins and take us into heaven to enjoy the new life, free from pain and death, which God has promised to the saints – the better life where there will be no more pain and death, and we shall be together again with all those we love and with the great Christian heroes of the past and present.

Universes

This gives a new meaning to the name of 'All Saints Day'; it means that all of us have the potential to become saints, and, with God's help, we almost certainly will. This raises a problem for those who believe in the literal truth of the Bible's poetry: where will there be room to put us all in the next life? Here again, the scientists may have helped us. They say that so many coincidences must have happened to cause a planet capable of supporting life to occur, and then to cause you and me to evolve, that there must be an infinite number of universes where everything that could happen does happen. Some of them say that somewhere there is another universe with two individuals who are exact replicas of you and me, except for one feature which is different. Well, I think that is ridiculous, and it is much simpler to believe that something we call God was micro-managing all those coincidences in order to produce creatures which could return his love. But it does enable us to conceive of another universe, where time and space are quite different from what they are in this universe, where there is room for the immortal souls of all those who have lived on this earth and anywhere else where life is possible. There, we shall all be saints. We can still have our heroes and heroines, whom we call *St* Francis and *St* Mary, but we also can take our place among the army, great beyond number, of forgiven sinners, who have now become . . . All Saints!

All-age worship

Pick one saint and find out all you can about them. Have you met anyone recently whom you would describe as 'a saint'. Can we imitate saints as role models?

Suggested hymns

For all the saints who from their labours rest; God, whose city's sure foundation; Ten thousand times ten thousand; Who are these like stars appearing?

Fourth Sunday before Advent   5 November
Principal Service   **Guy Fawkes**
(*For use if All Saints, is celebrated on 1 November, see p. 263 (All Saints' Sunday), and page 361 (All Saints' Day).*)
Micah 3.5–12 Judgement on society; Ps. 43 I will go to God's altar; 1 Thess. 2.9–13 A call to righteousness; Matt. 24.1–14 Predictions of the coming of Christ

> 'Hear this, you rulers of the house of Jacob and chiefs of the house of Israel, who abhor justice and pervert all equity, who build Zion with blood and Jerusalem with wrong!' Micah 3.9–10

Fireworks

> Remember, remember,
> the fifth of November,
> gunpowder, treason and plot!

This year 5 November falls on a Sunday, today, so 'I see of no reason why Gunpowder Treason should ever be forgot.' Well, in the United Kingdom, for one reason or another, the memory of this historical event seems to be indelibly printed on the national memory. Not that the people who let off fireworks at this time, or those who beg for 'A penny for the Guy', or whatever inflation now demands, know much about Mr Fawkes. Any excuse for a bonfire and a pyrotechnics display; indeed in multiracial areas we are already joined by Muslims celebrating Eid and Hindus observing Diwali in the same way. But for a long time, Guy Fawkes' Day was a divisive occasion, setting Roman Catholics against Protestants, and the English against the Scottish people. Was 'the greatest act of terrorism before 9/11', as it has been called, really planned on religious grounds, and was the national reaction against it actually a beastly attack on Roman Catholics? Christians on all sides should examine those questions carefully.

Politics

Going back a bit, we need to remember that Henry VIII was appointed 'Defender of the Faith', meaning the Roman Catholic faith. But he could not allow the pope, who was in league with the Spanish, to define the laws of an independent country, in particular the divorce laws. Henry broke with Rome for political reasons; only after he died did Archbishop Cranmer introduce the liturgy in the language of the people – which the Roman Catholics have now adopted also – and certain elements of Lutheran doctrine. Yet as power alternated in the reigns of Mary and Elizabeth, religion was claimed by both sides as an excuse for killing their fellow Christians. Those who clung to their Catholic faith were always suspected, with some justification, of wishing to overthrow the English monarch and bring in a foreign prince in their place.

Scots and plots

Many Roman Catholics managed to avoid suspicion by paying an annual fine; but 'James VI of Scotland and the first of England' was the son of Mary Queen of Scots, and became the focus of English prejudice against the Scottish people. In 1605, this led Robert Catesby to gather a group of a dozen others, all descended from old Catholic landowners in the Midlands, who felt they were losing their hereditary powers. They organized a plot which would destroy the entire English establishment of the king and the House of Lords. If it had gone as they intended, they would have gone on to kill 30,000 people, putting the few remaining Catholic peers into their place.

Fawkes

Guy Fawkes was an embittered man from humble origins in Yorkshire, who gladly agreed with the plotters to do their dirty-work for them. Fawkes acquired a cellar beneath the House of Lords, and brought there, under cover of darkness, 36 barrels of gunpowder, enough to reduce the entire building to rubble. The secret leaked out before they could let off their explosives; all the plotters were arrested, shot or executed. Most were hanged, drawn and quartered; Guy Fawkes was not burned, but managed to leap from the block and break his neck on the hangman's noose, avoiding the agony of being dismembered while still alive.

Aftermath

For centuries after that there was a special service in the Book of Common Prayer for Protestants to give thanks for the defeat of the 'Popish Plot'. Yet, like most so-called 'religious wars', it was not really about religious differences, so much as a struggle between competing empires for political power. So, while we enjoy the fireworks, Protestants must not lump all Catholics together in collective responsibility for this terrorist attempt; and we must repent for the way that each side treated the other in this and other countries in the succeeding centuries. Thank God that we are now able to live together as friends in the same community, with mutual respect for each other's history and culture. Pray to God, also, that similar inter-religious strife may never break out again.

All-age worship

Light sparklers to celebrate Christ the Light of the World, and pray that we may never be tempted to do the deeds of darkness.

Suggested hymns

Colours of day; Lord, the light of your love is shining; The Spirit lives to set us free; Thy hand, O God, has guided.

Fourth Sunday before Advent   5 November
Second Service   **Decline and Fall**

Ps. 111 The company of the faithful, 117 All you people; Dan. 7.1–18 Thousands attended; Luke 6.17–31 Sermon on the Plain

> *'I watched then because of the noise of the arrogant words that the horn was speaking. And as I watched, the beast was put to death, and its body destroyed and given over to be burned with fire.' Daniel 7.11*

Daniel

In the year 175 BC, Antiochus Epiphanes came to the throne in Syria. He ruled over the northern half of the Greek Empire of Alexander the Great. That meant that he was the colonial ruler of Israel, who bitterly resented the loss of their independence. So a rebellious book was written in the name of the prophet Daniel, describing the empires to which they had been subjected as horrible beasts. The number of years that each of the rulers would reign is correctly described in the book of Daniel, except for the last one. It was predicted that Antiochus Epiphanes would die soon after coming to the throne, handing over his reign not to another beast but to a human figure, 'one like a son of man'; and his empire would be destroyed by fire in Palestine. In fact he died peacefully in Persia 12 years later. The obvious conclusion, then, is that some Jew, speaking the late dialect of Aramaic, which Jesus also spoke, wrote under the pseudonym of Daniel, to encourage the Jews of his time that the long years of their persecution would not last much longer, and the occupying empires would be punished and destroyed. In fact it did not work out like that: there were five more Greek kings and then their empire was handed over to the Romans, and their puppet kings of the Herod family. When the Son of Man eventually was born, the Romans crucified him.

Punishment

But even though the historical events were not as the book of Daniel had predicted, the message it brings still rings true. Evil empires do

268

not last long; eventually they collapse, and their final leaders are often horribly punished. So be brave, says the Bible: unjust rulers do not have things their own way for ever, and many of them finish up enduring suffering like that which they had inflicted on others. You will be able to think of dictators in recent history, some of whom died in their beds, yet whose successors often suffered an awful death. But it is only in the long term that the picture becomes clear: the rise and eventual fall of empires. You can think of that as God's punishment on those who have not cared for the needs of their subjects. But you will ask, why are not all evildoers punished? Why does God not protect the innocent? Why does he take so long? To which I can only answer: the cost of God giving free will to you and me is that he must give the same power of choice to everyone, even to wicked dictators. Yet he has formed a world in which the eventual downfall of those who misuse their God-given freedom is inevitable.

Criminals

But this raises even more difficult questions. We have a legal system under which most people who commit criminal acts are eventually arrested and given some sort of punishment. Of course there is always room for improvement in the number of offenders who are detected and brought to justice. But many of the rich and powerful work out cunning ways of doing things which are manifestly unjust and cruel, causing unnecessary suffering to many, but are not actually illegal. Only by making our society more truly democratic can we fulfil God's will that evildoers are deterred from harming others by the awareness that the consequences of their actions will be unpleasant for themselves.

Purpose

For that is the purpose of punishment. God punishes evil empires by causing their downfall. But he punishes individuals who disobey his command to love their neighbours as much as they love themselves, by depriving them of that joy, which the rest of us have, of knowing that we are loved: loved by God as his precious and obedient children, and loved by our neighbours, who are grateful for the self-denying and loving way in which we serve them. The purpose of punishment is not to cause suffering to bad-seeming people, whose motives are always mixed; but to express society's disapproval of harmful acts; allow offenders to express their remorse; and deter them, and those who would imitate them, from doing bad things in the future. That is why God allows bad people and evil empires to be punished, and why he allows society to punish them; it is not so that we should impose on them a shallow tit-for-tat revenge on those who have hurt us, but to encourage virtuous living.

Suggested hymns

For the healing of the nations; Judge eternal, throned in splendour; O God of earth and altar; The kingdom of God is justice and joy.

Third Sunday before Advent   12 November
Principal Service   Changing One's Mind about Advent
(For a service that is not a Service of Remembrance.)
Wisd. 6.12–16 Wisdom described, *and Canticle*: Wisd. 6.17–20 Divine Wisdom; *or* Amos 5.18–24 Let justice roll down, *and* Ps. 70 A prayer for help; 1 Thess. 4.13–18 The resurrection from death; Matt. 25.1–13 Wise and foolish bridesmaids

> *'Therefore encourage one another with these words.'*
> *1 Thessalonians 4.18*

Literal

St Paul wrote his first letter to the Christians in Thessalonica in about AD 50, when he had been a Christian for about 17 years; and he wrote from Corinth, where he had only just arrived for the first time. He encouraged them to be full of hope, because whatever happened to them in this life, they would live again with Jesus in a better world to come. The words he used were very graphic; he believed that Jesus had promised certain historical events, and that this prophecy would be literally fulfilled at his Second Coming in just a few years' time. What Paul expected was that

> The Lord himself, with a cry of command, with the archangel's call and with the sound of God's trumpet, will descend from heaven, and the dead in Christ will rise first. Then we who are alive, who are left, will be caught up in the clouds together with them to meet the Lord in the air; and so we will be with the Lord forever. Therefore encourage one another with these words.

Spiritual

But only two years later Paul wrote, from Ephesus, his first letter to the Christians in Corinth, in which he uses astoundingly different words to describe the resurrection of all believers in Christ. He put it like this:

> There are both heavenly bodies and earthly bodies, but the glory of the heavenly is one thing, and that of the earthly is another . . . So it is with the resurrection of the dead. What is sown is perishable, what is raised is imperishable . . . It is sown a physical body, it is raised a spiritual body. If there is a physical body, there is also a spiritual body. But it is not the spiritual that is first, but the physical, and then the spiritual . . . What I am saying, brothers and sisters, is this: flesh and blood cannot inherit the kingdom of God, nor does the perishable inherit the imperishable. Listen, I will tell you a mystery! We will not all die, but we will all be changed, in a moment, in the twinkling of an eye, at the last trumpet. For the trumpet will sound, and the dead will be raised imperishable, and we will be changed. For this perishable body must put on imperishability, and this mortal body must put on immortality.

The message is still the same: don't lose heart, because one day we shall all be with Jesus in heaven. But the language has changed: in the first quotation Paul made a literal prediction of historical events; in the second, he writes of the coming of Christ in a metaphorical way, causing a spiritual change. It is so different that it is hard to believe the two passages were written by the same man.

Change

So what had happened to cause this change in St Paul? The first, literal, prophecy leads some American fundamentalists to put stickers on their cars reading, 'If this car has no driver, the rapture has come.' 'Rapture', or 'seizing' in this context, means that God has literally grabbed all the Christians and taken them up to a place above the clouds. But most Christians don't use such words, because scientifically educated people in the space age would only laugh at them. Paul had been laughed at by the educated Greek people of Athens, and then he started looking for ways of expressing the same truths in a metaphorical way, which would appeal to people all over the world.

271

Science-speak

We, too, must change our way of speaking the same old truths, in each new age and each different culture; otherwise we shall not pass on the message of Jesus, as he told us to. In the 2002 film *Solaris*, a widowed psychologist is sent to a remote space station to investigate unexplained phenomena, and receives visits from his dead wife. Eventually they decide that the nearby super-planet called Solaris is drawing their memories into another universe, with a different type of space and tine, and there is no such thing as death. The final words of the film, spoken by the resurrected wife, are 'Everything is forgiven.' There is no explicitly religious language, but the metaphor used by the film brilliantly stimulates people of the twenty-first century to a new understanding of the coming of Jesus, which we shall prepare for in the season of Advent.

All-age worship

Draw a space rocket taking dead people to heaven. In what way is this 'true'?

Suggested hymns

Christ is surely coming; Come and see the shining hope that Christ's apostle saw; Every star shall sing a carol; Soon and very soon.

Remembrance Sunday   12 November
'God with Us'

(*The readings of the day or those for 'The Peace of the World' or 'In Time of Trouble' can be used. These readings are for 'The Peace of the World'.*)
Isa. 9.1–6 Prince of Peace; Ps. 40.14–17 Deliver me; Phil. 4.6–9 Do not worry; Matt. 5.43–48 Love your enemies

'[Jesus said,] "You have heard that it was said, 'You shall love your neighbour and hate your enemy.' But I say to you, Love your enemies and pray for those who persecute you, so that you may be children of your Father in heaven."' Matthew 5.43–45

272

Remembrance

On Remembrance Sunday we try to keep two rather different ideas in our brains at the same time. First, we want to rejoice and thank God for the people, many of them volunteers, who laid down their lives for their friends in wartime. Jesus said that this is the greatest form of love, and we wish to honour them, to whom we owe so much. But second, we wish to find ways of preventing this terrible slaughter from ever happening again.

Evil

It is not just the problem of war which we confront. It is the whole problem of human evil: what causes war? What can we do to overcome it? How can we convince people that there are no ultimate winners, and that good can never be created by violence? That is not to say that evil can sometimes be held back, deterred, or postponed by a minimum display of strength, but we must not be tempted into escalating the killing. Pacifists would say that there are no circumstances in which violence is justified, even in self-defence.

God

The trouble is that people on both sides are convinced that God is on their side, and they are doing God's work by killing his enemies. In 1914, many German soldiers went into battle with the words on their helmets, *Gott mit uns*, 'God is with us.' On the allied side, the slogan was repeated often, 'We fight for God and King', as though there was an automatic alliance between these two powers, and if you were fighting under the orders of your king you must be fighting for God. But, including both sides, over 10 million people were killed in the 1914–18 war, and 20 million wounded, not to mention the widows and orphans that were created. This cannot surely be God's will! In the American Civil War someone said that they hoped God was on their side. Abraham Lincoln replied that, first of all, he prayed that they were on God's side.

Pride

The politicians are the ones who decide to go to war, and appoint the generals. But politicians are chiefly interested in being re-elected, so they think more of their own interests and less of how many will die. This is a particular form of pride, imagining that they know best. But it is the people who elect the politicians who bear the final responsibility, because they imagine that winning a battle will glorify their country. The generals think they have invented clever new strategies, and develop clever new weapons which will kill so many that they will bring the war to a speedy end. All these were misled by wicked and overweening pride: Jesus said, 'Blessed are the meek, for they will inherit the earth.'

Jesus

Jesus said, also in the Sermon on the Mount:

> You have heard that it was said, 'You shall love your neighbour and hate your enemy.' But I say to you, Love your enemies and pray for those who persecute you, so that you may be children of your Father in heaven.

So the root evil, the cause of all strife, is failing to love our enemies. It is easy, but wrong, to hate them. Instead we must learn to recognize that everyone, of every nation and religion, is a human being, and precious to God, who loves us all equally. That does not mean that you have to have an emotion of deep friendship as soon as you meet somebody who is fighting for the other side, or that you approve of everything that he or she is doing. Sometimes the most loving thing you can do for people is to imprison them, to prevent them from doing the same thing again, and to deter others from following their example. But you must learn to regard him, or her, as a human being like yourself, and as worthy of respect as you are. Remember this, before you shoot or shell your enemy, or destroy their homes or run over them with your tanks, or direct your drones at their cars.

Suggested hymns

For the healing of the nations; Judge eternal, throned in splendour; Make me a channel of your peace; O God of earth and altar.

Second Sunday before Advent   19 November
Principal Service   **Punished by God**

Zeph. 1.7, 12–18 The day of judgement; Ps. 90.1–8 [9–11] 12
Prayer, providence and faith; 1 Thess. 5.1–11 The day of the
Lord; Matt. 25.14–30 The parable of the talents

> *'At that time I will take a lamp and search Jerusalem. I will pun-
> ish the people who are self-satisfied and confident, who say to
> themselves, 'The Lord never does anything, one way or the other.'*
> *Zephaniah 1.12 (Good News Bible)*

Children

Parents worry about how to bring up their children. We want
them to be free to enjoy life; but because they are bound to make
mistakes, we want to protect them from the consequences. So we
warn them not to do things which will harm themselves or other
people. If we simply ignored what they do, they would think we
didn't care. Too much freedom would result in dangerous injury.
So we have to lay down some boundaries, in the certainty that our
kids will test those boundaries at some time by stepping over them.
Therefore, before they destroy themselves, we have to hold up a
threat of punishment. Naturally, at some point they will go beyond
that point, and the punishment has to be inflicted, or they will go
wild. We hope it will only be depriving them of some pleasure. At
the worst, it may involve a light slap on the wrist. Whereat, both
parent and child will burst into tears, at the agony of what has happened! Then they should flood each other with love, to restore the
broken relationship.

Punishment

So even the most loving relationship must contain the threat of punishment, if one party breaches their agreement. Does that apply to the
relationship between us and God? I think it does. Otherwise we would
conclude that God doesn't care what we do. There are verses in the
Bible like this, from today's Old Testament reading, where God says:

> I will punish the people who are self-satisfied and confident, who
> say to themselves, 'The Lord never does anything, one way or
> the other.'

Frequently God has no need to punish us, as we punish ourselves by our wrongdoing. But we must never slip into the assumption that God does not care what we do.

Vindictive

Yet it is a dangerous error to think that whenever anything unpleasant happens to us, it is because a vindictive God is taking his revenge. God promised Noah, 'I will never again curse the ground because of humankind.' Gradually God revealed his true nature, leading up to when Jesus said, 'Love your enemies, do good, and lend, expecting nothing in return. Your reward will be great, and you will be children of the Most High; for he is kind to the ungrateful and the wicked. Be merciful, just as your Father is merciful.' Those verses portray quite the opposite picture of God to the vindictive deity of some passages in the Old Testament.

HIV

The danger of the old approach was shown when some Christians spread the idea that HIV was God's punishment for unconventional sexual behaviour. The result of this teaching was that sufferers from this dreadful disease dared not report it, for fear of being ostracized, and HIV spread all the more rapidly. Things began to change when good-living people began to contract the disease, and the then Archbishop of Capetown said in 2004 that 'The Church is to blame for the stigma and the spread of HIV/AIDS, because a destructive theology linked sex with sin, guilt and punishment.'

Climate change

Similarly with climate change. One of the factors causing it must be human behaviour in increasing carbon emissions and destroying the forests which could absorb the CO_2 from the atmosphere. But in Bangladesh, some of the poorest communities are suffering from floods caused by increasingly vicious cyclones, and rising sea levels. Some preachers there told their congregations that this is God's punishment for their sexual behaviour. The result was that they had no motive for strengthening their houses and growing crops which float on the rising and falling surface of the water.

Human nature

So our Father God, like any other parent, weeps if he has to punish us his children. But he has to warn us that violence towards women and children, for instance, is so evil that God cannot ignore it. Yet the cross of Christ, surely, shows that God shares in the suffering which we bring upon ourselves by our sin, in order to reveal how much he loves us. Only in that way can God change us into loving people, who will try never to behave selfishly again.

All-age worship

Study global warming, its effects and its probable causes. What does God think about it?

Suggested hymns

Amazing grace; Be thou my guardian and my guide; God forgave my sin; There's a wideness in God's mercy.

Second Sunday before Advent 19 November
Second Service   Heirs and Successors
Ps. 89.19–37 David's greatness; 1 Kings 1.15–40 (*or* 1–40)
David chooses Solomon; Rev. 1.4–18 The heavenly Christ;
Gospel at Holy Communion: Luke 9.1–6 Apostolic authority

> *'From Jesus Christ, the faithful witness, the firstborn of the dead, and the ruler of the kings of the earth.' Revelation 1.5*

Henry VIII

King Henry VIII could have had as many mistresses as he wanted. But he felt obliged to divorce one wife after another because they did not bear him a legitimate male heir to inherit the crown. In countries where it was not clear who inherited the monarchy, the strife between different contenders for the throne reduced the country to chaos. Still today, when stocks and shares, not land, are where wealth is kept, numerous court cases argue over who is the legitimate heir of the deceased.

David

So when King David was dying, his many, many wives each raised a clamour demanding that *their* sons should be next in succession. Adonijah was David's fourth son, but he was the oldest one still living at this point; so he began to claim that he was to be the next King of Judah, and even organized a coronation feast for himself. Sure enough, this created an uproar.

Solomon

Bathsheba was David's favourite wife. He fell in love with her when he spied her having a bath on the rooftop, and had her husband killed so that he could marry her. So when she heard what was happening, she went to David to complain that he had promised the throne to her son, Solomon. King David gave the order, and before Adonijah could do anything, 'Zadok the priest and Nathan the prophet anointed Solomon King', as the music of Handel keeps reminding us. It was a secret, underhand and illegitimate coronation; but his rival realized he stood no chance against the dying king's stated wishes, and retired from the contest.

Heirs

From then on, the rulers of the combined kingdoms of Judah and Israel were known as 'Son of David'. Nobody could succeed to the throne unless he could prove that he was the legitimate descendant of the country's first monarch. The royal line continued until shortly after Israel returned from its exile in Babylon, about 500 years later. By that time most Israelites could claim to be descended in some way from David, and some did, with bloody consequences. But a hope grew up that one day there would be another legitimate heir sitting on David's throne, to be known as 'the anointed one', in Hebrew 'the Messiah', in Greek 'the Christ'.

Son of David

Jesus is described in the New Testament as 'the Son of David', or 'the Christ'; but he never claimed the title for himself, as, if he did so, the result would be a vicious war with the Romans, who claimed that only they had the right to rule over Israel. Yet Christians believe that only Jesus is entitled to inherit the throne of David, not only as King of Israel, but as 'King of kings'. St John, in the book of Revelation, calls him 'Jesus Christ, the faithful witness, the first-born of the dead, and the ruler of the kings of the earth'.

Inheritance

Among the doubtful songs which are sometimes sung at Boy Scout camps is one with the verse:

> David and Solomon led very naughty lives,
> with many, many concubines and many, many wives,
> but when they grew much older, their conscience gave them
>   qualms,
> so Solomon wrote the Proverbs and David wrote the Psalms!

But it is not their shady morality which Jesus inherited, but their unifying authority. If the 12 tribes who had left Egypt with Moses had remained divided, weak and squabbling, they would never have survived. It was David and Solomon, allegedly, who united them into one nation; and when they split up again, much of the Old Testament was written to persuade them to reunite.

King of kings

Monotheism, or belief in one God, was first revealed to the Jews. But at first they did not realize its implications. They thought it meant that every nation had its own God, but Jehovah was the greatest. It was St Paul who first explained, to the Greeks in Athens, that 'that same God whom you are worshipping, though without a personal relationship with him, is the God whose all-embracing loving nature we are revealing to you'. Since Jesus came, the Son of David and King of kings, we can no longer say to other nations, 'our God is the only god who really exists, while you merely worship idols'. We preach that every race worships the same God, but we can learn from each other about his loving, compassionate nature. And we owe a lot of that understanding to the unifying work of King David and King Solomon.

Suggested hymns

All glory, laud and honour; Hosanna to the Son of David; Once in royal David's city; You are the King of glory.

Christ the King   26 November
Principal Service   **Overseas Aid**

Ezek. 34.11–16, 20–24 God the shepherd; Ps. 95.1–7 We are his sheep, he is our shepherd; Eph. 1.15–23 Christ the head of all; Matt. 25.31–46 Sheep and goats

> *'[Jesus said,] "When the Son of Man comes in his glory, and all the angels with him, then he will sit on the throne of his glory. All the nations will be gathered before him, and he will separate people one from another as a shepherd separates the sheep from the goats."' Matthew 25.31–32*

King

In 1925, Pope Pius XI established the feast of Christ the King, in the aftermath of the First World War and the Bolshevik Revolution. He wanted to stress that the gentle rule of Christ, the crucified king, was more effective than any of the atheistic dictatorships in bringing peace and hope to the people of every land. If we follow Jesus as our leader, imitating his example of humility and self-sacrifice, then wars between nations on behalf of differing ideologies will end when the King of all the world ushers in his kingdom of peace. The date was set as the Sunday before Advent, to show that only when all nations submit to the one God shall we be ready to welcome his coming.

International

In today's Gospel reading, the 'Son of Man', meaning Jesus, is referred to a few verses later as 'the king'. Jesus prophesies that he will judge not just the Jews, or the Christians, but 'all the nations'. This word is translated elsewhere as 'the Gentiles', the races whom the Jews counted as their enemies. Then all are judged, not on our beliefs but on our actions. Whether you be a conservative Christian, an observant Jew or a submissive Muslim, what counts is whether you feed the hungry and heal the sick. That does not mean only the poor of your own nation, but of every nation, even of those whom you count as your enemies. The word 'stranger' would be better translated 'welcome the immigrant'. If you do this, says Jesus, whatever your faith, you will be counted among the sheep and welcomed into eternal life; but if you don't you will be condemned to punishment. Faith matters, though, because it gives you the motivation to behave compassionately.

Missions

The Christian missionary societies were founded in colonial times. Yet many brought not only the Gospel, but also hospitals and schools to improve the well-being of the poor, whether they were Christian or not. Secular development agencies today reject mixing religion with aid; but many people in the Global South see the separation of religion and social justice as an artificial construct of the irreligious North. So Christian missions have moved into development and relief work, helping the poor of all religions indiscriminately. Thus we witness to a God who so loved 'the world' – meaning the whole world, not just the 'most favoured nations' – that he gave his Son to die for us, that all who believe in him may inherit eternal life by loving all the poor indiscriminately, just as he did.

Advocacy

In Western Europe, though not elsewhere, the Christian population has shrunk so that we cannot make much of an impression on global poverty on our own. So we must persuade our governments to help us. But that's risky – governments expect a return for their investment, such as political influence, arms sales and trade agreements; they are also more subject to bribery and corruption than Christian organizations. But we can influence them by witnessing publicly to where aid is most needed, and in what form. We can also witness to the general public about the need for personal generosity to aid and development charities. This may involve advocacy for better environmental policies, as it is always the poor who suffer most when there is drought or flooding. It even includes intervention in the debate on immigration; for no amount of regulations will stop the hungry from seeking to enter our country to share in our relative wealth, unless we act urgently to raise the standard of living in theirs.

Politics

Yet as soon as we get involved in these issues, the cry goes up that Christians shouldn't meddle in politics. But we are only imitating Jesus, whose manifesto was to bring good news to the poor . . . to proclaim release to the captives and recovery of sight to the blind, to let the oppressed go free, to proclaim the year when the Lord liberates the slaves.

Yet what else would you expect from Christ the King, other than a challenge to politicians who think they have a monopoly on national policies? Then surely you and I, subjects of this king, cannot hold back from advocating international justice, and supporting the oppressed, just because it concerns controversial issues.

All-age worship

Prepare notes for a talk about Christian aid and development agencies.

Suggested hymns

For the healing of the nations; Judge eternal, throned in splendour; Lord of lords and King eternal; O God of earth and altar.

Christ the King 26 November
Second Service **Philosophers May Sing**
Morning Ps. 29 Enthroned, 110 The king at your right hand; Evening Ps. 93 God's majesty [97 The Lord is king]; 2 Sam. 23.1–7 The last words of David, *or* 1 Macc. 2.15–29 The beginning of the revolt; Matt. 28.16–20 Ascension authority

> *'Jesus came and said to [the eleven disciples], "All authority in heaven and on earth has been given to me."' Matthew 28.18*

Gondoliers

One of Gilbert and Sullivan's most popular comic operettas is entitled *The Gondoliers*. It is a story about a fictional nation called Barataria. When the King of Barataria became, and I quote, 'a Wesleyan Methodist . . . of the most bigoted and persecuting type', the Grand Inquisitor seized the King's young son and heir to the throne, and took him to Venice. There he was entrusted to a drunken 'gondolier', one of the boatmen who punt the gondolas up and down the canals there. But he muddled up the prince with his own son, of about the same age, and now nobody can remember which was which. When the operetta begins, the King of Barataria has just died; so the two boys, now grown to young men, gondoliers like their late father, have to act jointly as king until a witness can be found to identify which one is the true heir to the throne. Leaving out the romantic subplot, further comedy is drawn from the fact that the joint kings are both convinced republicans – that is, they believe that all nations should be ruled democratically with an elected president rather than a hereditary monarch. The second act begins as they sing a duet describing their rejection of kingly authority, and behaving as servants of the royal household. They sing:

Rising early in the morning,
we proceed to light our fire,
then our Majesty adorning
in its work-a-day attire,
we embark without delay
on the duties of the day.

Their song continues in this vein, then – and this is where it becomes relevant to the Sunday of Christ the King – next they sing the chorus:

Oh philosophers may sing
of the troubles of a king,
but of pleasures there are many and of worries there are none,
and the culminating pleasure
which we treasure beyond measure
is the satisfying feeling that our duty has been done.

Authority

Although most British people in those days were passionately loyal to Queen Victoria, Gilbert and Sullivan could not resist making fun in this operetta of both theories: monarchy *and* republicanism. Gilbert is here putting in another context what Shakespeare said: 'Uneasy lies the head which wears a crown.' This is especially so in the case of Jesus, who was crucified because Pontius Pilate thought Jesus was making false claims to be a king. To some extent, all of us long to hold a position of authority, but if we find one, we soon discover that the worries it brings far outweigh the pleasures. From the parent of a family to the CEO of a multinational company, we never stop trying to resolve disputes between those we hold authority over; worrying about those whose criticisms prevent us doing what we had planned; and fearing those who hope to dethrone us and steal our positions. Sad to say, it even applies to ministers of religion. A couple of years ago a survey showed that nearly a third of the clergy in the Church of England rate their morale from 'very low' to 'average', dreading the day ahead, and ending each day with regrets. This is probably because a few people who bear a grudge against another church member, or against God, sometimes express it in criticism of their clergy.

Grace

But because Christ the King suffered the extreme penalty for holding the responsible position of teacher and Saviour of the world, he sympathizes with us in our trouble. If we pray to him, Jesus will give us his grace to grin and bear it. It is essential to all of us that some people are willing to take up the burden of authority, or human society would collapse; but it is a burden, which can only be borne if you are prepared to make a sacrifice of your comfort and convenience for those whom you serve as their leader. The rest of us should hold back from glib criticism of those in authority, and assure them of our understanding and support. When we think they have made a mistake, we should reason with them in a friendly way. The two gondoliers sang, 'Oh philosophers may sing of the troubles of a king . . .', and the philosophers are usually right. So pray to God for your leaders, at all levels, and remember the suffering of Jesus, the Servant King.

Suggested hymns

Father, hear the prayer we offer; From heaven you came (The Servant King); I danced in the morning; Lead us, heavenly Father, lead us.

Sermons for Saints' Days and Special Occasions

SAINTS' DAYS

A great variety of people is celebrated on the various saints' days which are commemorated in our worship. They may be young or old, female or male, educated or simple, from any race under the sun. By considering their lives, and the manner of their deaths, we may acquire a broad understanding of human nature in all its richness. We should not be insular, thinking that we can only learn from 'people like us'; some of the saints in the calendar may be completely different, and indeed you may not like them much, but they all have something to teach us. They may also lead us to explore different strands of music. St Andrew will open the door to Scottish melodies, St David to Welsh, St Patrick to the Irish repertoire, St George to military, brass band music. Epiphany could inspire us to explore music from the East; feasts of the Blessed Virgin Mary to look at the variety of hymns to Mary which have been set to music, and so on. This need not be just curiosity, it can lead us to praise God for the variety of musical gifts he has given to different people, whether or not they believe in him.

St Stephen, Deacon, First Martyr

26 December 2016

Opposition

2 Chron. 24.20–22 The stoning of Zechariah, *or* Acts 7.51–60 The death of Stephen; Ps. 119.161–168 Persecuted without a cause; (*if the Acts reading is used instead of the Old Testament reading, the New Testament reading is* Gal. 2.16b–20 Crucified with Christ); Matt. 10.17–22 Persecution

> *'You are the ones that received the law as ordained by angels, and yet you have not kept it.'* Acts 7.53

Deacons

In the years after Christ's resurrection, the church in Jerusalem distributed free food to needy members. But just because they had become Christians, that did not mean that they were free from quarrelsomeness. There were disputes between Christians who spoke Greek and those who spoke Hebrew – the Greek-speaking widows complained that they were not getting as much food in the distribution as those who spoke Hebrew. The 12 apostles were fed up with trying to reconcile these two squabbling groups, and decided to choose seven others to take responsibility for the church's charitable works. In a diplomatic master-stroke they chose men with Greek names, who would therefore be sympathetic to the Greek-speakers. One of these was called Stephen, from the Greek word for a crown. These seven are often referred to as deacons, meaning 'servants', though they are never called that in the Bible; yet St Paul refers to other deacons, including Phoebe, the woman who ran the church in one of the ports near Corinth. But although the original task of the seven was administrative, they could not avoid being asked to speak out to enquirers about the new religion of Christianity. So Stephen was attacked and persecuted by the religious people of Jerusalem, for challenging their ancient traditions.

Persecution

Anyone who speaks up for Jesus today can expect to be persecuted. The movement for freedom of expression in this country has had the opposite effect. Those who call themselves 'secularists' attack any outward expression of religious faith, because they say it undermines their right to disbelieve! So symbols of Christianity, like a cross or a Christmas crib, are criticized, as are those who build them or display them. Teaching children about Jesus in schools is condemned as removing equality from those of other faiths. Mentioning eternal life in a hospital is called 'ramming religion down the throats of the patients'. Even if your friends hear that you go to church on Sunday, they may dismiss you as eccentric and old-fashioned. But like St Stephen, we should rejoice that we are privileged to suffer for Jesus' sake, and pray for our persecutors, 'Lord, do not hold this sin against them.'

Quarrelsomeness

But alas, there is still quarrelsomeness between different groups of Christians today. Different denominations pick holes in each other's doctrines and traditions, but cannot see any faults in their own. Non-Christians are put off from coming to church if we preach a gospel of love but cannot even love each other. Christians today, as in St Stephen's time, disagree over words, and like the Jews then, they persecute those they disagree with. Within a particular congregation, the traditionalists block the way of the progressives, and the liberals undermine the conservatives. Some years after St Stephen's martyrdom, St Paul found many of the congregations he wrote to divided irreconcilably between Jewish Christians who held to every detail of the Jewish tradition, and Gentile Christians who demanded total freedom from the moral law. In some congregations today there are feuds going back for several generations, between families who refuse to speak to each other. As for sitting in somebody else's seat in church, or arranging the flowers when it isn't your turn . . . enough said!

Caring for the carers

I must say, this congregation is very tolerant, and good at caring for each other. Sometimes when somebody is sick, or has suffered a family loss, the neighbours will anonymously leave a hot meal on their doorstep, so they don't have to worry about cooking for themselves. The church officers and ministers, like St Stephen, know when they offer themselves to the service of the Church that it will not all be plain sailing. But the officers devote many hours to ensuring that the church is well administered, the music is well performed, that enough money is raised to stop the building falling down, and that – although you cannot please all the people all the time – everybody feels consulted over important decisions. Those in ministry often devote their whole heart and soul into creating inspiring worship, developing new ways of caring for the needy, and making newcomers feel welcome so that the congregation will grow. Most people are very encouraging and cooperative. But it only takes a few who are critical and resistant to change, for a minister or officer to leave the church broken-hearted, feeling they have been a total failure. A warm thank you, then to all of you who are so supportive in caring for your carers.

Suggested hymns

For all thy saints, O Lord; Good King Wenceslas looked out; O thou who camest from above; Stephen, first of Christian martyrs.

St John, Apostle and Evangelist 27 December
The Beloved Disciple

Ex. 33.7–11a The tent of meeting; Ps. 117 Praise God, all nations; 1 John 1 The word of life; John 21.19b–25 The Beloved Disciple

> *'Peter turned and saw the disciple whom Jesus loved following them; he was the one who had reclined next to Jesus at the supper and had said, "Lord, who is it that is going to betray you?" . . . This is the disciple who is testifying to these things and has written them, and we know that his testimony is true.' John 21.20, 24*

Four or one?

Four people called John are mentioned in the New Testament. The dedication of this day to commemorate 'St John, Apostle and Evangelist', and the choice of the readings, implies thst these four were one and the same person. That could be true, but John was a very common name then, and the Bible doesn't definitely say that they were. The four people were:

1 John the son of Zebedee and brother of James; James and John were Galilean fishermen, nicknamed 'the Sons of Thunder', who were among the first to be chosen as members of the 12 apostles;
2 the author of the Fourth Gospel – that is what the word 'Evangelist' means, a Gospel-writer – who is referred to as 'the disciple whom Jesus loved';
3 the writer of the two letters of John, who calls himself 'the elder'; and
4 the author of the book of the Revelation, who calls himself John.

There's a detective story for you! The only clues are that the Gospel and the letters are written in literary Greek, though with a good knowledge of the Hebrew Scriptures, so could have been written by the same person. Against this, remember that the Beloved Disciple, as we usually call him, only wrote the first draft of the Gospel, and his friends who edited the final version could have polished up his rough fisherman's Greek for him. Perhaps I shall talk about the other three another time, but today I want to concentrate on the Beloved Disciple.

References

The disciple whom Jesus loved is mentioned in five verses in the Fourth Gospel.

1 At the Last Supper, he was reclining next to Jesus, and asked Jesus who it was who would betray him.
2 He was standing at the foot of the cross, and Jesus asked him to look after the Virgin Mary.
3 He was told by Mary Magdalene that the tomb of Jesus was empty, and was the first to get there and look inside.
4 He was the first of the disciples who had been fishing in Lake Galilee to recognize the risen Christ on the lakeshore.
5 Peter asked Jesus what would happen to the Beloved Disciple, and Jesus replied, 'If it is my will that he remain until I come, what is that to you? Follow me!', leading to the mistaken idea that he would live until the Second Coming. This is also the point at which it is stated that 'this is the disciple who wrote these things', that is, the first draft of the Gospel.

Beloved

In all these incidents it is quite possible that John the son of Zebedee could have been the person who is spoken of. John was named along with James and Peter among the select group of three who were with Jesus at the transfiguration, and in the Garden of Gethsemane, so he obviously had a special relationship with Jesus. But Jesus loved all his disciples, so it could have been any one of the Twelve, or even Martha, Mary and Lazarus, who are specifically stated to have been loved by Jesus – though they were not fishermen, so are unlikely to have seen Jesus on the lakeshore. So why does the author of the Fourth Gospel use this strange title to identify himself? Was he boasting that Jesus loved him more than any of the others? More likely it was an act of humility, an example which we all can follow. Maybe he didn't want to draw attention to himself by giving his name. All these wonderful things which had happened to him were not because he was especially clever, or wise, or brave, or spiritual; they happened just because Jesus loved him, the same as Jesus loves everybody else. As we look back on our lives, we should not claim any of the credit for ourselves. The good things happened because God loves us. And then we shall never be afraid, because we know we always live wrapped up in a warm blanket of God's love. The best thing I can hope to have written in my obituary is that I was a 'disciple whom Jesus loved'.

Suggested hymns

Immortal love, for ever full; Jesus, lover of my soul; Love came down at Christmas; My song is love unknown.

Holy Innocents   28 December
Child Death

Jer. 31.15–17 Rachel weeping for her children; Ps. 124 When our enemies attacked us; 1 Cor. 1.26–29 God chose what is weak; Matt. 2.13–18 The massacre

> *'God chose what is weak in the world to shame the strong.'*
> *1 Corinthians 1.27*

The Shack

I don't know if you are familiar with a little book called *The Shack* by William Paul Young. A bestseller all over the world, it tells the story of one man's journey to peace of mind. It is fiction, but its description of the human dilemma has struck a chord in many people who are trying to come to terms with the awfulness of life. It has a religious theme, told in terms which may turn your whole understanding of religion on its head. It is particularly relevant to today, the feast of the Holy Innocents, because it is about the loss of a child.

Sadness

In the story, Mack is grieving over his youngest daughter, Missy, who disappeared four years ago during a camping holiday. Subsequently, some evidence was discovered that she had been murdered in a hut, or shack, in the woods. Since then, Mack had felt as though an invisible, but terribly heavy, quilt was draped around his shoulders. He called it 'the Great Sadness'. His grief for Missy was like that of any bereaved parent, but made worse because he was uncertain what had happened to her. The weight of his sadness seemed to press continually on his shoulders. He described it to himself as like trudging through heavy mud, which turned the lightest of tasks into hard labour, and drained the colour out of everything. His eyes were seldom dry, and, waking up with a start, he would sit up in bed, covered in sweat. Exaggerated guilt and illogical regret swept across him in waves. Eventually, after four years of this, he paid his first visit to the shack where Missy had been murdered, met God, and his grief and anger came to a point of closure. To see how, you will have to read the book.

Bethlehem

Depression is a common experience among bereaved parents. For the atheist, there is nobody to shout at: the world is a wicked place, there is no cause, and no reason why it should not be. Yet attempts to grin and bear it are unbearably painful. For those who believe in God, or even worse, for those are not quite sure, anger against the Almighty wells up in their hearts. How can a God of love allow my child to die, when so many dreams and hopes for the future were as yet unfulfilled? Is he deaf to our prayers? The rural village of Bethlehem in the time of King Herod the Great must have been full of unhappy parents grappling with feelings like this. Is there any answer we can give to such people?

Answers

Those who have themselves been bereaved are the best qualified to help other bereaved parents, but others can humbly offer to share what they have learnt of God, while carefully avoiding giving a lecture. The first point is that death is not, in itself, a tragedy. Jesus assured us that after we die, there is a better world where there is no more pain, and all is love and happiness. 'In my Father's house', he said, 'there are many rest-stops,' suggesting that there is progress and growth after we die. When we meet our children in heaven, we shall recognize them, but they may have grown to a maturity far beyond our dreams. No, the tragedy is for those left behind, starved of the love and cuddles which our child used to give us. But God does love us. Essential to the world he created was that people should be free to commit wicked acts, and that predatory microbes should bring everyone face to face with death at some point. But God does answer prayer: he saves us from the messes we get ourselves into, or that are caused by others – not by taking away our free will, but by giving us the spiritual strength to come through them as better people. Not long ago, the majority of children died before they were 5 years old, and this is still true in many countries. God gave skill to the researchers to find cures for these diseases, and to change society so that the fighting and unhealthy habits, which caused so many children to die, have been reduced. We can never forgive those who harmed children, in the sense of saying it doesn't matter, but we can refuse to ruin our lives by bearing an endless burden of anger. And when we lose that, the weight of depression may also be reduced. Jesus was born in Bethlehem. I wonder whether he ever returned to comfort the bereaved parents there, and turn their horror into hope?

Suggested hymns

Lully, lullay, thou little tiny child; Morning glory, starlit sky; Unto us a boy is born; When Christ was born in Bethlehem.

Naming and Circumcision of Christ   1 January 2017

(Or 2 January 8; see note on page 33.)

Joking about Somebody's Name

Num. 6.22–27 Aaron's blessing; Ps. 8 From the mouths of babes; Gal. 4.4–7 Born under the Law; Luke 2.15–21 Naming and circumcision

> 'After eight days had passed, it was time to circumcise the child; and he was called Jesus, the name given by the angel before he was conceived in the womb.' Luke 2.21

Babies

How do you choose the name for a new baby? If you give your son the same name as his father, then you will have to call him John Smith Junior, and his father will become John Smith Senior, which is a nuisance. You don't often hear daughters named after their mother; if they are, it is usually by using Mother's first name as the daughter's second name. Calling the baby after an uncle, aunt or grandparent is not so bad, though it may lead to confusion in people who don't know the family well. And you remember that Zechariah and Elizabeth were thought odd for calling their son John, even though nobody else in the family had that name. But John acquired the nickname John 'the Baptist', and that often happens to a child with a very common name, particularly if some classmates have the same name. Or they may become known as Ann and Annie to distinguish them, or Mick, Mike and 'Mickey Mouse'. If you call your child after a film star, that could also become common; at one time there were several Waynes in every class, all of them nicknamed at Christmas time 'A-Wayne-in-a-Manger'! On the other hand, if you choose an uncommon name, your child will be bothered all their life by people asking how to spell it, and where it comes from. At one time, all Christians gave their children the name of a saint, or a hero in the Bible, which is nice, so long as they don't think it is an impossible challenge to live up to their name. A man was named after King David's father Jesse, who was spoken of as if he was a female, even at his funeral! Puritans had amazing names, including Praise-God Barebone and Fear-God Barebone, Fear-Not Helly, Die-well Sykes and his brother Farewell Sykes, Continent Walker and Humiliation Hynde. Pity the child whose first name was Fly-fornication.

Joking

That is the trouble with choosing first names: if you are not careful people will make fun of them. All you can do is grin and bear it. I think any parent who is expecting a baby in the coming year should make a resolution to be extremely careful in the choice of names. Worse still is if the name becomes used as a swear word. I can't think of any examples just now, and I wouldn't tell you if I could. The third of the Ten Commandments tells us not to take the name of God in vain, and it probably referred to swearing by the name of God in a law-court and then telling lies. Most people think it means using the names of God, Jesus or Mary as a swear word or obscenity. I doubt if God is bothered by such disrespect; more likely he pities the swearer for their ignorance. But I dislike it, and so do many Christians, because we love God. How would you feel if the name of somebody you love was used as a swearword? 'Oh my God' is frequently abbreviated to 'OMG' these days. I was thrilled to see that some churches now use the letters 'OMG' as a triumphal decoration, in one case with an arrow pointing to the crucifix, meaning 'Oh, Jesus is my God'.

Naming

A week after they were born, Jewish boys were circumcised and given their name. Modern Jews have a similar naming ceremony for little girls, but there was nothing for them in the old, sexist times. So, believing that Jesus was born on 25 December, the Church celebrated his naming and circumcision on 1 January. Jesus is a Greek translation of the common Hebrew name Joshua, or in the Aramaic dialect spoken then, 'Yeshua' (yeh-SHOE-ah). It means 'God saves'. So Jesus is our Saviour. What does he save us from? Sin and guilt, temptation, fear of death and hell. But most of all, Jesus saves us from ourselves. We are so selfish and self-centred that we never think of the pain our words and deeds cause to other people, and we blunder into temptation without even noticing it. We need to say, 'Lead us away from temptation.' We all encounter many pains, distresses and dangers in our lives. Perhaps we shall never know how many of them Jesus saves us from, but he can't remove them all. But when troubles come, he gives us spiritual strength to come through them. Thank God that his Son, as on this day, was named our Saviour.

Suggested hymns

All hail the power of Jesu's name; At the name of Jesus; Mary had a baby, yes, Lord; One more step along the road I go.

Epiphany   6 January

(Or may be transferred to Sunday 8 January; see page 37.)

The Star is Love

Isa. 60.1–6 Bringing gold and incense; Ps. 72.[1–9] 10–15 Kings will bow before him; Eph. 3.1–12 Preaching to Gentiles; Matt. 2.1–12 Visit of the Magi

> *'[The wise men asked Herod,] "Where is the child who has been born king of the Jews? For we observed his star at its rising, and have come to pay him homage."' Matthew 2.2*

Wise men

The story of the wise men teaches us a rather shocking lesson. Jesus was born a member of the Jewish nation, God's Chosen People. God had taught the Jews a great deal of wisdom, which they incorporated in their religion. They heartily despised all other races, whom they dismissed as *goiim* or Gentiles. As far as the Jews were concerned, all religions other than theirs were crass idolatry. And yet the first two groups to recognize the birth of the long-hoped-for Messiah, the King of the Jews, were:

1. a bevy of shepherds, ignorant and uneducated in the wisdom of the past; and
2. a coven of Iranian astrologers, superstitious devotees of God-knows-what system of oriental fortune-telling.

Religions

This message was surely to teach the Jews, and us, that there is good and bad in all religions, at least as they are now being practised by a mixture of good and bad people. The Jews didn't want to hear that, any more than many Christians do today. Something in the religion of the Magi had led them to bow before the feet of the baby Jesus. Magi, by the way, is the original name for Persian astrologers, which we translate as wise men. They were looking for a king to follow, and believed the star would lead them to him. There was much that was wrong in their beliefs, which they would have to unlearn – thinking that looking up your horoscope will tell you every detail of your future, for instance. But they were following the best they knew, in whatever direction it led them, and it led them to the child called 'Love'. What the Jews had learnt was there are not different gods for different nations, but one God for the whole earth, and the Jewish people had been chosen to spread that message to every nation. Christians have now taken on the task of evangelism, but nation still fights nation, often on the grounds of religion, and even Christians, who should know better, have sometimes tried to convert people by killing them.

Missionaries

But not all Christians are like that – tens of thousands have gone to other nations as missionaries, to share the good news of the God of love. They have brought teachers and doctors, and built hospitals and schools, to demonstrate that evangelism is best done by example; following God's call to be humble servants of others, no matter what their religion. Many would still be in the grip of disease and ignorance if it had not been for the missionaries. Most missionaries soon learn that what they say about Jesus will only be attractive if they say it not only in the language of their hearers, which they have to become fluent in, but also in the thought forms of their culture. It was the missionaries who studied the sacred books of the other nations, translated them into their own language, and in many cases prevented a culture from dying out. In return, wise men and women, from the countries the missionaries went to, began to rethink the Christian faith in terms of their own philosophies, bringing fresh insight into the teaching of Jesus. Even we from the so-called Christian nations have much to learn from these new interpretations.

The star is love

At the centre of Christianity is what Jesus taught us about love: God's love for us and our love for God; loving our neighbours, and even our enemies. Yet many who call themselves Christians still haven't learnt that, and try to spread their own culture by warlike means. We need the 'new Christians' from other cultures to shock us back into understanding what the gospel really means. Wise men from the East taught us, when we have grasped a truth, to follow that star wherever it leads. For them the destination was love; perhaps the star which led them to it was a symbol of love, too. So, no matter what culture you come from, search for the bright star of love, and follow it diligently till it brings you to the feet of Jesus. Then, if people of every nation bring with them the gift of their own, distinctive culture, we shall be able to enjoy a rainbow of cultural insights into the many-faceted love of God, so much nearer the one expressible truth than the monochrome version we have so far imagined to be all there is to say.

Suggested hymns

As with gladness men of old; From the eastern mountains; How brightly shines the morning star; We three kings of orient are.

Week of Prayer for Christian Unity   18–25 January
Post-denominational

Jer. 33.6–9a Judah and Israel; Ps. 100 All lands praise God;
Eph. 4.1–6 Maintain the unity; Matt. 18.19–22 If two agree

'I therefore, the prisoner in the Lord, beg you to lead a life worthy of the calling to which you have been called, with all humility and gentleness, with patience, bearing with one another in love, making every effort to maintain the unity of the Spirit in the bond of peace.' Ephesians 4.1–3

Appeals for unity

The Old Testament warns the two nations into which Israel had divided, now called Israel and Judah, that 'united we stand, divided we fall'. The Psalms have a vision of all nations united under one God. Jesus promised that if two Christians agreed, their prayers would be answered. He also prayed that all those who follow him should be one, that the world might believe. St Paul recognized tensions in the churches which he had founded, between those who liked to worship in one way and those who preferred another, between those who believed in freedom and those who wanted discipline. So he warned the Christians in Ephesus to 'make every effort to maintain the unity of the Spirit'. Paul wrote that the Church is the Body of Christ, and those who divide the Church into denominations, parties or factions are tearing Christ's body apart, causing Jesus to suffer again all the agonies he endured on the cross.

Urgency

So we have started an ecumenical movement: church leaders have joint conferences, and we have annual joint services in unity week, not very well attended. Then a couple of denominations pass resolutions proposing negotiations leading to reunion. But somehow these papers seem to get lost on somebody's desk, and nothing much happens. Therefore people are saddened who have read what the Bible says about unity. In some places there is cooperation between the denominations in caring for the outcasts of society, and occasionally joint evangelism. But although in some areas church attendance is growing, overall in this country it is falling, and we wonder why. There are many reasons, but one of them is that non-churchgoers look at our competing denominations and decide to ignore us as we can't even agree among ourselves as to what Christianity is.

Wake up!

So what the churches in this country need is a wake-up call! We need a sudden, short, sharp shock to remind us what we are doing to God by dividing his church into denominations. As I have said, every time we kneel down in our own denominational building, separated from other Christians in the neighbourhood who happen to belong to different traditions, we are tearing the Body of Christ into pieces – in effect we are re-crucifying our Saviour each week by our separation. We are preventing our neighbours learning about how Jesus loves them, because we are ignoring his call to be one 'that the world may believe'.

Post-denominational

So to jolt you all into ecumenical urgency, I invite you to think what Jesus wants his church in this area to be like. Let us call it post-denominational Christianity. So all the Christians in your locality will worship in one building. That means that those whose fussy ritual you can't stand, and the happy-clappies whose music you hate, will be worshipping with you, because that is what Jesus wants you to do. Not necessarily at the same time; but those who like the same form of worship as you do may meet at a less convenient time, and perhaps not every Sunday. Then gradually you may find that the variety of worship is more appealing than you expected, and you will enjoy being free to drop in on a different type of service when you feel like it. There will be no top-down organization, but each local church will be democratically run, independent but with a sense of mutual responsibility which causes the richer churches to offer their support to the poorer ones. People will be free to explore the Christian faith for themselves: so long as you believe in the one God of Love, and Jesus who reconciles us to him, you can put your faith into new words without being excommunicated as a heretic. No, I'm sure you wouldn't like it to begin with, but that isn't the point. Jesus would like it, and that is what matters. Eventually you will realize that post-denominational religion is better, in every way, than our present divided parody of what a church is meant to be. You are never going to get every Christian to agree with you, so you had better learn to live together in racial and every other type of mutual tolerance. Then get down to work, and bring the post-denominational church into being as quickly as you can – for Christ's sake!

Suggested hymns

Dear Lord and Father of mankind; Jesus, stand among us at the meeting of our lives; O thou who at thy Eucharist didst pray; Thy hand, O God, has guided.

Conversion of St Paul   25 January
From Jerusalem to Athens

Jer. 1.4–10 The call of a prophet; Ps. 67 Let all the peoples praise you; Acts 9.1–22 Saul's conversion (*if the Acts reading is used instead of the Old Testament reading, the New Testament reading is* Gal. 1.11–16a Called me through his grace); Matt. 19.27–30 The reward of eternal life

   'I appointed you a prophet to the nations.' Jeremiah 1.5

Tarsus

You never stop learning, do you? You think your opinions are firmly set, and then you have an argument, politely called a discussion, with somebody who disagrees with you. You never admit that you were wrong, but somehow, some of your opponent's verbal darts get absorbed into your own armoury, and suddenly your opinions have swung right round. So if that is what happens to you and me, why shouldn't it have happened to St Paul? He was born in Tarsus, a Greek-speaking university town, and the rowdy Greek students made fun of the snivelling little Jewish boy, and he was glad to leave the place when he went to university in Jerusalem.

Jerusalem

Jerusalem, where his final opinions would be formed, he thought. Based on a solid Old Testament background, he learnt that the Jews were the Chosen People, all the rest were rubbish, and anything which couldn't be said in Hebrew wasn't worth saying. So when he learnt that some Jews calling themselves Christians were speaking blasphemies, he realized that the Jewish Law was telling him to stone Stephen to death. So he arranged for that to happen. Yet afterwards he started feeling guilty. To silence his conscience, he got letters authorizing him to stone some of the Greek-speaking Christians in Damascus.

Damascus

But on the road to Damascus, Saul got sunstroke. He could have sworn that he had seen the dead prophet Jesus telling him that when he attacked his followers, he was persecuting their leader also. The sun made him blind, so his mates took him into Damascus, where a brave Christian called on him, healed him and baptized him into the Jesus movement, which he had sworn he would never have anything to do with. So much for fixed opinions!

Antioch

When Saul told the other Christians what had happened to him, they sent him off to Antioch, in south-east Turkey, to talk to some of the Greek-speaking Christians there, who wanted to share the gospel with Greek-speaking non-Jews. This was against Saul's principles, but he discovered that Antioch was the third biggest city in the Roman world; its stadium was where the famous chariot race in Ben Hur would later be set; and everybody, but everybody, spoke Greek. What a good idea it would be to convert some of them to Christianity; he was so pleased with himself for having thought of it.

Cyprus

Next, Saul's friend Barnabas took him to visit his home town in Cyprus. Saul's ideas were not well received in the synagogues, but he was summoned by the Roman Governor, Sergius Paulus, who was so impressed he asked Saul to baptize him, then suggested to Saul that he should take advantage of the Roman roads to travel all over the Empire converting people to Christianity. At this time the different cities worshipped different gods, but this would unite the Empire. Saul thanked the Governor for helping him to think up this splendid idea; and he changed his name to that of the Governor, Paulus, to show his gratitude, and said that from now on he would be concentrating on the non-Jews.

Pisidian Antioch etc.

There's no time to mention what he learnt in all the other places he visited:

- the chance to convert the surrounding tribesmen at places on the edge of Empire;
- the dangers of relying on Roman citizenship when he visited the old-soldier's settlement in Philippi, on his first visit to Europe, not to mention the value of a capable businesswoman like Lydia;
- the ineffectiveness of preaching about Christ coming on the clouds, in a Greek town like Thessalonica – later in Corinth he would say the opposite: that flesh and blood cannot inherit the kingdom of God.

Athens

The crucial stage in this journey of discovery was when he arrived in Athens, the city of philosophers. He realized he had to invent a whole new language, Instead of dismissing the worship of the Greek gods as meaningless superstition, he started where they were:

> Athenians, I see how extremely religious you are in every way ...
> What therefore you worship as unknown, this I proclaim to you.
> The God who made the world and everything in it, he who is
> Lord of heaven and earth ... made all nations to inhabit the
> whole earth ... so that they would search for God and perhaps
> grope for him and find him.

What a change from the 'only to the Jews' message he had been preaching 17 years before. We never stop learning, do we?

Suggested hymns

A heavenly splendour from on high; Disposer supreme, and judge of the earth; Hail, thou source of every blessing; We sing the glorious conquest.

Presentation of Christ in the Temple (Candlemas)
2 February
(or may be celebrated on Sunday 29 January)
Purification

Mal. 3.1–5 The Lord shall come to his Temple; Ps. 24.[1–6] 7–10 Open the gates for the Lord; Heb. 2.14–18 Jesus became like the descendants of Abraham; Luke 2.22–40 The presentation of Christ in the Temple

> 'When the time came for their purification according to the law of Moses, they brought him up to Jerusalem to present him to the Lord.' Luke 2.22

Purification

In the Book of Common Prayer, 2 February was called 'The Presentation of Christ in the Temple, commonly called The Purification of Saint Mary the Virgin'. Nowadays we usually call

302

it Candlemas, and often transfer it to the nearest Sunday. The old name was based on passages from the Old Testament, one of which was in the law book called Leviticus, where God allegedly gave some terribly sexist instructions to Moses. When a woman had borne a boy-child, she was what they called 'unclean' for 40 days, or if it was a girl, 80 days. This may have started as a humane recommendation to stay at home to avoid infection. But it got caught up with the assumption that the blood of menstruation and childbirth must not be found in the Temple. At the end of that time, she was to bring a sacrifice, when the priest would declare her fit to re-enter society. This was a lamb for a burnt offering and a young pigeon for a sin offering. I ask you! Surely God didn't think there is anything sinful or impure about childbirth. And anything *more* sinful in giving birth to a girl! But the laws of the Old Testament were based on the superstitions of a tribe of desert nomads. Though it makes it difficult for those who want to believe that the whole Bible was dictated by God.

Poor families

The sacrifice required would have been quite expensive, so poor families were allowed to sacrifice two pigeons instead of one pigeon and a lamb; this was known as 'the gift of the poor'. The fact that Mary was allowed to do this shows that Jesus was born into a poor family. He knew from first-hand experience the problems of hunger and a low income. He understood how hard it was to make a living. When we find life difficult, we should remember that Jesus, too, knew all about the hard grind of making ends meet.

Growing up

For there is no mention of Joseph when Jesus and his mother attended the wedding in Cana of Galilee. The obvious explanation was that he had died soon after taking Jesus to the Temple when he was 12 years old. This need not imply that Joseph was older than Mary, and that what the Bible calls Jesus's 'brothers and sisters' were actually Joseph's children by his first marriage. Working-class people died young in those days; what was remarkable was that Mary should have lived until her first born was 30; for most women the norm in those days was 'married at 13 and dead at 30'.

Supporting the family

If Joseph did die when Jesus was young, our Saviour must have had a hard time, going out to work while still a lad, to earn enough to feed his mother and his younger siblings. He told a parable about the unemployed waiting in the marketplace for someone to hire them; perhaps he had experienced that himself, and the loss of self-confidence it brings. Not until his brothers were old enough to go out to work on their own behalf would he be able to give up the hard grind and start his mission as a wandering preacher in the villages around Lake Galilee, at the age of about 27.

Children are lent

It cannot have been easy for Mary, either, as a young widow, to bring up a large family with no husband to help her. Particularly when she knew that one of them was the Son of God. Yet Mary 'the God-bearer', as she was later called, made a marvellous job of it. The Greek Stoic philosophers used to say that a child is not *given* to parents but *lent* to them. Mary endured the scorn of her neighbours for bearing a child when she was not married, the misogyny of the ceremonies which described childbirth as shameful, her struggle to bring up her family, and the loneliness when her son left home. Then came the greatest sacrifice of all, when the old lady had to give back the son that God had lent her, when she was one of the small number who watched his crucifixion. If we ever grumble about the trials of growing up or of parenthood, we should think again of Jesus and Mary.

All-age worship

Find out about the problems of single-parent families in your neighbourhood, and think what you can do to help.

Suggested hymns

Faithful vigil ended; Of the Father's love begotten; Sometimes a light surprises; Virgin-born, we bow before thee.

St David, Bishop of Menevia, Patron of Wales
c. 601   1 March
St David's Prayer

Ecclus. (Ben Sira) 15.1–6 Whoever holds to the law will obtain wisdom; Ps. 16.1–7 I have a goodly heritage; 1 Thess. 2.2–12 Entrusted with the gospel; Matt. 16.24–27 Take up your cross

> 'Jesus told his disciples, "If any want to become my followers, let them deny themselves and take up their cross and follow me. For those who want to save their life will lose it, and those who lose their life for my sake will find it. For what will it profit them if they gain the whole world but forfeit their life? Or what will they give in return for their life?"' Matthew 16.24–26

Biography

The earliest biography of St David that is known was written some 500 years after he died. No doubt much of it was faithfully passed down by word of mouth – as with the transmission of stories in the Bible, those who cannot read have a remarkably accurate memory for what they have heard. Nonetheless it is difficult to know which of the traditions and legends about him are true and which were invented by his devoted followers.

David's life

It is probable that St David was born in South Wales, in about AD 540, the son of King Sant, the ruler of South Wales, and his wife, later canonized as St Non. David was ordained as a priest, and lived the simple life of a Celtic monk. Later he became the Bishop of Menevia. Tradition tells us that on a pilgrimage to the Holy Land, he was consecrated by the Patriarch of Jerusalem to be the archbishop of the whole of Wales. He lived until he was about 60 years old, and during his lifetime he founded several monasteries. The monks, like St David himself, lived a simple life. They drank mostly water, and ate bread and salt with herbs and watercress. They prepared their fields with hand-drawn ploughs – no oxen – and ate honey from the bee-hives which they cultivated. In the evenings they studied the Bible and other holy books, and prayed together or alone. The monks in the monasteries which St David founded were not allowed to have any personal possessions, and were disciplined if they accidentally referred

305

to '*my* book' instead of '*our* book'. The monks were also renowned for their generous hospitality to passing pilgrims and other travellers, and those who lived in poverty in the nearby Welsh settlements. They shared their food and clothes with anybody who was in need.

Simplicity

Because of the simple life which he and his monks followed, St David became known as 'David the water-drinker'. His frugal vegetarian diet probably included leeks, which became a Welsh patriotic symbol; nevertheless he was healthy and strong, and taller than most. He had a loud voice, which made him heard by large crowds when he preached in the open air, and, being Welsh, also made him a powerful singer. Among other miracles attributed to David, it is claimed that he cured St Paulinus, his elderly teacher and mentor, of blindness. When he died, his body was buried in the grounds of his monastery, where St David's Cathedral now stands. On the Sunday before he died, St David preached a sermon calling his followers to live lives of simplicity after his example. He said:

> Be joyful, and keep your faith and your creed. Do the little things that you have seen me do and heard about. I will walk the path that our fathers have trod before us.

CAFOD

I cannot trace any prayers written by St David, but on the website of CAFOD, which stands for Catholic Aid For Overseas Development, I found a prayer addressed to St David, asking him for the gift of simplicity which he himself showed throughout his life. CAFOD is the official overseas development and relief agency of the Roman Catholic Church in England and Wales. They define their purpose as 'to raise awareness and inspire commitment to end injustice and poverty in developing countries'. This is similar to the role of Christian Aid in other churches, and in many areas the two organizations overlap. I have been unable to discover who wrote this prayer, but it shares the emphasis on simplicity and the 'little things' in life which St David showed in his last sermon. It goes like this:

> Saint David,
> you chose to live a simple life,
> and helped others whose lives were simple,

not through choice but circumstances.
I pray that I may consider my choices
and live more simply
in order to make a big difference to others.
Show me the way to make small tasks occasions of prayer.
Kindle in me a love of God
so that in everything I do,
I will keep that spirit of prayer.
Amen.

Suggested hymns

Father, hear the prayer we offer; Guide me, O thou great Redeemer (Cwm Rhondda); Love divine, all loves excelling (Blaenwern); We believe in God the Father (Ebenezer/Ton-y-botel)

St Patrick, Bishop, Missionary, Patron of Ireland c. 460 17 March
Ireland before Patrick

Deut. 32.1–9 Let my teaching drop like rain, *or* Tob. 13.1b–7 In the land of my exile; Ps. 145.1–13 Make known to all peoples; 2 Cor. 4.1–12 This ministry; Matt. 10.16–23 Warnings for missionaries, *or* John 4.31–38 Ripe for harvest

> *'Therefore, since it is by God's mercy that we are engaged in this ministry, we do not lose heart.' 2 Corinthians 4.1*

Irish Christians

The Roman occupation brought Christianity to England, and our religion grew and thrived there during that time and after the Roman legions withdrew. But Ireland was never part of the Roman Empire. There were Christians in Ireland before St Patrick arrived, but not in the area where he was enslaved and where he subsequently ministered. The south-eastern coast of Ireland was a busy area for shipping, and had contacts with traders from all over Europe and the Mediterranean coasts. Some foreign Christians settled in Ireland; some Irish people learnt about Jesus from them and were converted. But the organization of bishops, priests and deacons, and the areas known as dioceses, inherited from the Roman civil government, were unknown in Ireland at first.

Palladius

In the fifth century AD, a Briton named *Pelagius* started teaching what can best be described as 'self-help' Christianity. His opponents accused him of proclaiming that we can get to heaven by our own efforts, and ignoring our need of God's grace. Whether or not that is what he taught it is impossible to say, as the only surviving evidence is in the writings of his enemies. But Pope Celestine ordained a man called *Palladius*, made him a bishop and sent him to Ireland to preach against the Pelagian heresy to the Irish Christians, of whom there were apparently a good number at that time. Palladius landed in 431 at a town where Wicklow now stands, and is mostly associated with Leinster, around present-day Dublin. What happened next is very confused, and many of the deeds of St Palladius seem to have been wrongly attributed to St Patrick. Those who wrote Patrick's life story say that Palladius was soon banished by the King of Leinster, and returned to North Britain, where he died around 450 in Fordun, near Aberdeen. Palladius was accompanied by four companions: Sylvester and Solinus, who remained after him in Ireland; and Augustinus and Benedictus, who followed him to Britain, but returned to their own country after his death.

Patrick

Patrick, meanwhile, was born somewhere in the west of mainland Britain, in a Christian family. When he was 16 he was kidnapped by Irish traders and enslaved as a herdsman, probably in County Mayo, in Connaught on the west coast. He had plenty of solitude to pray and repent of his former life. Eventually he escaped, and travelled for 200 miles southeast to a port where he caught a ship. He then travelled widely in Europe, according to his autobiography. It used to be said that he received his training for the ministry on the island of Lérins, off the Cote d'Azur on the southern coast of France, though this is now questioned. Curiously, his tutor, a monk called Honoratus, had driven all the snakes from the island of Lérins; and although St Patrick is alleged to have banished snakes from Ireland, all the evidence suggests there never were any snakes in Ireland! So perhaps the story of Honoratus was wrongly attributed to Patrick. Patrick had no wish, he himself wrote, to return to Ireland, but God appeared to him in a dream or vision and instructed him to go and convert his former captors. The dates of his life are uncertain. One source gives: born in AD 385, kidnapped 400; escaped 407; returned to Britain 410; returned to Ireland 432; died 17 March 461. But other sources give the date of his death as 492, which would mean that his mission in Ireland fell between 460 and 492, 30 years later than in the original list of dates. In either case, Patrick's ministry in Ulster and Connaught was later than Palladius's visit to Leinster in 431, and they seem to have evangelized quite different areas.

Teamwork

There were other missionaries, whose dates are uncertain, who are claimed to have made converts in different parts of Ireland, and later on, pious biographers wanted to claim all the stories for the saint who founded the church in their area. Surely we should regard the conversion of Ireland as a team effort, with different missionaries sent by God to work in different areas. In that, it is a lesson for us today. We should thank God, who has sent us to spread the good news in our area, and thank him also for sending others to work in other places, regarding them not as rivals but as colleagues.

Suggested hymns

I bind unto myself today (St Patrick); I cannot tell why he whom angels worship (Londonderry); Inspired by love and anger (Salley Gardens); Lord, while for all mankind we pray.

St Joseph of Nazareth   20 March (transferred)
Adoption
2 Sam. 7.4–16 Descendants of David; Ps. 89.26–36 David's line; Rom. 4.13–18 Abraham's descendants; Matt. 1.18–25 Joseph's dream

> 'When Joseph awoke from sleep, he did as the angel of the Lord commanded him; he took her as his wife, but had no marital relations with her until she had borne a son; and he named him Jesus.' Matthew 1.24–25

Jesus

Jesus was adopted. Joseph was not his natural father, but Joseph married Mary after she had already borne her son, and by that action he became the legally adoptive father of baby Jesus. Joseph is to be commended for his courage; adopting a child commits you to years of caring, which may not be easy. Added to that, the scandal that Mary was not married when she became pregnant will have put Joseph in a very difficult position with his neighbours. When an adopted child eventually discovers that the people he or she knows as Daddy and Mummy are not his real parents, they often go through a period of rebellion, search desperately for their birth mother, and refuse to obey the instructions given to them by the adoptive parents. We have no evidence that Jesus was as naughty as that, but Joseph did not know that when he took on the responsibility, and must often have wondered how he would explain to the young lad who his real father was.

Adoption

Adoption was much more common in those days than it is now. If a couple had no sons, there was a problem as to who would inherit their property, their land and their business, when they died. They usually solved this by adopting a son, either an orphan, or the child of their brother or sister. Proprietors of a large estate of land needed a son to farm it or supervise the tenants, and parents would adopt a likely lad from a humble family to do so, even if his parents were still alive. This is why the New Testament so often speaks of God adopting us as his children; the readers will have realized that this gives us an extremely important position, and was a great privilege. And they will have thought that Joseph, even if he was only the proprietor of a carpenter's shop, had done a very generous thing by adopting Jesus.

Today

Things are very different today. Often a couple who have been longing to pour their affection over children of their own, when they find after a few years that none have been born to them, decide to go to an adoption agency. Though they would probably modestly deny it, this is a generous thing to do. They should regard Joseph as their patron saint. Sometimes when they have already brought up a family of their own, parents decide to share the parenting gifts they have learnt by fostering, or even adopting, one or more orphan children.

Orphans

I speak of the children as orphans, but it is more complicated than that. Some children, poor things, have lost both parents to disease or accident. Sometimes only one parent dies, but the survivor does not feel physically or financially able to bring up the children on their own. If they are fortunate they may find somebody who offers them a second marriage, and who is willing to become a step-parent. Not long ago, the extended family would have absorbed the orphan children, but families are so scattered these days that this may not be practical. Sometimes one or more parent is in prison or a psychiatric hospital, and not capable of raising their own children. So this is where the adoption agencies come in. Usually they do sterling work in finding and selecting suitable adoptive parents, though sometimes they ate criticized for taking so long that it discourages some couple from the whole process, and they die childless.

Encouragement

Of course, nowadays there is the alternative of IVF, but that, too, can take a very long time and by the time a couple have realized it is not going to work they feel too old to adopt. Yet adoption is a much more natural and traditional way of dealing with the problems of childlessness, and there are many lonely children out there who may spend their whole childhood in an institution because nobody has offered to adopt them. So, while all couples must feel entitled to make their own choices, and must be encouraged and affirmed whatever they choose, perhaps we should encourage more of them to look at the possibility of adoption. Like St Joseph, you never know what effects the loving care of a step-parent or adoptive or fostering parent may have on the future history of the world!

Suggested carols

As Joseph was a-walking, he heard an angel sing; Hail to the Lord who comes; Joseph was an old man (The Cherry Tree Carol); The great God of heaven is come down to earth.

Annunciation of Our Lord to the Blessed Virgin Mary 25 March
Divine Rape?

Isa. 7.10–14 The sign of Immanuel; Ps. 40.5–11 I love to do your will; Heb. 10.4–10 I have come to do your will; Luke 1.26–38 The angel's message

> *'Mary said to the angel, "How can this be, since I am a virgin?"'*
> Luke 1.34

Atheists

The story of the birth of Jesus is told in Matthew's Gospel and in St Luke, but nowhere else in the New Testament. The silence of Mark, John and Paul on this subject needs explaining. Some say Mary kept it secret until St Luke interviewed her. Others claim the story was invented to help Christians explain what they meant when they said that Jesus was the Son of God. The Qur'an says Mary was a virgin, but Muslims insist that 'Allah has no sons'. They imagine that Christians believe there was intercourse between God and Mary, which is not what the Bible says. But the atheist Christopher Hitchens, in his book *God Is Not Great*, brings up stories of miraculous births in other religions, as evidence that 'virgin birth' tales are fairly common in non-Christian religions around the world, and Christians have borrowed from them. A little study will reveal that this isn't so: many gods and goddesses, heroines and heroes have their births described as miraculous, but hardly any claim that the mother was a virgin. Even if it were true, it wouldn't disprove that Jesus was the Son of God; only that people in the Greek-speaking world wouldn't accept Jesus as a hero, unless his birth was unique – so God provided the miracle they expected, 'because nothing is impossible for God'.

Ancient religions

Hindus claim that Krishna descended into the womb of Devali and was born her son – but she had already borne seven children, so she was not a virgin. Two wives of King Pandu bore six children by six different gods, but this was more a story of divine rape than a miraculous birth. Some Buddhists say the Buddha was born fully grown when his former incarnation returned from Nirvana to enter the body of his mother. In Assyrian and Babylonian myths, relations between gods and goddesses resulted in the birth of yet more goddesses and gods, but no humans were involved. The Egyptian goddess Isis gave birth to the god Horus, who represents the rising sun; some versions call this a virgin birth, but in others the child's father is the god Osiris.

Greece and Rome

Greece and Rome begat many stories of miraculous births, but few of the mothers were virgins. Zeus invaded Danae's bedroom and 'cut the knot of her virginity', whatever that means. Hercules was the son of the god Zeus and the mortal Alcomene; Pan was the offspring of divine Hermes and some mortal shepherdesses. Perseus was born when his mother was impregnated by Jupiter, descending as a golden shower. Helen of Troy was born of the union between Leda and Zeus in the form of a swan. The Emperors Alexander, Ptolemy and Julius Caesar all claimed to be half-divine.

Jews

In Jewish legend, Moses spoke on the day he was born, and elderly Sarah gave milk to her friends' children to prove that she really had given birth to Isaac. In the crucial verse in Isaiah, which we translate as 'The virgin shall conceive and bear a son', the Hebrew word means 'a young woman'. Greek-speaking Jews mistranslated it. So, with apologies to Christopher Hitchens, the Bible isn't very interested in virginity.

Immaculate

The story that Mary herself was born as the result of an 'immaculate conception' is a tradition which was not written down until around AD 155, and states that she was conceived in the normal way only without the stain of sin. This doctrine was opposed by St Bernard, St Thomas Aquinas and others because it suggests that the sexual act is necessarily sinful, which is not what the Bible teaches.

Meaning

The virgin birth of Jesus, then, tells us that he was born not because Joseph wanted a son, but because God wanted a Saviour. The character of Jesus was more like that of God than any other human being's; as we say, 'like father, like son'. He addressed God as 'Abba', meaning Daddy, and it would have been cruel of God to have allowed the best human being that ever lived to die on the cross, unless in some sense, as St Paul says, 'God was in Christ, reconciling the world to himself.' The virgin birth story is there to draw our attention to this special relationship between Jesus and our heavenly Father. Whether it is historically true doesn't really matter; what is important is that, when Jesus was born, a little bit of heaven came down to earth, to convince us that God loves us all as his earthly daughters and sons.

Suggested hymns

Her virgin eyes saw God incarnate born; Love came down at Christmas; Tell out, my soul, the greatness of the Lord; The angel Gabriel from heaven came.

St George, Martyr, Patron of England c. 304
24 April (transferred)
Everybody Needs a Hero

1 Macc. 2.59–64 Be courageous, *or* Rev. 12.7–12 Michael fights the dragon; Ps. 126 Restore our fortunes; 2 Tim. 2.3–13 A soldier of Christ; John 15.18–21 They will persecute you

'Share in suffering like a good soldier of Christ Jesus.' 2 Timothy 2.3

Heroes

Everybody needs a hero. We want somebody we can look up to and admire. This is more than a celebrity, whom we may envy for their fame and riches, but is not a moral example we would wish to follow. A hero – and when I say hero I always include heroines – is someone who sets us a target of good behaviour for us to aim at; someone who stands up for what is right, and is prepared to suffer for it; somebody who cares for and protects the weak. Children may begin by making heroes of their parents, or one of their siblings. But eventually they will discover that their family are only human beings, and have faults like the rest of us. Then they may admire one of their schoolteachers, who set them an example which may last them their lifetime. But for true all-embracing heroism, we turn to fiction, whether it is on film, television, or in one of our childhood storybooks.

St George

St George, as we think of him today, is almost entirely fictional. Certainly a Christian of that name was martyred in Lydda in Palestine in about AD 304, and he may well have been a soldier. There was another George, who was martyred in Cappadocia in Turkey a little later, but apart from dying for his somewhat unorthodox faith, there was little that was admirable in his life. But most of the stories told about St George are legendary, to say the least. They have arisen because everybody needs a hero.

Beginnings

George is the Greek word for a farmer. From this may have sprung the custom in the region where he was martyred of praying to St George for the fertility of the fields In that area, women who wished to conceive a baby would go to one of the shrines to pray, with, until recently, Arabs and Christians praying side by side. The date of his name-day, close to the spring equinox, may have led to his association with the idea of rebirth. Then he became associated with the Islamic hero al-Khidr, who is said to have discovered the mythical Fountain of Eternal Youth. In the twelfth century he replaced in the popular imagination the Greek hero Perseus, who slew the dragon-like monster called the Kraken to rescue a young woman called Andromeda – near to where St George was martyred is the port city of Joppa, where the entrance to the harbour is marked by Andromeda's rock.

Crusaders

The Crusaders, finding that their enemies honoured a Christian martyr, attempted a takeover of St George, and marked a cross of red blood on their white tunics as his symbol. The Crusaders attributed many of their victories to St George, and when they returned to England, many of them dedicated to his honour the churches which they built to thank God for their safe homecoming. St George became a popular figure in the mummers' plays, and the patron saint of several of the trade guilds. A vision of St George was said to have been seen at the Battle of Agincourt, leading to Shakespeare's famous line,

'God for England! Harry and St George!' and at that time George was made the patron saint of England. But it is not only England which claims George as its patron: he is also claimed to watch over Armenia, Germany, Hungary, Lithuania, Malta and Portugal; he is the patron of Antioch, Barcelona, Genoa and many French towns; and the states of Georgia in Europe and in the USA are named after him.

Recently

The flag of St George became a symbol of the British Empire, alongside the Union Jack, and he is supposed to have appeared in visions to the British troops during the First World War. Since then the flag of St George has mostly been associated with football, with the England supporters waving it in the stands, and displaying it on their cars, their clothes and even their faces. For a while it was sadly associated with jingoism and xenophobia, which the Palestinian martyr would certainly not have approved of. But it is worth preserving the legend, as a symbol of heroism which anyone may be called upon to show at some time. Everybody needs a hero, to look up to and admire, whose example we can follow, a hero or heroine who sets us a target of good behaviour to aim at, who stands up for what is right, and is prepared to suffer for it, and who cares for and protects the weak.

Suggested hymns

Fight the good fight; Judge eternal, throned in splendour; O God of earth and altar; When a knight won his spurs.

St Mark the Evangelist 25 April
John Mark's Mother's House
Prov. 15.28–33 Good news, *or* Acts 15.35–41 Paul rejects Mark; Ps. 119.9–16 How can young people keep their way pure?; Eph. 4.7–16 The gift of an evangelist; Mark 13.5–13 Staying power

> '[Jesus said to his disciples,] "Brother will betray brother to death, and a father his child, and children will rise against parents and have them put to death; and you will be hated by all because of my name. But the one who endures to the end will be saved.'
> Mark 13.12–13

Anecdote

There is a charming story in the Acts of the Apostle where St Peter had miraculously escaped from prison, and went straight to the place where all the other Christians were holding an all-night prayer meeting. They were asking God to have Peter released. He knocked on the door, and a servant called Rhoda went to see who it was, and was so astonished that instead of letting Peter in, she ran back to tell everyone, leaving him still standing on the doorstep. The story continues like this:

> On recognizing Peter's voice, she was so overjoyed that, instead of opening the gate, she ran in and announced that Peter was standing at the gate. They said to her, 'You are out of your mind!' But she insisted that it was so. They said, 'It is his angel.' Meanwhile Peter continued knocking; and when they opened the gate, they saw him and were amazed.

You can just picture it, can't you? But the significant thing for us on this day, St Mark's Day, is that the place where this happened is described as 'the house of Mary, the mother of John whose other name was Mark'. Why was this detail remembered, unless it was told to everybody by John Mark himself?

Upper room

So now I want you to do a bit of detective work. Where could a large number of Christians gather in Jerusalem, which was well known to everybody and was the first place Peter thought of looking for them? I suggest that this was the upper room, where Jesus held the Last Supper. Of course we cannot prove it, but this idea is very probable. The fact that Mark's father is never mentioned implies that his mother was a widow, and having a maidservant suggests that she ran a hotel for pilgrims, which is why Jesus knew their upstairs guestroom was available for letting out. But the domestic work of an establishment like that was too much for a widow and a chit of a girl, so her fatherless son, John Mark, had to help with the housework, such as fetching the water from the nearest well, which was normally women's work. Which explains why both Mark and Luke in their Gospels say that Jesus told two of his disciples to

Go into the city, and a man carrying a jar of water will meet you; follow him, and wherever he enters, say to the owner of the house, 'The Teacher asks, Where is my guest room where I may eat the Passover with my disciples?' He [or possibly she] will show you a large room upstairs, furnished and ready. Make preparations for us there.

So Jesus was already known to Mark and his mother, and they must have been disciples; perhaps Jesus had stayed there on his previous visits to Jerusalem.

Speculation

That theory is quite possible. Now for two points which are pure speculation. Only Mark's Gospel mentions the young man who escaped arrest in the Garden of Gethsemane by slipping out of his cloak and running away naked. Maybe Mark mentions that trivial detail because he himself was the young man concerned. And why was the name of the maidservant, Rhoda, remembered? Perhaps because John Mark later fell in love with her and married her. Aah!

Cenacle

Pilgrims to Jerusalem today are taken to a building called 'the Cenacle', with the suggestion that this was the site of the upper room. There are probably some stones dating from the first century on this site, and a building here is shown on the mosaic map of Jerusalem at Madaba, in Jordan, from the sixth century, but the archaeology is inconclusive. Also in some early Christian writings there is mention of a church in Jerusalem called the Church of St Mary, 'the mother of all the churches'. It is just possible that this refers to the house of Mary, the mother of John Mark. But all this speculation is only valuable if we use it to form in our minds pictures of those early Christians as real people, not stained-glass saints. In which case, we stand a real chance of being able to copy the example of loyalty to Jesus, and to needy members of our own family, shown by John Mark the evangelist.

Suggested hymns

The kingdom is upon you'; The kingdom of God is justice and joy; The saint who first found grace to pen; We have a gospel to proclaim.

For biblical archaeology see http://www.bibarch.com.

SS Philip and James, Apostles   1 May
May Day
Isa. 30.15–21 This is the way; Ps. 119.1–8 The way of the Lord;
Eph. 1.3–10 The mystery of forgiveness; John 14.1–14 Show us
the Father

> *'Philip said to [Jesus], "Lord, show us the Father, and we will be satisfied."' John 14.8*

Pip and Jim

'Lord, show us the Father, and we will be satisfied.' Those words spoken by Philip the apostle are recorded in St John's Gospel only. St John also reports Philip's scepticism about being able to feed a large crowd with five loaves and two fish. John reports that Philip brought Nathanael to Jesus, and also some Greeks. Apart from that the name of Philip is only mentioned in the Gospels when they are listing the names of the Twelve. Yet although we know so little about him, there are many churches dedicated to St Philip, often together with St James, and they are celebrated together on 1 May. This is because what were believed to be the relics of these two saints were laid to rest together in a church in Rome which was dedicated on this day. They are referred to affectionately as 'Pip and Jim'.

Folk customs

The popularity of celebrations on 1 May is probably due to the number of folk customs which were practised on this date. In the Middle Ages it was thought of as the beginning of spring, and so many spring festivals were either continued in their pagan form, as a time for praying for the fertility of the fields by sympathetic magic, or Christianized – 'baptized' – as a time for asking God to give us a good harvest in the coming year. At the time when our ancestors scraped a meagre living from the soil, the day when the bitter cold days of winter were ended, and the crops began to appear, was a very special day. The old verse about 'Cast not a clout till May is out' is deliberately ambiguous: you will catch a cold if you leave off your warm winter clothes before summer begins. But whether that means the beginning of the month of May or the end of it, or when the May blossom appears on the hawthorn bushes, nobody knows. The statues of the saints, banished at the Reformation, were replaced by garlands of flowers in the church when spring arrived; and this was a time for dancing round the maypole. That said, the maypole may represent a pagan phallic symbol, but the young girls dancing with pretty ribbons, and the crowning of a May Queen, were only introduced into this country in the 1880s.

Labour Day

The first of May was adopted as International Labour Day at the first congress of the Second Socialist International in Paris in 1889. The idea was to celebrate the power of a united working class, arguing for such reforms as a maximum eight-hour working day. In the USA 1 May was already used for strikes in support for these reforms. Fortuitously, this ensured its popularity because many people were already accustomed to turning out in large numbers on that day, so it was a good opportunity to protest against the oppression of the working class by the newly rich capitalist bosses. When communism replaced socialism, May Day celebrations became more popular in Eastern Europe, but were frowned upon in Western Europe and the USA. Yet Jesus, with his identification with the poor and oppressed, would surely have approved.

Mayday!

All these folk celebrations are neutral in Christian eyes; we can join in them with prayer for the fertility of the crops, and welcome the growth of community which comes when people celebrate together. But there is another, more modern meaning to 'Mayday'. This is when the word is used as a cry for help, equivalent to SOS! This is the international telephonic distress signal to ships and aircraft, and comes from the French phrase, 'M'aidez', meaning 'help me'. This is something which Christians should be crying out to God every day of our lives, especially when things are going wrong in our lives, and we realize we cannot continue on our own, but need to call on our loving Saviour to help us. We should make it a regular part of our prayer to call out those words to Jesus, 'Help me! M'aidez! SOS!' To which Jesus will make the same reply as he made

to St Philip: 'Whoever has seen me' – even in their imagination –
'has seen the Father.'

Suggested hymns

Come my way, my truth, my life; Thou art the Way – by thee alone;
Twin princes of the courts of heaven; Tell me the old, old story.

St Matthias the Apostle   15 May (transferred)
Three Judgements

Isa. 22.15–25 Eliakim replaces Shebna; Ps. 15 Who shall dwell
in your house?; Acts 1.15–26 Mathias replaces Judas (*if the Acts*
reading is used instead of the Old Testament reading, the New
Testament reading is 1 Cor. 4.1–7 Stewards of God's mysteries*);*
John 15.9–17 I have appointed you (*If this sermon is used, the*
Isaiah reading is omitted, the first reading should be from Acts,
and the second reading from 1 Corinthians)

> *'Do not pronounce judgement before the time, before the Lord*
> *comes, who will bring to light the things now hidden in darkness*
> *and will disclose the purposes of the heart. Then each one will*
> *receive commendation from God.' 1 Corinthians 4.5*

Judas

St Matthias was chosen by God to take the place among the disciples of Judas Iscariot, who committed suicide after betraying Jesus.
But who are we to judge Judas? Let us see what St Paul says about
judgement.

Paul and Apollos

St Paul was writing to the Christians at Corinth, who were divided
into several factions. Followers of Paul were violently opposed to
another missionary called Apollos. They judged Apollos to be no
use as a Christian, whereas Paul was perfect in their eyes. But the
'Apollos freaks' idolized their own hero, and condemned Paul as a
walking disaster area. Paul wrote to them, urging the Corinthians
to judge nobody, least of all their fellow Christians.

Judgement

He distinguished three types of judgement to which all of us are subject from time to time:

1 judgement by other people;
2 judging yourself; and
3 being judged by God.

It is said that those who listen to other people's conversations never hear good of themselves. But although what others say about you is often downright wrong, it is sometimes revealing. We are all vain, but if we think about what impression we make on others, we might be more cautious to avoid causing offence. Yet we should never become depressed because others judge us. St Paul wrote: 'But with me it is a very small thing that I should be judged by you or by any human court.' If you have carefully compared the rights and wrongs of a situation, and have decided to follow what you believe to be the right course, you must not let yourself be put off because others criticize you. Stand up for what is right, and defend the weak against the strong.

Self-critical

We must always, however, be self-critical. Has it escaped your attention that what you are doing is morally dubious; are you aware of the harm that your actions may do to others? We have no right to be complacent about the way we live. A famous maxim of the Greek philosophers was 'Know yourself'. Yet, again, St Paul tells us not to allow self-criticism to go too far. He writes:

I do not even judge myself. I am not aware of anything against myself, but I am not thereby acquitted.

Lord and Master

For, writes Paul, we are all subject to a higher authority: 'It is the Lord who judges me,' he says. He starts from the premise that we are all servants, or stewards, in God's household. We have all been appointed to positions of responsibility in God's enterprise, and we must face a grilling from the boss one day over how wisely we have used the resources he entrusted us with: the world of nature; our knowledge and skills; the ability to love and be loved. Have we used these things

322

fully in God's service? If not, then our Lord and Master will judge that we have been idle servants in his house. But what does God do with sinners? Unlike other people who judge us to be beyond hope, and our own self-criticism, God only judges us so that he may forgive us.

Aunt Sally

So anyone who accepts a position of leadership or prominence in the Church or any other organization immediately makes of themselves an Aunt Sally. There are people who are angry with their circumstances or even with themselves, who deal with their anger by blaming somebody else. So they carp and they gossip, and eventually it comes to the ears of the person whose leadership they resent. That's human nature. But you mustn't let other people's criticism get you down. We are not judged by them, nor even by ourselves; our only judge is God, and he only judges us in order to forgive us.

Matthias

I am sure some of the apostles blamed Judas Iscariot for everything. I am certain that when Matthias took his place, he too became the butt of people's sarcasm. Many Christian ministers have this experience too. Hard as it seems, you have to just ignore it: God is our only judge, and when we repent, he declares us not guilty.

Suggested hymns

Teach me, my God and king; The highest and the holiest place; There's a wideness in God's mercy; They shall come from the east.

Visit of the Blessed Virgin Mary to Elizabeth
31 May
Modern Verse
Zeph. 3.14–18 Sing, daughter Zion; Ps. 113 Making her a joyous mother; Rom. 12.9–16 Hospitality; Luke 1.39–49 [50–56] Magnificat

> 'In those days Mary set out and went with haste to a Judean town in the hill country, where she entered the house of Zechariah and greeted Elizabeth.' Luke 1.39–40

[This could be read dramatically by two women; or a single reader could say 'Elizabeth says' or 'Mary replies' before each paragraph.]

Visit

You are now going to hear an updated version of the story we celebrate today, in verse. The idea of this is to make you think of the Blessed Virgin Mary (a teenager) and her cousin Elizabeth (a menopausal woman) as real people. This is not disrespectful, but helps us to admire them as ordinary people just like us, who were given by God a colossal task to fulfil, and did it magnificently. It is also meant to be entertaining: one anachronistic joke is to imagine that Elizabeth, whose son has not been named yet, uses the Welsh term 'brought up chapel' for anyone who belongs to the Baptist Church! Elizabeth speaks first:

ELIZABETH
Now Mary, dear, you're welcome here,
I hope you've come to stay.

MARY (*happy and excited*)
Dear cousin Liz, isn't it wiz?
We're both in the family way!

ELIZABETH (*laughing*)
An old man's wife, at my time of life;
it came as quite a shock!

MARY
And me not wed, with my maidenhead;
but God says that's no block.

ELIZABETH
Oh come here quick and feel him kick,
this babe within my womb!
Do what I will, mine won't keep still
while you're here in my room.

MARY
So let it be; this child's in me
according to God's word.

ELIZABETH
What joy is this, that I should kiss
the Mother of my Lord!

MARY
The angel came and said his name
is Jesus, but I'd rather
give him the name of Love, the same
as God's, his heavenly Father.
A secret name, which hides the shame
that Joe and I aren't married;
a special name that tells the fame
of the child that Mary carried,
who is the Son of the Eternal One
who stands on guard above him.
This name shall be known just to me . . .
and all of those who love him.

ELIZABETH (*reassuringly*)
Your secret, dear, is safe, no fear.
I've a secret, and I'll share it:
when the time draws on, I'll call mine John,
though none in the family bear it.

MARY
Your child is John the Baptist, on
whom all our hopes we place:
he'll preach and pray, and make a way
for God to bring his grace.

ELIZABETH
Zechariah's dumb, or else he'd come;
that's a thing with which he'll grapple.
But a Baptist? No, that can't be so;
we were none of us brought up chapel!

MARY
So let us all sing till the rafters ring
for the child whom God begat;
let each proclaim his secret name
and chant Magnificat.

MARY (*spoken, or sung to the carol tune 'The Seven Joys of Mary' with optional accompaniment from piano, organ or humming choir*)
My spirit magnifies the Lord, my soul is filled with love,
for God has sent his only Son, to earth from heaven above;
to earth from heaven above; so sing the birth of such a boy:
My spirit magnifies the Lord, my soul is filled with joy.

My spirit magnifies the Lord, my soul is filled with peace,
for God has sent his only Son, the pris'ners to release;
the pris'ners to release; and all the tyrants to destroy:
My spirit magnifies the Lord, my soul is filled with joy.

My spirit magnifies the Lord, my soul is filled with faith,
for God has sent his only Son, to break the power of death;
to break the power of death; and cleanse us all from sin's alloy:
My spirit magnifies the Lord, my soul is filled with joy.

My spirit magnifies the Lord, my soul is filled with grace,
for God has sent his only Son, the wealthy to displace;
the wealthy to displace and fill the hungry they annoy:
My spirit magnifies the Lord, my soul is filled with joy.

My spirit magnifies the Lord, my soul is filled with song,
for God has sent his only Son, to right all earthly wrong;
to right all earthly wrong that sinful people can deploy:
My spirit magnifies the Lord, my soul is filled with joy.

This could be followed by the whole congregation singing this song, with the words on duplicated sheets or a projector.

Suggested hymns

For Mary, mother of our Lord; Lord Jesus Christ; Lord of the home, your only Son; Tell out, my soul, the greatness of the Lord.

St Barnabas the Apostle   12 June (transferred)
Epistle of Barnabas

Job 29.11–16 Like one who comforts; Ps. 112 Generous; Acts 11.19–30 Barnabas encourages Saul (*if the Acts reading is used instead of the Old Testament reading, the New Testament reading is* Gal. 2.1–10 Barnabas and me); John 15.12–17 Love one another

> 'Some men of Cyprus . . . spoke to the Hellenists also, proclaiming the Lord Jesus . . . and a great number became believers . . . The church in Jerusalem . . . sent Barnabas to Antioch . . . for he was a good man, full of the Holy Spirit and of faith. And a great many people were brought to the Lord.' Acts 11.20–24

Which Barnabas?

Quite a lot of letters and sermons were written at the same time as those we know in the New Testament, but never quite made it into the Bible. Some are very exciting and revealing; others were rather dull. The so-called *Epistle of Barnabas* is, frankly, one of the boring ones. But the early Church made the decision about which books to include in the Scripture basically on whether or not they were written by one of the apostles. Therefore an excellent book called the *Didache* [DID-er-key], which did not claim apostolic authorship, was left out. The Revelation to John was borderline for a long time, because John was a common name, and nobody was sure whether the author of the Apocalypse was John the apostle or somebody else. And the *Epistle of Barnabas* was included in some of the early manuscripts, but was eventually omitted from the official list, because those first Christians decided it was by somebody else called Barnabas. In modern times, many people were undecided on this point, but now most agree that it is not by Paul's friend, Barnabas of Cyprus. It might be by someone called Barnabas of Alexandria, or by someone using Barnabas as a pseudonym. Don't be shocked at that, but in those days it was considered as a compliment to a famous person to write what they 'might possibly have written if they had been alive today'.

Better ignored?

So why am I preaching about this epistle by Pseudo-Barnabas today? Wouldn't it be better to ignore it? I think not, because it can show us a lot about how those early Christians, to whom we owe so much, lived and thought. And I thought it would make a change.

When, who and to whom?

The first question we must ask is, when was the *Epistle of Barnabas* written? In chapter 16, the *Epistle* reads:

[The Old Testament says], 'Behold, those who tore down this temple will themselves build it.' It is happening. For because of their fighting it was torn down by the enemies. And now the very servants of the enemies will themselves rebuild it.

So it was probably written between AD 70, when the Romans destroyed the Jerusalem Temple, and 132, when they finally defeated the Jews, leaving no hope that the Temple would ever be rebuilt. The *Epistle* is chock-full of Old Testament quotations, which means it was probably written by a Jewish Christian to Jewish Christians, as non-Jews would not have been impressed by scriptural arguments. Yet, whereas St Paul was careful to say that God had not abandoned the Jews, but had grafted the Gentile Christians into the vine of Israel, Pseudo-Barnabas was quite afraid of the Jewish authorities, who seemed at that time to be regaining power, so he writes that God's contract with the Jews was ended when they broke the Ten Commandments, and the Christians are the new Israel. Although the author was himself Jewish, his attitude led to a lot of anti-Semitism in the Middle Ages, and only now are we learning to see Christians and Jews as partners. His attempts to find a symbolic meaning in the Jewish food laws is quite amusing, but he is clear that they don't apply to us Christians in their literal sense.

The two ways

But the *Epistle of Barnabas* is most helpful to us when it describes 'the Two Ways'. Jesus said, 'This is the judgement, that the light has come into the world, and people loved darkness rather than light because their deeds were evil.' So Pseudo-Barnabas describes the

Way of Light, which is basically obeying the Ten Commandments, and the Way of Darkness, which is that of

> Idolatry, forwardness, arrogance of power, hypocrisy, double-heartedness, adultery, murder, robbery, pride, transgression, fraud, malice, self-sufficiency, enchantments, magic, covetousness, the lack of the fear of God; persecutors of the good, haters of the truth, lovers of lies, knowing not the reward of righteousness [and so on].

Phew! Curiously enough, exactly the same words occur in the *Didache*, which I mentioned earlier, though who borrowed them from whom we shall never know. But if we learn nothing else from the *Epistle of Barnabas*, it is the importance of ensuring that we are always walking in the Way of Light.

Suggested hymns

Come my way, my truth, my life; How bright these glorious spirits shine; The 'Son of Consolation'; Thou art the Way – by thee alone

Day of Thanksgiving for the Institution of Holy Communion (Corpus Christi)   15 June
Thicker than Water
Gen. 14.18–20 Melchizedek brought bread and wine; Ps. 116.10–17 The cup of salvation; 1 Cor. 11.23–26 The Last Supper; John 6.51–58 Living bread

> '[Jesus] took the cup . . . after supper, saying, "This cup is the new covenant in my blood. Do this, as often as you drink it, in remembrance of me."' 1 Corinthians 11.25

Blood

When their enemies heard the first Christians saying that they were eating the body of Christ and drinking his blood, they accused them of cannibalism. Now, we have got used to these terms in talking about the Holy Communion service. But non-churchgoers must still be baffled by the strange things we say, and not a few regular attenders are far from clear what this way of speaking means. So I suggest we approach it from a different direction, focusing on the words which Jesus used, referring to the wine as 'the new covenant in my blood'.

Covenants

In the early history of the human race, the family was all-important. In the family, you shared your limited resources when times were hard, brought up the children, cared for the sick and elderly. Without the family, many people would die; and then the family would become too small and they would all die. So it was your solemn duty to defend your family when it was attacked. They believed that what bound them together was that they all shared the blood of their common ancestors; and we still say today, when favouring our own relations, that 'blood is thicker than water'. If your family became too small to be viable, you made a contract with another family to form a tribe for mutual support and defence. The symbolic way of doing this was to share the same blood; so people from both groups would cut their hands and let the blood mingle. But this was a bit painful, so they hit on the idea of killing an animal, and both parties to the contract drinking from a cup of the animal's blood. Thus they were united by 'the blood of the covenant'. They became 'blood brothers' and 'blood sisters'.

With God

Then, each family had its own god. So when they made a covenant with another family, they also contracted with one of the gods, promising to all worship the same god in future. So they went to the temple, slaughtered a goat there; some of the blood they drank, and the rest was poured over the altar for the god to drink. Then you were not only blood brothers with the other family, but with your shared god. You had contractual obligations to obey and help the god, just as with the other family. The god was contracted to defend and protect both families.

Old Testament

There are many traces of these old customs in the Old Testament. Sacrifices were not seen as bribes, but as establishing a contract with the god. Moses signed a covenant in blood with God on Mount Sinai; the Ten Commandments were the terms of the exclusive contract. Jehovah agreed to care for them, provided that they kept their side of the deal. In the last chapter of Joshua, Joshua renews the covenant with Jehovah, bringing all 12 tribes into a 'blood-brother' relationship with each other. It implies that this was a frequent ritual.

Communion

At the Last Supper, Jesus emphasized that he was establishing the new covenant, or 'new testament' – the words both mean a type of contract. His death made Jesus equivalent to the sacrificial Lamb of God. In a humane gesture, he replaced the blood with wine, and the meat with broken bread, but the symbolism remained the same.

Sacrament

Think of that when you eat the bread and drink the wine. By eating the bread and drinking the wine, you are symbolically signing up to a contract with God, and also with Christians in every denomination who use a similar ritual in remembrance of Jesus and his death on the cross. God is promising to care for all who believe in Jesus, and to bring them at the last to heaven. We who drink the wine and eat the bread are signing a contract to obey God at all times. Yet unlike the ten rigid commandments of the old contract, this makes only two demands on you: to love God with all your heart, mind, soul and strength, and to love your neighbours, blood brothers and sisters as yourself. Much shorter and more flexible than the terms of the Old Testament; yet it will take you a lifetime to discover just how demanding those two clauses are. But after all, blood is thicker than water, and without the family, both the family at home and the wider family of Christ throughout the world, we could not survive.

Suggested hymns

All for Jesus; Bread of heaven, on thee we feed; God is here! As we his people; My God, and is thy table spread.

The Birth of St John the Baptist   24 June
Desert Saints

Isa. 40.1–11 A voice in the wilderness; Ps. 85.7–13 Salvation is at hand; Acts 13.14b–26 A baptism of repentance, *or* Gal. 3.23–29 The law our schoolmaster; Luke 1.57–66, 80 Birth of the Baptist

> *'[John the Baptist] grew and became strong in spirit, and he was in the wilderness until the day he appeared publicly to Israel.'* Luke 1.80

Prophets

John the Baptist lived in the desert from the time he left his parents' home until he was ready to make a public appearance with his message of repentance for his fellow Jews. St Matthew's Gospel adds that

> John wore clothing of camel's hair with a leather belt around his waist, and his food was locusts and wild honey.

This was his way of preparing himself for a difficult and controversial ministry, and was probably based on the stories of the prophets in the Old Testament. Zechariah describes the prophets' uniform as 'a hairy cloak', and Elijah is described as 'a hairy man, with a leather belt around his waist'. Elijah is also described as living on simple food which the ravens brought him when he lived by the brook called Cherith. Malachi has God saying,

> Lo, I will send you the prophet Elijah before the great and terrible day of the LORD comes. He will turn the hearts of parents to their children and the hearts of children to their parents, so that I will not come and strike the land with a curse.

Saints

Many Christians down the ages have retreated to wild areas to be alone with God. The wilderness is an area of stark and austere beauty, free from luxurious distractions, enabling the seeker to concentrate their mind upon God.

- St Antony was born to a rich family in Egypt, but gave away his wealth and in AD 286 he escaped the materialistic life of the cities to live an austere and solitary life among the wild bears in the Egyptian desert for 20 years. So impressed were the Christians at that time that many other pious people came to live in caves near his, to learn from him, until it was said, with permissible exaggeration, that the desert had become like a city.
- Many followed his example, and they became known as the Desert Fathers and Desert Mothers; their writings are treasured and made a significant impact on the thinking of Christians across the then-known world, even as far as the Celtic Christians of Ireland.
- St Benedict imitated Antony of Egypt, in a cave at Subiaco in Italy. Such a crowd of other hermits gathered around him that Benedict founded a community, living together in a monastery, bound by a strict rule of life, which is still observed by Benedictine monks and nuns to this day.
- From time to time, groups would break off from the original monastic orders because they thought they had become too worldly, such as the 'Discalced' – which means 'shoeless' – Carmelites.
- Then St Francis of Assisi, also the son of a rich family, gave up his wealth and began the life of a mendicant friar, wearing the simple brown tunic of the peasants, owning nothing, wandering along the roads of Italy and living on the food he begged from passers-by.

Challenge

Whether these desert saints were consciously imitating St John the Baptist we do not know. But their story shows that in every generation, holy people have found the distractions of wealth and materialism a hindrance in their search for holiness, and have identified with the poor whom Jesus called blessed. John returned from the desert when God called him to proclaim the need of all for repentance, and to prepare the way for the coming of the Messiah. Then, after baptizing Jesus, he handed over the leadership of his group and willingly took a back seat. But still he challenged immorality where he found it, including what he considered the incestuous marriage of Herod Antipas to his niece Herodias, for which temerity he was beheaded.

Example

The Baptist is an example to us all. It is too easy to become dragged down into the cesspool of materialism; and a silent retreat, and/or a Lenten fast, is a way of reminding us of our priorities. Very few of us could stand the extreme austerity of living in the desert, and without careful preparation it might kill us. But if John regarded that as a necessary preparation for the challenges of his later ministry, perhaps we all should look more closely at the value of lesser acts of self-denial and a simpler life, to prepare ourselves for whatever God wants to use us for.

Suggested hymns

God has spoken – by the prophets; Hark, a thrilling voice is sounding; On Jordan's bank the Baptist's cry; Lo, from the desert homes.

SS Peter and Paul, Apostles   29 June
Conflict in the Church

Zech. 4.1–6a, 10b–14 Two anointed ones; Ps. 125 Stand fast for ever; Acts 12.1–11 Peter released from prison (*if the Acts reading is used instead of the Old Testament reading, the New Testament reading is* 2 Tim. 4.6–8, 17–18 Poured out); Matt. 16.13–19 Peter recognizes the Messiah; *or for Peter alone*: Ezek. 3.22–27 Preaching to his own; Ps. 125; Acts 12.1–11 (*if the Acts reading is used instead of the Old Testament reading, the New Testament reading is* 1 Peter 2.19–25 Suffering for God); Matt. 16.13–19

> 'I said to [the angel], "What are these two branches of the olive trees, which pour out the oil through the two golden pipes?" He said to me, "Do you not know what these are?" I said, "No, my lord." Then he said, "These are the two anointed ones who stand by the Lord of the whole earth."' *Zechariah 4.12–14* (This sermon is suited to the first set of readings above.)

Zechariah

In the book of the prophet Zechariah, we read of two olive branches which symbolize two anointed people. They are pouring

334

out olive oil, presumably to anoint many other people in the service of the Lord. That is presumably why this was chosen as one of the optional readings for the Feast of St Peter and St Paul. These two apostles were a source of many blessings to the early Church, by their preaching, their writings, and by the fact they converted many others to the Christian faith, then sent them out to spread the gospel throughout the world.

Apostles

St Peter and St Paul were two of the most important figures in the early years which followed after the resurrection of Jesus. Both are described as apostles, which means missionaries. St Paul was not one of the Twelve, but he was anointed apostle to the non-Jews, while Peter was called the apostle to the Jews.

Disagreements

Yet, although we often speak of Peter and Paul together as friends, theirs was a strained relationship. St Paul went to Jerusalem to persuade the church leaders there that non-Jews who became Christians should not have to become Jews first, nor should they be bound by any of the laws in the Old Testament. The account in the Acts of the Apostles of this meeting reads like the minutes of a very heated gathering, and although they agreed that only four of the laws in the Old Testament are binding on us non-Jews, it is far from clear what those four laws were. It seems that Peter was unhappy with this compromise, and when he met Paul later they had, to be honest, a blazing row. As Paul described it himself, in his letter to the Galatians:

> When [Peter] came to Antioch, I opposed him to his face, because he stood self-condemned; for until certain people came from James, he used to eat with the [non-Jews]. But after they came, he drew back and kept himself separate for fear of the . . . faction [who insisted all Christians must become Jews] . . . I said to [Peter] before them all, 'If you, though a Jew, live like a [non-Jew] and not like a Jew, how can you compel the [non-Jews] to live like Jews? We ourselves are Jews by birth . . . yet we know that a person is justified not by the works of the law but through faith in Jesus Christ.

Factions

So there were clearly two factions in the early Church: first, the traditionalists, under James, of whom Peter was one, who, so their opponents said, insisted that the important thing about Christians was that they followed strict rules of behaviour. Second there were those whom their enemies called revolutionaries, under Paul; they were accused of teaching that people of any race who are inspired by the Holy Spirit can apply the commandment to love our neighbours in any way which is suitable to the society in which they live. That is an exaggeration, but you will find attitudes like that still in the Church today.

Reconciliation

Yet the important thing is that, in spite of their deep disagreements, Peter and Paul were reconciled at the last, martyred together in Rome, and both emphasized that preserving the unity of Christ's body the Church must override all other considerations. I expect there are Christians with whom you disagree profoundly. But Peter and Paul show us that there is room for many different opinions in Christ's family of love, and the only thing we cannot tolerate is intolerance. If we remember that, the oil of God's anointing will be poured equally on each of us.

Suggested hymns

Jesus, stand among us at the meeting of our lives; The church of God a kingdom is; Thy hand, O God, has guided; With golden splendour and with roseate hues of morn.

St Thomas the Apostle   3 July
Gospel of Thomas

Hab. 2.1–4 The righteous live by faith; Ps. 31.1–6 I trust in the Lord; Eph. 2.19–22 The foundation of the apostles; John 20.24–29 Doubting Thomas is convinced

> 'Look at the proud! Their spirit is not right in them, but the righteous live by their faith.' Habakkuk 2.4

Uncanonical

Despite his nickname, 'Doubting Thomas' was a great seeker after truth: he would not believe in the resurrection of Jesus until he had visible evidence. This year I decided to preach on the so-called *Gospel of Thomas*. This is a collection of the sayings of Jesus, not included in our Bibles, of which a translation into the ancient Egyptian language of Coptic was dug up in about 1945 near the village of Nag Hammadi in Egypt. Is it true, or is it not? The manuscript dates from the late fourth century AD, but it may be translated from an older Greek original. Some of the sayings are not found in Matthew, Mark, Luke or John; some of these could be the genuine words of Jesus. Some of the sayings reported in Thomas's Gospel, which are also in one or more of the Gospels in the New Testament, show signs which some people say indicate that they are nearer to the original words of Jesus than the versions we are familiar with. So we could possibly be dealing with an edited version of a collection of the sayings of Jesus gathered by St Thomas himself. But others show signs of teachings which were not found in Christian writers until at least a century after Jesus died, so 'Thomas', as I shall call the Gospel which goes by his name, is not a reliable source of Christian doctrine.

Similarities

As anyone who has attempted it knows, translation form one language to another is not an exact science. When you are choosing which word best corresponds to the original meaning, there is often a wide choice. A literal word-for-word translation may be either incomprehensible in the new language, or widely different in meaning, because the words you choose may have different nuances from what that word implied in the original language. So if *Thomas* comes up with a similar but slightly different phrase from that in one or more of the four Gospels in the Bible, that is an indication that it was probably a genuine saying of Jesus in Aramaic, translated into Greek and then into Coptic. For example:

Man is like a wise fisherman, who cast his net into the sea and drew it up from the sea full of small fish. Among them the wise fisherman found a large good fish. He threw down all the small fish into the sea; he chose the large fish without trouble. Whoever has ears to hear, let him hear.

Earlier

Some of the sayings of Jesus in *Thomas* are significantly different, and that is taken to mean that this Gospel is based on an earlier collection than those used by Matthew, Mark, Luke and John. For example: 'No prophet is acceptable in his village; a physician does not heal those who know him.'

New

Some of the sayings in *Thomas* are not known at all in the other Gospels, but could be genuine. What do you make of this?

Split a piece of wood: I am there. Raise up the stone, and you will find me there.

Heresy

But other sayings seem to have been invented long after Jesus died, in order to pretend that he was actually producing a quite different religion from what we know as Christianity, which is what we call a 'heresy'. This taught that God is not interested in the material world, and was only known to a select few who had been admitted into a secret society. It was called Gnosticism, spelt with a silent 'G' at the beginning, and is connected with our word 'knowledge', beginning with a silent 'k'. Christianity is open to everyone, so this book was never included in the Bible because of the dangerously narrow teaching found in some parts of it. It begins:

These are the hidden words which Jesus spoke . . . whoever finds the interpretation of the words will never taste of death . . . If you fast, you will beget a sin for yourselves; and if you pray, you will be condemned; and if you give alms, you will harm your spirits.

Importance

But if, like the apostle Thomas, we are eager for new truths about Jesus, and new evidence for what he taught, this book is worth a look – you can find it in paperback or on the internet – because the fact that the words of Jesus are known in several slightly different translations is an indication that they are true. The more we know about Jesus, the better we love him. Only be careful not to be led astray by false teaching.

Suggested hymns

Blessed Thomas, doubt no longer; Firmly I believe and truly; If you believe and I believe; Lead kindly light, amid th'encircling gloom.

St Mary Magdalene   22 July
Authority

S. of Sol. 3.1–4 Seeking and finding; Ps. 42.1–10 As deer long for water; 2 Cor. 5.14–17 A new creation; John 20.1–2, 11–18 Go and tell

> 'Jesus said to [Mary Magdalene], "Do not hold on to me, because I have not yet ascended to the Father. But go to my brothers and say to them, 'I am ascending to my Father and your Father, to my God and your God.'" Mary Magdalene went and announced to the disciples, "I have seen the Lord"; and she told them that he had said these things to her.' John 20.17–18

Authority

Was Mary Magdalene an apostle? She was not one of the Twelve. But not all the apostles were among the Twelve. Paul is an obvious example of that, and so are Andronicus and Junia, whom Paul mentions in his letter to the Romans as 'prominent among the apostles', And of course Junia also was a woman. One website tells us that Mary Magdalene was

> the first person sent to tell others of the resurrected Jesus [and that] in this sense she is the first apostle of the Gospel of the resurrection, not as one having authority, but as . . . the first person sent (which is what 'apostle' means) to tell others of the good news of His resurrection.

Now that's an interesting distinction, isn't it? An 'apostle . . . (but) not as one having authority'? But the writer misunderstands, of

339

course, the word 'authority', which is something different from power. Jesus 'spoke with authority' while Herod and Pilate spoke with power. You can't, however, be an apostle without authority. It would be like a postman without letters, a light bulb not plugged in. Whereas power is the ability to tell others what to do and expect to be obeyed without question, which is quite foreign to the Christian ethos of love. So what would be an apostle without authority? I suggest it's a contradiction in terms. To be an apostle, one who proclaims a resurrection faith, *is* to speak with authority; so there could be no apostleship without authority. Mary Magdalene spoke with the authority of a witness. Sometimes the frail, elderly human being in a wheelchair in a care home speaks with the authority of experience which no appointee can hope to match.

Change

The answer lies in the words Jesus said to Mary Magdalene, 'Do not hold on to me.' The invisible presence of Jesus is always with us, but sometimes we need to let go of the visible signs and accept challenge and change in our witnessing. God became flesh so that we might proclaim good news about God's presence not merely to a few individuals, but in multitudes, in a church, in sacraments. God is no longer willing to be limited by human boundaries, human distinctions, human laws and customs however ancient and honoured. He is present universally, present in the human flesh scattered in a wartime battlefield, present in the pre-teenage child fleeing rape and murder. We, like Mary Magdalene, are to bear witness to God present, Jesus present, often incognito, unknown, unrecognized but all around us and needing *our* witness to say 'Look here!' and 'Look there!' A witness free enough and strong enough to be able sometimes to let go of those beloved symbols of faith, that surely have their value, but can also blind us to a wider reality and hold us back from a wider worldwide witness.

Church

What is the role of authority in the Church? Do we need written authority from those at the centre to make small changes in our form of service? We should ponder the old slogan: 'Unity in necessary things; liberty in doubtful things; charity in all things.' Wikipedia tells us that those words are often misattributed to St Augustine of Hippo, but seem to have been first used in 1617 by – ironically – the Archbishop of Split in Croatia, in an anti-papal essay entitled 'The Republican Church'. I would like to suggest that the challenge of holding and proclaiming the 'necessary things' of the Christian faith has never been greater. We want and we need things to hold on to; we need, as always, material things to grasp – bread and wine – and the outward display of the liturgy. But there is much, also, that we cannot hold on to if we are to go and commend our faith to an indifferent world. I will not venture to be specific, but we need to ask ourselves, 'Do we need this or that or has it become an encumbrance that holds us back at the tomb when we need to go forward into the city?' Pray that God will enable us to let go of what is passing and hold on to what endures, so that we will be able to go and proclaim a living faith to a dying world.

Suggested hymns

Good Joseph had a garden; Lord, for the years your love has kept and guided; New every morning is the love; One more step along the world I go.

St James the Apostle 25 July
St James' Bones?

Jer. 45.1–5 Seeking greatness; Ps. 126 Sow in tears, harvest in joy; Acts 11.27—12.2 Herod kills James (*if the Acts reading is used instead of the Old Testament reading, the New Testament reading is* 2 Cor. 4.7–15 Treasure in clay pots); Matt. 20.20–28 Seeking greatness

> *'About that time King Herod laid violent hands upon some who belonged to the church. He had James, the brother of John, killed with the sword.' Acts 12.1–2*

Death of James

James, one of the two sons of Zebedee who were members of the 12 apostles, was executed on the orders of King Herod Agrippa I in AD 44. This is reported in the Acts of the Apostles, and confirmed not long afterwards by the Jewish historian Josephus. But neither of these sources tell us where he was buried. Yet bereaved people like to visit the graves of those we loved. These days, most Christians hold that the departed are invisibly close to us wherever we go; but it helps us to feel their nearness if we believe that we are close to their physical remains. This gave rise to Christians going on long pilgrimages to visit the shrines of the saints, and to the cult of relics.

Which James?

Then, in November 2002, an article was published in the *Biblical Archaeological Review* magazine, claiming that the remains of St James, the brother of Jesus, had been found. This raises two questions: is this the same James that we celebrate today, and were those really his remains? To the devout Christian, the answers don't make a jot of difference. We believe that God answers our prayers directly; but if it helps us to make them through an easily imagined saint, God allows that. The title of 'St James the Great', whom we commemorate today, is usually considered to refer to the Galilean fisherman, the son of Zebedee. But James the brother of Jesus is often mentioned in the New Testament as the leader of the church in Jerusalem, although he is assigned no commemoration day in the calendar. And the archaeologists are still arguing about whose remains were found in 2002.

Ossuary

So pray to whomever you like, wherever you wish, and God will hear you. But you may be interested to hear about the discovery, to help you decide whether or not archaeology confirms the Bible record. Around the time of Jesus, Jews usually buried their dead in caves, believing that there, they would be ready for the physical resurrection of all who had died, which they expected soon. When the bones were sufficiently decomposed, the remains were put into a marble box called an 'ossuary'. Nearly 900 burial caves have been found around Jerusalem, containing many times that number of ossuary boxes. Most of them were unmarked, and only 216 boxes are inscribed with the name of whoever was buried there. In 1980 a cave with ten ossuaries was found on the ridge south of Jerusalem, and among the inscriptions were names like Mary, Judah son of

Jesus, and Jesus son of Joseph. But these names were so common in those days that it is very unlikely that they refer to people in the Bible.

Brother of Jesus

But the ossuary found in 2002 had, quite deeply chiselled into the marble, the words 'James, son of Joseph', and then, not quite so deep, 'brother of Jesus'. It was all in an ancient form of letters, but possibly the second line was written later, and then dusted with chalk to make it look old. It belonged to a collector of antiquities called Oded Golan; he would not say where he got it. In 2003, the Israel Antiquities Authority declared that it is a modern forgery. Then, a German specialist came to the opposite conclusion. In 2007, Golan went on trial, and over 70 leading archaeologists were called to give evidence; they were equally divided, for and against! In 2012, Golan was convicted of illegally dealing in antiques, but acquitted of the forgery charges – the judge said the accusations had not been proved 'beyond reasonable doubt'.

Conclusion

So there you have it! Archaeology has come up with nothing to prove the words of the Bible wrong, and quite a bit to show that they are true. People named Jesus, Mary and James the brother of Jesus really did exist, as we thought; but what matters is what they said and did, and archaeology has no way of forming an opinion on that, as nothing can be proved one way or the other. We have to choose between believing that the Bible is basically true, which seems very likely, or that it is a pack of lies. If you prefer to believe that Jesus came from heaven to tell us that God loves us, then that will make you very happy; and you will almost certainly be right.

Suggested hymns

Father of heaven, whose love profound; For all thy saints, O Lord; Great God, your love has called us here; Love divine, all loves excelling.

The Transfiguration of Our Lord   6 August
(See page 200.)

The Blessed Virgin Mary   15 August
Human Rights

Isa. 61.10–11 As a bride, *or* Rev. 11.19—12.6, 10 A woman in heaven; Ps. 45.10–17 You shall have sons; Gal. 4.4–7 Born of a woman; Luke 1.46–55 Magnificat

> *'[Mary sang, "The Lord] has brought down the powerful from their thrones, and lifted up the lowly; he has filled the hungry with good things, and sent the rich away empty."' Luke 1.52–53*

Powerful women

'The hand that rocks the cradle rules the world,' they say. Certainly among the Jews at the time of Christ, though women were given no positions of authority, there were many powerful women who, by what they said and wrote, exercised a tremendous influence. One of these was the Blessed Virgin Mary, who, although she is sometimes held up as an example of meek submissiveness, wrote a song which we call the Magnificat, which is truly revolutionary. Perhaps we do not read it with sufficient understanding, but in any context these words would be seen as a call for the complete overthrow of the structures of society:

[The Lord] has brought down the powerful from their thrones,
and lifted up the lowly;
he has filled the hungry with good things,
and sent the rich away empty.

In the days of McCarthyism in the USA, that would have been banned as anti-American behaviour!

Justice

But no, the Virgin Mary was not calling for communism, but for a more just society. In most countries, still today, most of the power is in the hands of a few people, whether because they are rich, or they inherited the power from their parents, or they have become members of the ruling power group. These powerful people hold on to their positions by oppressing the poor and powerless. So those who believe in a God who is just and loving must seek ways of reducing the record difference between the rich and the poor which has emerged in many countries in recent years. We must support the human rights movement, which is a direct outcome of Mary's call for justice in the Magnificat.

History

This connection is ignored by most historians of the movement, who say that there was no concept of human rights before the end of the Middle Ages. There were early indications such as Magna Carta, and the Protestant Reformation was in part a call for freedom of conscience over the power of the Church. The writings of John Locke led to the English Bill of Rights and the Scottish Claim of Rights, both issued in 1689. The book titled *Rights of Man* was written by Thomas Paine in 1791. The writings of French philosophers led to the French Revolution. The American Declaration of Independence called for the right to life, liberty and the pursuit of happiness. William Wilberforce, a member of the evangelical Clapham Sect, fought for the abolition of slavery, and their Christian background was crucial to many of the African American men and women who struggled for the rights of black slaves in the South. The work of Christian women like Florence Nightingale, who cared for the wounded in the Crimean War, led to the Geneva Conference, with its regulations on how war could justly be committed, and the International Red Cross. The horrors of the Second World War and the Holocaust led to the Universal Declaration of Human Rights, passed by the United Nations Assembly in 1948.

Contents

That document listed the various types of freedom which humans are entitled to, and called on every nation to pass them into law. Each clause is in the spirit of the Magnificat, and would have delighted the Blessed Virgin. They say that everyone has a right to:

- life, liberty and security of their person
- privacy, asylum
- a fair trial, being presumed innocent until proved guilty
- work, with equal pay and just remuneration

- education
- freedom from slavery, torture, inhumane punishment, discrimination, and arbitrary arrest or exile
- freedom of speech
- freedom of assembly
- freedom of thought, conscience and religion
- freedom of movement, and
- a whole lot of other things which I have no time to mention.

It does not fail to mention that having rights imposes duties on everyone, too.

Score

What is the score on the human rights movement? I think most people would agree that we haven't achieved perfection on claiming these rights for everyone in our own country; and internationally we have a very long way to go. Yet this is the justice that Mary called for in her song, and it was a hymn of praise to her God. So we can be sure that this is the sort of society that God wants us to build, and he will help us build it if we let him. When that is achieved, we shall have something very close to the kingdom of God on earth, as it is in heaven.

Suggested hymns

Christ is the King! O friends, rejoice; Join the song of praise and protest; Tell out, my soul; Ye who own the faith of Jesus.

St Bartholomew the Apostle   24 August
Unknown Saints
Isa. 43.8–13 My witnesses; Ps. 145.1–7 Speak of your wondrous acts; Acts 5.12–16 The apostles heal (*if the Acts reading is used instead of the Old Testament reading, the New Testament reading is* 1 Cor. 4.9–15 The shame of the apostles); Luke 22.24–30 Judging the twelve tribes

> *'The greatest among you must become like the youngest, and the leader like one who serves.' Luke 22.26*

Unknown

What can we say about St Bartholomew? Not a lot! His name occurs in the list of the Twelve in the Gospels of Matthew, Mark and Luke, but not in John. 'Bartholomew' is a surname, meaning 'Son of Tolmai', so what was his first name? Some have suggested it was Nicodemus, who figures prominently in John but is not mentioned in the other Gospels. Legend suggests that he became a missionary in India, among other places, but it cannot be proved to be true. It is said that he was martyred by being flayed alive – having his skin whipped off him – and then beheaded with an axe. Many things have happened on St Bartholomew's Day down the ages:

- the St Bartholomew's Day massacre of Protestants in Paris in 1572;
- the passing of the Act of Uniformity in 1662, by which any Anglican priest who would not use the Book of Common Prayer and obey the bishops was excluded from his living – this led to the birth of the Free Churches;
- the St Bartholomew's Day fairs held at Smithfield in London from 1133 to 1855, which were also a carnival, with conjurers, including a very fat pig, the 'St Bartholomew's pig', which, blindfolded, could tell the time and choose any card out of a pack.

Then there is St Bart's Hospital, near to St Bartholomew's Church in London. Not to forget the cartoon hero Bart Simpson. Preachers have explored each of these themes to find a suitable subject for a sermon on St Bartholomew's Day.

Little-known saints

But the fact remains that, apart from his name, Bartholomew is one of the 'Unknown Saints' of the Christian Church. So I thought I would preach this year on that very subject: 'Unknown Saints'. The encyclopaedia called *Butler's Lives of the Saints* ran to 12 volumes when it was first published, and there have been several supplements since then. It includes biographies of all those officially recognized by the Roman Catholic Church. *Common Worship* adds more than 70 names of worthy people to commemorate, of all denominations.

347

Some have full hagiographies. Of others, we often know little more than the date and place of their death, and for a few, not even that. But it is worth studying the lives of the saints, great and small alike. Butler himself wrote:

> In the lives of the saints we see the most perfect maxims of the gospel reduced to practice.

Or to put it simply, Jesus told us how to live, the saints show us how it is done.

Unknown saints

But just as the 'tomb of the unknown soldier' in Westminster Abbey, and other places, reminds us that many people heroically gave their lives for their country, although we do not know how or where they died – little, in fact, apart from the fact that they never came back – so there have been many who have lived lives of triumphant Christian discipleship, of whom we may know little or nothing. And that, too, is a sign of their Christian humility, because it was sufficient to them that, with all their faults, they had pleased God, and had no wish to be honoured in this world after they had died and gone to a better one. Maybe you are proud to have known one or two people like that.

You?

So we have talked about unknown saints; finally, I want you to ask yourself, are you one? Yes, you; are you a saint? Of course you deny it, and that is a good start; humility is the first sign of sainthood. Jesus said, 'The greatest among you must become like the youngest, and the leader like one who serves.' The Bible tells us that we are all 'called to be saints'. Yet you protest that you have thought, said or done many bad things – well, so has every single saint in the calendar. But remember – you have asked and received God's forgiveness for each fault you have confessed. Your families may think you are a walking disaster zone – families often think that about people they love – but if you have sincerely tried to be loving and kind to everyone, and to do God's will, then God, at least, thinks you are a saint-in-the-making. Then at least he will say on your end-of-term report, 'Should try harder.' Because if you try to become an unknown saint, God will give you all the help you need.

Suggested hymns

Captains of the saintly band; God, whose city's sure foundation; Lord, it belongs not to my care; Rejoice in God's saints, today and all days.

Holy Cross Day   14 September
Salvator Mundi

Num. 21.4–9 The bronze serpent; Ps. 22.23–28 All the earth shall turn to the Lord; Phil. 2.6–11 Obedient to death on the cross; John 3.13–17 God so loved the world

> *'Just as Moses lifted up the serpent in the wilderness, so must the Son of Man be lifted up, that whoever believes in him may have eternal life.' John 3.14 –15*

Ouseley

There is a beautiful four-part anthem, simple enough for most choirs, called 'O Saviour of the World', the music by John Goss, who was organist of St Paul's Cathedral in the mid-nineteenth-century, and composer of at least two well-known hymn tunes, to 'Praise, my soul, the King of heaven' and 'See, amid the winter's snow'. There is another setting, even more beautiful but much harder to sing, by Sir Frederick Gore Ouseley, known as 'FAG Ouseley' to those who have sung his chants to the psalms. Ouseley was enthusiastic about restoring the English choral tradition in the nineteenth century when it was at a low ebb; and he founded St Michael's College, a choir school at Tenbury Wells, now sadly defunct. Other composers have also made settings, touched by the simple beauty of the words:

O Saviour of the World,
who by thy cross and precious blood hast redeemed us,
save us and help us, we humbly beseech thee, O Lord.
Amen.

Source

These words were first published in English as an anthem for the Order for the Visitation of the Sick in the Book of Common Prayer in 1549. This was a very long service to expect a dying person to pay close attention to, and I am sure the anthem was said, not sung, in the sick-room. But it is one of those little-known services of great beauty which are seldom used today. The First English Prayer Book was translated by Archbishop Thomas Cranmer, during the reign of King Henry VIII, from a number of Latin liturgies; this was from the Latin antiphon – words repeated before and after a psalm – at the service of Holy Unction, when a sick person was anointed with holy oil; and also at the Mass for the Exaltation of the Holy Cross. This is now celebrated by Roman Catholics on 14 September, which Anglicans call Holy Cross Day; but before 1960 it was held on 3 May. The Latin words begin *Salvator Mundi*.

The cross

Of course we celebrate Christ's death on the cross on Good Friday. But then we are swept along by the events of Holy Week, and there is hardly time to stop and meditate on the actual meaning of the cross itself. Crucifixion was the most barbaric and painful form of execution ever invented, and Jesus voluntarily chose to submit to it, when he could have easily escaped by fight or flight, or by lying about the kingdom of loving self-sacrifice which he was ushering in. Many words have been used for this act of atonement, and many theories propounded attempting to explain how it benefited us. All are meaningful to some people at most periods of history, but we must be careful not to use words which will be misunderstood today. This anthem speaks of redemption and blood. Redemption was the money that was paid to buy, for a slave, his or her freedom, and so we are reminded that through the cross, we gain freedom from our slavery to sin and selfishness. But we must be careful not to press the metaphor of a money transaction too hard, or it will sound too much as though Jesus was paying a bribe to God or the devil. It is essential to insist that it was God himself on the cross, eager to forgive us, and therefore keen to persuade us how serious our disobedience really is, and how it hurts our heavenly Father. The reference to blood, of course, connects the death of Christ on the cross with his giving of himself to us in the Eucharist or Holy Communion.

Paintings

The words *Salvator Mundi* are also used for a particular image in the fine arts. Paintings with this title have been made by Jan van Eyck, Hans Memling and Albrecht Dürer, and have been attributed to Titian and, recently, Leonardo da Vinci. In each of these beautiful works of art Christ's right hand is formed into a gesture of blessing, and in his left hand he holds a golden globe with a cross on top, similar to that held by British monarchs at their enthronement, symbolizing the world ruled by the cross. So these paintings illustrate the beautiful prayer asking Christ, the Saviour of the world, who by his cross and precious blood has redeemed us, to save us and help us.

Suggested hymns

In the cross of Christ I glory; Morning glory, starlit sky; Were you there when they crucified my Lord?; When I survey the wondrous cross.

St Matthew, Apostle and Evangelist
21 September
Love or Gold?
Prov. 3.13–18 Wisdom more precious than jewels;
Ps. 119.65–72 Better than gold; 2 Cor. 4.1–6 The open statement of the truth; Matt. 9.9–13 The call of Matthew

> 'Happy are those who find wisdom,
> and those who get understanding,
> for her income is better than silver,
> and her revenue better than gold.'
> Proverbs 3.13–14

Matthew

St Matthew was a tax collector, a Jew employed by the hated Roman army-of-occupation to raise funds from their Jewish friends to pay the Roman soldiers. No wonder the taxman was hated, then, as a traitor to his nation, a quisling, and a fraud who overcharged his friends and neighbours, keeping any balance left over for himself.

'All those taxmen ever think of is gold,' the Jews said bitterly; 'they have no idea of what friendship means.' A bit of an exaggeration, perhaps, but it was not far from the unpleasant truth. But Jesus called Matthew, and Matthew saw the wisdom of unselfishness, abandoned his ill-gotten gains, and followed Jesus as a penniless itinerant preacher. Jesus said he had come to call people, who knew they were sinners, to accept the forgiveness which follows repentance. Jesus could do nothing with those who thought they were perfect.

Capitalism

But what is wrong with going after money, you ask; don't we all try to feather our own nests? Yes, but that is because we live in a capitalist society, which has deceived us into believing that money-grubbing is natural. The Bible says that the desire for money is the root of all evil; wisdom more precious than jewels; and

> Happy are those who find wisdom,
> and those who get understanding,
> for her income is better than silver,
> and her revenue better than gold.

Gold

Yet for many people today, getting rich has become the main purpose of their lives. Supporting one's family is important, but not to the extent of having no spare time to spend with them. It is giving to others, not building a hoard of wealth, which leads to satisfaction in life. This message is taught by many fictional stories: there is a tale of a monkey who put his hand through some railings to grab some nuts, but couldn't get his full fists back through the narrow gap, so he went hungry rather than letting go. And another about the six-foot-long chopsticks issued in heaven and hell alike. The inhabitants of hell thought only of stuffing their own cheeks, but the tableware was too long for them to place the food in their own mouths; but those in heaven fed each other. In Charles Dickens' *Christmas Carol*, Scrooge is described as 'a squeezing, wrenching, grasping, scraping, clutching, covetous old sinner'. And it did not make him happy. Similarly greedy attitudes are inculcated by advertising campaigns, countless TV commercials, films and conversations.

Goodness

Yet unselfishness is recommended in the tales of Cinderella and Robin Hood, and by real-life heroes like Gandhi, Martin Luther King, Mother Teresa, Nelson Mandela and Desmond Tutu. *The Toast of New York* was a rather superficial movie of 1937 about a poor man whose greed for riches led him to buy up all the gold in the city, and then fix the price so as to bankrupt all the other rich men there. By this means he made himself hated by everyone in New York, and appalled the beautiful girl, whom to woo had been the object of his greed. Then he was shot, and the climax of the film is when he is dying, quite unrepentant, and speculates aloud, 'I wonder whether the gates of heaven really *are* made of gold?'

Wisdom

Greed makes fools of people, as it did of Matthew; most people know someone who had some fine elements in their character until they were swallowed up by the lust for riches. Whereas those who use what they can spare to make others happy are ennobled and enriched by their lives of compassion and generosity. St Matthew met Jesus and saw the error of his ways. He became wise enough to see that money would never bring him happiness; but serving the needs of other people would make him not only happy but wise. Wisdom in the Bible is not just book-learning; it is the common-sense ability to distinguish between right and wrong.

Love

The craving for 'filthy lucre' is the enemy of friendship, and before long it will destroy even the most devoted of loves. To be rich in cash and poor in compassion is to live in a fool's paradise, which will eventually collapse into dust and leave you alone, unloved and friendless. Given the choice between love and gold, always make the wise decision: choose what will go with you into heaven, not the one that will crumble into dust.

353

From heaven you came; Give thanks with a joyful/grateful heart; Great is thy faithfulness, O God my Father; O Lord of heaven and earth and sea.

St Michael and All Angels 29 September
Guardian Angels

Gen. 28.10–17 Jacob's ladder; Ps. 103.19–22 Bless the Lord, you angels; Rev. 12.7–12 Michael fought the dragon (*if the Revelation reading is used instead of the Old Testament reading, the New Testament reading is* Heb. 1.5–14 Higher than the angels); John 1.47–51 Angels descending on the Son of Man

> '[Jesus said,] "Very truly, I tell you, you will see heaven opened and the angels of God ascending and descending upon the Son of Man."' John 1.51

Euphemism

Angels are mentioned many times in the Bible, in several different ways. The Jews were scared of breaking the commandment against taking God's name in vain. So, instead of saying that God appeared to someone, they said, 'The angel of the Lord appeared to them.' For instance, Moses saw a bush which was on fire but not burnt up. The Bible says: 'There the angel of the LORD appeared to him in a flame of fire out of a bush . . .' But a few verses later, it is not an angel, but 'God called to him out of the bush . . .' Then a few verses after that, 'God said to Moses, "I AM WHO I AM."' It is as though the word 'angel' is a sort of euphemism to avoid using a word for which one might be punished.

Spiritual

But later the word is used for spiritual beings, distinct from God, who are God's servants. In the Old Testament angels are often called 'the heavenly host', an imaginary army of soldiers who fight for God against the forces of evil. They also sing God's praises. The Letter to the Hebrews asks, 'Are not all angels spirits in the divine service, sent to serve for the sake of those who are to inherit salvation?' Jacob 'dreamed that there was a ladder set up on the earth, the top of it reaching to heaven; and the angels of God were ascending and descending on it'. The angels in the dream were carrying the prayers of the people of Bethel up to God, and God's answers and blessings down to the people. In this case it was definitely a dream or a vision, which Jesus quoted from when talking about Nathanael praying under the fig tree.

Wings

The Bible does not describe what angels look like. Mostly, it seems, they looked just like human beings, so that Hebrews remarks that 'some have entertained angels without knowing it'. The seraphs, whom Isaiah saw in his vision in the Temple, had wings. But I cannot think of any other instances when wings are specifically mentioned in relation to angels in the Bible. Angelic wings, together with harps and haloes, seem to have been invented by the artists who painted them in the Middle Ages; which is when the idea that angels were female arose.

Guardians

The distinctive contribution which Jesus made to our thinking about angels was when he said, 'Take care that you do not despise one of these little ones; for, I tell you, in heaven their angels continually see the face of my Father in heaven.' The Jews, like the Persians, believed that every nation had its heavenly representative. The word 'angel' means a messenger, and the words of Jesus suggest that every human being has a spiritual being especially dedicated to asking God to forgive us our sins, and protect us from harm. It may be that our guardian angel also acts as our conscience, whispering in our ears a word of advice when we are tempted to do something wrong. This saying appears in the Gospels when Jesus has been talking about his 'little ones', which may mean small children. It is wonderful to reflect, as you look at the beautiful sight of a sleeping baby, that each child has their own heavenly representative, pleading with God to forgive them, and personally responsible for protecting this particular child from harm or distress. But Jesus sometimes seems to use the words 'my little ones' to refer to ordinary Christians like you and me. So if ever you wonder how God can possibly spare time to pay attention to the prayers of all the people who call upon him all the time – forgetting that God is infinite, and not limited by time or space – it is comforting to imagine that God has appointed one special spiritual being to keep an eye on you, seeing what your needs are – especially your spiritual needs – at any one moment and report back to God, who loves you as a unique individual. Have a word with your guardian angel on the way home, and thank him or her or it for rescuing you when, all oblivious, you were walking into disaster, and for warning you when you were about to harm yourself or other people.

Suggested hymns

Around the throne of God a band; As Jacob with travel was weary; Come, let us join our cheerful songs; Through all the changing scenes of life.

St Luke the Evangelist   18 October
Luke's Letter to Paul

Isa. 35.3–6 Healing in the new age, *or* Acts 16.6–12a The Macedonian call; Ps. 147.1–7 God heals the broken-hearted; 2 Tim. 4.5–17 Only Luke is with me; Luke 10.1–9 Sending out the 70

'Only Luke is with me.' *2 Timothy 4.11*

Here is an imagined letter as St Luke might have written to St Paul:

Dear Paul

As your medical advisor, I must warn you that you can't stay in that damp, waterfront prison cell in Caesarea Maritima any longer. When I visited you last week, your condition – your 'thorn in the flesh' as you call it – was nearly as acute as when you first employed me in Alexandria Troas, when you were having visions. Have you had any more recently? It's all very worrying, and I feel you're not taking the medical aspects of your imprisonment anything like seriously enough.

You're not an easy patient, but you must admit I travelled with you as your personal physician, to keep an eye on you. I realized then, and I still believe, that keeping you in good health is vital to the spreading of the gospel.

I needn't remind you how many journeys I made with you – I'd always longed to travel, but as soon as I step on a ship I feel seasick. I stuck by you until we reached Jerusalem three years ago. But what's a Jew like you doing, getting arrested again in the Jerusalem Temple?

Then you had to endure the nightride to Caesarea. And that cell! Physicians recommend sea air for some conditions, but that doesn't mean a cell on the quayside which gets soaked whenever there's a large wave, and goes on dripping from the ceiling for days afterwards. I'm sure that's what made you so much worse, and you have to get out of there soon or you'll be too ill to go on with your work. What use to God is a dead apostle?

Now, I pride myself that I write Greek quite well. And I'm careful about getting things into the right order. So why don't I write a history of the expansion of the Christian movement, and your part in it, for you to bring forward in evidence the next time your case comes up, to show that we're no threat to the Empire? Nobody would want to keep you in prison after reading that.

And I could carry the story right back to the beginning, by telling the good news of the life, death and resurrection of Jesus. So while my patient has been languishing in prison, I haven't been idle. I've been travelling around, questioning as many people as possible who actually met Jesus. Then I get an account, from each of them, of what he said and what he did. Then I write it all down for future use.

And do you know what? I found that there already is a collection of 'The Sayings of Jesus', in Greek, and I've got hold of a copy.

Peter's taken John Mark with him to Rome to be his interpreter. They tell me Mark, who is Pater's translator in Rome, has kept notes, in Greek, of what Peter says about his travels with Jesus. I am determined to get a copy, even if I have to travel to Rome to find it. I could add to that what I've collected from other disciples, and the things I have found out for myself, and I would have a full account of the life of Jesus.

And nobody seems to know much about the birth of Jesus. 'Born of a woman', you said once. That suggests there was something odd about it. Well, you'd expect the birth of the Son of God to be unusual. So I tracked down his mother to ask her about it. I'll tell you all about what Mary's told me when I come to see you soon. It's a strange story, but very beautiful.

Somebody said that, if the procurator keeps you in detention for too long without giving a verdict, then, as a Roman citizen, you have the right to appeal to have your case considered by the Emperor himself.

So I'm writing to say, don't do it! Doctor's orders!

Nero would take ages coming to a decision, without a bribe. Then you'd be sent to Rome, under escort, by sea. Of course I'd come with you, to look after your health, even though I hate sailing. But terrible things happen at sea. I want you out of that prison cell as soon as possible, but appealing to Caesar is the worst thing you could do. I wouldn't want to be responsible for what could happen to your health on a long sea voyage.

I'll see you soon, and share the results of my researches.

Your medical adviser and friend,
Doctor Luke

Suggested hymns

At even, ere the sun was set; Disposer supreme, and judge of the earth; From thee all skill and science flow; Sometimes a light surprises.

SS Simon and Jude, Apostles 28 October
A Shipwrecked Apostle
Isa. 28.14–16 A foundation stone; Ps. 119.89–96 I am yours, save me; Eph. 2.19–22 The foundation of the apostles; John 15.17–27 You have been with me

> 'You are citizens with the saints and also members of the household of God, built upon the foundation of the apostles and prophets, with Christ Jesus himself as the cornerstone.' Ephesians 2.19–20

Martyrs

'The Twelve' were also called 'apostles', which means those who are sent, or missionaries. As far as we know, they all went through danger and misadventure as they spread the gospel after receiving the Holy Spirit on the day of Pentecost, and many of them were martyred. But with St Simon and St Jude, we know nothing for sure about what happened to them. One 'tradition' says they travelled together to present-day Iran, where pagan priests slaughtered both men. Some accounts say that Simon was sawn in two, and others that he was stabbed to death. Jude was said to have been clubbed to death. Other legends say Simon died in battle when he was Bishop of Jerusalem, and yet others say that he trekked across North Africa until he reached the great age of 120 when he was finally martyred.

Christians

Paul, in his Letter to the Ephesians, tells us that we are all fellow citizens with the apostles – members of the same community. So we must not be surprised, but count it an honour if we suffer because of our faith, like them. St Paul the Apostle was shipwrecked at least four times. I should like to tell you the story of a contemporary Christian who was shipwrecked while going about his apostolic duties.

Archdeacon

He was born in the Seychelles Islands, in the Indian Ocean. His father had Chinese ancestors, so his surname was Chang Him. His mother was a Seychellois of mixed African and European ancestry, and he has a brownish-coloured skin. He said that his father sent his mother with instructions to register his birth under the Christian name of François, but she became confused and told the registrar her son was called Français. 'No such name', said the registrar – 'that is the French word for French people. You must call him "French"!' So when French Chang Him came to England to study for the ministry of the Anglican Church, some people came to meet him off the train knowing nothing about him except his name. They went down the train, asking anyone with a Chinese-looking face, 'Are you French?' Not surprisingly, they got no answer! He was ordained, and returned to his native islands, where, because he was the only priest to have been born in the Seychelles, the first Bishop of the Seychelles, George Briggs, wisely appointed him Archdeacon.

Shipwreck

But Archdeacon French was put in charge of the Anglicans on the small island of Praslin, and to come to the main island of Mahé, he had to travel across on a sailing-boat. One day the Bishop and a few others were worried when he was late for a diocesan meeting. He had telephoned that he was coming across on the schooner *Éro*, and the wind was unusually strong. They phoned a local airline which only had two small planes. They would not normally have taken off in such weather, but one of the pilots knew his mother was on the *Éro*, so he took off to look for it – and spotted the wreckage halfway between the two islands. He radioed the police, who sent a launch to fetch the survivors, while the plane circled overhead to point out where the pilot's mother had become separated from the rest. Just before the ship sank, the crew had made a raft of oil drums and planks, and everybody swam to it – except for the Captain and the Archdeacon who, realizing a small boy was trapped in the cabin, went back to rescue him, at the risk of their own lives.

Lessons

Archdeacon French told his friends later that he thought first of his new bride, whom he had married a few weeks previously, and prayed that she would not become a widow. Then he tried to minister the Christian gospel of hope to those who were floating beside him. He said his faith became much deeper as a result of facing the possibility of his own death. This shipwrecked apostle became the Bishop of Seychelles from 1974 to 2004, and Archbishop of the Indian Ocean from 1984 until 1995. He is a worthy successor to the church leaders in the New Testament, who faced shipwreck and death in the cause of sharing the gospel of Christ. Let us thank God, in silence, for all who have been willing to do the same, and pray that we may not face dangers like that, but that, whatever challenges we do encounter, God will give us the strength to come through them triumphantly.

Suggested hymns

Captains of the saintly band; God, whose city's sure foundation; Eternal Father, strong to save; Will your anchor hold?

All Saints' Day 1 November
Where Prayer Has Been Valid

(*If 5 November is not kept as All Saints' Sunday, the readings on p. 263 (All Saints' Sunday) are used on 1 November. If those are used on the Sunday, the following are the readings on 1 November*):

Isa. 56.3–8 My house for all people, *or* 2 Esd. 2.42–48 Crowned by the Son of God; Ps. 33.1–5 Rejoice, you righteous; Heb. 12.18–24 Come to Zion; Matt. 5.1–12 The Beatitudes

> '*You have come to Mount Zion and to the city of the living God, the heavenly Jerusalem, and to innumerable angels in festal gathering, and to the assembly of the firstborn who are enrolled in heaven, and to God the judge of all, and to the spirits of the righteous made perfect.*' Hebrews 12.22–23

Pilgrimage

John Bunyan describes the whole of life as a pilgrimage, in his book, *The Pilgrim's Progress*. The climax comes when the character called 'Christian' crosses the river into heaven:

> So he passed over, and the trumpets sounded for him on the other side.

Since Bunyan was a Puritan, he does not mention the saints, but there is no doubt that Christian will be met by a great crowd of witnesses on the other side. Bunyan wrote:

> There you shall enjoy your friends again, that is those who arrived before you; and there you shall also joyfully welcome everyone who follows after you into this holy place.

But the title of Bunyan's book is based on the great tradition which had grown up in the Middle Ages of making a pilgrimage to the place where some famous saint had been buried. Geoffrey Chaucer's *The Canterbury Tales* is a fiction about the stories told to each other by a group of pilgrims on their way to the place of martyrdom, and tomb, of St Thomas à Becket in Kent. Many people in those days thought that they could come closer to God when they came close to one of the saints, by visiting the place where they were buried. Pilgrims knew well that the souls of the saints are in heaven, not in the place where their mortal remains are interred. Nonetheless it seems easier to speak to the saints and ask them to pray for us when our imagination is stirred by visiting the place where they died.

Destinations

So there were pilgrimages to the empty tomb of Jesus in Jerusalem; to the supposed tomb of St James in Compostella; to the places where St Peter and St Paul are buried in Rome; to the grave of St Columba on the island of Iona off the Scottish coast, and many others. In later days pilgrimages began to the tomb of Bernadette Soubirous in Lourdes where she saw a vision of the Virgin Mary; Orthodox Christians make pilgrimages to many places, including the Lavra caves in Kiev in the Ukraine, founded by St Antony, a monk from Mount Athos; and so on.

T. S. Eliot

Recently, some people have begun to question the authenticity of some of these pilgrimage destinations. Although the archaeologists are not unanimous, in most cases the majority have agreed that most of the sites are probably genuine. But T. S. Eliot, in his *Four Quartets*, suggested that historical validity is not what matters most in a pilgrimage. He describes sitting in the chapel at Little Gidding, where one of the first Anglican religious communities was founded by Nicholas Ferrar in the seventeenth century. The atmosphere of prayer in such a holy place is palpable. Eliot warns us that we do not go on pilgrimage to places like that in order to check whether the location is historically accurate, or to satisfy our curiosity. He cautions in the *Four Quartets* that the pilgrim kneels in a place where 'prayer has been valid', and that the prayer of the dead is 'tongued with fire beyond the language of the living'.

Listening

So our devotion to the saints, whether on pilgrimage, in church or before an icon at home, is not an attempt to earn their favour, or bribe them to pray for us. God is more ready to hear than we to pray, and Jesus is the only mediator we need. No, we remember the communion of saints when we pray so as to listen to the lessons which their lives can teach us, and feel encouraged by the certainty of their presence around us when we pray. Then we can continue life's joyful pilgrimage, sure that we are surrounded by a cheering crowd of saints, and looking forward to meeting them face to face when we die.

Suggested hymns

Blest are the pure in heart; For all the saints who from their labours rest; Give us the wings of faith to rise; Let saints on earth in concert sing; O happy band of pilgrims.

Commemoration of the Faithful Departed (All Souls' Day) 2 November
Bereavement Trauma

Lam. 3.17–26, 31–33 New every morning, *or* Wisd. 3.1–9 Souls of the righteous; Ps. 23 The Lord my shepherd, *or* 27.1–6, 16–17 He shall hide me; Rom. 5.5–11 Christ died for us, *or* 1 Peter 1.3–9 Salvation ready to be revealed; John 5.19–25 The dead will hear his voice, *or* John 6.37–40 I will raise them up

> 'The Lord will not reject for ever. Although he causes grief, he will have compassion according to the abundance of his steadfast love; for he does not willingly afflict or grieve anyone.' Lamentations 3.31–33

Bereavement

Jesus said, 'This is indeed the will of my Father, that all who see the Son and believe in him may have eternal life; and I will raise them up on the last day.' He was not a man to lie or deliberately deceive us. So you would expect that in a Christian country, people would have a very positive attitude towards death; looking forward to our departure on a journey to a better world, where there is no more pain or grief; where we can meet again with those we love who have already passed over, and with our great heroes of the past; and with Jesus himself face to face and our loving heavenly Father. You would expect us to feel similarly delighted when our loved ones die, glad that they have gone to a better world, and looking forward to seeing them again when our turn comes. You might expect that, logically; but it isn't so, and it could never be so. Our emotions are not under our control, and whatever our brain tells us, our hearts will be full of grief. Aware that we shall face a long separation from someone who has been part of our daily life, we are not sure how we can cope. Heaven is for saints, we think; and our conscience rightly tells us that we have done many wrong things in our lives; we do not deserve heaven, and possibly neither did the person whose loss we are grieving over. So instead of being in a state of joy and hope, we are in a state of trauma, bereavement trauma, and it is entirely natural.

All Souls

That is why the day after All Saints is commonly called 'All Souls'; All Saints' Day is for those who have never sinned, we think, and 2 November is for the rest of us. Yet the canonized saints would be the first to insist that they, too, were not without sin, and it was only through the merciful grace of God that they achieved what they did. So let us not make invidious distinctions, but keep All Souls' Day to remember that all of us, with God's forgiveness, can qualify to enter into heaven.

Hope

Since everybody has their moments of doubt, it is wise to fill our memories with signs of hope. Read in the Bible how the disciples became convinced that they had seen the risen Christ, who once was dead, and is now alive. Read other books which tell of people having glimpses of the world to come; perhaps seeing departed loved ones in a vision or a dream. Have you had any moments when you yourself felt that the departed were very close to you? Cling to those memories; then you will be ready to face with courage the moment when death comes to you, the most natural thing in the world, and God calls you to join the heavenly party.

Coping

If you have accepted this, then you will be ready to cope with bereavement, when your loved ones pass on. Be gentle with yourself: cry if you want to, but don't worry if you can't at first; maybe it will come later, or maybe you aren't the crying kind. Accept that none of us is perfect, and ask God for strength to cope with the loneliness, knowing that God is always with us, and the departed are not far away, behind a kind of veil.

Caring

And if you are in a situation where you want to comfort a bereaved person, ask the Holy Spirit to give you the words to say. Be ready to ask questions, go over memories, then just sit in shared silence. If you get the chance, say how much your faith, feeble and hesitant as it is, has brought you through moments of sadness in your own life. Remind each other how Jesus has promised that there is room in heaven for everyone. Read from the book of Lamentations, one of the saddest but most hopeful books in the Old Testament:

> The Lord will not reject for ever. Although he causes grief, he will have compassion according to the abundance of his steadfast love; for he does not willingly afflict or grieve anyone.

Suggested hymns

All ye who seek for sure relief; Jesus lives! Thy terrors now; There is a green hill far away; There's a wideness in God's mercy.

Saints and Martyrs of (our own nation)
8 November
A Christian Nation?

Isa. 61.4–9 Build up the ancient ruins, *or* Ecclus. (Ben Sira) 44.1–15 Let us now praise famous men; Ps. 15 Who may dwell in your tabernacle?; Rev. 19.5–10 A great multitude invited; John 17.18–23 To be with me to see my glory

> *'Their descendants shall be known among the nations, and their offspring among the peoples; all who see them shall acknowledge that they are a people whom the Lord has blessed.' Isaiah 61.9*

> *Or: 'Let us now sing the praises of famous men, our ancestors in their generations.' Ecclesiasticus (Ben Sira) 44.1*

Patriotism

This day, a week after All Saints' Day, is called, in the calendar of the Church of England, a day to commemorate the Saints and Martyrs of England. I see no reason, however, why patriotic citizens of any other nation should not use it to remember the saints and martyrs who lived and died, to bring the gospel of God's love to their fellow citizens. It is good to be patriotic, and grateful to people who have made our nation what it is today. If we look through the church calendar or the history books we find many people mentioned to whom we must be deeply grateful.

Scriptures

There is a choice of two passages for the first reading at this service. Ecclesiasticus, written by a Jew called Ben Sira, comes from the Apocrypha, which is printed in some Bibles between the Old and New Testaments. It includes the famous words, 'Let us now praise famous men.' But if you don't have the Apocrypha in your Bible, you can read how Isaiah claims that all who see his nation will say that they are a people whom the Lord has blessed. I want to devote a few minutes today to examining what we should be proud of in our own nation.

Virtue

What the saints and martyrs of the past tried to bring to our country was the knowledge of a God of love, and of Jesus our Saviour. Therefore they laboured to change society here, to make it more like what Jesus called the kingdom of God on earth, as it is in heaven. So they tried to build a country which shows justice, mercy, compassion, and virtuous, self-sacrificing lives spent in the service of others. We should be proud that those virtues have taken root in our land as a result of the work and example of these great Christian preachers and teachers. Yet if anyone asked us, we should have to admit that we have a long way to go yet. Our nation is not perfect, and we are not unique. Many other nations are struggling to base their society on the pattern of Jesus, his words and his life. In some respects one country or another may have done better than we have, and to others our society is an example. Comparisons are odious, and strident nationalism is offensive.

Christian?

So the most Christian thing we can do is to try to make our nation better than it is. Some people are proud of their nation because they call it a 'Christian' country. And indeed, where the Christian virtues of faith, hope and love have shaped the way we treat each other here, and other nations overseas, that is certainly a thing to be grateful for. Christian saints have been an example to us, but we have learnt a lot from followers of other religious leaders like Mahatma Ghandi. In past ages, the majority of people here called themselves Christians; some, but not all of those, had a living faith in Jesus and based their lives on his. For the rest, it was a convention, but meant little in practice. But now, fewer people go to church, and in some schools the Bible is hardly taught at all. Because some have pretended that there is a conflict between science and religion, more people openly describe themselves as atheists or agnostics. So although we owe a lot to our Christian heritage, and would lose a lot by abandoning it, I think it is misleading to describe this as a Christian country.

Mission

Perhaps it would be more helpful to describe this as a *mission field*. The Christian mission never stops, because there is always a new generation of young people with whom we need to share our faith. We shall be more likely to enter into profitable debate with the unbelievers if we stop pretending that our society is perfect, and acknowledge that there is a lot more to do in making people more loving. And the only way of doing that is to reveal to them that each one of us is loved by God.

Suggested hymns

God, whose city's sure foundation; Judge eternal, throned in splendour; Lord, while for all mankind we pray; When a knight won his spurs.

St Andrew the Apostle   30 November
Instant Obedience

Isa. 52.7–10 The messenger who announces peace; Ps. 19.1–6 The heavens declare God's glory; Rom. 10.12–18 God's messengers reconcile Jew and Greek; Matt. 4.18–22 The call of the fishermen

'Immediately [Andrew and Peter] left their nets and followed [Jesus].' Matthew 4.20

Immediately

St Matthew's Gospel tells us that Jesus met Andrew and Peter, who were fishermen, on the shores of Lake Galilee, and called them to follow him, becoming fishers of men. And '*immediately* they left their nets and followed him'. This seems so preposterous that many people have speculated that somehow Peter and Andrew must have met Jesus before, and of course that is possible. But neither St Matthew's Gospel nor St John's say so. St John says that Peter was converted through his brother Andrew, but he doesn't contradict Matthew's suggestion that for both of them it was an instantaneous decision.

Psychology

This is disappointing for psychiatrists and psychotherapists who seek a psychological explanation. But they weren't interested in the whys and hows in those days; what they remembered was that when they first saw Jesus, his was such an authoritative presence that neither of them could have said 'no'. They couldn't even have said 'wait', or 'give me a day or two to think about it'. Jesus so clearly knew far more about life than they did, that when he gave them an order, they had no choice but to obey instantly.

Today

That is still true today. If you have not yet made up your mind to follow Jesus, or if you are having doubts about the faith which once seemed so clear to you, sit down by yourself, allowing nobody to interrupt you, and read one of the four Gospels from beginning to end at one sitting. Ignore the psychology; don't worry about how the Gospels came to be written; just picture Jesus standing in front of you and saying, 'Follow me.' Then refuse him if you dare!

Authority

The thing is, Jesus was quite different from any other person, and still is. Whether you meet him by Lake Galilee, or read about him in your bedroom, nobody can say 'no' to him. Of course, many things are left unexplained when you obey him, but that doesn't seem to matter, such is the obvious authority of the man. It would be more than your life is worth if you refused him; you would never forgive yourself if you said 'no'!

Following

Of course, the call of Jesus was horribly vague. He said to Andrew and his brother, 'Follow me', but what exactly does that mean? Then Jesus explained, 'I will make you fishers for people.' But what on earth does that mean? At some time in our lives, you and I hear the voice of Jesus in our brains saying, 'You there! Yes, you; you know who I'm talking to! Follow me. Now!' And we have no idea what it involves. Probably if we did, we would be so appalled to think that the task was completely beyond our powers that we would say, 'Not on your life!' It is just as well that we don't know what God has planned for us. Does he want us to help somebody who is ill, or to be a parent, a preacher or a schoolteacher, to talk to somebody about Jesus, or to work for a charity? 'Not me,' we think. 'You've made a mistake, Lord. You've got the wrong person. I could never do that!' And so we completely ignore the doctrine of grace, which says that whatever God wants us to do, he will give us the strength and wisdom we need for it, however low our self-esteem may be. 'Go on; give it a try,' says Jesus. And we are astonished to find we can do it.

Unworthy

Of course, you probably think that will never happen to you. You are just one of the 'also-rans'. Or perhaps you are too old. Don't you believe it! Just be alert to the voice of Jesus calling you, through circumstances or your conscience, and recognize the call when it comes. Then, in the words of the old hymn:

When we walk with the Lord
in the light of his word,
what a glory he sheds on our way;
while we do his good will,
he abides with us still
and with all who will trust and obey.
Trust and obey
for there's no other way
to be happy in Jesus
than to trust and obey.

369

That's what St Andrew did, and you can do it too! When Jesus calls you to do something for him, 'Trust and obey'. When push comes to shove, you will find that you quite enjoy it, too!

Suggested hymns

Amazing grace; Jesus calls us – o'er the tumult; When we walk with the Lord; Will you come and follow me?

Harvest Festival
Just Enough

Deut. 8.7–18 Do not forget the Lord, *or* Deut. 28.1–14 Blessings for obedience; Ps. 65 Thanks for earth's bounty; 2 Cor. 9.6–15 Generous sowing, generous reaping; Luke 12.16–30 The rich fool, *or* Luke 17.11–19 The thankful leper

> 'We shall be satisfied with the blessings of your house.' Psalm 65.3 (Common Worship)

Wishes

One of those emails which go round from time to time tells a touching story of a very elderly man wishing his daughter farewell as she departs at an airport. They accept that the next time she will come all the way home again will be for his funeral, and wish each other 'just enough'. A passer-by overheard this and asked why they used those words. The old man replied that they were the traditional greeting in his family. 'When we said, "I wish you enough,"' he replied, 'we were wanting the other person to have a life filled with just enough good things to sustain them.' Then turning towards the passer-by, he shared these words as if he were reciting them from memory:

- I wish you enough sun to keep your attitude bright no matter how grey the day may appear.
- I wish you enough rain to appreciate the sun even more.
- I wish you enough happiness to keep your spirit alive and everlasting.
- I wish you enough pain so that even the smallest of joys in life may appear bigger.
- I wish you enough gain to satisfy your wanting.

- I wish you enough loss to appreciate all that you possess.
- I wish you enough hellos to get you through the final goodbye.

It's a bit corny, like all such emails, but it has a point. We don't need to wish each other lavish riches and great fame; all we need wish them is 'just enough'.

Thanks

Conversely, when you come to thank God for all his gifts, you can thank him that he has given you 'just enough'. Because often at the back of your mind there is a nagging wish that God could have given you more. He could have made you as rich as this tycoon, or as famous as that celebrity. He could have given you perfect parents, a perfect partner and a perfect family. You wish you had a house as splendid as that of the Joneses. You know you don't really need any of these things; all you need is 'just enough'. In fact, if God had given you more than he has, it might have done you great harm, turning you into a spoilt brat, a troubled tycoon, or that rich fool that Jesus described so accurately in the parable.

Harvest

Thanking God for the harvest is a tradition which reaches right back to the beginning of an agricultural society. But in those days nature was completely unpredictable, and they had no refrigeration to preserve the produce of the good harvests to eat in the leaner years. When the harvest was in, the first priority was to provide seed for sowing next year, and food for the whole family until the next harvest-time. That was 'just enough to get by on'. Any surplus was sold in the market, to provide money to pay for house repairs, furniture, education for the kids, replacing worn-out clothing and so on. These things, though not luxuries, were items you had to forego in the slim years. We should thank God that our life today is better than theirs was then.

Poverty and plenty

But there are plenty of people around the world today who live on a similar knife-edge of poverty. Even in this country, there are those who slip through the net of the welfare state, whose only resource in emergencies is the loan-shark, which only drags them deeper into poverty. For these we should pray that God will bring their income up until it is 'just enough', at least, and ask ourselves if there is any way we could share our surplus with them in a way that would encourage them, rather than demoralize them. We have come to believe that essential to a full life are all the latest electronic gadgets, luxury food and clothes, and a shop-until-you-drop mentality. And this makes us greedy, and does us more spiritual harm than their poverty does to those who have less than enough. We must be 'satisfied with the blessings of God's house'.

Prayer

Let our prayer this harvest-tide be that God will give us just enough, and no more; and let us be profoundly grateful for what God does give us. And as you leave, greet each other saying, 'I wish you just enough of everything!'

All-age worship

For most foods, too little harms our health, and so does too much. Find out the levels of daily intake between which we have 'just enough' of meat, potatoes, sugar, salt, fresh fruit etc.

Suggested hymns

Father, Lord of all creation; For the fruits of his creation; Praise and thanksgiving, Father, we offer; We plough the fields and scatter.

Sermon for a Wedding
All Give, No Take
Romans 12.1–2, 9–13; Mark 10.6–9

> 'Dear friends, because God is so loving, make sacrifices . . . Love each other warmly as fellow Christians, and respect each other's personality.' Romans 12.1, 10 (personal translation)

Give and take?

Often people flood couples who are about to get married with advice. Most of it is very helpful, though most couples can remember very little of it a few days later. One of the best clichés is when they are told to remember that the secret of a happy marriage is 'give and take'. I am going to give you a variation on that, in the hope that it will flash back into the minds of each of you every time you are trying to work out what you should do, and every time you have a row.

Best man

It came to me through a Christian minister who said that on the night before he got married he held a stag party – though the only people attending were he and his best man, because all the other men were arriving on the wedding day itself. When they were nicely mellow, the best man said to the groom, 'You want your marriage to make you happy, pal? Forget it!' 'What do you mean?' asked the groom. 'That sounds a bit over-pessimistic. D'you mean there's no chance of ever being happy again?' 'No,' the best man continued, 'I am saying the very opposite. Your marriage *can* make you blissfully happy, but only if you forget all about being happy. Concentrate 100 per cent on making your wife happy. She'll be so pleased, she'll stop at nothing to make you happy in return. Then you'll both be blissfully contented, without thinking about yourselves at all. But if you try to make yourself happy, you'll only be miserable.' The minister spent all night trying to understand what his friend meant, and by dawn he thought he understood. So when anyone at the wedding reception said to him, 'The secret of a happy marriage is give and take,' he replied, 'Oh no it isn't. The secret is "All give, and no take." In planning our meals, our holidays and our career changes we must each think only of what will make the other happy. In bed and at board, in youth and old age, we must each put the other's wishes before our own. "All give, and no take," that's the secret.' And do you know, it works, in every marriage. If you think about what *you* want, you'll never get it. But if you make your partner happy, they will work out what you want, and give it to you on a plate! 'All give, and no take.' Or, perhaps, 'All give, and gratefully receive.'

C. S. Lewis

The Christian author C. S. Lewis, best known for his Narnia stories, also wrote a book called *Surprised by Joy*, in which he said that it was no use looking for joy in your life, but if you concentrate on giving joy to other people, you will be surprised at how happy it makes you. 'All give, no take.' 'Surprised by joy'!

Bible

And you know what, that advice is already in the Bible! St Paul wrote a letter to the Christians at Rome, who were always squabbling. He gave them some very down-to-earth advice, when he wrote, 'Dear friends, because God is so loving, make sacrifices . . . Love each other warmly as fellow Christians, and respect each other's personality.' Or, in the old translation, 'I beseech you therefore, brethren, by the mercies of God, that ye present your bodies a living sacrifice . . . Be kindly affectioned one to another with brotherly love; in honour preferring one another.' Jesus quoted the book of Genesis, where it says, 'That's why a man will leave his father and mother and be united to his wife, so that the two become one body.' Jesus explained it like this: 'Husband and wife are no longer two people, but one.' Jesus also said, 'Greater love than this, to lay down one's life for one's friends.' I very much doubt whether either of you will be required to die for the one you love, but that is what Jesus did for us, and he wants us to imitate his example of self-sacrificing love, in marriage and in all our other relationships: not 'Give and take', but 'All give, and no take'. 'All give, and gratefully receive.'

Suggested hymns

Come down, O love divine; Dear Lord and Father of mankind; For the beauty of the earth; Love divine, all loves excelling,

Sermon for a Baptism or Christening
Prince George

When Prince George was born in 2013, there was a huge public clamour for photographs and news. All babies are beautiful, but he seemed particularly so, and he an heir to the throne. Not long afterwards, he was christened, and although the ceremony was private, Archbishop Justin Welby published an article describing the Church of England's understanding of what christening means. Not surprisingly, this was followed by a surge in the number of parents applying to have their babies baptized in the C of E.

374

Church commitment

This is wonderful, for it means that both the church and the parents are taking seriously their responsibilities following the birth of a child. The church recognizes that it has to provide services to which the parents will feel welcome along with their growing children. These are needed on special occasions like Christmas and Harvest Festival, and also at regular services, sometimes called 'all-age worship', which have special activities for the children and songs for them to sing, so that they never feel bored. Many churches make their main Sunday service every week child-friendly; often children can sit with their parents at the beginning of the service, and go out with a few adults who help them to learn in what still goes by the misleading name of 'Sunday school'. At the end, the parents will be shown what the children have been up to, and marvel at the level of imagination to which they have been spurred.

Parents' commitment

Most parents also feel more deeply committed to ensuring that their children learn about the teaching of Jesus, the basis of our family and national life. People feel committed to this at various levels; at the very least, they decide to tell their children Bible stories, and bring them to church at least once a year at Christmas. They choose as godparents some good friends who will help them make sure their child spends time thinking about the deeper things of life, which are so often ignored in our superficial materialistic society. But you may feel that this is not enough, and want to keep the spiritual side of life in balance with the greedy pressures of the shop-till-you-drop modern world. So you need to set children an example of putting God first, by bringing your kids to church with you as often as you can. Then, when they begin to ask you deep questions, as all children do, you can refer them to friendly people at the church to suggest some answers. In the questions which the parents and godparents are asked in the christening service, you are encouraged to teach them by your words and example how to live a life of honesty and kindness, in which God's love for us and our love for other people are given first priority. Recently some simplified questions have been proposed, which will make it easier for people to understand what it is that they are promising to do. In some churches, baptism is delayed until teenagers or young adults make a conscious decision to give their lives to Jesus. Then they either have water poured over their heads, like the baby has in a christening service, or else they are dipped under the water in a small pool, as a symbol of the way Jesus washes our hearts clean when he forgives us all our selfish, sinful thoughts and actions. This symbolism is upheld in churches which baptize young children by pouring water over them at the christening service. In this case, the vital conscious decision to live like Jesus is postponed until, in their teens or shortly before, they confirm for themselves the promises their parents and godparents made for them, in a service which we call 'confirmation', and the bishop confirms their membership of the Church.

Urgency

You often hear people say, 'You don't need to go to Church to be a Christian.' That is absolutely true, if you mean living a life of love and kindness. But it is very hard to go on living like that unless you meet regularly with other people who are struggling to live like that, but know they can only do it by asking God to help them to. We all need to remind ourselves that God loves each one of us, and let his love flow through us into other people whom we love for God's sake. But in this country, where it is forbidden to teach religion in many schools, where else can children learn about Jesus and his love other than in church?

Welcome

Everybody, even atheists, is welcome in church; the only qualification is that you should realize you are not good enough yet, and want to be better. Only remember: the deeper your commitment, the more joy and satisfaction you will get out of life.

Suggested hymns

Amazing grace! How sweet the sound; Give me joy in my heart; He's got the whole world in his hands; It's me, it's me, O Lord.

Sermon for a Funeral or Memorial Service
The Lord is my Shepherd
Psalm 23 (Book of Common Prayer)

1 The Lord is my shepherd;
therefore can I lack nothing.
2 He makes me lie down in green pastures
and leads me beside still waters.
3 He shall refresh my soul
and guide me in the paths of righteousness for his name's sake.
4 Though I walk through the valley of the shadow of death,
 I will fear no evil;
for you are with me;
 your rod and your staff, they comfort me.
5 You spread a table before me
 in the presence of those who trouble me;
you have anointed my head with oil
 and my cup shall be full.
6 Surely goodness and loving mercy shall follow me
all the days of my life,
and I will dwell in the house of the Lord for ever.

[Or *this sermon can be adapted to refer to other readings.*]

Why we are here

As you all know, we are here for a funeral service. There are three reasons for holding a funeral. They are:

1 to be sad together;
2 to be thankful together; and
3 to be hopeful together.

Sadness

It is perfectly natural to be sad when somebody dies. People who are bereaved naturally feel bereft. So many things they had hoped to do together. So many ways of showing their love for each other which will no longer be possible. Loss, loneliness, anger, depression and confusion are all natural when somebody dies. But gradually it is possible to return to acceptance of things as they are, provided you are supported by the love of the rest of your family and your friends. For all who knew and loved the one who has been taken from us, this is a day of sadness, and we share in their grief in the hope that they will find our sympathy supportive.

Thanks

Second, we are here to give thanks for *his/her* life. [Here the preacher can refer to tributes made by family or friends, or read reminiscences which have been written down.]

Hope

Lastly, we are here to be hopeful. What we are doing today is to wish our friend goodbye, and *au revoir*, words which mean 'God be with you', and 'till we meet again'. We can't prove that there is an afterlife, but Christians have some evidence that makes it extremely probable. Jesus promised us eternal life, and over 500 people saw him alive again after he had died on the cross. Millions since then have prayed to Jesus and found their prayers were answered, which couldn't happen if Jesus was dead. Everyone has to make up their own mind; but if Jesus was not lying, we can end the sadness of this service on a note of quiet optimism.

Text

[As the writer of Psalm 23 puts it:

Though I walk through the valley of the shadow of death,
I will fear no evil;
for you are with me;
your rod and your staff, they comfort me. Amen.]

Suggested hymns

Any of the following:

Abide with me; All things bright and beautiful; Amazing grace; And did those feet (Jerusalem); Make me a channel of your peace; Morning has broken; Nearer, my God, to thee; O Lord my God (How great thou art); On a hill far away (The old rugged cross); The day thou gavest, Lord, is ended; The king of love my shepherd is; The Lord's my Shepherd, I'll not want.

Or see *Funeral Services* (Canterbury Press).

Address for an Atheist's Funeral
or Memorial Service
Socrates

An honour

It is always a great honour to be asked to speak at anybody's funeral. But it is a particularly significant compliment for a minister of religion, such as me, to be invited to preside at the funeral of somebody who claimed not to believe in God. I firmly believe that people have the right of choice, whether to believe or not in anything. I have had many discussions, usually very courteous, with people who say they cannot bring themselves to accept the arguments for the existence of God. Note that I say arguments, not proofs – nobody should be forced to believe. But we can have a logical discussion about probabilities one way or the other, and then leave it to each party to decide whether or not to make the experiment of believing, and see whether it has positive results.

Religion

You all know what I believe. Probably some of you think I am an old-fashioned simpleton to give any credence to such outmoded superstitions, but you are too polite to say so! But this is no time to preach religion. My object now is to bring some comfort to the bereaved, without necessarily expecting them to change their beliefs. That may or may not come later. I was puzzling how to do this, when I remembered that the Greek philosopher Socrates gave a very moving speech, when he was being put on trial before the judges of Athens for what they called 'atheism'. More likely they did not mean what we mean today by that word, but rather that he was telling his young pupils there was no need for them to believe the superstitious legends of the old Greek gods. He was facing the probability of a death sentence, but he spoke to the citizens of Athens there assembled in a very positive way about death. Listen to some extracts from his speech:

Socrates' speech

Let us reflect in another way, and we shall see that there is great reason to hope that death is a good; for one of two things – either death is a state of nothingness and utter unconsciousness, or, as men say, there is a change and migration of the soul from this world to another. Now if you suppose that there is no consciousness, but a sleep like the sleep of him who is undisturbed even by dreams, death will be an unspeakable gain . . . But if death is the journey to another place, and there, as men say, all the dead abide, what good, O my friends and judges, can be greater than this? . . . What would not a man give if he might converse with Orpheus and Musaeus and Hesiod and Homer? . . . For besides being happier than we are, they will be immortal, if what is said is true. Wherefore, O judges, be of good cheer about death, and know of a certainty, that no evil can happen to a good man, either in life or after death.

Support

End of quotation. What he says, in short, is that if there is no life after death, we shall have nothing to worry about, and if there is, we shall enjoy meeting with others. We all die sometime, and there is nothing to fear. What Socrates doesn't deal with, however, is how the bereaved are to deal with their loss. It is not easy, but we know what the answer is: they need a great deal of support and love from their family, friends and neighbours. So this is our opportunity to offer that support, at all times. Without intruding if we are not wanted, we promise that we shall all be available when needed, to give practical support in a difficult time, but more importantly, to provide a listening ear and a caring heart, so that they know that we shall not shrink away if they want to talk, and never condemn them for the intensity of their feelings. If I conclude by saying 'God bless you', you can take it in any way you choose. I don't think even Socrates would disapprove of that.

Scripture Index to Sermon Texts

	ch	v	page		84	9	73
Gen.	1	31	65		118	15–17	119
Ex.	15	1–2	116	Prov.	3	13–14	351
Num.	21	5–7	86		4	1, 5	256
Josh.	1	1, 7	90	Eccles.	11	7–9	261
1 Kings	6	11–12	198	S. of Sol.	8	6	121
	12	16–17	207	Isa.	5	1–3	106
	18	21	9		35	6	12
2 Kings	7	9	222		49	6	42, 108
Ps.	22	1–2	113		61	9	365
	23		376		63	9	33
	29	3	37	Jer.	1	5	299
	30	3	126	Lam.	3	31–33	363
	33	1, 3	49	Dan.	7	11	268
	34	17	54	Joel	2	13	76
	46	10	40	Amos	3	5, 7	63
	47	7	153	Micah	3	9–10	265
	50	14	81	Hab.	2	4	336
	65	3	370	Zeph.	1	12	275
	67	5	193				

Book	Chapter	Verse	Page
Hag.	2	9	131
Zech.	4	12–14	334
	8	4	145
Tobit	4	1–5	96
Ecclus. (Ben Sira)	44	1	365
Matt.	1	18	16
	1	24–25	309
	2	2	295
	3	1–2	7
	4	1	79
	4	20	367
	5	17	56
	5	27–28	61
	5	43–45	272
	9	35–36	167
	10	29, 31	171
	10	40–42	176
	11	28	181
	13	20–21	185
	13	31–32	195
	14	24–25	205
	15	14	210
	16	24–26	305
	17	1–3	71
	18	21–22	229
	20	1	234
	20	26–28	100
	22	17–21	254
	22	37–40	258
	24	23	4
	24	44	2
	25	31–32	280
	27	11–12	103
	28	18	282
Mark	13	12–13	316
	16	15	153
Luke	1	34	312
	1	39–40	323
	1	52–53	344
	1	80	332
	2	11	23, 30
	2	21	293
	2	22	302
	9	28	200
	11	24–26	169
	14	18	174
	17	33–36	178
	18	41–42	183
	20	1–2	188
	22	26	346
	24	15–16	128
John	1	51	354
	2	6–9	51
	3	14–15	349

	3	3,	
		16–17	83
	11	25–26	98
	14	8	319
	16	5, 7	163
	17	5	151
	20	17–18	339
	20	21–23	124
	21	20, 24	288
Acts	1	9	149
	2	17–18	158
	7	53	286
	11	20–24	327
	12	1–2	341
	13	5	203
	13	26	14
	16	14	212
	17	22–23	217
	19	19	226
	20	33–35	231
	26	12–15	236
Rom.	5	10	88
	8	18	190
	12	1, 10	372
	12	4–5	214
	12	12	219
	13	10	224

1 Cor.	1	10, 13	47
	1	27	290
	4	5	321
	11	23–24	111
	11	25	329
	12	4	156
2 Cor.	4	1	307
	13	11, 13	160
Gal.	1	15–16	44
Eph.	1	20–21	149
	2	13–14	135
	2	19–20	358
	4	1–3	297
	4	22–24	58
	5	8	93
Phil.	2	5–7	35
	2	7–8	239
	2	11	30
	3	12–14	244
	4	6	249
1 Thess.	4	18	270
2 Tim.	2	3	314
2 Tim.	4	11	356
Titus	3	4–5	25
Heb.	1	12	28
	12	22–23	361

1 Pet.	2	4–5	138
	2	25	133
	3	19	143
1 John	2	9–11	246
	2	22	241
	3	2	251

Rev.	1	5	277
	4	2	68
	7	9–10	263
	21	1–2	140
	22	20–21	19

Author Index

ALEXANDER, Eben, *Proof of Heaven* 123
ANON, 'Christmas is what man means by God . . .' 37
ANON, 'David and Solomon led very naughty lives' 279
ANON, 'Here lies one who feared God . . .' 173
ANON, 'How many people work in the Vatican?' 235
ANON, 'Many people want the protective clarity . . .' 64
ANON, 'Never try to teach anybody anything until . . .' 155
ANON, 'St David, you chose a simple life . . .' 306–7
ANON, *The Way of a Pilgrim* 46
ARISTOTLE, Accidental appearance 165
AUGUSTINE, 'Those who sing the praises . . .' xvii
BONAR, Horatius, 'Thy way, not mine, O Lord' 202
BROOKS, Phillips, 'O little town of Bethlehem' 18
BUNYAN, John, *The Pilgrim's Progress* 361
BUTLER, Alban, *Butler's Lives of the Saints* 348
CAMARA, Helder, 'Hope without risk is not hope' 221
CHAPMAN, M., 'Be bold, be strong' 92
CHURCHILL, Winston, 'Never give in . . .' 246
COLE, Nat King, 'There could be trouble ahead' 168
COUNSELL, Michael, *A Basic Christian Dictionary* 244
COUNSELL, Michael, 'Magnificat' 324–6
COUNSELL, Michael, 'The troubled town of Bethlehem' 18
CRAGG, Kenneth, *Sandals at the Mosque* 155, 195
DEARMER, Percy, 'Jesus, good above all other' 246
DICKENS, Charles, *Christmas Carol* 352
DICKENS, *David Copperfield* 240
ECKHART, Meister, 'To use God is to kill him' 221
ELIOT, T. S., *Four Quartets* 362
GILBERT, W. S. and SULLIVAN, A., *The Gondoliers* 282–4
GILBERT, W. S., 'The Disagreeable Man' 86
GOETHE, Wolfgang, 'I will not be as those . . .' 87
HERBERT, George, 'Teach me, my God and King' 235
HITCHENS, Christopher, *God Is Not Great* 312
HULL, John, '. . . the Church doesn't cope very well with disability' 184

IGNATIUS OF LOYOLA, 'Pray as if everything depended on God . . .' 235
IRENAEUS, *Against Heresies* 242
JACOBS, Rabbi Louis, *We Have Reason to Believe* 64
LEWIS, C. S., *Beyond Personality* 79
LEWIS, C. S., *Surprised by Joy* 373
LOCKE, John, *Rights of Man* 348
LUTHER, Martin, '. . . allowed to laugh in heaven . . .' 212
LUTHER, Martin, 'A safe stronghold our God is still' 174
MARKHAM, Edwin, 'He drew a circle to shut me out' 243
MCGRATH, Alister, *Mere Theology* 192
MENDELSSOHN, F., *Elijah* 11
MILTON, John, 'Ode on His Blindness' 93–5
ROBINSON, John, *Jesus and His Coming* 19
ROSSETTI, Dante Gabriel, *The Blessed Damozel* 68–70
SAMMIS, J. H., 'Trust and obey' 369
SCHULZ, Charles M., 'Don't worry about the world . . .' 5
SHAKESPEARE, William, *King Henry IV Part 2* 186
SHEPPARD, David, *Steps along Hope Street* 194
SINGH, Lekha and SPOTTISWOODE, Roger, *Beyond Right and Wrong* 229
SOCRATES, '. . . death is a good . . .' 379–80
WELLS, H. G., '. . . who began in a cave behind a windbreak . . .' 190–1
WILDE, Oscar, 'I can resist anything except temptation' 59
YEATS, W. B., 'The Indian upon God' 161
YOUNG, W. P., *The Shack* 291

Subject Index

Entries in *italics* are sermon titles

A light to the nations 42
Absence 139
Addiction 62, 172
Adoption 309
Adultery 61
Advent 270
Advocacy 281
Ageing 145
Agriculturalists 106
All give, no take 372
All the earth 153
Altruism 101
Angels 354
Anger 60, 109
Answers to prayer 119
Anti-Semitism 203
Apocalyptic 20
Apostles' Creed 143
Archaeology 342
Armour of God 91
Ashes 77
Athletes 244
Atoning sacrifice 83
Authority 188, 339

Be bold, be strong 90
Be still and know 40
Beloved Disciple 288
Bereavement trauma 99, 123, 145, 291, 363
Bethlehem 17
Betrayal 61
Beyond right and wrong 229
Biblical Archaeological Review 342

Bitterness 268
Blessed Damozel 68
Blind men and an elephant 155
Blindness 183
Blood 329
Bodies 124, 215, 252
Bonhoeffer, Dietrich 105
Born-again Christians 83
Builder 131

Calm down 175
Cappadocian Fathers 46
Caring for the carers 287
Casuistry 58
Catacombs 133
Causes of death 5
Celebrity 151
Change 50, 64, 127, 340
Chang-Him, Archdeacon French 359
Changing one's mind about Advent 270
Charismatic 157
Child death 290
Childbirth 96, 303
Chosen People 42
Christian nation? 29, 365
Christianity in Russia 44
'Christmas is what man means by God . . .' 37
Church and State 254
Church growth 196, 223
Church is the Body of Christ 214
Church music 49

Church, the new Temple 200
Churchgoing 73
Circular letters 26
Cleopas 129
Climate change 276
Code 20
Come, Lord Jesus 19
Coming of Christ 21
Communion 83
Communion of saints 74
Communist revolution 46
Communities 161
Community choirs xvii
Conflict in the Church 334
Constantine, Emperor 243
Contract with everyone 135
Conversations 238
Coping 192
Court of All Nations 108
Covenants 330
Creation 66
Crusaders 315
Cup of cold water 176
Cyril and Methodius, SS 45

Daily work 234
Damascus road 236
Darwin, Charles 220
David 278
'David and Solomon led very
   naughty lives' 279
Day of Atonement 82
Deadheading 178
Death 114, 122
Decline and fall 268
Dementia 146
Democracy 189
Demons 169
Desert saints 332
Destined to grow 195
Developing world 6
Devil 80
Dimensions 253
Disabled 184
Disagreements 47

Discipline 71
Discrimination 154
Distractions 40
Divine rape? 312
Do not be afraid 171
Do or die 224

Ecumenical movement 298
Elijah and Mendelssohn 9
Emmaus 129
Empowerment 160
Empty tomb 111
End of the world 5
Ephraim 208
Epistle of Barnabas 327
Eternal life 147
Evangelism 43, 126, 154, 197, 222
Everybody needs a hero 314
Everybody's slave 100
Evidence for the resurrection 128
Exile 42
Exorcism 169
Expedient 55
Exultet 116

Faith 29, 99
Family 136
Fathers' wisdom 256
Fear 146, 171
Fellowship 160
Feminist 160
Ferrar, Nicholas 362
Fiction 91
Forgiveness 229
From Jerusalem to Athens 299
Fundamentalism 64

*Gallons of guilt and gallons of
   grace* 51
Gentiles 42, 193
Gifts of the Spirit 156
Giving and receiving 231
Giving to God 65
*Gloom family's Christmas circular,
   The* 25

Glory 152
Gnosticism 338
God knows best 190
God speaks to us 236
God with us 272
God's help 34
God's idea of humanity 35
God's strategy 224
God's will, not mine 200
God-fearers 14
Gospel of Thomas 336
Goss, John 349
Grace 53, 57, 227
Gratitude 249
Gravity 205
Greed 352
Grumbling 86
Guard 111
Guardian angels 354
Guilt 52

Hallucinations 127
Harmful sin 246
Hatred 248
Have faith 28
Headship 188
Healing 227
Heaven 70, 112, 122, 149, 252
Hebrew Bible 71
Heep, Uriah 240
Heirs and successors 277
Hell 143
Hellenists 203
Henry VIII 277
Heresies 241, 338
Hermes 134
Herod's Temple 131
Heroes 314
History 237
HIV/AIDS 276
Holy Spirit 125, 156
Hope 221
'How do I get into Carnegie Hall?' 175

'How many people work in the Vatican?' 235
How to read music xix
Human rights 344
Humble 239
Humour and holiness 24, 210

Illegal legalities 103
Imagination 238
Immaculate conception 313
Impossible miracle 205
Incarnation 34, 36
Incomprehensible 163
Innocent until proved guilty 72
Instant obedience 367
Insults 60
Internationalism 43
Ireland before Patrick 307
Is anyone there? 119
Is the world coming to an end today? 4
Isaiah chapter 12
Islam 217

Jerusalem destroyed 3, 17, 141
Jesus speaks to us 39
Joel 78
John Mark's mother's house 316
John the Baptist 8
Joking about somebody's name 293
Judah 208
Judgement 322
Just enough 370
Just say no 3
Justice 71

Kiev 45
Kindness 60
Kingdom of God/heaven, the 3, 167, 196

Language of science 197
Laughter 211
Law and the prophets 71
Law of Moses or law of love 56

Laws 224
Lazarus 98
Leadership 189
Learning 154
Lesser of two evils 58
Letter to Paul from Philippi 212
Likeness 35
Listening 38
Litany 76
Living stones 138
Logic 63
Lord hears them? 54
Lord is my shepherd 376
Love 234
Love and death 129
Love, long life and happiness 84
Love or gold? 351
Loved ones 253
Luke Warm, Mark Time and Percy Vere 245
Luke's letter to Paul 356
Lust 122
Lying 60

Magic 226
Man 249
Marginalized 158
Masada 131
Materialists 121
Matthew's vision 2
May Day 319
Mediator 89
Mendelssohn, Felix 10
Menstruation 303
Miletus 232
Milton's 'Ode on His Blindness' 93
Mind of Christ 239
Miracles 183, 206
Miserable 87
Miserable sinners 76
Missions 281, 296, 367
Modern verse 323
Modernism 64
Monarchies 149
Money 66

Moses 56
Motherliness 96
Motives 104
Multicultural 154
Music 49
Muslims 194

Naming 34
Nature 237
Nature miracles 206
Near-death 123
Negative theology 79, 164
Neighbours 259
'Never try to teach anybody anything until . . .' 155
New beginnings 33
Nicene Creed 243
Nicodemus 347
Nightingale, Florence 345
Noah 143
Non-Jews 203

Old age 145, 261
Old and new 59
Old Believers 46
Old Jerusalem and new 140
Old life and the new life 58
On screen 23
One day in your courts 73
One-way telephone conversation 119
Opposition 286
Orphans 311
Other faiths 193, 295
Ouseley, Frederick Gore 349
Overseas aid 280

Pain and hope 115, 219
Palliative care 146
Paparazzi 151
Parables 196, 211
Paradox 28
Parenthood 304
Pastoralists 106
Patience 94